Enterprise Reform in China
Ownership, Transition, and Performance

Edited by Gary H. Jefferson and Inderjit Singh

Published for The World Bank

Oxford University Press

Oxford University Press

OXFORD NEW YORK ATHENS AUCKLAND BANGKOK
BOGOTA BUENOS AIRES CALCUTTA CAPE TOWN CHENNAI
DAR ES SALAAM DELHI FLORENCE HONG KONG ISTANBUL
KARACHI KUALA LUMPUR MADRID MELBOURNE MEXICO CITY
MUMBAI NAIROBI PARIS SAO PAULO SINGAPORE
TAIPEI TOKYO TORONTO WARSAW

and associated companies in
BERLIN IBADAN

Published by Oxford University Press, Inc.
198 Madison Avenue, New York, N.Y. 10016

Oxford is a registered trademark of Oxford University Press.

Manufactured in the United States of America
First Printing December 1998

Cover: The Chinese characters that appear on the cover and that open each chapter (pronounced *chigai*) mean enterprise reform.

Library of Congress Cataloging–in–Publication Data

Enterprise reform in China : ownership, transition, and performance / edited by
    Gary H. Jefferson, Inderjit Singh.
       p.   cm.
    Includes bibliographical references and index. 1?02347229
    ISBN 0-19-521120-0
    1. Industries—China—1976– . 2. Industrial productivity—China.
    3. Government ownership—China. 4. Government business enterprises—
    Government policy—China. I. Jeffereson, Gary H.
    II. Singh, Inderjit, 1941–
    HC427.92.E58   1998
    338.0951—ddc21
                                                              97-36569
                                                                  CIP

Contents

Acknowledgments

We can only attempt to thank the many people who contributed to the preparation of this volume. The list is long, in part because this project, which began nearly a decade ago, entailed the collection and analysis of multiple sets of survey data and withstood several administrative reorganizations within both China and the World Bank.

Chief among the contributors to this volume are those who prepared papers for the book and who exhibited the enormous patience along the way required to see their work through an extended process of several reviews and revisions. Their names and institutional affiliations appear on the contributors list.

Many other individuals and their organizations have substantially helped in the research that went into this volume. This project originally began as a joint venture among the World Bank, the Institute of Economics in the Chinese Academy of Social Sciences (CASS), the State Economic System Reform Commission, and the Rural Development Research Center. Along the way the project expanded to include numerous other collaborating organizations. Specifically, we wish to thank:

- The Institute of Economics (CASS) and its Director Lin Qingsong and staff Zhang Ping and Zhang Xuejun
- The Institute for Technical and Quantitative Economic Research (CASS), including its director Li Jingwen and our colleague, Zheng Yuxin, and his staff
- The State Economic System Reform Commission including Peng Zhaoping
- The Rural Development Research Center including Du Ying, Qiu Jicheng, and Luo Xiaopeng;
- The Development Research Center of the State Council, including Chen Jianbo and Li Guodu

- The State Statistical Bureau including Lu Chunheng, Li Qiming, Xing Junling, Zhang Shouqing, and former staff member, Liu Li
- The Ministry of Metallurgy, including Zhang Xinchuan and Xue Chuanzhao.

In the World Bank we are grateful to Mr. Javid Burki, former director of the China Department, for his early and continuous support for the project, which was initiated in his department; Shahid Yusuf, former chief economist of the department; and Richard Stern, former director of the department's Industry and Energy Division. Chen Kang, Xiao Geng, Zheng Decheng, and Dilip Ratha provided enthusiastic and capable research support. We also appreciate the generous and able administrative support of Cecilia Guido-Spano and Vesna Petrovic.

The efforts of those at the publishing stage who helped to bring this volume to publication are deeply appreciated. These include Nancy Levine of the World Bank and Meta deCoquereaumont, Barbara Karni, Daphne Levitas, Glenn McGrath, and Donna McGreevy of Communications Development Inc. Several anonymous inside and outside reviewers contributed invaluable criticisms and suggestions that made this volume far better than it appeared in its initial incarnations.

The overall quality of the book also benefited greatly from persons who prepared working papers or offered review and comment on earlier manuscripts. These include V.K. Chetty, Richard H. Day, Zvi Griliches, Thomas Rawski, Wang Zhigang, Calla Wiemer, and Zou Gang.

We also appreciate the extensive and conscientious research assistance of Xu Wenyi, Wang Benzhou, John Zhao, Albert Hu, and Bai Huamao, all currently or formerly at Brandeis University. Also, Claire Cincotta and Mary Smith in the Department of Economics at Brandeis helped in innumerable ways to support the logistics of this project; they specifically helped to arrange the visits of numerous Chinese collaborators to the States and to Brandeis.

We would like to thank Alan Gelb, former chief of the Transition Economics Division of the World Bank, who not only provided valuable guidance, but also participated in the research and was a constant source of patient support and encouragement for research in a comparatively new area of transition economics. The division allowed the project to benefit from the wealth of intellectual interaction with other colleagues and scholars passing through it. Research by others in the division also provided us with a useful and comparative frame of reference from other country experiences and continuously challenged us to show how China's experience was different and why it mattered.

In addition to the financial support of the World Bank, we deeply appreciate support from the Henry Luce Foundation, the American

Council of Learned Societies, the Chiang Ching-Guo Foundation, and the Brandeis Mazer Fund.

Finally, and most important, we would like to thank our families for their encouragement, patience, and support over the many years when it seemed that our work would never finish.

Contributors

The affiliations shown are those pertaining at the time of writing.

Chen Jianbo	Rural Development Research Center, State Council, China
Albert G. Z. Hu	Department of Economics, Brandeis University
Gary H. Jefferson	Department of Economics, Brandeis University
Lu Mai	Harvard University Institute for International Development and Development Research Center, State Council
Frances C. Perkins	East Asia Analytical Unit, Department of Foreign Affairs and Trade, Canberra Australia
Mark M. Pitt	Department of Economics, Brown University
Louis Putterman	Department of Economics, Brown University
Thomas G. Rawski	Department of Economics, University of Pittsburgh
Inderjit Singh	Transition Economics Division, World Bank
Wang Benzhou	China Everbright Financial Holdings, LTD, Hong Kong
Xing Junling	State Statistics Bureau, China
Zhang Ping	Economic Research Institute, Chinese Academy of Social Sciences
Zhang Shouqing	State Statistics Bureau, China
John Z. Q. Zhao	Department of Economics, Brandeis University
Zheng Yuxin	Institute of Quantitative and Technical Economics, Chinese Academy of Social Sciences

Overview

Gary H. Jefferson and Inderjit Singh

The transformation and growth of China's economy, which raised living standards for one-fifth of the world's population and provided indirect benefits for many more, stands among the most significant economic developments of the late twentieth century. This book rests on two premises. The first is that the key to China's dramatic economic transformation is that country's industrialization. The second is that the real story of China's industrialization is unfolding at the level of the individual Chinese enterprise and factory.

This volume seeks to document the impact of economic reforms on China's industrial sector and to explain why China's reforms, which appear meager relative to the more ambitious reform programs of Eastern Europe and even Russia, have had such wide-reaching effects. This book differs from much of the research and analysis of China's economy in several ways:

- It provides the first in-depth comparative look at different ownership systems, going well beyond the standard state/nonstate contrast to illustrate the real organizational, behavioral, and performance differences among China's systems of ownership.
- It analyzes the extent to which specific reforms have altered the behavior and performance of Chinese enterprises across different forms of ownership.
- It examines how the millions of enterprises in China interact with their institutional and international environments to create a dynamic reform process that has greatly magnified the impact of reform initiatives from the center.
- It attempts to distinguish, evaluate, and reconcile various perspectives or schools of thought regarding the nature of China's reform.

The story of the industrial enterprise, the most basic unit of organized production, affords the deepest and most comprehensive insight into the

1

progress and problems of China's economic transition. Through its connection to other parts of the economy, the enterprise provides a window through which the reform of China's labor markets, banking system, social insurance system, systems of foreign trade and investment, and legal and regulatory system can be viewed and understood. Because the enterprise stands at the nexus of so many other economic institutions, reform of the industrial enterprise is synonymous with China's economic reform.

This book is the outgrowth of a World Bank project that began in the late 1980s. That project commissioned two large-scale enterprise surveys. One survey covers 1,200 state-owned enterprises and collective-owned enterprises in the "urban system"; the other includes 300 township and village enterprises. Both surveys span the period from the early 1980s through 1991–92 and include detailed information about the management systems of the participating enterprises. A third data set, produced by China's State Statistical Bureau, includes about 5,000 of China's large and medium-size enterprises for the period 1988–92, nearly one-third of the total during that period. For one year, 1993, the data include the entire population of 18,500 large and medium-size enterprises, spanning 14 different ownership types. This State Statistical Bureau data set enables us to extend our analysis to the important foreign sector, which contains both foreign-funded and overseas Chinese–funded enterprises, sometimes collectively referred to as foreign-invested enterprises. Two additional surveys were designed to investigate the dynamics of technical innovation and of foreign trade in China's industrial enterprises. One or more of these five data sets provides the empirical foundation for most chapters in this book. They also provide a rich source of statistical material that is being made available to a wide range of scholars.

These survey data, which capture the experience of more than 7,000 enterprises, create a record from which researchers can document the ways in which China's enterprises, both old and new, have responded to changes in their institutional and policy environment. The statistical records of these enterprises document the experience of each individual enterprise and allow us to construct a broad picture of the program, process, and outcome of China's overall reform experience. While the data upon which most chapters in this book are based will be "antiquated" before long, these data and the analysis that follows provide a critical record of a period that is likely to define the Chinese economy for decades to come.

In addition to this overview, the book contains 11 coordinated studies that document and analyze changes in the governance and performance of China's industrial enterprises. Chapter 1 presents an overview of the structure of China's industrial economy. Chapter 2 extracts key aspects of the survey data to describe, compare, and contrast the systems of governance of key ownership types. Chapters 3 through 5 should be read together. Chapter 3 describes the special features of China's economic and institutional structure that create a kind of dynamic endogenous reform process, characterized by the authors as an "industrial innovation ladder." The ladder has two interactive dimensions. The first is technical innovation, which is modeled and empirically tested in chapter 4. The second is institutional change, or enterprise reform, which is viewed in chapter 5 as arising from both conditions within the industrial system and the efforts of central reformers. Chapters 6 and 7 assess the performance of Chinese industry—chapter 6 through a general review of the literature on Chinese enterprise reform and chapter 7 by comparing the performance of state-owned enterprises and township and village enterprises. By controlling for policy and firm-specific differences, chapter 7 seeks to identify the "pure ownership" effect on productivity.

Like chapter 7, chapters 8 through 11 present formal models and technical econometric work. Each of these chapters seeks to examine the behavior of one or more samples of enterprises with respect to a particular enterprise function. Chapter 8 focuses on the comparative wage-setting and employment behavior of state-owned enterprises, urban cooperatives, township and village enterprises, and foreign-invested enterprises. Chapter 9 targets township and village enterprises and some private rural enterprises to investigate whether enterprises in this important and poorly understood sector overemploy, underemploy, or choose more-or-less profit-maximizing levels of employment. Examining the investment process, chapter 10 asks a key question, perhaps the most important for any transition economy: are the most successful enterprises capturing scarce investment resources in order to expand their share of production? Chapter 11 examines the impact of various open door policies on export performance among state-owned enterprises and foreign-invested enterprises.

For the reader focused on the "idea" of China's economic reform, three "high-concept" essays in this volume may be of particular interest. Appendix A develops the analogy between the optimal reform strategy and the investment decision of the firm, looking at reform from the perspective of the social welfare–maximizing leader or reformer. Chapter 3 looks at China's industrial economy as a system. It extends the product cycle and quality ladders of Vernon (1966) and Grossman and Helpman (1991) to China's domestic industrial economy to portray a dynamic process of institutional change as well as technical innovation. The section in chapter 5 entitled "Implications: the commons, coase, and a property rights market" extends the notion of a public good and social externalities to state enterprises and argues for the application of the logic of the Coase theorem to the reform of Chinese industry. This prescriptive material identifies the establishment of a property rights market as the central policy priority implied by the two other essays.

Highlights of China's reforms

Volumes have been written describing and characterizing China's economic reform program.[1] This account cannot substitute for these excellent descriptions of China's reform program. The brief discussion below is intended simply to orient the less familiar reader to key elements of China's reform program and to alert the more knowledgeable reader to those initiatives that constitute the essential ingredients of China's dynamic reform process.

Much of the impetus for China's industrial transformation originated with two highly successful reform initiatives—the Open Door policy and the rural reform program—the outline of which became clear in the late 1970s and early 1980s. The massive impact of these complementary initiatives was not anticipated by China's early reformers. The Open Door policy opened China's coastal provinces to foreign trade, investment, and an influx of new technologies, managerial initiative, and foreign exchange. The rural reform program led to immediate productivity gains in rural agriculture that, in turn, vastly expanded the supply of domestic savings and surplus labor while unleashing individual and local government entrepreneurial initiative. Together the Open Door policy and the rural reform program created a surge of new industrial enterprise formation, intense competition within many product groups, and pressures for both technological and institutional change. These conditions have forced China's centrally controlled trading system, its institutions of factor allocation, and its industrial enterprise system to adapt continuously to the requirements of a modern market-oriented economy.

The Open Door policy and the rural reform program created a fertile environment that allowed for the formation and entry of new capital, labor, managerial initiative, and firms, thereby creating effective competition throughout most of Chinese industry. Two other reforms—the devolution of managerial autonomy to the firm, and the two-track price system—created the necessary incentive structure. Allowing firms to retain profits and provide bonuses established a powerful, if uneven, set of incentives for workers and managers to expand and accumulate financial surpluses. By exposing decisions at the margin to market forces, the dual-track price system served two functions. First, it enabled smaller new firms to secure the necessary market access and producer goods from established firms to enter the market and grow. In addition, it afforded firms already operating in the state sector the product and market space into which to expand and restructure their operations in search of financial gain.

A critical prerequisite for the efficacy of these meta- and microinitiatives has been the creation of a comparatively stable macroeconomic environment, which Chinese authorities have maintained through a mix of direct and indirect instruments. Recollection of the high political and economic costs of rising inflation during 1989 are likely to motivate China's political leaders and policymakers to sustain macroeconomic stability into the foreseeable future.

China's industrial performance

China's industrial economy created $340 billion of value added in 1995, about a fifth of the U.S. figure for that year (World Bank 1997). By other measures, however, the size of China's industrial economy overwhelms that of every other nation. By the mid-1990s more than 7 million industrial enterprises in China employed more than 140 million workers, up from about 50 million in 1978 and nearly equal to the combined industrial work forces of the 28 OECD economies.

China's economy is adding more industrial production each year than any other economy in the world, including the United States. Most of the average annual industrial growth of 14 percent during the 15-year period 1980–95 was powered by three factors: the growth in the industrial work force by 90 million workers, two-thirds of whom have moved from China's agricultural sector; a doubling of the industrial sector's fixed assets every four to five years, fueled in large part by the nation's domestic savings rate, which rose from 25 percent in 1965 to 35 percent by 1980 and now stands at more than 40 percent; and overall industrial productivity that has grown by 3–4 percent a year (chapter 6, this volume; World Bank 1997).

While growth in China's state-owned industry has been rapid by world standards, averaging nearly 8 percent between 1980 and 1995, two emerging sectors have served as the principal engines of China's industrial growth and transformation. The first is the rural township and village sector, which reported annual real rates of growth of nearly 22 percent over this 15-year period, increasing its share in industrial output to more than one-quarter by 1995 (see table 1.3). While township and village enterprises served as the engine of industrial growth during the 1980s, the so-called "other" sector, comprising individual enterprises, joint stock companies, domestic joint ventures, and foreign-invested enterprises (both joint and wholly owned ventures), emerged as the principal source of growth in the 1990s.

The variety of ownership forms in this "other" sector confounds the conventional public-private dichotomy. While much of the original capital in this sector was publicly owned (most notably the state and collective enterprises that have been converted to joint ventures or joint stock companies), most of the conversions themselves were made possible by injections of private capital, both domestic and foreign. More than 90 percent of enterprises in the sector are small, wholly privately owned firms classified as "individual" or "private."

By the mid-1990s China's industrial structure could be broadly characterized as one-third state-owned, one-third collective- and township and village–owned, and one-third joint public-private or wholly privately owned. This burgeoning growth of township and village enterprises, foreign-invested enterprises, and public-private enterprises, not the privatization of public enterprises, has accounted for the greatest source of change in China's industrial ownership structure.

Chinese industry: what needs to be explained?

The extraordinary performance of China's industrial economy has been widely acknowledged. There is not, however, unanimity concerning the causes and sustainability of this growth. Many observers are puzzled by three paradoxes:

- Relative to other transition economies and to the general notion shared by most economists of what constitutes an effective set of market institutions, China's industrial reforms have been partial and piecemeal. As a result key institutions, including bankruptcy law, the banking system, and the social insurance system, remain undeveloped. Nevertheless, China's industrial growth has been robust and appears likely to continue.
- China's economy has been dominated by publicly owned firms, both state- and collective-owned. Although these factories display many of the negative characteristics that economists ascribe to public ownership, they accounted for most of the extraordinary growth of Chinese industry during the critical early years of transition.
- Most literature on productivity in Chinese industry, principally in state industry, reports that productivity is growing. Yet profitability in state industry is declining, and the number of loss-making enterprises is on the rise.

One approach to resolving these paradoxes is simply to dismiss them. Sachs and Woo (1997), for example, contend that rising productivity in state industry is illusory and that China's publicly owned enterprises, including its township and village enterprises, are inherently flawed and destined to fail—

sooner rather than later. They believe that China's robust economic growth is unsustainable without rapid, comprehensive, and immediate reform.

Another approach to resolving these paradoxes is suggested by the proponents of gradual reform. Nolan (1995), for example, argues that incremental reform creates the conditions for effective transition, whereas a "big bang" destroys the institutions needed for transition with growth. The improving performance measures of China's state and collective enterprises should not be surprising, he maintains, since "a wide variety of property rights regimes can now be seen to be compatible with effective economic performance" (1995, p. 317). Others, including McKinnon (1994) and Murphy, Schleifer, and Vishny (1992) offer "second best" reform models in which the relaxation of certain government controls leads to instability in the context of incomplete liberalization.

Our view is that these paradoxes do exist: China's economy has performed impressively despite inadequately reformed economic institutions, the intrinsic weaknesses of public ownership, and extensive loss-making in China's state industry. A central purpose of this volume is to clarify and resolve each of these three paradoxes.

What are the major findings?

The conclusions put forth in this volume are organized around several basic questions:

- What are the key features of China's economic reform process? What is the motive for continuing and widening the reform process? Why has such limited reform initiative from the center had so much effect? How do we resolve the paradox of rapid growth with limited reform?
- What changes in governance and the institutional environment are most responsible for changes in enterprise conduct and performance? What is the role of ownership in accounting for differences in conduct and performance among enterprise types? Can we account for the paradox of high-performance publicly owned enterprises?
- How well are China's industrial enterprises performing? Has the performance of state-owned enterprises improved? How can the paradox of rising productivity and falling profitability throughout Chinese industry, most notably in the state sector, be resolved?
- In what ways has the behavior of the Chinese firm been altered with respect to employment and wage-setting behavior, investment activity, innovation, and export orientation? Are enterprises increasing efficiency by responding to incentives and relative price changes?

The key findings of the volume are summarized below.

Growth and reform

Reform strategy. Uncertainty over its vision of the future and aversion to risk help explain China's initial "groping" reform strategy. Advantageous initial conditions and fortuitous early reform initiatives have facilitated China's transition, and success has sustained the continuity of a gradual or evolutionary approach to reform.

Success has many fathers. Not surprisingly, numerous interpretations of China's successful experience have been offered. Emphasizing the importance of initial conditions, Sachs and Woo (1997) argue that the dominance of an agricultural sector comparatively free of subsidies and social services allowed China's underdeveloped economy to respond to the meager, incoherent reform agenda more as a developing country than as an industrial socialist economy encumbered by the weight of ubiquitous subsidies and useless fixed assets. Jefferson and Rawski (chapter 3 and appendix A) also emphasize the importance of China's prereform endowment (that is, its initial conditions) that has allowed for the emergence of intense competition and powerful incentives for managers and local governments. These conditions, which are built into the system, are, in turn, creating a dynamic process of endogenous reform. For Groves, Hong, McMillan, and Naughton (1994), the creation of effective incentives, particularly managerial incentives, explains China's ability "to grow out of the plan."

Although these interpretations may have different policy implications, as explanations of China's rapid industrial transformation none is inconsistent with the others. We combine these interpretations to create a synthesis of explanations that points to initial conditions, competition, and incentives. All of these conditions have enabled limited reform to have substantial impact; all also create pressures for new rounds of reform. Naughton (1994) observes that there is a "generally consistent logic to the way [planned economies] dissolve" (p. 306). The view that emerges from this volume is that within a competitive economic setting, there is also a consistent logic to the process by which China is replacing its planned economy with a market economy.

A more rapid reform scenario may have been possible, but it would have exacted additional costs and risks. Day, Wang, and Zou (1994) develop several policy reform scenarios based on a dynamic adaptive model of enterprise behavior. They conclude that under a rapid reform scenario, in which prices were freed more rapidly and greater financial resources were redirected to facilitate more rapid restructuring, China's economy would have been more susceptible to inflation and fluctuations and would have experienced more layoffs.

In their general theory Jefferson and Rawski (chapter 3 and appendix A) liken the reform process to the firm's investment decision, in which the pace of reform cum investment depends on technical relationships between (reform) inputs and (social welfare) outputs, uncertainty, risk, and costs of adjustment. In their view reform, like investment in fixed assets, cannot be costlessly reversed. Hence, in a world of uncertainty in which there is learning by doing, something less than a "big bang" is optimal. From this perspective the lack of a clear vision of the outcome of the reform process in China demanded a "groping" strategy. (In contrast, in Eastern Europe, where the desired state of the world—that is, Western Europe—was clear, "big bang" reform was adopted in order to reach the desired state more rapidly.) Moreover, in China various initial conditions magnified the marginal returns to these partial reform instruments. Finally, the 9–10 percent real rates of annual growth are widely viewed within China as sufficient. Thus far China has been able to achieve high growth with stability. The expectation is that continued high growth will require ongoing reform but not a radical big bang solution.

Technical change. Market-based technical change is widespread in China where competition and market incentives foster widespread product innovation. Moreover, emerging markets in R&D resources (funds and engineers) are generating high and surprisingly uniform returns across state-owned and township and village enterprise industry.

Jefferson and Rawski (chapter 3) portray a dynamic process through which innovation spills over into China's economy from international markets through joint ventures and China's larger publicly owned enterprises. Through a process of imitation by less technologically sophisticated, lower-cost producers, new products and processes filter down the ladder, creating competitive pressures that move up the ladder, thereby forcing new rounds of innovation by firms at the top of the ladder. A central prediction of this industrial innovation ladder is that competition motivates a rising incidence of technical change. Moreover, R&D resources are expected to move down the ladder, where they can generate competitive, or superior, rates of return.

In chapter 4 Jefferson, Rawski, and Zheng demonstrate how, at least in the late 1980s, China's township and village enterprises were engaged in an intense process of technical catch-up with state enterprises, which were widely viewed as the technological leaders across a range of product groups. In terms of the sheer volume of innovation, township and village enterprise spending on R&D and technicians generated higher returns than comparable activity by state-owned enterprises. In terms of the quality of innovation, measured by the profitability of new products, the allocation of R&D spending and technicians within China's industrial economy appears to have been efficient.

Institutional innovation. De facto property rights have devolved to China's publicly owned enterprises, creating a coherent set of decision-making rights and incentives for some enterprises. While the devolution of rights to enterprises and managers varies substantially, so that many state enterprises enjoy more extensive rights than do some township and village enterprises, property rights are generally more devolved and congruent within the township and village enterprise sector.

Relative to the prereform period, most of China's publicly owned industrial enterprises have enjoyed a substantial expansion of property rights, although these changes are often specified through implicit rather than explicit contracts. Changes in property rights include expanded decisionmaking authority for the enterprise, designated authority for a central contracting agent within the enterprise, and a redistribution of residual claimant authority toward the enterprise and its central agent or manager. If these rights are not congruent (if, for example, there is substantial enterprise autonomy but fragmented internal authority and weak incentives), reform may be counterproductive. Within the enterprise samples studied, decisionmaking rights and the incentive structure were found to be more devolved and coherent within the township and village enterprise sector, which may help explain its relatively robust performance.

Clarifying property rights in both state and collective industry, including township and village enterprises, is a top reform priority among academics and Chinese policymakers. The case study of the Hengdian Company (appendix B), a township conglomerate, demonstrates how an intricate contracting system that embodies a strong incentive structure can, in some settings, effectively substitute for conventionally defined private property rights. Friction between the Hengdian town government, which continues to claim ownership of the company, and company officials and workers has been muted, in substantial part by the extraordinary force and success of a single individual and the rapid growth of production and incomes. The disappearance of one or more of these conditions is likely to reveal the cost of the company's poorly defined property rights. Concern about poorly specified property rights is motivating thousands of enterprises within the township and village enterprise sector to "individualize ownership," that is, to distribute shares to managers, workers, and local residents, sometimes leaving a substantial portion of the shares in the hands of local government, thus reducing but not eliminating the ambiguity of formal ownership.

Causality in the reform process. Virtually all of the literature on enterprise reform examines the impact of reform on performance. Causality also operates strongly in the other direction. Poor or declining performance, particularly among enterprises operated at lower levels of government, motivates new rounds of reform. Indeed, the industrial innovation ladder predicts that causality should run from enterprise performance to reform.

The industrial innovation ladder portrays competition squeezing financial performance and motivating a search for more efficient forms of corporate governance, as well as new technologies and markets. This process is at the heart of the concept of endogenous reform. Using enterprise data, Jefferson, Lu, and Zhao (chapter 5) find evidence in support of the endogenous reform model, particularly among state-owned enterprises that display poor productivity and financial performance and face a competitive environment and supervisory body at a lower level of government. These circumstances motivate new rounds of enterprise reform. These findings reinforce the view that China's industrial reform should be viewed as a process that is driven by forces within China's industrial system as well as a sequence of reforms inspired by officials at the center. But jurisdictions converting larger firms to joint ventures or shareholding firms tend to select the most successful state-owned enterprises. This evidence demonstrating that performance drives reform creates vexing simultaneity issues, which make it difficult to discern the direction and magnitude of the relationship between reform and performance.

Policy implications. The emergence of a dynamic industrial innovation ladder may be China's most valuable transition resource. To enable individual entrepreneurs, firms, and local levels of government to respond to pressures and opportunities for reform that are generated within the industrial system, the Chinese government should embrace the logic of the Coase theorem. Within a context of competition and incentives for reform, clarifying property rights and lowering transactions costs will enable entrepreneurs, firms, and local governments to more easily negotiate efficiency-enhancing exchanges of control rights and industrial assets.

China's industrial innovation ladder—an immense population of heterogeneous firms seeking to survive and grow within a system of substantial and growing competition and incentives—is arguably the most important of China's transitional institutions. It also carries certain policy implications, outlined by Jefferson, Lu, and Zhao (chapter 5) in their discussion of a Coasian approach to reform. From this perspective, by creating weak authority and incentives for monitoring within the firm, dispersed public ownership often displays characteristics similar to those of public goods (nonexcludability, in which managers, workers, and public officials take more from the enterprise than they give; and nondiminishability, in which governments employ fiscal and financial subsidies to replenish these exactions). These subsidies, in turn, give rise to social externalities involving publicly financed subsidies, inflation, and inefficient resource allocation.

Externalities arising from dispersed public ownership can be limited by applying the logic of the Coase theorem, which effectively argues for the creation of a property rights market by clearly assigning property rights and reducing transactions costs. Better-specified property rights and lower transactions costs—achieved by increasing competition through tighter budget constraints, improving transparency, and making contracting easier—enable agents to spontaneously negotiate efficiency-enhancing exchanges of control rights and industrial assets. In China where competition and local incentives for financial gain exist, creation of a set of institutions ensuring property rights can facilitate the decentralized, spontaneous exchanges between individual entrepreneurs and local governments needed to allocate property rights more efficiently. Already the incidence of mergers, acquisitions, privatization, and managerial contracting is growing. The potential for creating productive gains by expanding and reducing the costs of such exchanges is immense.

Industrial performance

Total factor productivity. Across all sectors of Chinese industry total factor productivity has improved. Between 1980 and into the early 1990s, total factor productivity grew at an average annual rate of 2–4 percent in state industry; rates in the collective sector were higher. Some preliminary evidence of a slowdown in the early 1990s should be carefully watched to determine whether it reflects cyclical or structural conditions.

Jefferson, Singh, Xing, and Zhang (chapter 6) identify 12 studies of productivity growth in China's state sector. Eight of these report total factor productivity growth rates that fall within the range of 2–4 percent; two lie above this range and two lie below it. Another comprehensive survey (Wu 1993) also finds widespread evidence of substantial productivity gain. In this volume Perkins (chapter 11) finds evidence of rising productivity in both state enterprises and foreign-invested joint ventures. Comparative studies of total factor productivity growth in the state and collective sectors, including those by Jefferson, Rawski, and Zheng (1992, 1996) and Wu and Wu (1994) show higher growth rates of total factor productivity among collective enterprises, particularly in the township and village enterprise sector, where productivity growth appears to have been 1.5–3.0 times that of the state sector.

These findings run counter to conventional wisdom, which holds that efficiency at state enterprises cannot increase unless ownership is changed and that it is not possible to improve performance substantially at publicly owned enterprises, including China's collectives and township and village enterprises (see, for example, Galal and Shirley 1995). In China the performance of state-owned enterprises and collectives contradicts both of these propositions: measured by the growth of real output and productivity in physical terms, state enterprises and collectives have performed well.

Increasing numbers of studies are linking this improved productivity performance to specific reforms. Hay and others (1994) and Jefferson, Singh, Hu, and Wang (chapter 8) cite the importance of profit retention, bonuses, and various reforms within the wage-employment system. Groves and others (1994) underscore the importance of managerial incentives. Hay and others (1994) and Jefferson, Hu, and Singh (chapter 10) find growing correspondence between performance, investment, and retained earnings. Perkins (chapter 11) demonstrates the impact of autonomy, incentives, and the trade regime on enterprise export performance. Jefferson, Lu, and Zhao (chapter 5) and Jefferson and Rawski (1997) attribute efficiency gains to ongoing exchanges negotiated within China's fledgling property rights market. The combination of these mutually reinforcing changes has enabled both state-owned enterprises and urban and rural collective-owned enterprises to substantially improve their performance.

Profitability. In all sectors of the industrial economy profitability has declined. Profitability is lower in the state sector than in the collective, foreign-funded, and shareholding sectors but comparable to the overseas Chinese–funded sector. Assessments of performance must distinguish between productivity, which may rise, and profitability, which may fall, even as productivity rises. While other explanations deserve consideration, the central, most fundamental explanation of the industrywide decline in profitability in China is rising competition. Profitability in state industry has fallen more than elsewhere, in part because productivity in that sector is rising relatively more slowly than elsewhere.

The simultaneous rise in productivity and fall in profitability is one of the striking paradoxes of China's industrial transition. Measured as the ratio of total profits plus taxes to total capital, overall pretax profitability in Chinese industry fell from about 25 percent in 1980 (Naughton 1994) to 20.5 percent in 1988, 9.5 percent in 1992, and 7.1 percent in 1996 (table 1.9). Much of this decline has resulted from heightened competition. That profit rates are lowest in the small-firm sector, which is most exposed to competition, is evident from table 6.8, which shows 1996 pretax profit-to-revenue rates of 12.8 percent for large firms, 6.4 percent for medium-size firms, and 5.9 percent for small firms. The low rates of profit reported by the overseas Chinese—funded sector may reflect the concentration of small firms in export-oriented light industry.

In state industry the pattern of decline was similar to overall industry until after 1992. By 1995 the ratio of profit plus tax to total assets had declined to 6.6 percent. During the early 1990s about one-third of China's industrial state enterprises were reporting losses. Two types of factors may explain the relative decline in profitability in state industry.

The first is the entry of nonstate enterprises into industries that had enjoyed quasi-monopoly profits. Two sets of results, both reported in chapter 6, find that the entry of nonstate producers has driven down profits in the state sector. This phenomenon has been most acute in recent years, as overcapacity has driven down prices, especially in the consumer goods sector.

The relative decline in profitability of state-owned enterprises reflects the rise in their productivity, which nevertheless lags behind that of the nonstate sector. Hence, although the long-run average cost curve in state industry is shifting downward, costs in the nonstate sector and prices generally are declining faster. Productivity among state-owned enterprises is not rising fast enough to prevent growing losses that arise from increasing domestic and international competition, which is causing demand for China's industrial goods to become increasingly price elastic.

Low and falling rates of profit in state industry reflect other factors relating to state industry in itself; Jefferson, Singh, Xing, and Zhang review these in chapter 6. The limited means of exit in state industry restricts the ability of state industry to shed chronic loss-making enterprises, thereby fattening the loss-making tail of profit distribution in that sector. At the same time conversion of the most successful state enterprises to forms of nonstate ownership is thinning the tail at the high-profit end of the distribution. Overall, profit rates in state industry are also depressed by the continued concentration of subsidized housing and social services in the sector. Finally, low real rates of interest and a lack of discipline in the financial system appear to be encouraging overinvestment in state industry, which is depressing profitability and levels of capital productivity.

Enterprise conduct

In a variety of ways state-owned, urban collective, and township and village enterprises demonstrate a surprising degree of consistency with the behavior predicted of the neoclassical firm. During the 1980s and 1990s wages have become more strongly associated with labor productivity, bonuses have become more strongly associated with profits, investment and innovation activity have become more closely linked with profitability, and autonomy and export-oriented incentives have been used to spur export activity.

Both chapters that examine wage-setting behavior in Chinese industry find significant links between reward and effort. In their chapter on wage and employment behavior (chapter 8), Jefferson, Singh, Hu, and Wang concur with a major conclusion of Hay and others (1994) that "the standard neoclassical model seems to fit these firms, even though imperfect adjustment and/or lags are clearly evident" (p. 143). Hay and others limit their analysis to state industry; Jefferson, Singh, Hu, and Wang extend the conclusion to enterprises of all ownership types. They find that state-owned enterprises are more constrained by past values of the wage bill, basic wage, employment, and bonuses, while joint ventures generally demonstrate greater short-run responsiveness to price changes. Yet in the long-run, state-owned enterprises adjust substantially—perhaps more fully than other ownership types—to changes in relative prices. The incentive effect of wages and bonus are most evident in state industry, where the threat of layoff is weak; less so in the collective sector; and hardly evident in the joint venture sector.

In chapter 9 Pitt and Putterman examine the widely held view that both state and collective enterprises in China overemploy labor. Comparing actual employment levels to those projected to be profit-maximizing given outside wages and estimated technical parameters, their results suggest that, if anything, township and village enterprises are biased against, rather than toward, employment creation. This striking result, combined with related research on state-owned enterprise (Dong and Putterman 1997), indicates that during the 1980s both state and township and village enterprises experienced monopsony power in labor hiring. The work of Dong and Putterman (1997) also suggests that state industry's monopsony power has ended as the rapid expansion and diversification of China's industrial base and relaxation on labor mobility have created more competitive and unified labor markets.

Jefferson, Hu, and Singh (chapter 10) find a robust fit between the survey data and various investment functions derived from neoclassical principles. They conclude that their findings "provide encouraging evidence that capital's marginal revenue product, enterprise profitability, and relative prices are significantly affecting patterns of capital accumulation." Various data sets consistently demonstrate a substantial and growing link between enterprise performance and investment, a pattern that appears to be just as much in evidence in state industry as it is in urban collective enterprises, township and village enterprises, and joint ventures. This is one of the most important findings in the literature on Chinese enterprise reform. Over the long run, robust economic growth requires a close statistical link between enterprise economic performance and investment, the principal avenue for expanding production capacity. The authors' conclusion that in general the stronger state-owned enterprises are capturing most of the investment resources in that sector needs to be reconciled with Jefferson, Rawski, and Zheng's finding (1996) of an overall decline in capital productivity in state industry beginning in 1988 and continuing into the early 1990s.

Perkins (chapter 11) finds that policies intended to encourage export activity are, in fact, raising total factor productivity and expanding exports. The major determinants of export activity appear to be enterprise decisionmaking autonomy and exposure to freer domestic markets. Provision of duty drawbacks and tax and other privileges enjoyed by firms in the Special Economic Zones expose enterprises to international markets and promote exports. These are a powerful set of conclusions. While Perkins does control, in some measure, for obvious simultaneity problems, the conclusions should nonetheless be viewed somewhat tentatively.

The role of ownership

The collective sector has outstripped the state sector in terms of productivity growth and profitability, and average levels of total factor productivity appear to be higher in the collective and joint venture sectors than in state enterprises. Some of this disparity results from policy differences that are not intrinsic to ownership. These include less marketization, more social overhead, and less reformed management systems among state-owned enterprises. The fact that these factors constrain productivity and profitability in the sector suggests that further gains are achievable through policy reform that stops short of outright privatization.

Within all five enterprise samples virtually all the enterprises are either wholly publicly owned or include substantial public ownership; the sample of purely privately owned enterprises was not large enough to allow performance by private firms to be compared with performance by the various types of publicly owned enterprises. Such analysis represents the next important frontier of research on China's industrial enterprises.

Jefferson (chapter 7) indicates that in 1989, total factor productivity in township and village enterprises was either greater than or comparable to that of their state-owned enterprise industrial branch counterparts. If, as the evidence suggests, the township and village enterprise sector has continued to experience more rapid productivity growth, the sector now enjoys higher productivity levels than state enterprises. It is difficult to appreciate fully the reasons for the superior productivity performance of the township and village enterprise sector. Chapters 6 and 7 attempt to identify sources of differing performance among state industry, township and village enterprises, and other forms of ownership.

The statistical work in both of these chapters indicates that part of the disparity in measured productivity can be explained by differences in market exposure and contracting arrangements. Differences in production scale and industrial branch composition also matter. Disparities in productivity and profitability can also be explained in part by differences in social overhead and pension obligations. Relative to state–owned enterprises, township and village enterprises also generally enjoy property rights that are more devolved and coherent.

While controlling for these conditions tends to narrow the performance gap between state enterprises and township and village enterprises, the gap nevertheless persists. As Perkins notes (chapter 11), "even controlling for policy differences (including decision autonomy), urban collective, township and village, and foreign-funded enterprises are all significantly more successful exporters than state enterprises."

It may be that whether the factors that continue to depress efficiency by state enterprises relative to nonstate enterprises are extrinsic to state ownership or not is immaterial. If the state is unable to unshackle state industry from the constraints of social obligations, blocked exit, and impeded competition, the "pure ownership effect" will remain entangled with policy variables.

Three views of ownership can be distinguished. The first, held by Nolan (1995) and Rawski (1994), among others, is that the form of ownership is less important than a level playing field, on which state and collective enterprises can hold their own. Others, including Sachs and Woo (1997) and Galal and Shirley (1995), view publicly owned enterprises as inherently flawed and thus urge their disbandment. A third view is agnostic. From this perspective, held by Weitzman and Xu (1994), who see township and village enterprises as sustained by a "culture of cooperation," some publicly owned enterprises may be able to compete successfully in the foreseeable future. Regardless of which of these views one embraces, the appropriate policy response is to focus on constructing an efficient property rights market that consistently subjects all firms, regardless of ownership, to a market-based performance test. This view, propounded by Jefferson (1998), argues for leaving the ownership issue to a property rights market that provides clear, unencumbered avenues through which unsuccessful firms and ownership types can exit or be acquired by more successful firms. It suggests that the Chinese government may wish to retain or assign ownership rights to various units of government. Whether or not a substantial publicly owned sector survives in China outside of the natural monopoly industries should depend on the ability of these publicly owned enterprises to compete and innovate within China's emerging property rights market and, more generally, its industrial innovation ladder.

Sustainability

Enterprise performance has improved as a result of a continuous, if gradual, sequence of reforms. Expanding competition, encouraging marketization and exposure to international trade and investment, increasing fiscal and financial discipline, and supporting evolving property rights markets while maintaining a stable macroeconomic environment are key to sustaining economic reform and a growing industrial economy. These are also the measures most needed to strengthen and capitalize on China's industrial innovation ladder. Strengthening the industrial innovation ladder, in turn, will serve to build in pressures throughout the industrial system for steady, ongoing reform.

In the medium term, productivity gains can be achieved through reductions in static inefficiency associated with further marketization and property rights reform under existing ownership arrangements. This potential should not be underestimated. Through a continuing process of factor reallocation, bankruptcy, and merger, the resources of the more than 7 million enterprises in China will gradually be consolidated, so that economies of scale and scope comparable to those realized in the industrial economies are achieved. Beyond this vast potential for static efficiency gains, China's high savings rates and increasing openness to international trade and investment are motivating and financing the adoption of improved physical and human capital, which is needed to support ongoing rapid technical progress within China's more advanced industrial sectors.

Productivity gains in China's state-owned enterprises have enabled the state enterprises to serve as a useful transitional device by providing a guarantee of social insurance to China's urban population and a source of producer goods to the emerging nonstate sector. The conversion of state-owned enterprises to joint ventures and to large shareholding enterprises has fueled the growth of these new ownership forms, while increasing numbers of smaller state-owned enterprises are being fully privatized. As a declining proportion of state enterprises is able to compete effectively with other ownership forms and as new social insurance arrangements are put in place, the pace of conversion is accelerating, both through the market and at the direct initiative of Chinese government.

Jefferson and Rawski's model of an innovation ladder (chapter 3) represents one perspective on the sustainability of reform. In this model a competitive process of "natural selection" is built into the economy, in which enterprises and local governments must search for new governance structures and new technical innovations in order to remain competitive and solvent. The speed and efficiency with which the Chinese economy and people realize the potential gains already embodied in their industrial system will depend on the capacity of a competitive, well-functioning property rights market to mediate the millions of exchanges required to match supplies of labor, capital, technology, and entrepreneurship. Clarifying the assignment of property rights within China's industrial system, expanding competition, and reducing transactions costs will increase the efficiency of China's industrial innovation ladder.

Even as a property rights market develops, however, various forces will curtail high rates of growth. These include the following:

- *Stable or declining savings rates.* During the past two decades China's savings rate has risen to more than 40 percent. The increase in the savings rate has contributed to rising rates of capital formation and rising living standards; stabilization of the rate of savings will slow growth. During the next two decades savings rates will likely fall as China's dependency ratio rises. That ratio is likely to rise as children of the "one-child" policy increasingly dominate the work force, the retirement population swells, and the one-child policy is relaxed under a more liberal political regime.
- *Declining export growth.* Starting from a low base, China's exports have grown dramatically. With or without comparable rates of import growth, China is unlikely to be able to sustain the rate of export growth of 10 percent a year that helped drive GDP growth during the first two decades of reform. While China's trade ratio will continue to rise, its rate of increase will slow.
- *Slower technological advances.* Most of China's industries remain far from the international technology frontier. In some branches, notably apparel, footwear, and consumer electronics, however, Chinese industry is approaching the frontier, so that gains will require increasing shares of costly innovation rather than comparatively inexpensive imitation. As with all developing countries, growth slows as manufacturing capabilities increasingly embody best available practice.

The issue is not whether China's robust economic growth will moderate; it will. The question is whether within these broad constraints of changing demographics, international markets, and available technology the Chinese economy will create and continuously refine a set of economic institutions that enable it to achieve the living standards of the most advanced nations. The perspective in this volume is that China has made an impressive start in that direction in a relatively short period of time. By virtue of its immense size and diversity and its proximity to overseas resources, the Chinese economy enjoys a dynamic process of reform and innovation that, with the evolution of a complementary set of political institutions, should allow it to achieve economic prosperity. The key to understanding this transformation entails more than measuring the performance of Chinese enterprise; it involves understanding the process of China's industrial transition and the institutions that drive that process.

Note

1. At the risk of omitting worthy sources on the subject, we venture to note several books, including Findlay, Watson, and Wu (1994); Naughton (1992); J.Y. Lin (1992); and Nolan (1995). Articles include Naughton (1992), Chen, Jefferson, and Singh (1992), and Gelb, Jefferson, and Singh (1993).

References

Chen, Kang, Gary H. Jefferson, and Inderjit Singh. 1992. "Lessons from China's Economic Reform." *Journal of Comparative Economics* 16(3): 201–25.

China State Statistical Bureau. Various years. *China Statistical Yearbook (Zhongguo tongji nianjian)* (in Chinese). Beijing: China Statistical Publications Office.

Day, Richard H., Zhigang Wang, and Gang Zou. 1994. *A Dynamic Analysis of Chinese Enterprise Behavior under Alternative Reform Regimes.* Research Paper Series. World Bank, Socialist Economies Reform Unit, Washington, D.C.

Dong, Ziao-Yuan, and Louis Putterman. 1997. "China's State-Owned Enterprises in the First Reform Decade: An Analysis of a Declining Monopsony." Working Paper. Brown University (Providence, R.I.) and University of Winnipeg (Ontario).

Findlay, Christopher, Andrew Watson, and Harry X. Wu., eds. 1994. *Rural Enterprises in China.* New York: St. Martin's Press, Inc.

Galal, A., and M. Shirley. 1995. *Bureaucrats in Business.* New York: Oxford University Press.

Gelb, Alan, Gary H. Jefferson, and Inderjit Singh. 1993. "Can Communist Economies Transform Incrementally? The Experience of China." *Macroeconomics Annual 1993.* Cambridge, Mass.: MIT Press.

Grossman, Gene M., and Elhanan Helpman. 1991. "Quality Ladders and Product Cycles." *Quarterly Journal of Economics* 106(9): 557–86.

Groves, Theodore, Yongmiao Hong, John McMillan, and Barry Naughton. 1994. "Autonomy and Incentives in Chinese State Industry." *Quarterly Journal of Economics* 109(1): 1–27.

Hay, Donald, Derek Morris, Guy Liu, and Shujie Yao. 1994. *Economic Reform and State-Owned Enterprises in China, 1979–1987.* Oxford: Clarendon Press.

Jefferson, Gary H. 1998. "China's State-Owned Enterprises: Public Goods, Externalities, and Coase." *American Economic Review: Papers and Proceedings* 88(2): 428–32.

Jefferson, Gary H., and Thomas G. Rawski. 1993. "A Theory of Economic Reform." Working paper. Department of Economics, Brandeis University, Waltham, Mass.

———. 1994. "How Industrial Reform Worked in China: The Role of Innovation, Competition, and Property Rights." *Proceedings of the World Bank Annual Bank Conference on Development Economics.* Washington, D.C.: World Bank.

———. 1996. "Chinese Industrial Productivity: Trends, Measurement Issues, and Recent Developments." *Journal of Comparative Economics* 23(2): 121–46.

———. 1997. "China's Enterprise Reform as a Market Process." Working Paper 76. William Davidson Institute, University of Michigan Business School, Ann Arbor, Mich.

Jefferson, Gary H., and Wenyi Xu. 1994. "Assessing Gains in Efficiency Production among China's Industrial Enterprises." *Economic Development and Cultural Change* 42(3): 597–616.

Jefferson, Gary H., Thomas G. Rawski, and Yuxin Zheng. 1996. "Chinese Industrial Productivity: Trends, Measurement Issues and Recent Developments." *Journal of Comparative Economics* 23(2): 146–180.

Lin, Justin Yifu. 1992. *The Chinese Miracle: Development Strategy and Economic Reform.* Hong Kong: Chinese University of Hong Kong Press.

McKinnon, Ronald I. 1994. "Gradual versus Rapid Liberalization in Socialist Economies: The Problem of Macroeconomic Control." *Proceedings of the World Bank Annual Conference on Development Economics 1993.* Washington, D.C.: World Bank.

Murphy, Kevin M., Andrei Shleifer, and Robert W. Vishny. 1992. "The Transition to a Market Economy: Pitfalls of Partial Reform." *Quarterly Journal of Economics* 107(3): 889–906.

Naughton, Barry. 1992. "Implications of the State Monopoly over Industry and Its Relaxation." *Modern China* 18(1): 14–41.

———. 1994. *Growing Out of the Plan: Chinese Economic Reform, 1978–1993.* New York: Cambridge University Press.

Nolan, Peter. 1995. *China's Rise, Russia's Fall.* New York: St. Martin's Press.

Perkins, Dwight H. 1992. "China's 'Gradual' Approach to Market Reforms." Paper presented at a conference on "Comparative Experiences of Economic Reform and Post-Socialist Transformation," July 6–8, El Escorial, Spain.

Rawski, Thomas G. 1994. "Progress without Privatization: The Reform of China's State Industries." In Vedat Milor, ed., *Changing Political Economies: Privatization in Post-Communist and Reforming Communist States.* Boulder, Colo.: Lynne Rienner Publishers.

Sachs, Jeffrey, and Wing Thye Woo. 1994. "Structural Reforms in the Economic Reforms of China, Eastern Europe and the Former Soviet Union." *Economic Policy* April: 101–45.

———. 1997. "Understanding China's Economic Performance." Working Paper 5935, National Bureau of Economic Research, Cambridge, Mass.

Vernon, Raymond. 1966. "International Investment and International Trade in the Product Cycle." *Quarterly Journal of Economics* 80(2):190–207.

Weitzman, Martin, and Chenggang Xu. 1994. "Chinese Township-Village Enterprises as Vaguely Defined Cooperatives." *Journal of Comparative Economics* 18(2): 121–45.

Woo, Wing Thye, Gang Fan, Wen Hai, and Yibao Jin. 1993. "The Efficiency and Macroeconomic Consequences of Chinese Enterprise Reform." *China Economic Review* 4(2): 153–68.

World Bank. 1997. *World Development Report 1997: The State in a Changing World*. New York: Oxford University Press.

World Bank, Resident Mission in China. 1993. "China: Recent Economic Development." *Economic Note*. February.

Wu, Harry X.Y., and Yanrui Wu. 1994. "Rural Enterprise Growth and Efficiency." In C. Findlay, Andrew Watson, and Harry Wu., eds., *Rural Enterprises in China*. London: MacMillan.

Wu, Yanrui. 1993. "Productive Efficiency in Chinese Industry." *Asian-Pacific Economic Literature* 7(2): 58–66.

Ownership Change in Chinese Industry

1

Gary H. Jefferson and Thomas G. Rawski

The rapid pace of real growth of China's industrial sector during its first two decades of reform has paralleled dramatic changes in the structure of ownership. This transformation of ownership structure has both caused and resulted from fundamental changes throughout Chinese industry in the patterns of investment, employment, productivity, profitability, and sectoral composition. The purpose of this chapter is to document and interpret these changes. Specifically, this chapter describes the formal classification of ownership within Chinese industry. It also provides a statistical overview of changes in the structure of ownership, compares and contrasts the performance of Chinese industry by ownership, and examines the functional complementarities among various ownership types that cause these ownership types to fit together into a dynamic system.

The ownership composition of Chinese industry

China's State Statistical Bureau divides Chinese enterprises into four broad ownership categories: state-owned enterprises, collective-owned enterprises, individual-owned enterprises, and "other" ownership forms (box 1.1). Collective-owned enterprises include urban collectives, township enterprises, village enterprises, and cooperatives. "Other" ownership forms include domestic joint ventures, privately owned enterprises, foreign-funded joint ventures, overseas-funded joint ventures, foreign-funded wholly owned firms, overseas-funded wholly owned firms, foreign-funded cooperatives, overseas-funded cooperatives, and shareholding enterprises.

Individual-owned firms *(geti)*, which account for about 80 percent of the more than 7 million enterprises in China, are privately owned firms that employ no more than seven workers. Private firms that employ eight or more workers are classified as "privately owned" *(siying)*.

23

Box 1.1 Ownership classifications of Chinese enterprises

STATE-OWNED ENTERPRISES*

COLLECTIVE-OWNED ENTERPRISES*
  Urban collectives
  Township-owned enterprises*
  Village-owned enterprises*
  Cooperatives

INDIVIDUAL-OWNED ENTERPRISES*

OTHER*
  Privately owned enterprises
  Domestic joint ventures
  Foreign-funded enterprises*
    Foreign-funded joint ventures
    Foreign-funded wholly owned enterprises
    Foreign-funded cooperatives
  Overseas-funded enterprises*
    Overseas-funded joint ventures
    Overseas-funded wholly owned enterprises
    Overseas-funded cooperatives
  Shareholding enterprises*

* Included in China State Statistical Bureau 1996.

China's statistical office distinguishes between firms with foreign direct investment from Hong Kong,[1] Taiwan (China), and Macao, which it calls overseas-funded firms, and firms with foreign direct investment from elsewhere, which it calls foreign-funded firms. In 1996 the number of overseas Chinese–funded firms exceeded the total number of foreign-funded firms by one third (table 1.1). Most of China's foreign- and overseas-funded joint ventures were created by combining foreign direct investment with state- or collective-owned enterprises that are reclassified as joint ventures.

The *China Statistical Yearbook* compresses these 15 ownership classifications into a smaller number, which varies from year to year. In the 1996 *Yearbook* the large grouping of collective-owned enterprises is subdivided into three subgroups: township, village, and joint enterprise. (Thus the sum of these subgroups is less than the total for collective–owned enterprise, with the difference representing urban collective–owned enterprise.) The "other" category includes detailed data for just three of its nine subcategories: shareholding, foreign-funded, and overseas-funded. Presumably, the foreign- and overseas-funded subcategories include joint ventures, wholly owned enterprises, and cooperatives.

TABLE 1.1

Number of enterprises, selected years, 1980–96
(thousands)

Type of enterprise	1980	1985	1990	1995	1996
State-owned	83.4	93.7	104.4	118.0	113.8
Collective-owned	293.5	367.8	1,668.5	1,475.0	1,591.8
Township-owned	186.6	217.1	228.7	228.8	202.3
Village-owned	—	632.6	680.8	689.9	678.4
Cooperative	—	741.7	596.6	371.6	518.6
Individual-owned	—	3,347.8	6,176.0	5,688.2	6,210.7
Other	0.4	1.7	8.8	60.3	70.2
Shareholding	—	—	—	5.9	8.3
Foreign-funded	—	—	—	18.0	19.8
Overseas-funded	—	—	—	26.9	24.5
Total	377.3	3,811.0	7,957.8	7,341.5	7,986.5

— Not available.
Note: Includes both independent accounting units and nonindependent accounting units.
Source: China State Statistical Bureau 1986 (p. 233), 1993 (p. 409), 1996 (pp. 401, 407), and 1997 (pp. 411, 416–17); China State Statistical Bureau, *China Industrial Economy Statistical Yearbook* 1991 (p. 23).

Since 1980 the number of enterprises has increased in every category, including state industry, where the number of enterprises rose from 83,400 in 1980 to 113,800 in 1996. The number of collective-owned enterprises rose from 293,500 in 1980 to 1,591,800 in 1996, with most of the growth coming from village or joint township-village enterprises.

The most explosive growth of new enterprises occurred in the individual sector, which did not exist in the late 1970s but which grew rapidly in the 1980s after rural reform began. The number of individual enterprises rose from 3.3 million in 1985 to 6.4 million in 1991 and then leveled out to about 6 million during the mid-1990s. The number of "other" enterprises rose from just 400 in 1980 to 70,200 by 1996. Nearly half of the enterprises in this sector are overseas-funded firms, followed by foreign-funded firms and shareholding firms.

Most striking about this picture is the fact that the number of enterprises in China rose from 377,000 in 1980 to nearly 8 million in 1996. This phenomenon of rapid business formation outside the state sector, across virtually all ownership forms, reflects the relatively free entry of new business in China.

Differences in growth rates by form of ownership

Chinese industry grew at an overall inflation-adjusted rate of about 15.8 percent between 1980 and 1996 (table 1.2). State industry grew at 7.7 percent—slightly more than half the overall rate—while the collective sector grew at 21.5 percent a year. The individual sector grew by 80.0 percent a year and the "other" sector grew at 46.8 percent a year.

TABLE 1.2
Growth of real output in Chinese industry, selected years, 1980–96
(1980=100)

Type of enterprise	Index of real output				Average annual growth rate (percent)	
	1985	1990	1995	1996	1980–96	1990–96
State-owned	148	210	313	329	7.7	7.8
Collective-owned	247	554	1,858	2,246	21.5	26.3
Individual-owned	21,752	126,057	973,103	167,724	80.0	44.9
Other	492	3,530	37,663	46,615	46.8	53.7
Total	176	328	893	1,040	15.8	21.2

Source: China State Statistical Bureau 1996 (p. 403) and 1997 (pp. 411, 424).

Chinese industrial statistics are widely viewed as overstating the growth of real output (Rawski 1991; Field 1992; Jefferson 1992). The causes of upward statistical bias, summarized in Jefferson, Rawski, and Zheng (1996), include the use of the current price of new products to stand for the constant price measure of output, which biases implicit price deflators; a movement away from the "excessive integration" of the planned Chinese industrial enterprise, which reduces the net-to-gross output ratio and increases double counting of industrial production; and falsification of output statistics, particularly in rural areas. This tendency to overstate production was confirmed by the 1995 industrial survey, which found fewer township and village enterprises and substantially less output than had been officially reported. These biases suggest the need for a small downward adjustment to officially reported rates of growth for state industry and a more substantial adjustment for township and village enterprises.

Changes in the composition of output by form of ownership

State industry's share of gross industrial output has fallen dramatically since reform began (table 1.3). In 1980 more than three-quarters of gross industrial output was provided by state firms; by 1995 the figure had fallen to 34 percent and by 1996 it had dropped to less than 29 percent. Over the same period the share of output produced by the collective, individual, and other sectors rose by more than 15 percentage points. Two-thirds of this increase in the output share of the "other" sector came from foreign and overseas-funded enterprises.

While the robust township and village enterprise sector largely accounted for the expanding output share of nonstate industry during the 1980s, the individual and "other" sectors enjoyed the largest gains during the 1990s. The township and village enterprise sector expanded

TABLE 1.3
Gross industrial output, selected years, 1980–96
(percent)

Type of enterprise	1980	1985	1990	1995	1996
State-owned	76.0	64.9	54.6	34.0	28.5
Collective-owned	23.6	32.1	35.6	36.6	39.4
Township-owned	—	7.8	10.2	13.0	11.8
Village-owned	—	6.8	10.0	12.9	16.0
Individual-owned	0	1.8	5.4	12.9	15.5
Other	0.5	1.2	4.4	16.6	16.6
Shareholding	—	—	—	3.0	3.3
Foreign-funded	—	—	—	5.2	6.6
Overseas	—	—	—	5.3	5.4
Total	100	100	100	100	100

— Not available.
Note: Total may not equal 100 percent because of rounding.
Source: China State Statistical Bureau 1936 (pp. 409, 412), 1996 (pp. 401, 414), and 1997 (pp. 411, 424).

its output share by almost 8 percentage points during 1990–96, while the individual and "other" sectors expanded their combined share by better than 22 percentage points.

Differential rates of growth by ownership type and changing ownership shares have altered the state and nonstate shares across individual industries. In 1987 state industry accounted for at least 80 percent of output in 13 of the 29 industries for which data were reported (table 1.4). In only one industry—furniture—was the share of state-owned enterprises less than 20 percent. By 1995 state industry accounted for at least 80 percent of output in only 6 of 39 industries; in 9 industries the share of state industry fell to less than 20 percent. The most dramatic declines in the share of output by the state occurred in food manufacturing, chemical fibers, plastics, metal products, timber, telecommunications equipment, and electrical equipment.

Changes affecting Chinese industry

The transformation of Chinese industry has been driven by the restructuring of China's existing state-owned enterprises as well as by the rapid entry of millions of new enterprises operating under a variety of forms of ownership. These mutually reinforcing changes constitute the centerpiece of China's evolving enterprise system.

Rapid growth outside the state sector

The reported output of the collective sector exceeded that of state-owned industry in China by 1995. Exports by China's rural firms, which

TABLE 1.4
State share of gross industrial output, by industry, 1987 and 1995
(percent)

Industry	1987	1995	Industry	1987	1995
Coal	83.3	77.7	Pharmaceuticals	—	51.2
Petroleum	99.4	95.4	Chemical fibers	89.4	34.7
Ferrous metals	70.8	45.3	Rubber	70.0	40.0
Nonferrous metals	79.5	56.9	Plastics	26.0	12.4
Nonmetal mining	37.9	31.9	Nonmetal mineral		
Other minerals	—	37.9	products	52.9	32.4
Logging	97.0	96.3	Ferrous smelting	89.2	68.9
Food processing	—	18.9	Nonferrous smelting	84.2	55.4
Food manufacturing	83.1	38.1	Metal products	28.9	13.8
Beverages	75.8	53.2	Machinery	70.3	40.1
Tobacco	98.2	96.8	Special equipment	—	50.7
Textiles	62.6	39.6	Transport equipment	74.4	51.5
Garments	—	6.9	Electrical equipment	50.9	22.8
Leather	—	8.4	Telecommunications		
Timber	52.5	17.6	equipment	69.7	25.1
Furniture	13.3	8.9	Office machines	64.3	32.9
Paper	—	37.3	Other manufacturing	—	8.1
Printing	—	40.7	Electricity	97.6	77.6
Stationery	—	10.7	Gas	82.0	89.7
Petroleum processing	97.5	88.2	Water	93.0	84.8
Raw chemicals	82.4	56.0			

— Not available.
Note: Independent accounting enterprises only.
Source: China State Statistical Bureau 1988 (pp. 318, 377, 389), 1996 (pp. 414, 418).

dominate the collective sector, reached $40 billion in 1994, about a third of total exports, up from $3.9 billion in 1985 (Lardy 1992; *China Daily* 6 May 1996).

During the 1980s the fastest growth was in the township and village sector; during the 1990s the individual and "other" sectors, which include many former state-owned enterprises, have burgeoned. These sectors, which were of marginal importance in 1985, surpassed state industry in terms of output in 1996, accounting for nearly one-third of industrial production (China State Statistical Bureau 1997).

The number of small enterprises outside the state sector has proliferated, and nonstate enterprises have begun to establish a presence among China's largest industrial enterprises. During the 1980s virtually all of China's large and medium-size enterprises were state-owned. This profile had changed dramatically by 1993, when one-fourth of the 18,471 large and medium-size enterprises in China were classified as nonstate enterprises. This number included about 2,800 collectives and 350–400 joint stock companies and foreign and overseas joint ventures (China State Statistical

Bureau 1994). By 1995 the collective sector had grown to include 528 large firms and 3,540 medium-size collectives (Census of China 1997).

The dominant role of public enterprise

The decline in state industry's share of industrial output did not reflect stagnation in the state sector, which grew by almost 8 percent a year between 1980 and 1995. Rather, the decline reflected the spectacular growth of other ownership forms. Despite the decline in state industry's output share, public sector industry—the combined state and collective sectors—accounted for about two-thirds of China's industrial economy in 1996.

If individual enterprises are assumed to be fully privately owned and about half of the assets of the "other" sector are assumed to be privately owned, about 70 percent of industrial output originates with public ownership, 15 percent with private ownership, and 15 percent with joint public-private ownership.[2] Many privately owned enterprises "wear a red hat" (*dai hongmao*) and are formally designated as collectives. The need to disguise private ownership to avoid harassment has diminished since the early reform years, and during the mid-1990s many township and village enterprises have begun to "individualize ownership" (*gerenhua suoyouzhi*) through the distribution of shares to managers, workers, and residents.

Measuring ownership shares in terms of underlying assets rather than sales also overstates the dominance of the public and state sectors. While state industry's share of industrial output in 1996 fell to 29 percent, it accounts for nearly two-thirds of the total reported net industrial assets for that year (China State Statistical Bureau 1997).

The decentralization of public ownership

A significant by-product of the proliferation of public enterprises is the decentralization of ownership and control to local units of government. This has occurred through two means.

The first is the proliferation and expansion of the township and village sector. In 1978, 85 percent of industrial output originated from industry; by the mid-1990s, 40 percent of industrial output was produced by China's nearly 1.5 million publicly owned collective enterprises, most of which are controlled by local government.

The second channel through which public ownership has become increasingly decentralized is through devolution of the control of state industry to provincial and local governments. Beginning in the 1960s and continuing through the 1970s and into the reform era, control of all but the largest state enterprises has been increasingly decentralized to subnational jurisdictions. This decentralization of control has been further reinforced by the policy of "retain the large, release the small" (*juada, fangxiao*), in which the state is increasingly leaving the disposition of all but the largest enterprises to provincial and local levels of government.

The devolution of public enterprise control to China's 31 provinces, more than 600 cities, and 48,000 townships and villages has far-reaching implications for the behavior of Chinese industry. Although public ownership dominates Chinese industry, the center can no longer monopolize production and pricing, except in certain natural resource and defense sectors. As a result of relaxation of barriers to entry through the liberalization of commodity, capital, and labor markets, most industries have entered an era of intense competition, driven in substantial part by widespread overcapacity. Local governments have become active agents of business planning and strategy, but none appears able to exercise substantial or sustainable market power.

Decentralization of public enterprise control has also contributed to the development of a property rights market, and it is motivating the decentralized exchange of ownership and control over industrial land, plants, equipment, and whole companies. Mergers and acquisitions have become everyday occurrences in China's industrial economy (Howson 1997). Chapters 3 and 5 in this volume demonstrate how this local restructuring of property rights is motivated in substantial part by the competition that has resulted from the decentralization of enterprise control.

Performance of Chinese enterprises

Data describing the technical and financial performance of Chinese industry are examined in the following sections, which try to explain the apparent contradiction between rising productivity and falling profitability.

Productivity

Total factor productivity in Chinese industry grew substantially during the early to mid-1980s and continued to grow between 1988 and 1992, albeit at a slower rate for both the state and collective sectors (table 1.5). Some of the apparent industrywide slowdown may reflect the choice of reference years, which occur at different points in the business cycle (Jefferson, Rawski, and Zheng 1996). During 1988 inflation accelerated rapidly in industrial sectors operating well above normal capacity. In contrast, in 1992 relative price stability resulted from a more normal level of capacity utilization.

The more pronounced slowdown in total factor productivity growth in state industry reflects two conditions. The first is the relative decline in capital productivity in the state sector—the result of overinvestment (see table 6.9). The second is the growing tendency for the most productive state-owned enterprises to become joint ventures or joint stock companies and therefore to drop out of the state ownership classification (see table 6.2).

Data on total factor productivity growth for the individual and "other" sectors are not available. Single factor productivity levels can be compared across ownership types, however (table 1.6). These data, which are limited to independent accounting units (enterprises with formal state-sanctioned accounting procedures), omit enterprises below the township level from the collective-owned enterprise category and individual enterprises from the "other" category. The "other" category is therefore dominated by shareholding enterprises and foreign and overseas joint ventures.

These data show an uneven pattern of single factor productivity in which the productivity of labor is highest within the "other" category, next highest within large and medium-size state-owned enterprises, and lowest within collective-owned enterprises. Capital productivity is highest within collective-owned enterprises, next highest within the "other" category, and lowest within state-owned enterprises. The productivity of intermediate inputs is highest within large and medium-size state-owned enterprises and lowest within the "other" category. No single ownership type dominates along all three measures of single factor productivity, but

TABLE 1.5

Growth rates of output, inputs, and total factor productivity for state and collective industry, 1980–92
(percent)

Type of enterprise	Real output	Deflated net fixed assets	Labor	Real value of intermediate inputs	Total factor productivity
State-owned					
1980–92	6.90	1.38	0.33	2.69	2.50
		(6.73)	(2.73)	(3.98)	
1988–92	5.11	1.75	0.20	1.59	1.58
		(8.53)	(1.64)	(2.35)	
Collective-owned					
1980–92	12.36	1.36	0.37	7.19	3.43
		(10.20)	(3.19)	(9.60)	
1988–92	7.90	1.03	0.03	3.86	2.98
		(7.71)	(0.29)	(5.15)	

Note: Numbers within parentheses are growth rates for factor inputs. The (normalized) values of the weights for capital, labor, and intermediate inputs used in these calculations are 0.205, 0.120, and 0.675 for the state sector and 0.134, 0.117, and 0.749 for collective industry. The figures for collective industry were obtained by recalculating real output for collective industry, applying the price index for state sector industrial output used in Jefferson, Rawski, and Zheng (1996) to the official figures for nominal output of collective industry.
Source: Jefferson, Rawski, and Zheng 1996.

TABLE 1.6
Single factor productivities, value added ratios, and average firm size, 1996
(current yuan)

Type of enterprise	Value added of labor	Value added of net fixed assets	Value added of gross industrial output	Gross industrial output/ number of enterprises
State-owned	21,836	0.43	0.33	38,497
Large and medium-size	25,054	0.43	0.34	103,796
Collective-owned	18,211	0.99	0.26	6,788
Other	38,720	0.58	0.25	34,868

Note: Independent accounting units only.
Source: China State Statistical Bureau 1997.

measured in terms of value–added productivity the "other" sector clearly dominates the state sector.

While the 1980s was characterized by a surge of new business formation, the 1990s has been characterized by a growth of firm size. Individual enterprise production rose 45 percent a year during 1990–96 (see table 1.2), even as the number of individual enterprises remained relatively stable (see table 1.1). During this period real average firm size increased by more than 600 percent in the individual sector, by 280 percent in the collective sector, by 40 percent in the state sector, and by 20 percent in the "other" sector. The growth of average firm size between 1991 and 1996 suggests that rising competition is forcing all of Chinese industry to move toward minimum efficient scale. (For a review of various productivity studies of state and nonstate industry, see chapter 6.)

Profitability

Before profitability is compared across ownership types, various shortcomings of the profit data should be noted. (These are discussed in more depth in chapter 6.) Profitability data can be misleading for a variety of reasons, most of which lead to an understatement of the relative performance of state enterprises:

- Price controls in coal, mining, and crude oil reduce profitability significantly in major state enterprises, such as the Daqing oilfields.
- State enterprises face extremely high average and marginal tax rates, which typically exceed the tax burdens imposed on other types of firms. This gives state enterprises a powerful incentive to conceal profits. Expansion of capital flows among industrial firms, multiplication of financial intermediaries, and growing internationalization provide unprecedented opportunities for concealing profits.

- State enterprises are burdened with social service and insurance costs, including pensions, unemployment insurance, and health and education expenses, which far exceed comparable outlays for firms outside the state sector (tables 1.7 and 1.8). Transfer of social programs to government budgets is under way but remains far from complete.
- The most successful state enterprises avail themselves of financial opportunities outside the state sector by converting themselves into joint ventures or shareholding corporations (see table 6.2). At the same time, many of the least successful enterprises remain trapped in the state sector (despite bankruptcy legislation). Both trends act to reduce average measures of profitability in state industry.
- State enterprises may benefit from interest rate subsidies, tax breaks, or loan forgiveness provisions that are less frequently extended to firms outside the state sector. These benefits effectively reduce costs and increase profitability within the state sector.

TABLE 1.7
Welfare costs of Chinese state enterprises, 1992

Cost	State-owned enterprises	Collective units[a]	Foreign-invested units[a]
Welfare costs			
Per yuan of output (yuan)	0.012	0.006	0.003
Per worker (yuan)	490	149	272
Total (billions of yuan)	22.1	8.7	0.6
Industrial output (billions of yuan)	1,782.4	1,410.1	206.6
Year-end work force (million)	45.2	58.3	1.4/0.8[b]

a. Includes all units, not just industrial units.
b. First number represents foreign-funded enterprises; second number represents overseas-funded enterprises.
Source: China Labor Statistics Yearbook 1993 (pp. 483–97); China Industrial Economy Statistical Yearbook 1993 (pp. 3, 36).

TABLE 1.8
Pension costs of Chinese state enterprises, selected years, 1978–96

		State-sector share of		Active workers	
Year	Retirees (million)	Retirees[a] (percent)	Pension[a] outlays (percent)	Industry productivity (percent)	Number per retiree
1978	3.1	79.0	88.5	77.6	30.3
1983	12.9	78.6	86.0	73.4	8.9
1988	21.2	72.8	82.4	56.8	6.4
1992	26.0	75.9	83.7	48.1	5.7
1996	32.1	78.3	84.3	38.0	4.6

a. Includes all units, not just industrial units.
Source: China Labor Statistics Yearbook 1993 (pp. 483–97); China Industrial Economy Statistical Yearbook 1993 (pp. 3, 36).

Profitability has fallen consistently in China's industry since 1988 (table 1.9). In state industry, profits declined from nearly 18 percent to 10 percent of output between 1988 and 1999; profits by collective industry fell from nearly 11 percent to less than 6 percent. Profits as a percentage of total assets (net value of fixed asstes plus circulating capital) declined even more steeply. Using this measure of profitability, the capital-intensive state sector is the second least profitable sector in the economy (after the overseas Chinese sector).

After-tax profit data show a strikingly different picture (table 1.10). Profit as a percentage of output was just 2.6 percent for state industry in 1995, much lower than the 11.1 percent pretax rate enjoyed by state enterprises that year. As a percentage of assets, profits were just 1.9 percent after taxes. This pretax/after-tax differential is substantially higher for state industry, implying an average tax rate of about 71 percent on state enterprises versus rates of 60 percent for collective enterprises and 39 percent for foreign-funded enterprises. These effective tax rate differentials raise a further measurement issue, in that tax evasion can be expected to be higher among enterprises subject to high rates than among those with lower rates, leading to an underestimate of pretax profitability of state and collective enterprises relative to foreign-funded enterprises.

TABLE 1.9
Pretax profitability in Chinese industry, selected years, 1988–96
(percent)

Type of enterprise	1988	1992	1995	1996
(Profit + tax)/gross value of industrial output in current prices				
State-owned	17.8	11.4	11.1	10.0
Collective-owned	10.7	7.6	6.6	5.9
Township	10.1	7.9	—	—
Other	13.2	9.5	—	—
Shareholding	—	—	13.4	11.5
Foreign-funded	—	—	8.8	7.7
Overseas	—	—	5.9	5.8
Total	15.7	10.1	9.2	8.2
(Profit + tax)/(net fixed assets + average balance circulating funds)				
State-owned	20.6	9.2	6.6	6.5
Collective-owned	19.8	9.8	8.1	8.1
Township	18.8	11.8	—	—
Other	24.7	10.7	—	—
Shareholding	—	—	9.5	9.2
Foreign-funded	—	—	8.3	8.4
Overseas	—	—	5.1	5.6
Total	20.5	9.5	8.3	7.1

— Not available.
Note: Numbers for 1988 are retained profits; numbers for 1992 and 1995 are after-tax profits.
Source: China State Statistical Bureau 1989 (pp. 273, 320), 1993 (p. 414), and 1997 (pp. 424, 427).

TABLE 1.10
After-tax profitability in Chinese industry, selected years, 1988–96
(percent)

Type of enterprise	1988	1992	1995	1996
Profit/gross value of industrial output in current prices				
State-owned	3.3	3.1	2.6	1.5
Collective-owned	2.3	3.5	2.4	2.3
Township	2.4	4.2	—	—
Other	2.5	6.2	—	—
Shareholding	—	—	7.4	5.9
Foreign-funded	—	—	4.6	3.9
Overseas	—	—	2.9	2.8
Total	2.9	3.5	3.0	2.4
Profit/(net fixed assets + average balance circulating funds)				
State-owned	3.8	2.5	1.9	1.0
Collective-owned	4.1	4.5	3.2	3.1
Township	4.5	6.3	—	—
Other	4.7	7.0	—	—
Shareholding	—	—	6.3	4.7
Foreign-funded	—	—	5.1	4.3
Overseas	—	—	2.8	2.7
Total	3.9	3.3	2.7	2.1

— Not available.
Note: Numbers for 1988 are retained profits; numbers for 1992 and 1995 are after-tax profits.
Source: China State Statistical Bureau 1989 (pp. 273, 320), 1993 (p. 417), and 1996 (pp. 414), and 1997 (pp. 424–27).

Among independent accounting units, losses were widespread in 1996. Overall, 23 percent of the 390,000 enterprises reported losses. Losses were suffered by 38 percent of state enterprises, 40 percent of large and medium-size state enterprises, 18 percent of collectives, and 34 percent of "other" enterprises (China State Statistical Bureau 1997). Striking is the fact that the proportion of firms suffering losses in the "other" sector approaches that in the state sector, even though barriers to exit are not as formidable in the shareholding and foreign-invested firm sectors.

Some observers are puzzled by this apparent contradiction of reported rising productivity and falling profitability (Bai, Li, and Wang 1997). Naughton (1992, 1994) and Jefferson and Rawski (1994) argue that the widespread decline in profitability reflects increasing competition, which has eroded monopoly rents. Growth of the nonstate sector substantially reduced the market power of state industry, which had already been diminished by past efforts to build "complete sets" of industries in every province. Eight-firm concentration ratios (table 1.11) reveal levels of product and industry concentration that are considerably lower than comparable figures for Japan and the United States.[3] Moreover, these ratios generally declined over the period 1980–88.

TABLE 1.11

Eight-firm concentration ratios in China, Japan, and the United States, selected years, 1980–88

Product or industry	China 1980	China 1985	China 1988	Japan 1980	United States 1982
Beer	16.2	8.1	10.2	98.9	64.0
Cement	5.7	3.8	2.5	46.0	24.0
Cotton yarn	4.1	3.9	2.8	28.0	44.0
Diesel engines	22.6[a]	15.6[a]	16.2[a]	60.1	—
Machine tools	12.5	10.5	—	—	22.0
Nylon	76.0	62.4	51.2	—	78.0
Refrigerators	42.3	35.7	26.1	73.3	82.0
Steel	37.1	34.7	32.5	65.0	—
Structural glass	40.6	33.6	25.6	100.0	90.0
Televisions	35.8	21.2	19.8	59.2	59.2
Average	29.3	23.0			
	24.3[b]	20.1[b]			

— Not available.
a. Three-firm concentration ratios.
b. Omits machine tools.
Source: Jefferson and Rawski 1994.

If profitability among state enterprises fell as a result of increasing competition—the competition hypothesis—the decline should have been most marked in those regions and industries in which the entry of nonstate producers during recent years was most rapid. Tests of the competition hypothesis, reported in chapter 6, confirm that declining entry barriers have depressed industry profitability.

The other source of rising competition is, of course, the international sector. Spurred by successive tariff reductions that have cut average import duties from 40 percent to 17 percent since 1990, imports have risen more than 250 percent, jumping from $53 billion in 1990 to $139 billion in 1996 (China State Statistical Bureau 1997). Although some imports service export production in China's Special Economic Zones and thus do not compete directly with domestic products, many enter the domestic market, with painful consequences for local suppliers. Between 1990 and 1994, for example, the domestic market share of machine tools made in China plunged from 67 percent to 38 percent (*China Daily* 6 June 1995).

While rising competition is probably the most important cause of declining profitability throughout Chinese industry, the decline in profitability by state industry is accounted for by two additional factors. These are a lag in productivity growth behind the nonstate sector, created in substantial part by overinvestment and declining capital productivity in state industry (see table 6.6) and the growth of unfunded pension obligations, as reflected in the decline in the number of active workers per retiree (see table 1.7).

Functional complementarities: how different enterprise types contribute to industrial reform

Does ownership matter? Do the major ownership groupings tend to crowd one another out, or do they interrelate to create complementarities within Chinese industry? State-owned and collective-owned firms, foreign and overseas joint ventures, and private firms, including individual-owned domestic firms, share important complementary relationships that are critical to the overall dynamism of Chinese industry.

State-owned enterprises

Despite their falling share of output (see table 1.2), state-owned enterprises retain a central position in China's industrial economy. Their ranks include the largest producers of coal, steel, power-generating equipment, and other key commodities.

State enterprises provide essential resources to newly emerging domestic industry. At the outset of reform in the late 1970s, most of the technical capabilities of China's industrial sector resided in the equipment, facilities, and personnel controlled by large and medium-size state enterprises (see chapter 4).

State firms are responsible for large flows of commodities and services that have been essential to the increasing organizational diversification that is a critical component of China's reform dynamic. Through the sale of secondhand equipment, reverse engineering, and the provision of technical services and "Sunday engineers" to the collective sector, state enterprises have become an important conduit for the diffusion of technology within China's industrial economy. One such example is that of the Hengdian Company (appendix B), whose original silk and magnetic manufacturing operations were supported by the technology, capital, and engineering resources of state enterprises.

China's Open Door policy started an ongoing process of upgrading within state industry, partly through independent state enterprise initiatives and partly through participation in joint ventures with overseas businesses. Firms that have approached the international frontiers of quality and technology have enriched the domestic supply of engineering, management, and marketing techniques available to China's emerging enterprise sector.

Conversions of state enterprises are a vital source of joint venture and joint stock companies. In addition to providing continued support for rural industry, state enterprises have increasingly contributed to the creation and expansion of new forms of enterprise, operating at much higher levels of technological sophistication. Labor, equipment, and technical personnel of state enterprises provide an important component of joint venture operations. Many of these joint ventures have made profitable use of equipment, design and engineering, and managerial services provided by the Chinese partners, even in sectors in which domestic firms operate far from international technical frontiers.

A growing number of state enterprises, including the most successful large and medium-size firms, are reorganizing themselves into joint stock companies, some of which are now listed on stock exchanges in Shanghai, Shenzhen, Hong Kong, Singapore, and New York. Ownership conversions that result in the departure of successful firms from the state sector have intensified the competitive pressures facing the remaining state enterprises, accelerating the pace of reform in some instances and clearly revealing the failure of reform in others.

State industry's profits represent a vital source of fiscal revenues. Throughout the two decades preceding reform, China's state industry served as the government's main source of revenue. By controlling prices of agricultural and raw material inputs to the industrial sector, the government was able to generate surpluses within state industry, some of which it captured and recycled into industrial investment. Although state enterprises have become increasingly squeezed by price reform—which has, in general, driven up input prices relative to product prices—and by competition from the burgeoning nonstate sector, state industry continues to provide a substantial share of central and local government revenues. In 1994, 65 percent of industrial taxes were paid by state industry; these taxes represented about 30 percent of total government revenues, even after accounting for subsidies to loss-making state enterprises. The fact that the effective tax rate in the state sector was 72 percent in 1995 (much higher than the 60 percent paid by collectives and the 39 percent paid by foreign-invested firms) underscores the continuing inability of the fiscal system to tax the nonstate sector efficiently. This unbalanced tax burden in turn creates disincentives to state enterprise and financial sector reform (see *International Herald Tribune* 3 July 1997).

State enterprises have served as an important transition device in providing insurance against the extensive social risk arising from the potential destabilizing effects of a shift from plan to market. While government developed a publicly managed system of unemployment, health, and pensions, and the nonstate sector created nearly 100 million industrial jobs during the 1980s and 1990s, state industry employed, housed, and insured a labor force of 40.6 million in 1996, down from 45.2 million in 1992 (China State Statistical Bureau 1992; 1997).

Figures from the early 1990s indicate that 93 percent of employees in state industrial firms are provided with housing, with 51 percent of urban residents occupying housing furnished by state enterprises (Du and Shang 1993). The costs of state firms include massive social outlays that have grown rapidly with rising medical costs and the aging of the state enterprise work force. Under a pay-as-you-go system, state enterprises must draw on current revenues to support the pensions and medical expenses of retirees. State enterprises also run schools that educate tens of millions of children.

Collective-owned enterprises

The development of rural collective industry is among the most important of China's reform achievements.[4] Perhaps the most important effect of this growth is its contribution to energizing state firms. Coddled by official favoritism and accustomed to monopolistic control over product markets, state-owned enterprises in a growing range of industries found their market dominance shattered by the relaxation of competitive constraints on collective sector rivals, who began with a 1978 base of 265,000 enterprises, three times the number of state-owned enterprises. In addition to food processing, garments, and labor-intensive assembly manufacturing, rural firms have begun to challenge state-owned enterprises in a range of industries. China's second-largest cement producer is a township and village enterprise; by 1994, 30 of China's top 500 firms (ranked by sales) came from the township and village enterprise sector (*China Daily* 6 September 1995).

Expansion of the collective sector has served as a lever forcing state firms to adopt market-oriented behavior. By eroding profits of state industry, the burgeoning collective sector set in motion a process of "creative reduction," as market share, profits, and investment resources are diverted away from less efficient state enterprises (see Jefferson and Singh 1996). As well as expanding the number of firms and overall competition, collective enterprises are contributing to a wider diversity of forms of corporate ownership, organization, and management that provide the foundation for a dynamic selection process.[5]

Joint ventures

Joint ventures, which scarcely existed before 1980, have emerged as a major force in China's international trade. They include a variety of organizational forms but typically involve a cooperative manufacturing effort in which a foreign or overseas firm joins forces with one or more Chinese entities—typically a state enterprise manufacturer—to create an independent producer that is directed, funded, and managed under working arrangements determined by the parent firms. Although tax and regulatory relief to joint ventures was curtailed during the mid–1990s, these benefits continue to provide substantial incentives to Chinese firms to seek out joint venture partners.

Many joint ventures operate in duty-free export zones and produce mainly for foreign markets. As a result their economic impact is most notable in export trade, more than one-fourth of which is accounted for by these firms. Joint ventures have strongly influenced the process of industrial reform by bringing foreign firms, with their access to offshore pools of funds and intimate knowledge of advanced technology, market intelligence, and management systems, into partnership with Chinese enterprises. The impact of novel product designs, manufacturing processes, marketing techniques, information systems, and management styles has begun to ripple through China's business community through supplier networks, competitive pressures, and the rotation of Chinese personnel to and from foreign-linked enterprises.

In addition to its direct impact on partners, rivals, suppliers, and employees, expansion of the Chinese operations of overseas firms contributes to China's ongoing information revolution and to the absorption of new concepts, standards, and organizational structures into China's domestic economy. Building codes, environmental standards, job safety standards, packaging standards, distribution systems, chain stores, market research, mass advertising, and labor relations practices are among the many areas in which joint ventures provide a transmission mechanism between international business practice and China's domestic economy.

Private enterprise

Private enterprise, long the bane of socialist propagandists, is booming in China today. Chinese industry includes 5.5 million individual enterprises that employ no more than seven workers each. Private enterprises employing eight or more workers number only several thousand firms, but growth of this category promises to be rapid, as many smaller private enterprises expand.

While township and village enterprises were principally responsible for spurring the robust growth of Chinese industry during the 1980s, joint ventures, the child of the Open Door policy, and individual and private enterprises, the child of rural reforms, together are providing the most dynamic source of growth during the 1990s. Private enterprise provides the crucible for the development of China's future entrepreneurship.

Conclusions

A significant portion of China's industrial growth reflects complementarities that create a technologically and organizationally rich, diverse, and functionally linked industrial system. The different enterprise types create a kind of ladder, linked by a hierarchy of technological capabilities, governance, cost structures, resource flows, and competition. This system, based on a set of functional complementarities, causes the whole to be greater than the sum of its parts and creates the institutional context for a process of endogenous reform. This phenomenon is analyzed more closely in chapter 3, which shows how the various ownership types in China fit together to form a kind of innovation ladder in which technologies and modes of governance move from more sophisticated to less sophisticated enterprises.

State industry served as a useful transitional device in the early phases of the reform program. But the ensuing ownership diversification and employment growth, rising overall industrial productivity, and comparative fiscal and social stability have made the state sector an increasingly dispensable feature of China's industrial landscape.

Notes

1. Hong Kong refers to the Hong Kong Special Administrative Region, People's Republic of China.

2. About 40–60 percent of enterprises classified as joint ventures or joint stock companies appear to be privately owned. For most publicly listed shareholding companies, the Chinese government appears to have retained majority ownership.

3. Concentration ratios must be interpreted within the context of the degree of product market integration. Although product markets are certainly more integrated in Japan and the United States, the rate of product market integration in China during the 1980s and 1990s has exceeded the rates in those two countries. For a fuller discussion, which focuses on "contributions" rather than "complementaritites," see Jefferson and Rawski (1994).

4. China's small and declining urban collective industry is not examined here.

5. Despite their success it is too soon to conclude that China's collectives represent an enduring organizational innovation. The dependence of the sector on resources from the state sector, the tendency for collective-owned enterprise operations to cluster at the low end of the technology spectrum, and problems of vaguely defined property rights all suggest that rapid collective-owned enterprise gains owe much to specific circumstances of China's economy in the 1980s. Indeed, the number of village enterprises declined 13 percent in just one year from 1994–95, suggesting the beginning of a shakeout in collective industry.

References

Bai, Chong-en, David D. Li, and Wang Yijian. 1997. "Enterprise Productivity and Efficiency: When Is Up Really Down?" *Journal of Comparative Economics* 24(3): 265–80.

Census of China. 1997. *Data of the Third Industrial Census of the People's Republic of China (Zhonghua renmin gongheguo 1995 nian di san ci quanguo gongye pucha ziliao huiban: guoyou—sanzi—xiangzhen juan).* Beijing: China Statistical Publications Office.

China State Statisctical Bureau. Various years. *China Industrial Economy Statistical Yearbook (Zhongguo gongye jingji tongji nianjian)* (in Chinese). Beijing: China Statistical Publications Office.

————. Various years. *China Labor Statistics Yearbook (Zhongguo laodong tongji nianjian)* (in Chinese). Beijing: China Statistical Publications Office.

————. Various years. *China Statistical Yearbook (Zhongguo tongji nianjian)* (in Chinese). Beijing: China Statistical Publications Office.

Du, Haiyan, and Shang Lie. 1993. "Distribution of Fringe Benefits for Employees of State-owned Enterprises." *Research on Chinese Industrial Economics* (in Chinese) 2(30):46–52.

Field, Robert Michael. 1992. "China's Industrial Performance since 1978." *China Quarterly* 131: 577–607.

Howson, Nicholas C. 1997. "New Acquisition Structures in China: M & A Comes to the Middle Kingdom." New York: Paul, Weiss, Rifkind, Wharton & Garrison.

Jefferson, Gary H. 1992. "Growth and Productivity Change in Chinese Industry: Problems of Measurement." In M. J. Dutta, ed., *Research in Asian Economic Studies. Asian Economic Regimes: An Adaptive Innovation Paradigm.* Vol. 4B. Greenwich, Conn.: JAI Press.

Jefferson, Gary H., and Thomas G. Rawski. 1994. "Enterprise Reform in Chinese Industry." *Journal of Economic Perspectives* 8(2): 47–70.

Jefferson, Gary H., Thomas G. Rawski, and Yuxin Zheng. 1996. "Chinese Industrial Productivity: Trends, Measurement Issues, and Recent Developments." *Journal of Comparative Economics* 23(2): 146–80.

Jefferson, Gary H., and Inderjit Singh. 1996. "Ownership Reform as a Process of Creative Reduction in Chinese Industry." In *China's Economic Future: Challenges to U.S. Policy,* pp. 176–202. Study papers submitted to the Joint Economic Committee, Congress of the United States. Washington, D.C.: U.S. Government Printing Office.

Lardy, Nicholas R. 1992. "Chinese Foreign Trade." *China Quarterly* 13: 691–720.

Li Mingzhi, and Cao Hongbo. 1990. "Price Factors as a Link to Overestimates of China's Industrial Growth Rate" (in Chinese). *Price Theory and Practice* 5:12–14.

Naughton, Barry. 1992. "Implications of the State Monopoly over Industry and Its Relaxation." *Modern China* 18(1): 14–41.

————. 1994. *Growing Out of the Plan: Chinese Economic Reform 1978–1993.* New York: Cambridge University Press.

Qi Jingfa. 1995. "Emphasize Quality and Efficiency: Support, Develop, Raise and Stabilize and Advance the Favorable Trend in Rural Industry." *China Township Enterprise, Beijing* 2:11–17.

Rawski, Thomas G. 1991. "How Fast Has Chinese Industry Grown?" Research Paper Series 7. World Bank, Country Economics Department, Socialist Economies Reform Unit, Washington, D.C.

Structure, Authority, and Incentives in Chinese Industry

2

Gary H. Jefferson, Zhang Ping, and John Z. Q. Zhao

This chapter draws on data from two World Bank surveys (see page 2 of this volume and World Bank 1992) to compare and contrast the structure, decisionmaking authority, and incentives in state, collective, and town and village enterprises in China. Specific areas of comparison include enterprise autonomy, internal authority, management systems, wages and incentives, and the market environment.

Characteristics of sample enterprises

Between 1991 and 1992, as part of the survey process, China's state statistical bureau mailed 1,600 questionnaires to state enterprises, urban cooperatives, and township and village enterprises. More than 95 percent of these surveys were completed and returned. State enterprises constitute about 60 percent of the sample: the balance is about evenly divided between urban and rural collectives. A small number of enterprises fall into the "other" category, which consists of joint ventures and privately owned firms.

The surveys covered an extensive geographic area. The state enterprise and urban cooperative sample covers more than 40 cities in 26 provinces. The township and village enterprise sample covers 15 coastal and interior provinces.

The industry codes of urban enterprises are based on the three-digit coding system introduced in 1985. Aggregated to the two-digit level codes, the sample for urban state-owned enterprises and urban cooperatives covers 36 of 40 industrial branches. Using the old industrial coding system, the township and village enterprise sample covers 12 of 15 industries, with petroleum, electric power, and forest products excluded.[1]

The National Standard of Urban Enterprises establishes standards for classifying enterprises as small, medium-size and large. Using those standards, the sample of urban enterprises (state-owned enterprises and urban collectives) contains 378 large enterprises (30.8 percent), 402 medium-size enterprises (32.7 percent), and 448 small enterprises (36.5 percent). Larger industrial enterprises are substantially overrepresented in the sample. In 1992 only about 14 percent of China's 105,000 state-owned enterprises were classified as large and medium-size enterprises. In terms of share of output and fixed assets, however, these larger enterprises play a dominant role in Chinese industry: in 1992 large and medium-size enterprises accounted for about 45 percent of China's total industrial output and more than three-quarters of output originating from state industry.

Larger and older enterprises are also overrepresented in the township and village enterprise sample. In 1990 the average township and village enterprise in the sample reported annual sales of 4 million yuan and employed 269 people, while the average township and village enterprise in China as a whole had sales of 2 million yuan and employed 150 people.

Reform of corporate governance

Three types of control rights—assignment of rights to the enterprise, intra-enterprise assignment of rights, and control of the residual—are examined here in order to evaluate the extent to which property rights have been transferred to the enterprise. While each of these rights is important in itself, they also share important complementarities (see chapter 5).

Assignment of decision rights to the enterprise

The World Bank Enterprise Surveys (World Bank 1992) identified 11 types of decisions and asked respondents to indicate which of the following described the distribution of authority for each type of decision: the enterprise has the decisionmaking right (there is no limit on the authority of the enterprise), the decisions are made jointly by the enterprise and its supervisory body (there is some limit on the enterprise's authority), or the supervisory body has the decisionmaking right (the enterprise has no authority).

The survey results indicate that during 1991–92 township and village enterprises enjoyed considerably more production, sales, and pricing autonomy than state-owned enterprises (table 2.1). Only 29 percent of the state-owned enterprises report having the unfettered right to set production plans, about half the percentage reported by township and village enterprises. State-owned enterprises were also found to be more constrained than their township and village enterprise counterparts in terms of choosing customers, setting sale prices, and selecting suppliers.

TABLE 2.1
Allocation of decision rights, 1992
(percentage of sample)

Type of decision	State-owned enterprises (n = 915–930)	Urban cooperatives (n = 246–296)	Township and village enterprises (n = 282–285)
Set production plans			
Enterprise	28.8	32.1	57.7
Consultation	43.6	37.5	20.4
Supervisory agency	27.6	30.4	21.8
Set prices			
No limit	19.6	46.5	66.6
Somewhat limited	54.1	41.7	23.3
Completely limited	26.3	11.7	10.1
Choose customers			
No limit	75.1	90.0	90.2
Somewhat limited	19.8	7.6	4.9
Completely limited	5.0	2.4	4.9
Choose suppliers			
No limit	71.3	86.2	90.2
Somewhat limited	24.6	10.4	6.3
Completely limited	4.2	3.4	3.5
Set bonus levels			
Enterprise	62.8	60.5	54.4
Consultation	18.2	23.1	27.0
Supervisory agency	18.9	16.3	18.6
Set wage differentials			
Enterprise	43.6	93.5	79.2
Consultation	19.8	3.1	11.7
Supervisory agency	43.6	3.4	9.2
Set bonus differentials			
Enterprise	93.3	50.0	86.9
Consultation	4.4	19.7	8.2
Supervisory agency	2.3	30.3	5.0
Appoint leaders			
Enterprise	1.1	6.1	15.8
Consultation	17.9	18.8	24.2
Supervisory agency	80.9	75.9	60.0
Recruit employees			
Enterprise	22.6	40.8	66.7
Consultation	50.0	44.9	29.8
Supervisory agency	27.4	14.3	3.5
Dismiss employees			
Enterprise	62.8	54.8	72.2
Consultation	26.4	34.6	23.6
Supervisory agency	10.8	10.6	4.2
Make investment decisions			
Enterprise	14.4	37.1	24.5
Consultation	57.1	48.4	59.6
Supervisory agency	28.6	14.5	16.0

Source: World Bank 1992 (Enterprise Surveys).

According to the surveys, state-owned enterprises enjoy less autonomy in setting wage differentials than township and village enterprises but have more authority to set bonuses and bonus differentials. State-owned enterprises may enjoy more authority in determining bonuses because they have relatively limited authority to set wage differentials. Although state-owned enterprises enjoy some autonomy in fixing employees' compensation, their authority to change the membership of the production team is more limited. Like township and village enterprises, state-owned enterprises enjoy a substantial measure of authority to dismiss employees, but within the enterprise dismissal authority is exercised largely by employee councils. State-owned enterprises are limited in their authority to recruit employees, and both state-owned enterprises and township and village enterprises are still more limited in their authority to appoint upper-level managers, who are typically appointed by the supervisory agency, with little consultation with enterprise management. Within the state sector then, the data reveal considerable unevenness in the authority of the firm to exercise the full range of decision authority required to motivate the work force. Township and village enterprises enjoy a broader range of discretion regarding personnel decisions.

Relatively few enterprises have authority to alter the firm's capital stock through the investment process. For the majority of state-owned enterprises and township and village enterprises, this decision is made jointly by the state and the enterprise.

Figure 2.1 displays the distribution of a composite measure of enterprise decision autonomy for both state enterprises and township and village enterprises. On average, township and village enterprises enjoy decisionmaking authority in more areas than do state-owned enterprises. Unlike state-owned enterprises, which typically represent but one of several hundred enterprises in the portfolio of a provincial government whose capital is some distance from the enterprise, township and village governments generally own and supervise a small number of enterprises. In some cases these enterprises are managed as a conglomerate, in which the enterprise can be viewed as a division rather than as an independent management and accounting unit (Qian and Xu 1993). In these cases, although respondents may indicate that the supervisory body has the decisionmaking right, local governments may be able to avoid the information asymmetries and monitoring difficulties that lead to inefficiencies in the conventional central planning hierarchy.[2]

In general, the devolution of decision rights to collective-owned enterprises falls between that of state-owned and township and village enterprises, although urban collectives have more autonomy in setting

FIGURE 2.1

Histogram of decisionmaking authority in Chinese enterprise: distribution of authority between the enterprise and the state
(percentage of firms)

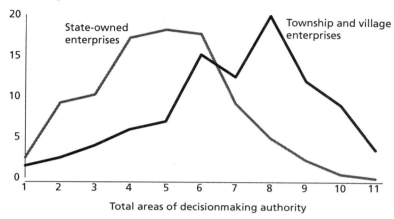

Total areas of decisionmaking authority

Source: Based on data in table 2.1.

wage differentials among employees and less autonomy in setting bonus differentials. This finding suggests that substantial limits on the use of one instrument of compensation (wages) are compensated for by substantial flexibility in the use of another (bonuses). The urban collectives in the sample also appear to enjoy greater investment autonomy than either state-owned enterprises or township and village enterprises.

Creation of intrafirm decision rights

The literature on the theory of the firm underscores the important role of a central contracting agent (see, for example, Alchian and Demsetz 1972). The establishment of an effective central contracting, or monitoring, agent within the enterprise requires not only that the firm be a locus of decisionmaking but that within the firm rights are exercised by a clearly defined agent. The contract responsibility system embodies this principle, so that, broadly speaking, the signatory within the enterprise is expected to perform as the manager or central contracting agent within the enterprise.

The enterprise responsibility contract is widely used as the formal instrument for allocating decision authority and residual control rights between the supervisory authority and any one of several possible contracting agents (Koo 1990). These agents may include a single director, a management group, or all the personnel of the enterprise (table 2.2).

Although individual directors dominated state-owned enterprise contracting during the first period, covering 1986–88, a broader set of representatives served as contractors during the second round of contracting. The proportion of state enterprise contracts signed by individual directors declined from 66 percent in the first round to 48 percent in the second, while those signed by groups rose to nearly 30 percent in the second round and signatories involving "all personnel" rose to more than 20 percent. The tendency for the central contracting agent to shift from individual directors to groups and all personnel was also apparent for urban collectives. In contrast, in both the first and second rounds almost 90 percent of the contractors in township and village enterprises were individual directors or management groups, with management groups dominating the contracting process. Contracts signed by all personnel in township and village enterprises represented less than 10 percent of the total.

Enterprise directors throughout most of China's publicly owned industrial sector are appointed by the supervisory agency (table 2.3). During 1991–92, 93 percent of directors in state-owned enterprises were appointed by the supervisory agency; supervisory agencies appointed enterprise directors in 83 percent of urban cooperatives and 78 percent of township and village enterprises. Directors were elected by employee congresses in 10–11 percent of urban collectives and township and village enterprises, more than three times as often as in the state-owned enterprise sample. Within all ownership types, a bidding process was used to recruit directors in only 3–5 percent of enterprises.

In practice, the principal decisionmaker is not always the individual or group signing the responsibility contract. The survey distinguished four parties within China's enterprises: the director, the management group, the party secretary, and the employees' council. For various areas of decision

TABLE 2.2
Designated contractor
(percentage of sample)

Contractor	State-owned enterprises		Urban cooperatives		Township and village enterprises	
	First round (n=846)	Second round (n=788)	First round (n=248)	Second round (n=212)	First round (n=231)	Second round (n=214)
Director	65.5	47.6	62.1	47.2	23.8	26.2
Group	17.7	29.6	23.8	27.4	64.5	63.1
All personnel	15.6	21.2	13.3	23.1	8.2	7.5
Other	1.1	1.5	0.8	2.4	3.5	3.3

Source: World Bank 1992 (Enterprise Surveys).

TABLE 2.3
Selection of enterprise director
(percentage of sample)

Method of selection	State-owned enterprises (n=889)	Urban cooperatives (n=297)	Township and village enterprises (n=282)
Appointed by supervisory agency	92.8	83.2	78.4
Elected by employee council	3.3	11.1	10.3
Selected through bidding	3.4	5.1	4.3
Recommended by contractors	0.4	0.7	2.5
Other	..	..	4.6

.. Zero or negligible
Source: World Bank 1992 (Enterprise Surveys).

authority the survey asked respondents to identify which of these parties exercises principal decisionmaking authority within the enterprise.

Across all nine decision areas township and village enterprise directors exercise exclusive authority in nearly 20 percent or more of the enterprises (table 2.4). For state-owned enterprises, although the individual director is the contractor in nearly 50 percent of state enterprises, he or she enjoys exclusive authority in fewer than 5 percent of the enterprises.

Combining the first two categories (director and management group) into a broader category (called simply "management") reveals that for township and village enterprises this broader management category dominates all nine areas of decisionmaking authority. For state industry, "management" exercises dominant authority in a majority of firms in only five areas. Management's authority is diluted principally by employees' councils, which exercise the control over employee dismissals, and party secretaries, who play a key role in appointing upper-level personnel, particularly assistant directors and middle-level cadres (see chapter 5).

Figure 2.2 portrays the distribution of a composite measure of internal decision authority within state-owned enterprises and township and village enterprises. We can see from this figure that for the plurality of township and village enterprises (about 40 percent), all nine decision rights are vested in management. For the plurality of state-owned enterprises, however, only six of the nine decisionmaking rights are vested in a manager. Relative to township and village enterprises, the distribution shown in figure 2.2 generally indicates a dispersed pattern of decisionmaking authority within state-owned enterprises.

The management group has more decision authority in urban collectives than in state-owned enterprises, but less than in township and village enterprises. Workers in urban-based enterprises, both state-owned

TABLE 2.4
Distribution of decisionmaking authority within enterprises
(percentage of total respondents)

Function	State-owned enterprises	Urban cooperatives	Township and village enterprises
Fix production plans			
Director	4.3	9.1	19.4
Management group	76.3	78.4	72.7
Party secretary	8.8	7.4	6.8
Employees' council	10.6	5.1	1.1
Set bonus levels			
Director	4.0	8.3	20.4
Management group	62.1	63.4	63.6
Party secretary	9.3	8.3	12.0
Employees' council	24.6	20.0	4.0
Set bonus differentials			
Director	3.2	8.3	19.6
Management group	60.1	63.4	68.9
Party secretary	10.1	8.3	7.5
Employees' council	26.7	20.0	3.9
Set wage differentials			
Director	1.8	4.8	19.9
Management group	48.4	52.2	68.1
Party secretary	16.2	13.3	7.6
Employees' council	33.6	29.6	4.4
Allocate retained profits			
Director	5.5	11.2	19.6
Management group	65.8	63.9	60.7
Party secretary	14.6	13.0	18.2
Employees' council	14.1	11.9	1.4
Appoint assistant directors			
Director	3.4	11.4	19.7
Management group	9.7	13.9	32.0
Party secretary	85.0	70.3	47.2
Employees' council	1.9	4.4	1.1
Appoint mid-level cadres			
Director	3.1	14.6	31.2
Management group	23.5	38.4	52.8
Party secretary	72.8	44.9	13.5
Employees' council	0.7	2.0	2.5
Recruit new employees			
Director	5.2	7.7	28.2
Management group	73.1	72.7	59.3
Party secretary	13.8	14.0	9.6
Employees' council	7.9	15.6	2.9
Dismiss employees			
Director	1.7	3.5	22.0
Management group	31.3	25.3	50.2
Party secretary	14.6	12.8	13.4
Employees' council	52.4	58.3	14.4

Source: World Bank 1992 (Enterprise Surveys).

FIGURE 2.2

Histogram of decisionmaking authority in Chinese enterprise: distribution of authority within the enterprise
(percentage of firms)

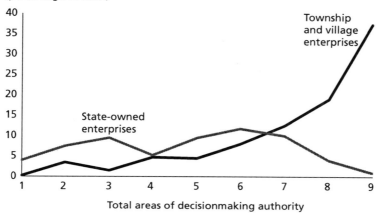

Total areas of decisionmaking authority

Source: Based on data in table 2.4.

enterprises and urban cooperatives, exercise more authority within the enterprise than their counterparts in rural enterprises.

Incentive structure

The third area of property rights reform is the incentive structure for the firm in general and the central contracting agent and work force in particular. The incentive structure is critical: where incentives to increase revenues, economize on input costs, and limit the diversion of enterprise surplus and assets are weak, they will limit or erode the firm's net worth, especially where decision authority has been ceded to the firm.

Principal types of contracts. The contract responsibility system is the most widely used form of management system in Chinese industry. Other management systems used include the asset management system, a variant of the contract responsibility system in which there is explicit emphasis on using profits to maintain or expand the assets of the enterprise; the contract lease system, in which managers lease enterprises; and the joint stock system, in which the enterprise is corporatized and shares are issued.

Management system reform was initiated much earlier in the township and village enterprise sector than in the urban sector (table 2.5). Not surprisingly, since the enterprise contract responsibility system is an outgrowth of the agricultural household responsibility system, nearly 50 percent of township and village enterprises were operating under the contract responsibility system in 1984. State-owned and urban

TABLE 2.5
Type of management system, selected years, 1984–90
(percentage of sample)

Year	Type of enterprise	Joint stock	Contract responsibility	Contract leasing	Asset management	Other
1984	State-owned	0.5	12.3	0.1	12.4	74.6
	Urban cooperative	1.5	13.1	0.4	15.4	69.6
	Township and village	3.6	48.6	0.0	—	47.8
1987	State-owned	0.3	19.6	0.1	11.5	68.5
	Urban cooperative	2.8	41.6	1.8	11.4	42.4
	Township and village	3.0	58.7	0.4	—	38.0
1990	State-owned	0.2	82.9	0.7	6.2	10.1
	Urban cooperative	2.4	70.2	3.7	8.8	14.9
	Township and village	1.8	71.1	0.7	—	26.4

— Not available.
Source: World Bank 1992 (Enterprise Surveys).

collective–owned enterprises had begun to experiment with the contract responsibility system by 1984, but it was not extensively implemented until 1987. As of 1991 nearly 90 percent of urban state-owned enterprises, 80 percent of urban cooperatives, and 70 percent of township and village enterprises were using the contract responsibility system or asset management system.

By 1990 only a small proportion of enterprises of all ownership types had been converted to joint stock companies or were leased out to independent managers. This system has gained widespread popularity during the 1990s, both for township and village enterprises and for the largest and most successful state-owned enterprises, for which shares are being offered on public exchanges.

Distribution of profits. A key reform of the management system was the early innovation that expanded the right of the firm to residual profits. From virtually zero before reform, the average profit retention rate of state-owned enterprises and township and village enterprises reached about 35 percent during 1989–90 (table 2.6). But retention rates varied widely during 1986–90, ranging from 0 to 100 percent for the state-owned enterprises and from 0 to 98 percent for the township and village enterprises. Effective retention rates continue to vary because of profit remittances by publicly owned enterprises to their supervisory bodies and a variety of local or ad hoc taxes.

Within the contract responsibility system, four forms of management contracts are used by all enterprise types: (a) the contract specifies a profit remittance quota and allows the contractor to retain all above-quota profits; (b) the contractor retains profits at a progressive rate; (c) the con-

TABLE 2.6
Incentive structure

Measure	State-owned enterprises	Urban cooperatives	Township and village enterprises
Retention rate (average share of gross profit retained)	33	36	35
Bonus share (share of total wage and bonus)	22	17	16
Bonding expenses (percentage required)	20	29	30
Average amount (yuan)	14,258	16,349	42,524

Source: World Bank 1992 (Enterprise Surveys).

tractor receives a fixed profit quota and a share of above-quota profits; and (d) the contract is written so that the contractor has an incentive to reduce losses. State-owned enterprises and urban collectives also use contracts such as the "two guarantees and one link"—which links the level of retained profit to the satisfaction of negotiated output and productivity targets. Township and village enterprises also use certain contractual forms unique to that sector. The key distinction among these contracts is the arrangement for distributing profit.

The use of these types of contracts varies across sectors, and no single form of contract dominates (table 2.7). Moreover, no clear relationship exists between the form of ownership and the type of contract used. The most common form of contract among state-owned enterprises is the

TABLE 2.7
Forms of profit sharing
(percentage of sample)

Contract type	State-owned enterprises	Urban cooperatives	Township and village enterprises
Contractor retains all above-quota profits	15.5	15.2	20.7
Contractor retains above-quota profits at progressive rate	17.7	32.5	9.1
Contractor shares above-quota profits at fixed rate	28.4	23.2	46.0
"Two guarantees and one link"[a] (total profit is remitted)	19.4	15.6	9.8
"Second stage tax for profit"[b]	10.9	8.0	13.0

a. Refers to system in which the level of retained profit is linked to the satisfaction (guarantee) of agreed-upon output and productivity targets. Applies to state-owned enterprises and urban cooperatives only.
b. Refers to system in which the tax rate is negotiated in lieu of profit remittance. Applies to state-owned enterprises and urban cooperatives only.
Source: World Bank 1992 (Enterprise Surveys).

fixed rate scheme, but this scheme is used in only 38 percent of enterprises. Urban cooperatives most often retain profits at a progressive rate, with about a third of enterprises using this type of contract. More than half of urban collectives allow contractors to retain excess profits at fixed or progressive rates. Among township and village enterprises 46 percent of firms allow contractors to retain excess profits at a fixed rate, and 21 percent allow them to retain all profits above the quota level.

Use of bonuses. Bonuses play and important role in state industry where they represent 22 percent of total cash compensation (see table 2.6). As Jefferson, Singh, Hu, and Wang show in chapter 8, a 1 percent increase in gross profit per worker translates into about a 0.33 percent increase in the per worker bonus within state-owned enterprises. The survey data do not distinguish between the allocation of bonuses to workers and managers. If the share of bonuses in total cash compensation is at least as great for managers as for workers, however, the incentive effect of bonuses is likely to be substantial.

For township and village enterprises the share of bonuses in total cash compensation is lower—16 percent—probably because the basic wage is itself more flexible than in state industry. In about 90 percent of the township and village enterprises in the sample, managerial income was limited to a fixed ratio of the average worker's wage. Regulated income ratios varied widely, with managerial income ranging from 1 to 12 times that of the average wage. Because state enterprise managers secure substantial bonuses while operating under relatively uniform regulated income ratios, the ratio of the bonus to total compensation is a better measure of their incentive structure.

Demand for collateral. Managers are often required to commit their own collateral as a form of performance guarantee. These guarantees, termed "bonding expenses" by Jensen and Meckling (1976), are intended to insure against agents engaging in certain actions, such as asset stripping, that would harm the interests of the supervisory agency or the public. Enterprise losses can be partially financed from these bonds. About 20 percent of the signatories in state-owned enterprises and 30 percent in township and village enterprises report having committed some amount of collateral (see table 2.6). For state-owned enterprise managers the average payment was 14,258 yuan; for township and village enterprise managers the average was 42,524 yuan.[3]

A comparison of incentive structures across enterprises and ownership types should include each of the elements discussed—contract provisions, retained profits, bonuses, and collateral. Without a theory of how to combine each of these elements, employing different units and weights, we initially simplify the construction of an incentive index by using only the retention rate. The distribution of retention rates, rescaled over the interval 0–10, is shown in figure 2.3.

From this survey of incentive mechanisms it is apparent that a multifaceted incentive structure is emerging in the state-owned and township and village enterprise sectors in which managers are becoming substantial risk bearers. Comparison of the two systems indicates that their basic structures are similar: managers are appointed by supervisory bodies, collateral is a common requirement, and profit retention rates are similar. The major difference between the two sectors is that wages are relatively inflexible in state-owned enterprises, so that bonuses paid from profits are used more extensively. In contrast, wages are highly variable in township and village enterprises.

Contract provisions

The survey revealed surprising results regarding respondents' rankings of the importance of various contract provisions (table 2.8). About 65 percent of the state enterprise respondents identified a financial provision relating to profit, loss, and its distribution as their most important contract provision. These include total realized profit and tax (35 percent), profit delivery and tax payment to the state (27 percent), and loss reduction and

FIGURE 2.3

Histogram of decisionmaking authority in Chinese enterprise: incentive index for state enterprises and township and village enterprises
(percentage of firms)

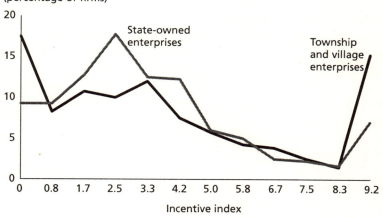

Source: Based on data in table 2.6.

TABLE 2.8
Most important contractor provision
(percentage of sample)

Objective	State-owned enterprises		
	Most important	Second most important	Third most important
Increase output, expand scale, and improve quality	33.8	19.1	18.1
Increase total realized profit and tax	35.1	34.6	5.1
Decrease profit delivery and tax payment	27.2	22.4	17.9
Develop new products	0.5	5.7	15.0
Construct, innovate, and acquire assets	0.2	9.8	22.5
Reduce losses and repay loans	2.9	6.5	10.1
Earn foreign exchange	0.1	1.5	3.0
Upgrade enterprise	0.2	0.4	7.9
Other	..	..	..
Sample size	867	849	825

.. Zero or negligible.
Source: World Bank 1992 (Enterprise Surveys).

repayment of loans (3 percent). Only 41 percent of urban cooperatives and 43 percent of township and village enterprises assign top priority to a financial objective.

Commitments to meet contract provisions specifying output value, production quality and variety, and labor productivity targets are cited as the most important contract provision for 51 percent of urban cooperatives and 49 percent of township and village enterprises. Only a third of the state-owned enterprises identified this provision as most important.

For both state-owned enterprises and urban cooperatives, the third most important contract provision appears to be investment and product innovation. State enterprises place more emphasis on investment. This result is consistent with information gleaned from interviews with enterprise managers, who report the widespread desire in state industry to replace old, inefficient equipment. In contrast, township and village enterprises place relatively little importance on new product development, although improving product variety and quality is a priority (presumably with more of an emphasis on imitating products rather than developing new products).

Managerial objectives

Managers of state-owned enterprises cited increasing profits, increasing output and expanding scale, and meeting contract targets as their top objectives (table 2.9). Urban cooperatives and township and village

Urban cooperatives			Township and village enterprises		
Most important	Second most important	Third most important	Most important	Second most important	Third most important
51.0	23.8	10.3	49.0	19.2	19.2
40.1	48.4	2.1	32.7	38.8	14.7
0.7	13.5	19.3	10.2	15.1	26.9
0.0	7.5	32.1	0.8	4.5	5.3
0.4	3.2	16.9	..	..	1.6
03	2.0	7.4	..	0.8	1.6
0.0	0.8	3.3	0.4	..	1.6
0.4	0.4	8.2	6.1	21.2	27.8
..	..	..	0.8	0.4	1.2
257	252	243	245	245	245

enterprises place comparatively more combined emphasis on increasing output, expanding scale, and improving quality and on upgrading the enterprise.

Several conclusions can be drawn from this profile of contract provisions and managerial objectives. The fact that state-owned enterprises place most importance on financial performance whereas urban cooperatives and township and village enterprises focus on expanding scale, product mix, and productivity runs contrary to conventional wisdom, which would reverse the assignment of priorities. Within the context of the contract responsibility system, the strong incentive of state-owned enterprises to expand profit and taxes presumably reflects a central objective of their supervisory bureaus. This emphasis on realized profit and tax in state industry may reflect the fact that the decline in profit rates, most pronounced in smaller state-owned enterprises, has affected local governments, which rely on state industry for revenue generation. Declining profitability should cause both enterprises, whose bonuses depend on profit, and their supervisory bodies, whose revenues depend on industry profit, to be more attentive to profit and tax objectives. For urban and rural collectives the emphasis on product variety and quality, output, and labor productivity measures may reflect their relatively early stage of business development. Local entrepreneurs may be relatively focused on eliminating the scale and technological advantages of state-owned enterprise competitors.

TABLE 2.9
Managerial objectives
(percentage of sample)

Objective	State-owned enterprises		
	Most important	Second most important	Third most important
Increase output, expand scale, and improve quality	31.3	17.8	9.9
Increase profits	41.4	40.3	6.8
Create job opportunities	0.2	1.8	4.6
Increase employee's income	2.3	2.9	49.1
Meet contract targets	23.0	16.0	17.4
Upgrade enterprise	1.3	2.6	10.6
Use local resources	0.4	0.5	1.5
Sample size	910	910	907

.. Zero or negligible.
Source: World Bank 1992 (Enterprise Surveys).

Differences in corporate governance across ownership forms

In terms of enterprise autonomy, internal authority, and incentives, on average, township and village enterprises enjoy greater autonomy, more concentration of internal authority, and a stronger incentive structure than their urban enterprise counterparts. Within the urban system, on average, urban collectives enjoy a more evolved distribution of property rights than state-owned enterprises. Along each of these dimensions, however, a substantial number of state-owned enterprises enjoy more rights and incentives than their urban cooperative or township and village enterprise counterparts. Overall assessment of the relative quality of property rights reform across ownership types requires an examination of the extent to which enterprises of each ownership type enjoy evolved rights along all three dimensions of reform, an issue addressed in chapter 5.

Labor and incentives

An effective incentive system requires that managers have at their disposal a set of instruments to motivate workers. In its initial stage Chinese enterprise reform emphasized worker incentives. As a result of the declining effectiveness of the "iron rice bowl" system of employment guarantee, across-the-board bonuses for whole industries were reinstated during the late 1970s and early 1980s. Wages and bonuses were later tied to performance.

In setting wages enterprises face two issues. The first is to establish the overall wage bill; the second concerns its distribution to workers within the firm. Many enterprises, particularly state-owned enterprises, operate

Urban cooperatives			Township and village enterprises		
Most important	Second most important	Third most important	Most important	Second most important	Third most important
41.3	19.8	7.7	24.7	16.0	13.2
36.6	48.0	3.4	29.6	36.6	17.4
1.0	1.7	8.7	5.9	6.3	8.4
2.3	19.5	52.0	2.8	15.3	30.3
15.8	8.7	14.4	15.3	13.6	12.9
2.3	2.3	17.4	21.3	12.2	17.8
0.7	..	1.3	0.3	..	..
298	298	298	287	287	287

under strict formulas that tie their wage bills to performance. About 37 percent of state-owned enterprises operate under compensation schemes in which total income is tied to profit and tax payment (table 2.10). Collective-owned enterprises appear to enjoy more autonomy in setting total compensation: just 20 percent of urban cooperatives and 6 percent of township and village enterprises are constrained to link their wage bill to profit and taxes.

Under the internal wage system, once the enterprise has established the overall wage bill through external standards or negotiations, it enjoys comparative autonomy in setting wage differentials among employees. Within the sample studied, 69 percent of township and village enterprises had established an internal wage system, substantially more than urban cooperatives and state-owned enterprises, among which just 8–9 percent report having internal wage systems.

TABLE 2.10
Wage system
(percentage of sample)

System	State-owned enterprises (n=912)	Urban cooperatives (n=297)	Township and village enterprises (n=277)
Per piece wage rate	25.5	39.5	82.3
Time wage	51.8	48.8	8.7
Wage and bonus tied to profit and tax payment	36.6	20.4	5.8
Internal wage system	8.5	8.7	69.3

Source: World Bank 1992 (Enterprise Survey).

Wage systems in township and village enterprises and urban enterprises differ substantially. Township and village enterprises, which constituted 82 percent of the sample, mainly use per piece wage rates, which may explain why fewer enterprises take advantage of the flexibility afforded by the internal wage system. About 40 percent of urban collectives and 25 percent of state-owned enterprises use per piece wage rates. About half of urban collectives and state-owned enterprises use time based wages, used by only 9 percent of township and village enterprises. Because differences in compensation schemes reflect differences in industrial technology, not just differences in enterprise management style, it is not surprising to find piecework concentrated in township and village enterprises and in urban cooperatives that tend to specialize in light industry involving apparel and assembly.

The market environment

In the absence of a competitive market environment, the reform of enterprise management systems may affect enterprise conduct and performance in only limited ways. If resource allocation and scarcity are administratively determined, rather than coordinated by market competition, autonomous, highly motivated managers may direct their energies to rent-seeking behavior rather than to innovations designed to cut costs and improve product quality. Several indicators of market structure and pricing behavior are examined below.

Price autonomy

Government price regulation played an important role among state-owned enterprises as late as 1991 and early 1992 (table 2.11). Among state-owned enterprise managers 36 percent cited government price con-

TABLE 2.11
Determinants of price
(percentage of sample)

Objective	State-owned enterprises		
	Most important	Second most important	Third most important
Government price regulation	36.0	40.0	23.9
Product cost	47.2	46.4	6.3
Market supply-demand	51.9	42.4	5.7
Price of similar product of other enterprises	12.2	65.1	22.7

Source: World Bank 1992 (Enterprise Surveys).

trols as most important. Just 24 percent of urban cooperatives and 15 percent of township and village enterprises assigned similar importance to price controls, indicating a lower (but nevertheless significant) incidence of price controls in nonstate industry. Price autonomy varied substantially among the three groups. A majority of state-owned enterprises and urban cooperatives identified supply and demand conditions as being very important determinants of product prices, while township and village enterprises placed somewhat more importance on product cost.

Market conditions: oversupply and response

The survey was conducted in 1991–92, following a period of austerity that began in the second half of 1989. More than half of the enterprises that survived indicated that production supply had exceeded demand over the previous three years, causing inventory buildup. In response to weakened demand and unanticipated inventory accumulation, most enterprises resorted to "improving product quality" and "strengthening sales effort and improving service." In the face of inventory buildup, urban enterprises, both state-owned enterprises and urban cooperatives, tended to place less importance on reducing output and more importance on securing government purchase of excess inventories. Township and village enterprises indicated a greater willingness to reduce price.

Competition

Nearly all (95 percent) state-owned enterprises and urban cooperatives indicated that they belong to a competitive industry, with 65 percent of those respondents indicating that competition is very severe. Nearly 50 percent of state-owned enterprises, 40 percent of urban cooperatives, and 20 percent of township and village enterprises reported producing money-losing products in 1991, the last year of the austerity program. On average,

Urban cooperatives			Township and village enterprises		
Most important	Second most important	Third most important	Most important	Second most important	Third most important
23.6	38.2	38.2	14.8	32.5	57.9
55.5	42.8	1.7	52.8	41.1	6.0
58.1	38.8	3.1	45.6	49.5	4.9
16.4	60.4	23.2	12.4	68.1	19.5

losses persisted for about five years in state-owned enterprises and urban cooperatives and three years in township and village enterprises.

Among urban cooperatives and township and village enterprises the most common explanation for losses was "extremely competitive markets," an explanation cited more often by urban cooperatives than by township and village enterprises. Fifty percent of the state-owned enterprises reporting losses and 25 percent of the urban cooperatives claimed that they were policy-related. Both state-owned enterprises and urban cooperatives reported that losses are useful for obtaining policy-related subsidies. For many township and village enterprises, but not for state-owned enterprises or urban cooperatives, money-losing products were often by-products of profitable products. This result is surprising, given that fewer multiproduct producers are likely to occupy the ranks of township and village enterprises than urban enterprises.

Capacity to adjust

To survive and grow in market competition, enterprises must improve their competitive capabilities by improving both their short-run efficiency and their long-run technological capabilities. A variety of factors prevent firms from raising productivity (table 2.12).

Township and village enterprises cite external factors, such as shortages of capital, raw materials, electricity, technicians, and skilled workers. Although state-owned enterprises are also sensitive to external constraints, they more frequently cite conditions specific to the enterprise,

TABLE 2.12
Impediments to raising productivity
(percentage of sample)

| | State-owned enterprises | | |
Impediment	Most important	Second most important	Third most important
Shortage of raw materials	14.6	5.5	4.3
Shortage of electricity and other energy inputs	5.7	6.3	4.4
Shortage of technicians and skilled workers	9.7	14.7	10.5
Shortage of good managers	10.7	14.1	12.2
Lack of effective incentives	7.0	6.7	9.0
Poor market conditions	15.7	8.0	11.2
Shortage of capital or technology	8.5	12.6	10.7
Too much production under mandatory plan	1.8	2.4	1.1
No authority to set prices and production	3.1	5.0	3.6
Excessive profit handed over to the state	5.5	6.2	6.8
Little authority over personnel	3.3	4.0	3.9
Outdated equipment	14.4	14.5	21.3

.. Zero or negligible.
Source: World Bank 1992 (Enterprise Surveys).

such as the lack of effective incentives and the lack of good managers, excessive profit remittance, and outdated equipment. Township and village enterprises cite "little authority over personnel" as a significant obstacle to raising productivity. This apparent contradiction may reflect, relative to state-owned enterprises, high expectations on the part of township and village enterprise managers for labor market discipline and flexibility in adapting the work force to changing market conditions.

Conclusions

This broad statistical profile of the institutional arrangements governing China's key ownership types reveals a range of organizational and behavioral differences. With few notable exceptions the survey data confirm the widely held perception that township and village enterprises enjoy more evolved property rights than their urban counterparts and that within the urban system, urban cooperatives enjoy somewhat more autonomy and stronger incentives than their state-owned enterprise counterparts.

Relative to state-owned enterprises and, to a lesser degree, to urban cooperatives, township and village enterprises exhibited more enterprise autonomy; more concentrated authority for a central contracting agent; and somewhat stronger incentives for managers and workers, as a result of more wage flexibility and more extensive reliance on bonding for managers and piecework for laborers.

Urban cooperatives			Township and village enterprises		
Most important	Second most important	Third most important	Most important	Second most important	Third most important
17.2	3.7	5.8	14.3	7.4	5.3
3.0	5.4	4.4	7.7	11.2	10.6
16.8	22.1	8.5	12.2	13.3	20.1
17.8	21.1	10.5	17.5	16.1	9.5
4.4	5.4	7.8	0.7	0.4	1.4
14.1	9.4	13.6	13.3	9.5	9.9
12.5	14.1	16.6	21.3	23.9	12.7
0.0	1.0	0.3	1.4	2.5	2.5
1.0	1.7	2.0	2.1	4.9	5.3
3.7	4.4	4.4	0.3	0.4	2.8
3.0	2.3	2.4	6.6	10.2	19.0
6.1	9.1	22.4	2.4	..	0.7

Other distinctions emerged clearly. State-owned enterprises assigned greater importance to fulfilling the terms of profit remittance than did their counterparts in collectives. Township and village enterprises appeared to be more concerned with growth, product quality, and product mix. This difference may reflect the fact that these enterprises are at a different phase in their life cycle. Survey results showed that during 1991–92 state-owned enterprises were more likely to be subject to price controls but that these affected urban cooperatives and township and village enterprises as well. Finally, the surveys identified impediments to raising productivity (see table 2.12): for state-owned enterprises ineffective incentives and excessive profit remittance were relatively more significant barriers to raising productivity, while for township and village enterprises shortages in energy inputs, skilled labor, technology, and capital were more important. These differences are not surprising, since state-owned enterprises suffer from a range of governance issues and rural enterprises operate within an environment in which factor markets are relatively underdeveloped.

Notes

1. The urban and rural surveys used different classification schemes. Currently, China's industrial enterprises are subject to a uniform code. At the time the survey was conducted, township and village enterprises used the old code, which included just 15 industrial branches. The urban survey used the new code, which includes 40 industrial branches.

2. The author thanks Louis Putterman for this perspective.

3. In 1991, when the survey was conducted, the exchange rate was 4.78 yuan to the U.S. dollar.

References

Alchian, Armen, and Harold Demsetz. 1972. "Production, Information Costs, and Economic Organization. *American Economic Review* 62(5): 777–95.

Jensen, Michael, and William Meckling. 1976. "Theory of the Firm: Managerial Behavior, Agency Costs, and Ownership Structure." *Journal of Financial Economics* 3(4): 305–60.

Koo, Anthony Y. C. 1990. "The Contract Responsibility System: Transition from a Planned to a Market Economy." *Economic Development and Cultural Change* 38(4): 797–820.

Qian, Yingyi, and Xu Chenggang. 1993. "Why China's Economic Reforms Differ: The M-Form Hierarchy and Entry/Expansion of the Non-State Sector." *Economics of Transition* 1(2): 135–70.

World Bank. 1992. "Enterprise Surveys." China and Mongolia Department and the Socialist Economies Unit. Washington, D.C.

China's Industrial Innovation Ladder: *3* A Model of Endogenous Reform

Gary H. Jefferson and Thomas G. Rawski

China's dynamic economic growth has taken place within an institutional and policy environment that is far different from that prescribed by economists as necessary for reform. This chapter investigates how China's unorthodox reforms have unleashed a burst of economic activity that has outpaced progress in other former socialist economies and in most developing nations.

Many economists view the reform of former socialist economies as a process of replacing old institutions with new structures in an organized top-down fashion. In this view of reform, the self-interested response of agents within the economy is expected to stimulate profit-seeking behavior and market activity. If progress is inadequate, planners can impose further rounds of reform.

This style of centrally directed reform, which we attempt to characterize in appendix A, undoubtedly played an important role in China's economic transition. It was China's central leadership that initiated economic reform in the late 1970s by expanding the role of prices and market allocation, rolling back long-standing barriers to international trade and investment, transferring authority from central planners to enterprise managers and local governments, creating a unique system of dual (plan and market) pricing for industrial goods, and so on. But unlike postcommunist leaders in countries such as Poland and the Czech Republic, China's policymakers embarked upon a path of reform with no clear vision of what a restructured economy should look like and no consensus about the appropriate policy mix or institutional arrangements (Hua, Luo, and Zhang 1993; Shirk 1993; Naughton 1994).

Policy announcements from the center were partial and tentative. The center ratified but did not direct the momentous shift from collective to household farming. Central initiatives in the reform of industry focused on incremental relaxation of controls over state-owned enterprises. Even the revolutionary Open Door policy, embodied in a sequence of central decisions that shattered long-standing barriers to China's participation in the world economy, concentrated on expanding trade and investment activity in a small number of provinces and special zones along China's southeast coast.

Many economists find China's recent economic gains remarkably large given the modest reform initiatives adopted by the central government. This chapter tries to explain this apparent anomaly by showing how technical innovation, economizing behavior, market-leaning institutional changes, and a multitude of cumulative and mutually supporting choices by administrators, managers, and workers reinforced and eventually overshadowed Beijing's partial reform efforts. It focuses on industry both because industry is the largest sector in China's economy and because industry is at the core of China's reform program.

Industrial reform—what needs to be explained?

Three characteristics of Chinese industry appear inconsistent with high rates of economic growth and therefore require explanation:

- Public sector enterprise continues to dominate the economy.
- Performance by the public sector enterprises—including performance by old-line state firms—has improved, despite the absence of a plan or the credible threat of privatization or bankruptcy.
- The institutional infrastructure remains flawed by several important defects.

Each of these apparent paradoxes is addressed in the following sections.

The dominant role of public enterprise

Although the public sector, including urban and rural collectives, accounted for 68 percent of China's output in 1996, the share of output produced by state-owned industry plunged between 1980 and 1996, falling from 76 percent to less than 29 percent of output (see table 1.3). The decline reflected the extraordinary increase in the share of industrial output produced by collectives, especially township and village enterprises. The share of output produced by private firms, although still small relative to the public sector share, rose more than fivefold between 1985 and 1994.[1]

The improved performance of state enterprises

No one disputes the scale and significance of the contribution that township and village enterprise industry has made to the growth of production, exports, productivity, employment, incomes, and material welfare. The success of these public sector firms belies the assumption that prompt dissolution of official influence on enterprise management, preferably through early and comprehensive privatization, is a necessary early ingredient in the reform of socialist systems.

But the inconsistency between recent Chinese industrial experience and free market orthodoxy runs even deeper. Many of China's old-line state enterprises have responded to ongoing partial reform by behaving less like passive bureaucratic followers and more like profit-seeking commercial businesses. The impact of reform on objectives, incentives, and "corporate culture" within state firms, while neither universal nor complete, has brought substantial improvements in performance. Given the size of state industry, which accounted for more than half of industrial output and absorbed a large share of aggregate fixed investment at the end of the 1980s, China's recent economic gains could not have occurred if state industry had served only as a drag on economic progress.

This chapter does not present a detailed review of the evidence supporting these assertions. Instead it limits it scope to examination of the following propositions about state industry, each of which rests on substantial empirical foundations for which considerable empirical support is presented throughout this volume:

- State-owned enterprises, once devoted to plan fulfillment, now take profit as their chief objective. Data on state-owned enterprise performance reveal increasingly robust statistical relationships of the kind expected from profit-seeking firms operating in a competitive market.
- State-owned enterprises have achieved substantial increases in labor productivity and steady, albeit modest, increases in total factor productivity.
- Exports of state-owned enterprise manufactures, which increased at an estimated annual rate of 18 percent between 1985 and 1992, reflect the impact of greater attention to quality, variety, customer requirements, and cost control.
- State-owned enterprises have sharply increased the pace of their R&D efforts, new product development, and process innovation (see chapter 4). They furnish an important and often crucial source of technology, equipment, funds, information, expertise, and marketing opportunities essential for the successful development of township and village enterprise industry.

The persistence of institutional weaknesses

The challenge posed by China's broadly based industrial advances arises precisely because these advances have occurred without the benefit of features that many economists regard as core ingredients of a market system. Chinese industry continues to operate in an environment in which property rights are not fully specified. Rules of commerce are neither clearly defined nor consistently enforced. Competing firms in the same industry or locality face widely differing legal, fiscal, and regulatory regimes. Government intervention in business affairs still extends well beyond the boundaries observed in heavily regulated market economies (such as Japan and the Republic of Korea), and official involvement frequently has the effect of softening budget constraints. These difficulties restrict innovation and productivity growth, particularly, although not exclusively, in the state sector. They have also prolonged the life of insolvent and hopelessly inefficient state enterprises that waste vast amounts of productive resources and require subsidies on a scale large enough to affect macroeconomic stability (Sachs and Woo 1994; Woo and others 1993). The cost of institutional shortcomings, although difficult to quantify, appears large.

A model for analyzing induced industrial reform

A model of China's industrial transformation is presented here in which competition and technical and institutional innovation create a mutually reinforcing circle of reform. Reform is a cumulative process that begins when partial relaxation of institutional constraints associated with socialist planning initiates competition in the markets for industrial products. Competition reduces profits, creating financial pressures that induce technical innovations, promote economizing behavior, and stimulate fresh rounds of market-leaning institutional change. The model rests on four key institutional features of China's industrial economy: decentralized supervision, incipient competition, fiscal dependence on industrial profits, and a hierarchy of heterogeneous enterprise types.

Decentralized supervision

Central control of China's industrial enterprises was never as tight as in Eastern Europe and the Soviet Union (Granick 1990). Decentralization increased during the late 1960s and 1970s, as the central government transferred the supervision of many firms to provincial and municipal governments. This system of decentralized supervision encouraged provinces and localities to create and pursue their own industrial development strategies. When reform began, decentralized decisionmaking also made it possible to introduce piecemeal reforms and to conduct local policy experiments without disrupting the whole economy. Successful local reforms inspired widespread emulation.

Incipient competition

The term "incipient competition" describes the circumstances of domestic Chinese markets for industrial products on the eve of reform. Actual competition was sharply limited by policies that created strong barriers to entry. Removal of these barriers, however, quickly revealed multiple competitors in nearly every product line. Unlike in Russia, the other former Soviet republics, and Eastern Europe, deregulation in China led to industrial competition, not monopoly.

Once liberalization commenced, competitive pressures arose from four sources. Rural industry developed widely in the decades before reform, but it was largely confined to fabricating local materials into goods for local buyers (Perkins 1977). Entrepreneurial leaders in hundreds of counties and thousands of production brigades were poised to take advantage of deregulation by bursting into markets they had coveted for years. China's southern regions, which had been excluded from large-scale industrial investment during three decades of central planning, took advantage of the new Open Door policy to promote industrial growth with the aid of capital, skill, and commercial contacts from overseas Chinese, most of whom trace their ancestry to the southern coastal provinces. Defense conversion brought strong new entrants into a number of civilian industries; by the early 1990s at least two-thirds of output from defense industries consisted of civilian products (Blasko 1994). Finally, China's long-standing policy of building complete sets of state-owned industries in most provinces provided a ready-made source of competition.

Fiscal dependence on industrial profits

Taxes on industrial profits are a key component of fiscal revenue at every level of government. State enterprises contributed 80 percent or more of "adjusted budgetary revenues" in every year during 1978–87; state industry accounted for 73 percent of profits and profit taxes from all state enterprises (Sicular 1992).

The fiscal reforms of the 1980s created a system in which each level of government collected taxes from enterprises under its jurisdiction, turned over a contractually specified amount to the next higher level of government, and retained the residual. The result was "a shift toward local fiscal power at the expense of the center, as the center's proportion of total government revenue fell" from 50 percent in the 1970s to less than 30 percent in the 1980s (Walder 1994).

Chinese industry as a hierarchy of heterogeneous enterprise types

Vernon (1966) and Grossman and Helpman (1991) have developed models of international product cycles and quality ladders that focus on interactions between innovative firms in the "North" and imitators in the "South." Northern firms rely on product innovations to support their high-cost manufacturing operations. Southern firms, with lower production costs, can capture markets from Northern rivals by replicating Northern products. The North retaliates with fresh rounds of innovation. Rivalry among different types of producers leads to an ongoing evolution of product characteristics, while the locus of manufacturing activity may shift back and forth between firms located in the "industrial" North and the "developing" South.

This model explains China's recent industrial history once its concepts are extended to encompass the existence of product cycles and quality ladders within the domestic economy of nations participating in global trade as well as across high- and low-wage economies. Chinese industrial goods rarely match the quality and characteristics of products manufactured by global leaders. But the most accomplished Chinese firms, on their own or with the cooperation of foreign partners, can produce reasonable substitutes at low cost. Rapidly growing exports of textiles, garments, footwear, machinery, and consumer durables illustrate China's participation in international quality ladders.

China's industrial sector is characterized by extreme heterogeneity and a hierarchy of firms. At the top of the international quality ladder are the overseas firms that set the innovative pace in global markets. They are followed by domestic state enterprises, urban and rural collectives, and smaller private businesses, which occupy the lower rungs of the ladder. These groups of firms exhibit systematic differences in technological capabilities, cost structures, and institutional arrangements. Among domestic firms state-owned enterprises have the greatest technical strength. They also face the highest labor costs and suffer the greatest restriction from institutional constraints. Township and village enterprises are least affected by institutional limitations. The interaction of these different enterprise types creates a kind of innovation and competition ladder up and down which the hierarchy of firms generates domestic versions of the rivalries, flows, and pressures associated with global product cycles.

During the 1980s and 1990s a well-defined hierarchy of domestic technological capabilities extended downward from joint ventures to state-owned enterprises and collective-owned enterprises. Among purely domestic firms state-owned enterprises enjoy superior endowments of equipment, laboratory facilities, and skilled and educated workers, technicians, and managers. This resource differential shows up in the outcome of quality inspections. In the fourth quarter of 1993, 90 percent of "big state enterprises" but only 62 percent of "township and private manufacturers" passed inspection (*China Daily* 20 January 1994). Managers of urban cooperatives and township and village enterprises (as well as state-owned enterprises) overwhelmingly identify state firms as the domestic technological leaders in their own industries (see table 4.7).

As in the transnational versions of the product cycle, technology percolates down China's domestic quality ladder. The example of bar coding illustrates how links with international markets necessitate the mastery of suitable technologies and the achievement of specific quality standards that gradually spread into the domestic economy. Export-oriented firms have learned to use bar codes, which they see as "tickets to foreign supermarkets." In 1994, China announced its intention "to have bar codes on all its exported goods and 60 percent of domestic commodities" (Sun 1994, p. 8).

One important and widely overlooked aspect of Chinese quality ladders is the dependence of many township and village enterprise producers on funds, equipment, product designs, technical information, management skills, and subcontracting opportunities obtained from state-owned enterprises (Jefferson and Rawski 1994). In southern Jiangsu Province (near Shanghai), a center of booming rural enterprise development, "more than two-thirds of township and village enterprises ... have established various forms of economic and technical cooperation arrangements with industrial enterprises, research units, and higher educational institutions in larger cities" (Xu, Mao, and Yuan 1993). Officials attempting to develop industry in poor localities are encouraged to pursue "joint operations with scientific research organizations or large- and medium-scale enterprises" (Du, Huang, and Chen 1992).

The domestic quality ladder also resembles its international counterpart in that firms with greater technological capabilities usually have higher costs and vice versa. According to one manager of a shirt factory, "in the area of product quality, household producers can't match collectives and collectives can't match state enterprises; but as for costs, state enterprises can't match collectives and the collectives can't match individual households" (1994 interview with author). Wage costs are highest in foreign-invested enterprises and lowest in township and village enterprises (table 3.1). The cost advantage of collective-owned enterprises over state-owned enterprises is a staple topic of discussion in Chinese newspapers and economic journals, which emphasize the extra burden of pensions, taxes, redundant workers, fringe benefits, and welfare responsibilities borne by state-owned enterprises, especially compared with township and village enterprises. The extra costs are large and, in some cases, growing rapidly.

TABLE 3.1
Average wages in China's textile industry, 1989–91
(yuan per person-year)

Type of enterprise	1989	1990	1991
Joint venture	3,663	4,232	5,674
State-owned enterprise	2,069	2,252	2,377
Urban cooperative	1,368	1,688	1,862
Township and village enterprise	1,132[a]	—	—

— Not available.
a. Average wage figure for all township and village enterprise industries.
Source: Jefferson, Rawski, and Zheng 1994.

National data (probably excluding the farm populace) show that the ratio of retirees to active workers increased from 1:26 in 1978 to 1:6 in 1990 (Du and Shang 1993). Since state-owned enterprises are obliged to pay retirement benefits out of current income, these obligations are costly. A sample of enterprises polled in 1989 showed that the average firm paid about 232 yuan per worker for annual medical costs; a similar study conducted in 1993 (Li and Qin 1993) reported average annual medical costs of 1,201 yuan, equivalent to 37 percent of money wages.

The dynamics of partial reform in Chinese industry

Hirschman's (1958) analysis of unbalanced growth is used here as a framework for examining the dynamics of partial reform in China's industry. The elements of the dynamic process that transforms partial reform into improved performance are simple and direct:

- The government implements partial reform measures that reduce entry barriers and lower the cost of many types of transactions. These initiatives have a differential impact on the opportunity sets available to different groups of firms. Partial reform accelerates the domestic product cycle by facilitating the transmission of cost pressures and technologies up and down the hierarchy of industrial enterprises.

- The differential impact of reform efforts destabilizes the existing division of industrial resources and product markets among different types of firms. Competition in industrial product markets intensifies.

- Stronger competition diminishes flows of quasi-rents derived from the enforcement of entry barriers and market segmentation. At the microeconomic level, reduced profitability limits the growth of wages and bonuses for some firms and causes others to suffer financial losses. At the macroeconomic level, erosion of profits limits the growth of revenues accruing to local and provincial authorities and to the central government.

- Firms react to financial pressures by restructuring operations, lobbying for further deregulation to facilitate profit-seeking initiatives, or lobbying for government subsidies or official intervention to restore the initial financial position.
- Governments also react to financial pressures that reduce their share of total output and destabilize the distribution of fiscal revenue across regions and administrative levels. Officials face conflicting lobbying efforts, some demanding further autonomy and deregulation, others seeking protection from the effects of earlier reforms.
- The induced responses of firms and governments further erode entry barriers and reduce transactions costs. These beneficial feedback effects accelerate every dimension of the reform process by intensifying competition, further diminishing quasi-rents and motivating additional reform efforts by the enterprises and governments. These changes set in motion additional rounds of technical development, economizing efforts, and incremental reform.
- The entire process affects the attitudes of enterprise personnel and government officials, pushing them in the direction of reform. Changing attitudes affect the objectives and strategies of all participants.

Not every industrial policy initiative undertaken since the beginning of reform represents an endogenous response to the initial partial reform effort. Many policy changes, such as the partial commercialization of bank lending and the reduction of budgetary appropriations for industrial research and development projects, probably represent a combination of endogenous response and exogenous initiative.

There is no guarantee that partial reform will succeed. If governments act to stifle competition, equalize financial outcomes for winners and losers, or alter regulations to restore the prereform status quo in product markets, the endogenous process linking initial reforms with innovation, economizing, and further institutional change may stall.

The endogenous component has been important in China's reform accomplishments; this cumulative process is the key to explaining how China recorded unexpectedly strong achievements in both growth and institutional change despite modest reform initiatives by the central government. Several specific propositions about Chinese industrial reform correspond to each element of the model.

Proposition 1: Partial reform erodes market segmentation, thereby lowering barriers to technology and resources

China's reforms of the late 1970s restored household agriculture and reopened rural markets; expanded China's participation in global markets for commodities, capital, and technology; and began to loosen controls in the industrial sector. Each of these policy shifts eroded barriers to competition in industrial factor and product markets.

Agricultural reforms provided a big boost to China's rural industries by simultaneously increasing the supply of labor, the supply of raw materials, and, following the quick rise of farm incomes, the demand for output. As Sachs and Woo (1994) point out, China's comparatively large rural sector creates possibilities for rapid productivity growth that are not accessible to more urban states, such as the Czech Republic, Poland, and Russia.

The Open Door policy rapidly increased imports of industrial goods, many of which competed directly with domestic products. Partial liberalization of the external sector sharply reduced the transactions costs associated with international inflows of capital, technology, market information, managerial skills, and equipment. New policies sped the transfer of capabilities and cost pressures across China's borders and throughout the hierarchy of domestic enterprises. The pace of change was particularly rapid in regions of south China that benefited from accelerated deregulation and proximity to Hong Kong.

Although intended to stimulate state-owned enterprises, these measures had their greatest impact in the township and village enterprise sector. The two-track system enabled township and village enterprises to obtain producer inputs previously reserved for clients of the state plan and to penetrate markets outside their home areas. The relaxation of restrictions on information sharing, consulting, and technical ties across urban-rural administrative boundaries made it easier for collective and township and village enterprises to adopt new technologies and produce substitutes that could compete with products produced by state-owned enterprises. These changes shattered constraints that had previously restricted township and village enterprise growth. The result was an unexpected growth explosion in China's rural industries.

These partial and uneven reforms substantially eroded barriers that had long obstructed flows of resources and products across the boundaries separating different types of firms and different administrative and bureaucratic jurisdictions. As old distinctions gradually blurred, resources, products, funds, and information began to circulate in new directions. The new market channels soon narrowed differences in factor returns among different enterprise groups, especially among enterprises with the greatest market exposure (Jefferson and Xu 1994).

The bright growth prospects and high rates of return enjoyed by township and village enterprise firms at the start of reform attracted a large inflow of funds that served to push down returns to township and village enterprise capital (table 3.2). Naughton (1992) documents a relat-

TABLE 3.2
Profit-capital ratios in Chinese industry, selected years, 1980–92
(percent)

	Pretax rate of return			After-tax rate of return		
Year	State-owned enterprises	Collective-owned enterprises	Township and village enterprises	State-owned enterprises	Collective-owned enterprises	Township and village enterprises
1980	24.8	26.6	32.5	16.0	18.5	26.7
1982	23.4	22.0	28.0	14.4	13.8	20.2
1984	24.2	22.3	24.6	14.9	13.9	15.2
1985	23.8	24.5	23.7	13.2	15.3	14.5
1988	20.6	19.7	17.9	10.4	11.3	9.3
1990	12.4	—	13.0	3.2	—	5.9
1992	9.7	—	14.2	2.7	—	7.2
1995	6.6	8.1	—	1.9	3.2	—

— Not available.

Note: Rate of return is the ratio of the sum of profit figures (positive or negative) for all firms to the sum of net (of depreciation) value of fixed assets plus average amount of working capital in use.

Source: State-owned enterprise data for independent accounting units are calculated from China State Statistical Bureau 1991 (p. 416) and 1992 (p. 437). Collective-owned enterprise data for independent accounting units are calculated using data from the following sources: for 1980–84, *China Industrial Economy Statistical Yearbook 1984* (p. 85); for 1985, *China Industrial Economy Statistical Yearbook 1986* (p. 87); for 1986, *China Industrial Economy Statistical Yearbook 1987* (p. 128). Data for 1988 are from China State Statistical Bureau. Township and village enterprise data for all enterprises are calculated from China State Statistical Bureau 1991 (pp. 377–79) and 1993 (pp. 396–97).

ed phenomenon, the convergence of rates of return to capital across different branches of industry. These changes occurred before the creation of organized capital markets, which remain embryonic even today.

Access to high-level technical personnel offers another example of declining market segmentation. A comparison of data from China's 1985 industrial census with 1989 survey data (China State Statistical Bureau 1992) reveals a large increase in the share of technicians outside the state sector (see table 4.11). Using 1989 data Jefferson, Rawski, and Zheng (chapter 4) show that the marginal profitability of upper-level technicians within state-owned enterprises, township and village enterprises, and urban cooperatives in three branches of industry is comparable.

Proposition 2: Reform intensifies competition in markets for industrial products

On the eve of reform Chinese industry was characterized by "incipient competition," with large numbers of potential entrants poised to intensify product market competition. Partial reform rapidly turned this potential into a reality. Booming imports of manufactures, swift expansion of joint ventures and other foreign-linked enterprises, and rapid erosion of economic and administrative barriers preventing domestic state-owned enterprises from raiding each other's customers all contributed to the upsurge of competition. The greatest impetus to competition, however, came from the growth of township and village enterprise production, which accounted for nearly 28 percent of total industrial output in 1996 (see table 1.3).

Competition expanded most rapidly in markets directly affected by the growth of township and village enterprise output, but competitive pressures extended to other markets as well. By 1997 mandatory plans controlled less than 10 percent of industrial output and few firms remained immune from competition. The experience of the Luoyang Tractor Works, China's largest manufacturer of wheeled tractors and bulldozers, is illustrative. According to *China Daily,* Luoyang "is trying to improve the quality of its products as well as its marketing and publicity techniques in a bid to offset ... sluggish domestic sales.... The sluggish market ... provoked incessant price undercuttings by producers.... The Luoyang tractor complex had been forced to sacrifice more than half of its profits in trying discounts, lotteries, and free delivery of goods to boost sales" (28 May 1990, p. 4).

Concentration ratios (see table 1.11) reveal the broad structure of China's domestic markets for industrial products. These ratios are low and declining, and they are below comparable ratios for Japan and the United States. With competition from manufactured imports on the rise and barriers to domestic trade increasingly porous, it is clear that partial reform has firmly installed competing product markets as a regular feature of everyday operations for most of China's industrial enterprises.

Proposition 3: Competition erodes profits and curtails the growth of fiscal revenues

Reform has brought a large decline in industrial profits. Rates of return (including taxes) for state-owned enterprises and township and village enterprises in 1992–95 were less than half of what they were in 1980 (see table 3.2). After-tax rates of return for various industries confirm the fact that profits are declining (table 3.3). Rates of return also reveal the powerful impact of township and village enterprise competition on industrial profitability. In the early years of reform, profits fell fastest in branches with the greatest township and village enterprise activity. During 1980–85 falling profitability was concentrated in industries using agricultural raw materials, especially beverages, tobacco, textiles, and apparel. During the second half of the 1980s and early 1990s downward pressure on profitability extended to industries with little direct township and village enterprise competition,

TABLE 3.3

Rates of return to capital in Chinese industry, selected years, 1980–93
(percent)

Type of enterprise	1980	1985	1991	1994
Industry	25.5	23.8	11.9	9.8
Light industry	49.1	31.8	15.0	11.4
Farm materials	54.7	32.0	15.9	—
Nonfarm materials	39.1	31.5	13.0	—
Heavy industry	18.5	20.3	10.2	9.2
Active township and village enterprise				
Food processing	20.4	17.5	9.7	3.2
Beverage	48.5	28.4	18.6	15.1
Tobacco	326.9	207.4	113.6	73.8
Textile	69.0	26.5	6.6	3.9
Apparel	46.0	26.0	11.7	3.4
Leather, hides	30.3	19.4	5.6	–0.4
Handicrafts	43.0	27.4	12.0	—
Plastics	31.6	21.2	9.1	2.1
Average[a]	41.3	23.8	10.5	4.6
Limited township and village enterprises				
Power	20.6	16.0	13.0	10.8
Chemicals	22.0	21.7	14.0	5.3
Ferrous metals	18.3	25.8	15.5	5.9
Machinery	13.0	19.3	7.9	5.1
Electronics	14.0	24.9	8.5	5.2
Average	17.6	21.5	11.8	6.5

— Not available.
Note: Rate of return equals tax plus profit as a percentage of net (of depreciation) value of fixed assets plus working capital.
a. Average excludes the tobacco industry.
Source: Data for 1992 and 1993 are from Government of China 1994. Other data are from *China Industrial Economy Statistical Yearbook 1992* (pp. 168–78).

including power, chemicals, iron and steel, machinery, and electronics, although erosion of profitability was deeper in industries with intense township and village enterprise activity. Excluding the tobacco industry, average profit rates in industries with high rates of township and village enterprise participation fell from 41.3 percent in 1980 to 4.6 percent in 1994; in industries with relatively little township and village enterprise participation, profits fell from 17.6 percent to 6.5 percent.

Proposition 4: Enterprises react to market pressure by searching for financial gain

An enterprise facing competition and declining profit margins may employ one or more of the following three strategies to strengthen its financial position: improve the performance of the firm within its existing institutional limits, pressure the government to extend greater autonomy and incentives to the firm, or pursue rent-seeking alternatives by capturing direct subsidies or soft loans to offset losses or by lobbying for restrictions to stifle competition. Each of these strategies is examined below.

Improve performance within existing institutional limits. China's state-owned enterprises, particularly those facing severe competition and declining profit margins, have demonstrated a substantial capacity to economize and innovate. Since state-owned enterprises came under increasing competitive pressures in the 1980s, total factor productivity has improved steadily (*China Daily* 1 March 1994). Singh, Ratha, and Xiao (1994) establish an explicit link between competitive pressure and productivity growth by using provincial data for 1982–90 to show that total factor productivity in state industry rose most rapidly in provinces with the largest shares of nonstate production in total (Q/L) industrial output.

The association between competition and state-owned enterprise efficiency is tested using the following regression equation with 1990 enterprise data:

(3.1)
$$\ln(Q/L) = -1.25 + 0.63*\ln(K/L) + 0.09*\text{COMP} + 0.65*\text{PCOMP} - 0.11*(NK/K)$$
$$(3.04)\ (13.94) \qquad\qquad (2.55) \qquad\quad (4.72) \qquad\qquad (2.54)$$
$$R^2 = 0.32, n = 496$$

where Q/L is labor productivity, K/L is the capital-labor ratio, and NK/K is the fraction of nonindustrial capital held by the enterprise. COMP is the firm's estimated demand elasticity for the firm's major product; PCOMP reflects the firm's assessment of the overall competitive pressure it faces. Whether panels of provincial data or a cross-section of enterprise data are used, competitive pressures are consistently found to motivate firms to improve overall efficiency.

In a 1992 survey of 10 percent of China's large and medium-size industrial enterprises, 92 percent of the 954 respondents reported innovating products or processes. More than half reported major modification of their main products; 81 percent had new products in the marketplace; 61 percent were engaged in major product innovation; and 66 percent were implementing new production technologies (Ma and Zhao 1993).

A second set of panel data covering 249 enterprises in the textile, electronics, and equipment industries provides information on output of new products (but not on the intensity of competition). These results show the impact of changes in profitability during 1984–86 on new product innovation during 1986–88. (A two-year lag between changes in profitability and shifts in the output share of new products is assumed.) Product innovation is constrained by two factors: diminishing returns to product innovation—captured by NPS_{86}, the initial 1986 share of new products in total output; and financial capacity—represented by PRO_{86}, the 1986 ratio of profit (including tax) to sales. The estimation yields the following result:

$$(3.2) \quad NPS_{8886} = 0.005 - 0.320\ PRO_{8684} - 0.443\ NPS_{86} + 0.371\ PRO_{86}$$
$$(0.617) \quad (1.970) \qquad\qquad (7.908) \qquad\quad (5.921)$$
$$R^2 = 0.250, n = 210$$

NPS_{8886} is the change in the share of new products in output value during 1986–88, and PRO_{8684} is the change in the profit-sales ratio during 1984–86. These estimation results confirm that declining profitability creates an incentive to innovate, conditional on the enterprise's financial capability and the diminishing returns to innovation.

Seek to expand institutional limits. In addition to trying to improve performance within existing institutional limits, financially pressed enterprises seek greater autonomy and a larger share of residual earnings. Through the mid-1980s the circumstances and opportunities available to enterprises in the state sector were widely regarded as preferable to those facing collective or private firms. In the late 1980s both published materials and interviews with factory managers revealed a gradual shift toward the view that the autonomy associated with collective ownership outweighed the privileges available within the state sector, leaving state-owned enterprises at a competitive disadvantage in China's domestic markets. As state firms complain of administrative interference and cost-inflating obligations that township and village enterprises and joint ventures often escape, managers in the state sector have gradually emerged as active agents for reform.

Seek rents in the form of direct subsidies or soft loans. A third avenue of response for financially distressed enterprises is to seek rents in the form of direct subsidies, soft loans, and competition-stifling resumption of regulation. Whenever such assistance is available, enterprises will pursue opportunities for rent seeking as long as the expected payoff exceeds the cost of lobbying. From this perspective governments' attitudes control the distribution of enterprises' resources between economizing and innovation on the one hand and rent seeking on the other. The following section considers whether reform has reduced the availability of various types of direct and hidden subsidies for enterprises experiencing financial distress.

Proposition 5: On balance, government policy toward industry extends autonomy, increases market exposure, and hardens budget constraints

The central facts of life for Chinese public finance in the 1980s included a slowdown in revenue growth, especially at the central level; significant hardening of budget constraints for subnational governments at all levels (Walder 1994); and repeated episodes of macroeconomic instability, attributable to fiscal deficits and excessive monetary expansion.

The erosion of industrial profits, a by-product of growing competition, has curtailed the growth of government revenues, which have declined sharply as a share of total output, falling from about 30 percent in the early 1980s (as reform began) to 14 percent in 1992 (Wong, Heady, and Woo 1993). Although revenue shortfalls have not been as serious for subnational governments as for the central government, even rich localities have generally been less willing than their counterparts at the center to subsidize weak firms and industries. The reason is simple: fierce competition among development-conscious subnational jurisdictions. Diverting resources from developmental spending to subsidies threatens to undercut the ability of provinces, cities, counties, townships, and villages to attract domestic and foreign investment. With local revenues increasingly tied to the growth of profits from local industry, slow growth of investment endangers the revenue prospects of the same bureaus and officials faced with requests for subsidies and protection.

Under these circumstances how do officials respond to the pleas of firms whose financial interests are damaged by competition? Two main options exist: granting direct or indirect subsidies or pushing enterprises toward the market. Although various forms of subsidies continue, evidence shows that government policy has gradually tilted toward "sending enterprises to market."

Macroeconomic data suggest a distinct shift away from bailouts. Chronic loss-making township and village enterprises are closed and their workers dismissed. Information on subsidies to loss-making firms in state industry shows a tightening of budget constraints. At the start of reform state-owned enterprises typically expected full compensation for losses. By 1986 the ratio of subsidies to losses for state-owned enterprise industry had dropped to 0.81 (table 3.4). Another sharp falloff in compensation occurred in connection with the retrenchment of 1988 and 1989. Although different sources create some confusion about the exact timing and scope of the decline, after a decade of partial reform, a declining scale of partial compensation has emerged as the general rule for loss-making state industrial firms.

TABLE 3.4
Losses and subsidies for Chinese state enterprises, 1986–91
(monetary data in billions of yuan)

Year	Figures for all state enterprises			Figures for state industry		
	Loss	Subsidy	Ratio	Loss	Subsidy	Ratio
1986	41.71	32.5	0.78	4.71	3.5	0.81
1987	48.17	37.5	0.78	5.07	3.7	0.72
1988	52.06	44.6	0.86	7.13	5.2	0.73
1989	74.96	59.9	0.80	12.80	9.5	0.74
1990	93.26	57.9	0.62	27.88	11.8	0.42
1991	93.11	50.6	0.54	30.02	14.5	0.48

Sources: Data on public enterprises are from Hwa 1992; data on subsidies are from World Bank 1992; data on state industries are from Wong, Heady, and Woo 1993.

Direct subsidies are not the only avenue of government support for weak enterprises. Public officials can use tax concessions, regulatory protection, and soft bank credits to sustain loss–making firms. Tax concessions are limited by the same factors that constrain subsidies. The increasingly high opportunity cost of scarce fiscal resources causes large concessions or protective trade restrictions to be widely viewed as undesirable and infeasible. In the words of Chen Qingtai (1994), Vice Minister of the State Economic and Trade Commission, "In the past enterprises turned to the government when they ran into difficulty because the government could lower taxes and allowed them to retain more profits. This road has now been basically closed."

This leaves the banking system as the main vehicle for large-scale indirect support of weak firms. China's banks face strong official pressure to advance funds to weak borrowers. "Policy loans," viewed as unrepayable from the start, are extended to both large and small industries at the behest of powerful official interests. Financial officials indicate that "policy loans" account for about 30 percent of new lending, with most of the soft credits destined for investment projects.

Policy lending is an important component of Chinese industrial policy, but it is subject to very real restrictions. Increases in bank lending have the same inflationary potential as government deficits. Furthermore, the banks, which have developed systems of credit ratings as part of their own profit-seeking agenda, have already cut the "policy" component of current lending to less than 10 percent. Banks can be expected to defend their business autonomy with increasing tenacity.

The growing reluctance of government agencies to support weak enterprises is reflected in microeconomic data. Survey data analyzed by Hay and others (1994) show that despite an increase in the absolute level of subsidies, budget constraints for state firms hardened considerably during the late

1980s. Other data support the hypothesis that enterprises facing strong competition move (or are pushed) toward the market in the expectation that greater independence will help them resolve their own financial problems.

Equation 3.3, a regression based on 1990 data for state enterprises surveyed in late 1991 and early 1992, evaluates the impact of market conditions on the government's grant of decisionmaking autonomy (DMA) to the enterprise:

$$(3.3) \quad \text{DMA} = 1.73 + 0.12*\text{COMP} + 0.10*\text{PCOMP} - 0.27*\text{PROFIT} + 0.02*\text{IND}$$
$$\qquad\quad (19.40) \ (5.02) \qquad\quad (3.69) \qquad\qquad (2.17) \qquad\qquad (0.46)$$
$$R^2 = 0.10, n = 572$$

In this regression DMA is a composite measure of enterprise control over production and marketing decisions in 1991; COMP is the firm's estimated demand elasticity for the firm's major product; PCOMP reflects the firm's assessment of the overall competitive pressure it faces. PROFIT represents profitability, the ratio of profit (or loss) to the gross value of output in 1990. To control for differences in autonomy that are specific to the light-heavy industry mix, the equation includes IND, a dummy variable in which 0 represents heavy industry and 1 represents light industry.

The regression results show that competition (measured by the firm's estimate of the elasticity of demand for its products and of the degree of competitive pressure from its rivals) is associated with a relatively high degree of managerial autonomy, which can be interpreted as synonymous with greater exposure to market forces. Low or negative profits also contribute to a greater transfer of production control and marketing rights to enterprise management.

Recent developments in the woolen textile industry illustrate the government's propensity to assist troubled firms with offers of deregulation rather than direct or indirect subsidies. The requirement that exporters of textiles sell through foreign trade corporations had insulated them from international market changes and led to the accumulation of large inventories and losses during 1990–91. In response to these losses and to pressures from producers, the government allowed woolen textile companies to export directly to overseas customers. Direct marketing allowed Chinese producers to produce semifinished inventories that could be more quickly transformed into final goods that conformed to specifications and just-in-time production requirements of overseas customers.

Although government intervention continues to cushion some firms, especially state-owned enterprises, against the consequences of weak performance, limited resources, fear of inflation, and changing attitudes have increased the likelihood that firms and their workers will bear the financial consequences of market outcomes. The gap between financial outcomes for successful and unsuccessful firms is widening. Loss-making industrial enterprises, once routinely eligible for full compensation, face growing difficulties under China's steadily expanding reforms. In the rural sector, losses result in quick exit for enterprises and dismissal for workers. Subsidies continue, but even for urban state-owned enterprises the ratio of subsidies to losses has dropped by 50 percent. Workers associated with loss-making enterprises face a growing probability of sanctions, such as slow wage growth, deterioration of bonuses, erosion of health benefits and other nonwage income, layoffs with no more than partial wage payment, delayed payment of wages, compulsory transfer to ancillary units, and, most recently, dismissal.

Proposition 6: Feedback mechanisms amplify and extend the reform process

The consequences of partial reform are not limited to a linear progression in which new policies intensify competition, reduce profits and fiscal revenues, and create pressures for better industrial performance. At every stage, feedback mechanisms reinforce the momentum of beneficial change. The success of some enterprises in reducing costs or developing new products reverberates up and down the domestic quality ladder, escalating the pressure on rival enterprises to follow suit. Every reform increment that relaxes institutional constraints on market entry, enterprise autonomy, or technological change shortens the distance separating adjacent rungs along the ladders of technology and cost, increases the probability of competition-enhancing innovation, and raises the costs suffered by enterprises that are slow to reform themselves. Reductions in fiscal resources caused by falling profits or tax evasion (itself an outcome of reform-induced expansion of enterprise autonomy and financial mechanisms) increase pressures on enterprises by reducing the chances of successful rent seeking, further widening the gap between "winners" and "losers."

Groves and others (1994) provide a quantitative illustration of feedback mechanisms by showing that state enterprises use grants of autonomy to strengthen work incentives and raise productivity. Their analysis of sample data indicates that enterprise autonomy is associated with large shares of discretionary payments in worker compensation and with high shares of untenured contract workers in the labor force. Their statistical analysis confirms the expected positive link between these changes to incentives and productivity growth. Thus incremental grants of enterprise autonomy appear to feed back into faster productivity growth, which, in turn, intensifies competition, and so on.

Proposition 7: China's decision to create a market-based economic system is an endogenous outcome of the partial reform process

China's initial reform efforts sought to improve economic performance but there was no clear picture of what a postreform economy should look like. Partial reform initiated a learning process that expanded the horizons of all participants. Competition among firms organized under heterogeneous institutional arrangements opened the door to a dynamic and interactive reform process in which specific policy initiatives have different effects on the opportunity sets of firms facing different institutional as well as technological constraints. Enterprises adopted competitive strategies designed to capitalize on the advantages conferred by their institutional as well as technical endowments. Competition forced participants to compare the merit of alternative institutional arrangements in exactly the same way that managers analyze the profit consequences of different product designs, machines, or compensation arrangements. Heterogeneity encouraged a culture of envy in which firms and managers now demand access to more attractive institutional possibilities to "level the playing field" in their competition with rivals operating under different institutional arrangements (*China Daily* 18 September 1993).

The experience of partial reform created promarket sentiments among former advocates of central planning. Shirk shows how managers of large-scale industry changed their views: "[These leaders] were at first leery of market reforms that threatened to shake them out of their comfortable dependence on the state. But the wrenching experience of the 1980–81 readjustment ... gave them a new appreciation of the opportunities offered by the market, and their envy of the benefits of reform enjoyed by smaller enterprises and nonstate enterprises motivated them to demand that these benefits be extended to their own enterprises.... Large state factory managers changed from lazy conservatives coddled by the state to active reformers challenging the state" (1993, p. 288; see also Rawski 1994). Government officials and political leaders experienced a similar change of opinion.

The rise of promarket sentiments among the political and administrative elite represents the greatest feedback mechanism of all in China's partial reform process. In the early 1990s these changes coalesced into a stunning reversal of deep-seated attitudes. Ideas that only 10 years earlier stood far beyond the limits of permissible discussion took center stage, as the government announced huge staff cuts, ambitious young bureaucrats began leaving the government to pursue private business careers (*Wall Street Journal* 26 January 1994), and China's Communist Party in 1993 formally announced a national goal of creating a decentralized market economy.

This remarkable change in values, combined with intense fiscal pressures, has sparked a series of policy innovations aimed at relieving governments of the burden of supporting loss-making enterprises. Although official documents rarely use the terms "ownership reform" or "privatization" to describe these changes, recent initiatives amount to a policy of endogenous or induced privatization. Under these new policies various ministries, provinces, and localities have begun to lease state-owned industrial firms to private agents (including foreign as well as domestic companies). Some loss-making firms are forced to merge with stronger enterprises, with substantial loss of jobs; others are simply auctioned off to the highest bidder. The government has also begun to encourage a variety of organizational innovations designed to reorganize state-owned enterprises as limited-liability entities owned by government, corporate, and private shareholders.

Conclusions

The gradual, cumulative reform process that has taken place in China differs markedly from the top-down, exogenous, centrally planned reforms proposed by international organizations (and endorsed by many economists). The differences between the two approaches are similar to those between the "balanced" growth approach (Rosenstein-Rodan 1943; Nurkse 1953) and the "unbalanced" development (Hirschman 1958) approach.

The balanced growth approach portrayed economic growth as an event—a "big push" or "great leap"—rather than a process; it downplayed the developmental potential of inherited economic structures and ignored international as well as domestic linkages. The subsequent export success of such economies as those in Japan, Taiwan (China), and the Republic of Korea, which were wrongly identified as "basket cases" on the basis of low initial levels of capability and atypical institutional arrangements, thus came as a surprise to many balanced growth proponents. Although several years of experience have muted the "all or nothing" approach, a tendency to repeat the mistakes of the balanced growth approach by underestimating the complexity of imposing market systems from above remains.

James Buchanan insists that "a market is not competitive by assumption or by construction" but "*becomes* competitive, and competitive rules *come to be* established as institutions emerge" to shape behavior (1979, p. 29, emphasis added). Buchanan believes that economics should focus on this "process of becoming." This orientation seems highly appropriate for the study of socialist reform. China's gradual and partial path of industrial reform was not determined by a few top officials. Industrial reform evolved from sequences of decisions made by tens of thousands of enterprises and millions of administrators, managers, and workers. The large number of participants and the extended duration of the reform process, which gave people ample time to evaluate alternatives and reconsider their initial views, eventually built a constituency for market-directed change that was far stronger than any official announcement could have achieved. This process is very different from Western parliamentary democracy, but it has produced a durable reform constituency that easily rebuffed high-level efforts to roll back reform in the wake of the inflation scare and political repression of 1989.

Before reform, government officials set the agenda for China's industrial firms. Today, enterprises, managers, and workers design strategies for success, and the state finds itself reacting to the outcome of decentralized efforts to implement a multitude of uncoordinated agendas. Enterprises and individuals no longer await the government's announcements but struggle to shape government involvement in ways that suit their own plans. In short, despite subsidies, soft loans, tenured state enterprise workers, and numerous other divergences from the textbook ideal, China's industrial economy looks increasingly like a market system.

Notes

Research for this chapter received support from the Henry Luce Foundation, the John S. Guggenheim Foundation, the University of Pittsburgh's University Center for International Studies, Brandeis University's Mazer fund, and the World Bank's Project on Industrial Reform and Productivity within Chinese Enterprises. The authors acknowledge the research assistance of John Zhigiang Zhao and the data, comments, and suggestions provided by Shahid Javaid Burki, Athar Hussain, E.C. Hwa, Nicholas R. Lardy, Wei Lo, Boris Pleskovic, Penelope Prime, Inderjit Singh, Nicholas Stern, Wing T. Woo, and Shahid Yusuf.

1. The output share of private domestic firms is the sum of shares for individual enterprises employing fewer than eight people *(geti qiye)* and larger private firms. The share rose from 2.8 percent in 1989 to 8.9 percent in 1992 and more than 15 percent in 1994.

References

Blasko, Dennis J. 1994. "Review of Paul Folta, From Swords to Plowshares? Defense Industry Reform in the PRC." *Far Eastern Economic Review* (March): 37.

Buchanan, James M. 1979. *What Should Economists Do?* Indianapolis: Liberty Press.

Chen, Qingtai. 1994. "Vice Minister on New Enterprise Reforms." *Daily Report: China,* January 27, pp. 48–49. U.S. Department of Commerce, Foreign Broadcast Information Service.

China State Statistical Bureau. Various Years. *China Industrial Economy Statistical Yearbook* (*Zhongguo gongye jingji tongji nianjian*) (in Chinese). Beijing: China Statistical Publications Office.

————. Various years. *China Statistical Yearbook* (*Zhongguo tongji nianjian*) (in Chinese). Beijing: China Statistical Publications Office.

————. Various years. *China Statistical Yearbook* (*Zhongguo tongji nianjian*) (in Chinese). Beijing: China Statistical Publications Office.

————. 1992. *China Labor Statistics Yearbook* (*Zhongguo laodong tongji nianjian*) (in Chinese). Beijing: China Statistical Publications Office.

————. 1992. *Innovation Survey*. Beijing: China Statistical Publications Office.

Du Haiyan, and Shang Lie. 1993. "Distribution of Fringe Benefits for Employees of State-owned Enterprises." *Research on Chinese Industrial Economics* (in Chinese) 2(30): 46–52.

Du Miaodeng, Huang Shiqiu, and Chen Xuewen. 1992. "On the Management of 'High Starting Point' Enterprises in Poor Townships and Districts." *Economic Management* (in Chinese) 12:55–57.

Government of China. 1994. "Communiqué on the National Economy and Social Development in 1993 by the State Statistics Bureau of the PRC." *People's Daily* (in Chinese) March 1, pp. 2–3.

Granick, David. 1990. *Chinese State Enterprises: A Regional Property Rights Analysis*. Chicago: University of Chicago Press.

Grossman, Gene M., and Elhanan Helpman. 1991. "Quality Ladders and Product Cycles." *Quarterly Journal of Economics* 106 (2): 557–86.

Groves, Theodore, Yongmiao Hong, John McMillan, and Barry Naughton. 1994. "Autonomy and Incentives in Chinese State Enterprises." *Quarterly Journal of Economics* 109(1): 183–209.

Hay, Donald, Derek Morris, Guy Liu, and Shujie Yao. 1994. *Economic Reform and State-Owned Enterprises in China, 1979–87*. Oxford: Clarendon Press.

Hirschman, Albert O. 1958. *The Strategy of Economic Development*. New Haven, Conn.: Yale University Press.

Hua, Sheng, Xiaopeng Luo, and Xuejun Zhang. 1993. *China: From Revolution to Reform*. Houndsmills: Macmillan.

Hwa, Erh-cheng. 1992. "Enterprise Reform in China." World Bank, China Department, Washington, D.C.

Jefferson, Gary H., and Thomas G. Rawski. 1994. "Enterprise Reform in Chinese Industry." *Journal of Economic Perspectives* 8(2): 47–70.

Jefferson, Gary H., and Wenyi Xu. 1994. "Assessing Gains in Efficient Production in China's Industrial Enterprises." *Economic Development and Cultural Change* 42(3): 597–616.

Jefferson, Gary H., Thomas G. Rawski, and Yuxin Zheng. 1994. "Institutional Change and Industrial Innovation in Transitional Economies." *Journal of Asian Economics* 5(4): 585–604.

Li Dianjing and Qin Chengdiao. 1993. "Survey on Conditions of Reimbursement of Employee Medical Expenses." *China Price (Zhongquo wujia)* (in Chinese). 11:33–34.

Ma Ke and Zhao Yuchuon. 1993. "Our Country's Large and Medium-Size Enterprises' Technical Innovation Activity: General Opening." *China Statistics* 4:10.

Naughton, Barry. 1992. "Implications of the State Monopoly over Industry and Its Relaxation." *Modern China* 18(1):14–41.

————. 1994. *Growing Out of the Plan: Chinese Economic Reform, 1978–1993*. New York: Cambridge University Press.

Nurkse, Ragnar. 1953. *Problems of Capital Formation in Underdeveloped Countries*. New York: Oxford University Press.

Perkins, Dwight H. 1977. *Rural Small-Scale Industry in the People's Republic of China.* Berkeley: University of California Press.

Rawski, Thomas G. 1994. "Progress without Privatization: The Reform of China's State Industries." In Vedat Milor, ed., *The Political Economy of Privatization and Public Enterprise in Post-Communist and Reforming Communist States.* Boulder, Colo.: Lynne Rienner.

Rosenstein-Rodan, P. N. 1943. "Problems of Industrialization of Eastern and South-Eastern Europe." *Economic Journal* (June–September). Reprinted in A. N. Agarwala and S. P. Singh, eds., 1963. *The Economics of Underdevelopment.* New York: Oxford University Press.

Sachs, Jeffrey, and Wing Thye Woo. 1994. "Reform in China and Russia." *Economic Policy* (April): 101–45.

Shirk, Susan L. 1993. *The Political Logic of Economic Reform in China.* Berkeley: University of California Press.

Sicular, Terry. 1992. "Public Finance and China's Economic Reforms." Harvard Institute of Economic Research Discussion Paper 1618: Cambridge, Mass.

Singh, Inderjit, Dilip Ratha, and Geng Xiao. 1994. "Non-State Enterprises as an Engine of Growth: An Analysis of Provincial Industrial Growth in Post-Reform China." World Bank Research Paper Series, China CH-RPS#20.

Song, Lina. 1990. "Convergence: A Comparison of Township Firms and Local State Enterprises." In William A. Byrd and Qingsong Lin, eds., *China's Rural Industry: Structure, Development, and Reform.* New York: Oxford University Press.

Sun, Hong. 1994. "Public Merchants Learn to Have Bar Codes." *China Daily Business Weekly* February 21, p. 8.

Vernon, Raymond. 1966. "International Investment and International Trade in the Product Cycle." *Quarterly Journal of Economics* 80(2): 190–207.

Walder, Andrew G. 1994. "Local Governments as Industrial Firms: An Organizational Analysis of China's Transitional Economy." *American Journal of Sociology* 101(2): 263–301.

Whiting, Susan H. 1993. "Market Discipline and Rural Enterprise in China: A Principal-Agent Approach." Paper presented at conference on "The Evolution of Market Institutions in Transition Economies," University of California at San Diego, May 8.

Wong, Christine, Christopher Heady, and Wing Thye Woo. 1993. "Economic Reform and Fiscal Management in China." Draft manuscript. University of California, Davis.

Woo, Wing Thye, Gong Fan, Wen Hui, and Yibiao Jin. 1993. "The Efficiency and Macroeconomic Consequences of Chinese Enterprise Reform." *China Economic Review* 4(2):153–68.

World Bank. 1992. *China: Reform and the Role of the Plan in the 1990s.* Washington, D.C.

Wu, Yanrui. 1993. "Productive Efficiency in Chinese Industry." *Asia-Pacific Economic Literature* 7(2):58–66.

Xu Fengxian, Mao Zhichong, and Yuan Juying. 1993. "New Development a la Sunan." *Economic Research* (in Chinese) 2: 49–55.

Innovation and Reform in China's Industrial Enterprises

4

Gary H. Jefferson, Thomas G. Rawski, and Zheng Yuxin

Industrial firms in most socialist economies generally have poor records of innovation and technological change. Production efficiency and product quality have taken a back seat to efforts to increase the physical volume of output. Industrial growth has been driven by the rapid accumulation of capital, labor, and energy inputs at the expense of efforts to control costs, improve quality, and satisfy customer requirements (Berliner 1976, 1991). Unless pressed by administrative superiors, socialist firms have tended to eschew innovation, preferring "the administered security of government control to the uncertainty and risks of the market" (Lee and Nellis 1990). When planners do emphasize innovation, the task is generally defined in terms of quantitative targets rather than market-driven outcomes. Recognizing these difficulties, the proponents of China's industrial reform program have attempted to motivate industrial enterprises to become successful innovators.

Although substantial productivity gains can accrue from improving resource allocation across enterprises as economies move away from central planning and toward markets and profit-seeking behavior (as shown by Jefferson and Xu 1994), in the absence of technical innovation, living standards will no longer rise once a Pareto efficient allocation is achieved. Continuous, ongoing improvements in living standards can be achieved only through continuous product and process innovation. Roemer (1994) has argued persuasively that conventional measures of economic growth substantially undervalue the considerable welfare gains that accrue from new product innovation. If China is to develop, manufacture, and market new products in order to move toward the international technology frontier and continue to close the gap in living standards with the world's advanced economies, its reforms must substantially enhance the innovative capabilities of the nation's industrial enterprises.

Economic transition involves both reform of the traditional state sector (the core) and the emergence or growth of a nonstate sector (the

89

periphery), consisting of both privately and collectively owned domestic enterprises and foreign-invested enterprises. In their model of innovation ladders and endogenous reform, Jefferson and Rawski (chapter 3) emphasize the importance of interaction between the core and the periphery. Through the entry of millions of new enterprises—principally, publicly owned township and village enterprises during the 1980s and foreign-invested and domestic privately owned enterprises during the 1990s—a kind of innovation ladder has developed in which innovation (including imitation of international technologies) by more technically sophisticated enterprises is mimicked by less sophisticated enterprises. Competition and the diffusion of technical capabilities down the ladder motivate new rounds of innovation at the top of the ladder.

In this innovation cycle the emergence of a periphery and the reform of the core are complementary phenomena. Growth of the periphery expands competition and erodes the state's monopoly over production. At the same time the development and growth of a periphery depends both on its ability to access increasingly sophisticated technologies and on the resources and goods supplied by established industry. Without access to producer goods provided by state industry through the dual-track system, China's township and village enterprise sector would not have flourished as it did during the 1980s.

Many sectors of China's industrial system appeared to have entered a period of fierce Schumpeterian competition by the early 1990s. The Open Door policy resulted in a rush of foreign investment, managerial and technical expertise, and rapid export growth. At the same time China's successful rural reforms generated domestic savings and surplus labor, and they nurtured an entrepreneurial spirit. These changes resulted in the formation of more than 6 million new industrial enterprises during the 1980s. Although bankruptcy remains rare in China's state sector, it is common outside the state sector. Within the state sector mergers, private sales, and conversions to joint stock companies and joint ventures are everyday occurrences.

The lack of exit and business failure in state industry suggests that Chinese industry is best described as undergoing a process of "creative reduction" (Jefferson 1996) rather than of "creative destruction" (Schumpeter 1950). The share of China's state sector in total industrial output fell from about 80 percent in 1978 to 55 percent in 1990 and less than a third in 1995. This dramatic shrinkage occurred despite 7–8 percent annual rates of growth in the output of state industry over the past 15 years (*China Statistical Yearbook* 1995). Creative reduction requires that the best-performing enterprises—those that generate the highest return on capital, labor, and other inputs—capture the lion's share of resources at the margin. Investigating this relationship between investment and profitability, Jefferson, Singh, Hu, and Wang (chapter 8) find strong evidence in support of this critical link in Chinese industry, no less in state industry than elsewhere. Through this process of resource allocation and reallocation, the most successful enterprises, both state and nonstate, expand capacity most rapidly; the least successful enterprises either stagnate or restructure through management reform, ownership reform, or merger (see Naughton 1995).

This chapter examines the pattern of new product innovation across state industry, collective industry, and rural township and village enterprises. The statistical analysis is based on a survey that was administered by China's State Statistical Bureau (1992). The survey was administered to 254 industrial enterprises in and around seven large Chinese cities (Beijing, Guangzhou, Nanjing, Shanghai, Shenyang, Wuhan, and Wuxi) during 1990/91. The sample was evenly divided among three industrial branches—cotton textiles, electronic components, and industrial equipment—and among three types of firms—state-owned enterprises, urban collective-owned enterprises, and township and village enterprises. Using these survey data, the chapter investigates the following questions:

- Is there evidence of an increase in innovation even among the large and medium-size enterprises that occupy the upper echelons of the innovation ladder in China?
- Is there evidence to support the paradigm that rising competition spurs innovation by causing profitability to decline?
- Are China's scarce R&D resources being effectively distributed between the core and the periphery, or are these resources being squandered by a hopelessly ineffective innovation system in state industry?

The mismatch hypothesis versus the catch-up hypothesis

The fundamental unit of technical innovation is the new product, defined in the World Bank Enterprise Surveys as "any new product introduced during the past five years by enterprises in heavy industry and, for light industry enterprises, any product introduced within the past two years" (World Bank 1992). This definition is laxer than that specified by China's State Statistical Bureau, which requires that new products meet more demanding physical requirements than existing products. The definition used in the survey is a highly localized definition of new product, since it may include production of products that are already well established in the market but only recently adopted by particular enterprises.

If the share of new product production in the gross value of industrial output is used to measure innovation, significant differences in performance are evident across ownership types (table 4.1). Just 9 percent of the production of state enterprises during 1987–89 was of new products—slightly lower than the 11 percent figure for urban cooperatives and less than half the 20 percent for township and village enterprises. These figures suggest that the periphery is substantially more innovative than the core.

Two competing hypotheses—the mismatch hypothesis and the catch-up hypothesis—may explain this apparent disparity in innovative activity between the core and the periphery. Under both hypotheses the process of technical change is viewed as consisting of three complementary inputs: incentives, autonomy, and resources. Because these three categories of innovation resources enter a kind of R&D production function in a complementary, or multiplicative, form, scarcity of any one input reduces the marginal product of the other two inputs. If, for example, incentives are weak in state industry but the supplies of R&D resources are abundant, the overall level of innovation can be increased

TABLE 4.1
Measures of innovation and capacity to innovate

| Item | State-owned enterprises | | Urban cooperatives | Township and village enterprises |
	All enterprises	Large and medium-size enterprises		
Value of products as share of gross output value (percent)				
1980	10.1	11.2	11.8	16.1
1985	10.1	10.0	9.9	19.1
1987–89	9.2	9.5	11.5	20.1
Number of observations for 1989	57	45	45	24
Autonomy[a]	2.61	—	2.64	2.65
Resources				
Number of upper-level technicians as share of total 1989 work force (percent)	4.0	3.9	2.4	2.2
Number of observations for 1989	86	68	67	34
Expenditures for technical innovation as share of net value of industrial output 1985–89 (percent)	8.2	9.1	8.3	11.5
Number of observations for 1989	69	57	41	19

— Not available.
a. Average combined score on 13 measures of enterprise autonomy (see table 4.4). Higher score represents greater autonomy.
Source: China State Statistical Bureau 1992 (Innovation Survey).

substantially either by introducing greater incentives within state enterprises or by reallocating resources for innovation to enterprises with a greater abundance of incentives and autonomy.

The mismatch hypothesis starts from the premise that incentives and autonomy are relatively weak within the state sector and strong within the nonstate sector; resources for innovation, both technicians and R&D expenditures, are assumed to be more abundant in state industry and scarce in the nonstate sector (table 4.2). These disparate factor intensities explain why innovative activity, measured by new product shares, is low in state industry and high in nonstate industry.

The catch-up hypothesis begins by distinguishing between the qualitative nature of innovation at the core and at the periphery. According to this hypothesis, innovation at the core is more often "frontier," or "leader," innovation, whereas innovation at the periphery is more often "follower" innovation or simply imitation. In this view the social contribution of innovation at the core exceeds that at the periphery, as does the profitability of innovation. Rather than reflecting primarily mismatches of complementary inputs, the higher incidence of innovation at the periphery results from an emphasis on catch-up that is comparatively easy relative to developing new products for a global or domestic market.

The two competing hypotheses bear significantly different economic and policy implications. The mismatch hypothesis implies the presence of market segmentation in which state enterprises are relatively shielded from fierce product competition while engineers are unresponsive to the lure of profitable innovation opportunities in the periphery. It predicts that the marginal revenue product of engineers and R&D spending should be higher at the periphery than at the core. In contrast, the catch-up hypothesis acknowledges that markets for R&D resources are sufficiently fluid to erode large disparities between returns to innovation resources at the core and the periphery. According to the catch-up hypothesis, disparities in these returns narrow when measured in terms of the profitability of new products.

TABLE 4.2
Index of engineers and technicians in the work force
(index for all firms = 100)

Type of enterprise	1989 sample	1985 census
State-owned large and medium-size	119.2	212.9
Small	111.9	126.5
Collective-owned	94.5	22.5
Township and village	79.8	23.3

Source: Sample data are from China State Statistical Bureau 1992 (Innovation Survey). Census data are from Census of China 1989.

Findings from the enterprise survey

Survey data from 254 industrial enterprises in seven large Chinese cities were collected to test these hypotheses. The sample was divided among three branches of industry: cotton textiles, electronic components, and industrial equipment. Within each branch the sample was split across three different types of ownership: state enterprises, urban cooperatives, and township and village enterprises. The survey was administered by China's State Statistical Bureau in 1990 and includes 96 statistical items for the years 1980 and 1984–89 as well as separate questionnaires designed to gauge the status of management, autonomy, and new products and process innovation in 1990.

Three complementary factors—incentives, autonomy, and resources—contribute to innovative activity. Since innovation is difficult, expensive, and risky, enterprises, managers, and workers will innovate only if they face incentives to do so (that is, they expect to gain from successful innovation or they fear the consequences of failing to innovate). Whatever their motivation enterprises cannot innovate unless they have the authority to experiment with new designs, resource combinations, production arrangements, sales or procurement agreements, labor redeployment, and so forth; excessive regulations can easily stifle innovation. Finally, innovation requires access to resources, including information, manpower, funds, materials, and equipment.

Incentives. Results of the survey sample and information from other sources confirm that raising profits has become the leading objective among Chinese enterprises. Almost 80 percent of enterprises surveyed cited "raising profits" as an "important" incentive for developing new products (table 4.3). All 49 firms that indicated that raising profits was not "most important" designated it as "somewhat important" in motivating product innovation; none indicated that raising profits was "not important."

These results are confirmed by most researchers who have engaged in extensive on-site interviewing. Based on his survey work in the mid-1980s, for example, Granick (1990, p. 189) found that at state firms "both middle and senior managers are quite as concerned with earning profits as are their Western counterparts."

Although all branches and types of enterprises rank profit above other objectives, significant differences exist by branch and ownership type. Producers of industrial equipment place much more weight on fulfilling plans than do their counterparts in the textile and electronic component branches. Also noteworthy is the relatively strong (although distinctly secondary) emphasis on plan fulfillment reported by township and village enterprises, which attach greater importance to this objective than

TABLE 4.3
Incentives for new product innovation

| | | Enterprises by ownership | | |
Incentive	All enterprises	All	State-owned enterprises	Township and village enterprises	Equipment industry
Raise profits	1.79	1.77	1.84	1.75	1.80
Fulfill Plan	0.96	0.87	0.92	1.12	1.20
Increase worker income	0.59	0.60	0.57	0.61	0.60

Note: Figures are averages based on 0 = "not important," 1 = "somewhat important," and 2 = "important" reasons for pursuing innovations.
Source: China State Statistical Bureau 1992 (Innovation Survey).

do state and urban collective enterprises. This last result should serve as a warning against assuming too quickly that township and village enterprise managers are always more focused on profit and more independent of bureaucratic directives than their collective and state counterparts.

Considerable evidence suggests that reforms have created new links between enterprise profits and employee compensation. Increased levels of profits and retained earnings are strongly associated with higher compensation for workers (table 4.4). In 1989 one additional yuan of gross profit translated into a quarter yuan of additional wages, and labor and management together captured about half of the increase in retained earnings. Similar results are reported in chapter 8.

Autonomy. Enterprise respondents were asked to indicate whether "the supervisory bureau decides," "the enterprise and supervisory bureau talk it over," or "the enterprise decides itself" in 13 areas of decisionmaking. The results indicate that most enterprises believe that they enjoy a relatively high degree of autonomy across most decisionmaking areas (table 4.5).

Market exposure, particularly the right to sell products outside the plan, is an important stimulant to innovation. Firms for which the state is not a key customer or buyer of last resort are required to "keep one eye on the market." They must therefore make decisions to improve their product appeal and reduce costs in order to avoid losing market share and profit and suffering low wage and income growth. For all ownership types, by 1990 the right to "sell products outside the plan" seemed to be nearly universal among all participating enterprises (the right to sell products outside the plan did not necessarily imply the unfettered right to set prices, however).

The survey results support three conclusions concerning enterprise autonomy. First, all three types of enterprise believe that they have a high degree of autonomy over a wide range of decisions. Even in the state

TABLE 4.4

Relationship between the wage bill (dependent variable) and profits and retained earnings (independent variables) of state-owned enterprises, selected years, 1980–89

Year	Pretax profit		Retained earnings	
	b	R^2	b	R^2
EI sample[a] (n = 400)				
1980	0.80	0.37	2.55	0.41
1983	0.16	0.56	0.79	0.67
1984	0.19	0.56	0.70[b]	0.06
1985	0.26	0.59	0.89	0.82
1986	0.23	0.43	0.69	0.76
TGS sample[c] (n = 800)				
1986	0.18	0.60	0.00	0.00[d]
1987	0.18	0.59	0.43	0.60
1988	0.24	0.74	0.43	0.26
1989	0.26	0.64	0.54	0.62

Note: Wage bill includes bonuses. Regression equation: Wage bill = C + b*X, where X = profit or retained earnings (RE).
a. Economic Research Institute (EI) data come from EI308; wage bill = D8; profit = D39; retained earnings = Db151.
b. t-ratio = 4.26; t-ratios for other b coefficients in this sample > 9.0.
c. Economic System Reform Institute (TGS) data come from TGS309; wage bill = V6; profit = V31; retained earnings = V33.
(TGS)
d. t-ratio = 0.52; t-ratios for other b coefficients in this sample > 15.0.
Source: Economic Research Institute and Economic System Reform Institute data.

sector the typical firm believes it has sufficient authority to adjust its product mix, move into new markets, redeploy its work force, and determine its wage bill. Areas in which autonomy is perceived as more limited (that is, the average score is less than 2.5) related to trade and the setting of total employment and bonuses. Second, although the relative degree of autonomy across the three types of enterprise shows that state-owned enterprises enjoy the least (self-reported) autonomy and township and village enterprises enjoy the most autonomy, the differences, on average, are not significant. Finally, the main advantage of township and village enterprises appears to be their ability to choose suppliers of raw materials, an area in which they indicate virtually complete autonomy. Among state enterprises a substantial minority cannot alter their suppliers without some form of consultation with or permission from their administrative superiors.

Before the beginning of the reform process, supervisory bureaus would have made most of these decisions, or enterprises would have "talked the decision over" with their supervisory bureau. Despite the survival of mandatory planning through the end of the 1980s and beyond, the persistence of intrusive regulation, and the ubiquity of administrative approval

TABLE 4.5
Measures of enterprise autonomy

Decision	State-owned enterprises	Urban cooperatives	Township and village enterprises
Begin making new products	2.72	2.76	2.67
Stop making old products	2.72	2.72	2.60
Sell products outside the plan	2.91	2.93	2.96
Determine outside plan price	2.69	2.72	2.74
Sell products outside existing sales area	2.91	2.86	2.99
Export products	2.49	2.60	2.43
Determine total wage bill	2.87	2.91	2.92
Determine total bonuses	2.37	2.33	2.31
Determine total employment	2.46	2.46	2.41
Distribute and appoint workers within the enterprise	2.87	2.91	2.92
Choose enterprises for supplying raw materials	2.59	2.67	2.99
Import raw materials	2.37	2.33	2.31
Import equipment	2.04	2.15	2.18
Average	2.61	2.64	2.65

Note: Figures show averages for all firms in each category. Responses were coded as follows: 1 = supervisory bureau decides; 2 = enterprise and supervisory bureau talk it over; 3 = enterprise bureau decides.
Source: China State Statistical Bureau 1992 (Innvotion Survey).

processes, Chinese managers appear to have gained substantial control over industrial operations during the second half of the 1980s.

Although the survey does not find substantial differences in the average level of autonomy of state enterprises and township and village enterprises, the physical and bureaucratic proximity of local township and village industrial authorities to the enterprise may cause the nature of supervision to be qualitatively different from that exercised by the supervisory authorities of state enterprises, who may be physically remote (situated in Beijing or a provincial capital). Both the proximity and the limited scale of township and village enterprise supervisory bodies can serve to economize on bounded rationality and attenuate opportunism, thereby helping to overcome problems of information impactedness that typify the classic central planning model (Gelb 1990; Williamson 1985).

Resources. In 1989 the distribution of resources for innovation across ownership types was mixed (see table 4.1). The average proportion of upper-level technicians was higher in the state-owned enterprise sector than within the urban cooperative or township and village enterprise sector in 1989, but state industry spent relatively less on technical innovation between 1985 and 1989 (8.2 percent) than did urban cooperatives (8.3 percent) or township and village enterprises (11.5 percent).

Moreover, expenditures by state enterprises appeared to be concentrated among the larger enterprises. These results may reflect a segmented market in technical services, in which university graduates and engineers are concentrated in urban areas and assigned to state industry, a pattern that existed in the past and may persist today.

A model of innovative activity

Incentives, autonomy, and resources complement one another; that is, the marginal product of each input depends on the supply of the other two. To capture complementarities in the innovation process, the innovation function can be represented by equation 4.1:

$$(4.1) \qquad O = A^\alpha I^\beta R^\gamma e^{\sum_i a_i X_i} \varepsilon$$

in which O represents a measure of innovation output, A represents autonomy, I represents incentives, and R is a measure of R&D input. The X_i are industry dummies ($i = 1,2,3$), and ε captures the error structure, which is assumed to have a log-normal distribution.

In principle, the measures of enterprise autonomy shown in table 4.5 could be used to construct measures for incentives for each enterprise and to estimate equation 4.1. Instead, equation 4.1 is simply estimated with categorical measures of ownership that are assumed to capture the essential differences in incentives and autonomy among enterprises of different ownership types. Allowing $Z^\theta = A^\alpha I^\beta$ (that is, combining the incentive and autonomy measures for each ownership type), equation 4.1 can be rewritten in logarithmic form:

$$(4.2) \qquad \ln O = \theta \ln Z + \gamma \ln R + \sum_i a_i X_i + \varepsilon$$

where $\ln Z$ can be interpreted as a constant, or dummy, that captures the ownership (read incentive and autonomy) effect. Equation 4.2 is used to test two competing hypotheses or the differences in innovation activity among state enterprises, urban cooperatives, and township and village enterprises.

The mismatch hypothesis

The mismatch hypothesis is tested by defining O, the measure of innovation output, as the share of new products in gross industrial output. A three-year average of R&D resources and innovation output is used, with each average assumed to represent a proxy for the true underlying stock of R&D input and R&D output. One advantage of this approach of using synthetic stock variables is that it reduces the need to specify a dynamic time structure that relates the flow of inputs to the flow of outputs.

The resource input, *R*, has two measures, expenditures on new product development and the availability of upper-level technicians. For each estimate of the innovation function using a subset of the sample data by ownership type, $\ln Z$ is simply a constant.

The estimates of the elasticity of innovation output with respect to resource input and the share of new products in gross output are used to estimate the marginal revenue product of spending on new product development. The mismatch hypothesis predicts that because the relative supply of R&D resources is abundant in state enterprises and scarce in township and village enterprises while the supplies of incentives and autonomy are scarcer in state enterprises, the marginal revenue product of R&D resources should be higher in township and village enterprises than in state enterprises and that of the urban cooperative sector should fall somewhere in between.

The results indicate that the marginal productivity of expenditures on new product development in the state and urban cooperative sectors is comparable: 1 yuan of new product development expenditure generates about 5 yuan of new product output (table 4.6). As predicted by the mismatch hypothesis, relative to the expenditures within the state and urban cooperative sectors, expenditures on new products within the township and village enterprise sector yield substantially higher returns (22 yuan of output for each yuan of expenditure). The marginal physical productivity of spending on new product development among township and village enterprises thus exceeds the figures for state and collective firms by a factor of about 4.

A generally consistent result emerges from analysis of the relative productivity of upper-level technicians (table 4.7). Measured in terms of the proportion of technicians, the marginal productivity of innovation resources in township and village enterprises surpasses that in state enterprises by a factor of 2.5 (25.98 versus 10.59). In contrast to the results on R&D spending, in which returns to state enterprises and urban cooperatives were comparable, the marginal productivity of technicians in urban cooperatives is similar to that in township and village enterprises and well above that in state enterprises.

These results appear to provide support for the mismatch hypothesis. They are consistent with the view that incentives and autonomy are systematically stronger in state-owned enterprises than in township and village enterprises. They also suggest a kind of market failure, in which innovation resources are captured by state industry, interfering with the diffusion of R&D funds and technicians to the periphery, where they could capture higher returns.

These findings have important policy implications. They suggest that to accelerate the pace of industrial innovation, China's government must

TABLE 4.6

Contribution of expenditures on new product development to new product output

Item	All enterprises	State-owned enterprises	Urban cooperatives	Township and village enterprises
Constant	3.209	3.644	2.804	3.088
	(4.697)	(3.721)	(1.409)	(5.240)
Electronics industry	−1.753	−1.002	−2.693	−1.960
	(1.872)	(0.728)	(1.028)	(2.155)
Equipment industry	−1.073	0.050	−2.502	−1.936
	(1.121)	(0.034)	(0.984)	(2.125)
Expenditures on new product development	0.777	0.554	1.066	1.198
	(7.034)	(3.555)	(3.413)	(10.868)
R^2	0.404	0.287	0.401	0.907
Marginal revenue product	6.30	5.18	4.44	21.72

Note: Regression equation: $\ln GNPV = a + b\ BRANCH + c\ \ln EXPEND + \varepsilon$, where GNPV = gross value of new product production (average of available observations, 1987–89), BRANCH = dummy variable for the electronic and equipment industries (constant represents cotton textiles); and EXPEND = expenditures on new product innovation (average of available observations, 1987–89). Figures in parentheses are t-statistics.
Source: China State Statistical Bureau 1992 (Innovation Survey).

TABLE 4.7

Contribution of upper-level technicians to new product innovation

Item	All enterprises	State-owned enterprises	Urban cooperatives	Township and village enterprises
Constant	2.365	0.470	3.211	3.931
	(2.932)	(0.209)	(3.781)	(2.337)
Electronics industry	−0.858	−0.264	−2.664	−3.137
	(0.802)	(0.171)	(1.040)	(1.180)
Equipment industry	−0.662	−0.832	−2.812	0.127
	(0.596)	(0.502)	(1.105)	(0.043)
Upper-level technicians	0.658	1.112	1.301	0.698
	(4.148)	(1.665)	(3.523)	(1.766)
R^2	0.193	1.085	0.415	0.246
Marginal revenue product	7.21	10.59	21.00	25.98

Note: Regression equation: $\ln GVPV = a + b\ BRANCH + c\ \ln TECH + \varepsilon$, where BRANCH = dummy variable for the electronic and equipment industries (constant represents cotton textiles); TECH = number of technicians at or above the intermediate level (average of available observations, 1987-89). Figures in parentheses are t-statistics.
Source: China State Statistical Bureau 1992 (Innovation Survey).

dramatically improve incentives and autonomy within state industry and simultaneously initiate measures to enhance the access of township and village enterprises to resources that complement their relative independence and entrepreneurial drive.

The catch-up hypothesis

Estimates of equation 4.2 using shares of new products in gross output as the dependent variable support the notion that China's township and village enterprises are more innovative than either state enterprises or urban cooperatives. This intuitive finding must be reconciled with the seemingly contradictory finding that firms of all ownership types generally identify state enterprises as the most technically advanced in their product line (table 4.8). One possible explanation is that although township and village enterprises are innovating aggressively, they are involved in a process of catch-up, with much of their innovation involving mere imitation.

If, in fact, product innovations by state enterprises are frontier innovations, then the profit captured by these first-in-the-market innovations should exceed the profit of township and village enterprises that subsequently adopt these innovations. Although the marginal product of innovation resources used by the township and village enterprise sector measured in terms of volume exceeds that of the state sector, comparison of the marginal profitability of innovative activity between the two sectors may reveal superior performance by state enterprises.

Examination of average profit rates for total production and for new products alone reveals two interesting patterns (table 4.9). First, new products are initially more profitable in state enterprises than in the other two sectors. Relative to the township and village enterprise sector, new products introduced by state enterprises enjoy about a 4 percentage point productivity advantage. Second, 1989 profit rates for these products show significant erosion in the innovation rents captured by the state sector: by 1989 profit rates on these products were

TABLE 4.8
Enterprises identified as most technically advanced in product line

Respondent	State-owned enterprises	Urban cooperatives	Township and village enterprise
All enterprises	299	47	11
State-owned enterprise	116	14	4
Urban cooperative	83	17	7
Township and village enterprise	100	16	0

Source: China State Statistical Bureau 1992 (Innovation Survey).

TABLE 4.9
Profit rates for total production and new product production
(percent)

| Type of enterprise | Average profit rate 1989 | Profit rate on new products | | Difference between profit rate in year introduced and township and village enterprise profit rate in 1989 |
		Year product introduced	1989	
All enterprises	8.7	15.4	12.2	3.2
State-owned enterprise	9.0	17.0	11.1	5.9
Collective-owned enterprise	8.1	15.4	14.7	0.7
Township and village enterprise	9.1	13.3	10.7	2.6

Source: China State Statistical Bureau 1992 (Innovation Survey).

comparable to rates in the township and village enterprise sector. This decay of rents within state industry is consistent with a process in which nonstate enterprises are imitating new products developed by the state sector, possibly at lower cost.

The marginal profitability of expenditures on new product development is estimated by substituting, for the dependent variable in equation 4.2, gross profits from the production of new products (a qualitative measure of innovation) for new product production (a quantitative measure).[5] The marginal revenue product of new product expenditures, measured in terms of new product profit, is then calculated. Measured in terms of ability to develop profitable products, R&D expenditures generate substantial positive returns in the state sector (table 4.10). Based on a statistically insignificant elasticity estimate, the estimate of returns to R&D spending in the township and village enterprise sector is lower than in the state sector. Estimated returns to expenditures for innovative activity in the urban cooperative sector are positive but not as large or as statistically robust as estimates of the returns in the state sector.

Estimates of the marginal contribution of upper-level technicians to enterprise profitability contrast with estimates of their contribution to new product production (table 4.11). While the marginal product of technicians in the township and village enterprise sector, measured in terms of new product production, was about 2.5 times that in the state sector in terms of profit, the two sectors are comparable. Returns to technicians measured in terms of profit are not statistically robust in the township and village enterprise sector. Estimates of returns to technicians in the state and urban cooperative sectors are both positive and significant, however. Surprisingly, in light of the previous results, the

TABLE 4.10

Contribution of spending on new product development to new product profits

Item	All enterprises	State-owned enterprises	Urban cooperatives	Township and village enterprises
Constant	3.086	3.995	1.971	2.295
	(6.652)	(6.359)	(1.877)	(2.519)
Electronics industry	−1.011	−1.535	0.221	−0.645
	(2.016)	(2.258)	(0.197)	(0.792)
Equipment industry	−1.551	−1.595	−0.303	−1.532
	(2.631)	(1.674)	(0.254)	(1.757)
Expenditures on new product development	0.524	0.497	0.396	0.480
	(4.428)	(3.117)	(1.884)	(1.121)
R^2	0.240	0.278	0.119	0.279
Marginal revenue product	2.48	2.75	1.21	1.52

Note: Regression equation: lnPROFIT = $a + b$ BRANCH + c lnEXPEND + ε, where PROFIT = [profit rate of a major new product (QB6-13B)/(QB6-1B)] x [gross value of total new product output (V4, averaged over available observations, 1987–89)]. Figures in parentheses are t-statistics.
Source: China State Statistical Bureau 1992 (Innovation Survey).

marginal product of technicians among all three ownership types appears to be highest in the collective sector.

The results suggest that the mismatch hypothesis requires substantial qualification. The township and village enterprise sector demonstrates a higher propensity for innovation, as measured by new product

TABLE 4.11

Contribution of upper-level technicians to new product profits

Item	All enterprises	State-owned enterprises	Urban cooperatives	Township and village enterprises
Constant	1.989	1.128	0.208	3.201
	(4.769)	(1.547)	(0.216)	(4.123)
Electronics industry	−0.527	−1.205	0.780	−0.600
	(1.457)	(2.520)	(0.869)	(0.688)
Equipment industry	−0.468	−0.854	0.734	−0.373
	(1.038)	(1.534)	(0.747)	(0.358)
Upper-level technicians	0.772	1.066	1.140	0.171
	(6.881)	(5.849)	(2.199)	(0.458)
R^2	0.323	0.449	0.267	0.042
Marginal revenue product	4.49	5.66	11.46	2.22

Note: Regression equation: lnPROFIT = $a + b$ BRANCH + c lnTECH + ε. Figures in parentheses are t-statistics.
Source: China State Statistical Bureau 1992 (Innovation Survey).

share. Relative to innovative activity in the state sector, township and village enterprises tend to adopt "follower" innovations, drawing heavily on frontier innovations made within the state sector. When adjusted for differences in the profitability of innovative activity across the three sectors, the contribution of new product expenditures and technicians is greater in state industry than in the township and village enterprise sector. These results suggest that innovation within the township and village enterprise sector during the 1980s may not have been generating innovation rents. Instead, innovation by township and village enterprises appears to have focused on imitation, which contributed to growth and product diversity within the township and village enterprise sector and added to producer and consumer surplus within China's economy more by reducing costs than by introducing new products.

Conclusions

This chapter has attempted to establish a systematic approach to thinking about the innovation process in a transitional economy. Although it should be read more as a template for the study of transitional innovation rather than as a definitive study, its findings do provide evidence to support several conclusions:

- Spurred by rising industrial competition, the incidence of profit-motivated innovative activity within Chinese industry, including state industry, is rising. While the incidence of product innovation in the township and village enterprise sector is higher than in state industry, differences in the profitability of innovation in the two sectors indicate that town and village enterprises tend to imitate while state enterprises tends to innovate.
- Measured in terms of the incidence of innovation, returns to innovation resources—R&D expenditures and technicians—are significantly higher in the township and village enterprise sector than in state industry.
- Measured in terms of the profitability of new product innovation, the advantage of township and village enterprises disappears. By 1990 returns to innovation resources in the two sectors appear to have become comparable.

These results support the notion that China's industrial transformation is being driven by an industrial innovation ladder, which the entry of nonstate enterprises that imitate and efficiently produce products creating competitive pressures that motivate innovation in state industry. Within Chinese industry R&D resources appear to be efficiently deployed so as to take advantage of profitable product development opportunities. These findings lend strong support to the model of an industrial innovation ladder outlined in chapter 3. Chapter 5 investigates the extent to which rising industrial competition in Chinese industry drives institutional innovation as well as technical change.

Notes

The authors gratefully acknowledge financial support from the Henry Luce Foundation, the Chinese Academy of Social Sciences, the World Bank, the American Council of Learned Societies, the Chiang Ching-Kuo Foundation, Brandeis University's Mazer Fund, and the University of Pittsburgh's China Studies Endowment. They benefited from the assistance of Wenyi Xu at Brandeis University and Hong Ji at the Chinese Academy of Social Sciences in Beijing. The survey work drew heavily on the knowledge and experience generously shared by colleagues at the China State Statistical Bureau, particularly Chunheng Lu, Li Liu, and Jianyi Xu.

1. Within the smaller sample of state-owned enterprises, no increase was found in the reported share of new products during the 1980s. However, because that survey used a definition of new products that differs from the standard definition used in China's statistical system, comparisons of new product innovation between 1980 and the survey period, the late 1980s, may not be accurate.

2. To avoid upward bias in measures of the new product share caused by new entrants, each enterprise in the survey was required to have been established and producing by 1980.

3. The cities were Beijing, Wuhan, Guangzhou, Wuxi, Shenyang, Shanghai, and Nanjing.

4. A score of less than 2.50 implies that more than half of the firms must discuss decisions with their supervisory bureau or that more than one-fourth lack the right even to discuss the matter jointly, while the others have unfettered autonomy in decisionmaking.

5. Since direct measures of the profitability of all new products are not available, the product of the gross value of the new product output of each enterprise and the profit rate reported by that firm for a major product innovation is used.

References

Berliner, Joseph. 1976. *The Innovation Decision in Soviet Industry.* Cambridge, Mass.: MIT Press.

———. 1991. "Economic Structure and Technological Innovation." Paper presented at the conference on "Technology and Transition in the USSR," September 17–20, University of Birmingham, Alabama.

Census of China. 1989. *People's Republic of China 1985 Industrial Census Materials.* Abbreviated summary volume (in Chinese). Beijing: China Statistical Publications Office.

China State Statistical Bureau. 1992. "Innovation Survey." Beijing: China Statistical Publications Office.

———. Various years. *China Industrial Economy Statistical Yearbook (Zhongguo gongye jingji tongji nianjian).* Beijing: China Statistical Publications Office.

————. Various years. *China Statistical Yearbook* (*Zhongguo tongji nianjian*) (in Chinese). Beijing: China Statistical Publications Office.

Gelb, Alan. 1990. "TVP Workers' Incomes, Incentives, and Attitudes." In William A. Byrd and Qingsong Lin, eds., *China's Rural Industry: Structure, Development, and Reform*. New York: Oxford University Press.

Granick, David. 1990. *Chinese State Enterprises: A Regional Property Rights Analysis*. Chicago: University of Chicago Press.

Jefferson, Gary H. 1996. "Ownership Reform as a Process of Creative Reduction in Chinese Industry." In Joint Economic Committee, *Future Economic Challenges: Challenges to U.S. Policy*. Washington, D.C.: U.S. Government Printing Office.

Jefferson, Gary H., and Wenyi Xu. 1994. "Assessing Gains in Efficiency Production among China's Industrial Enterprises." *Economic Development and Cultural Change* 42(3): 597–616.

Lee, Barbara, and John Nellis. 1990. "Enterprise Reform and Privatization in Socialist Economies." World Bank, Private Sector Development Department, Washington, D.C.

Naughton, Barry. 1995. *Growing Out of the Plan*. New York: Cambridge University Press.

Roemer, Paul. 1994. "New Goods, Old Theory and the Welfare Costs of Trade Restrictions." *Journal of Development Economics* 43(1): 5–38.

Schumpeter, J. A. 1950. *Capitalism, Socialism and Democracy*. New York: Harper.

Williamson, Oliver. 1985. *The Economic Institutions of Capitalism: Firms, Markets, Relational Contracting*. New York: Free Press.

World Bank. 1992. *Enterprise Survey*. China and Mongolia Department and the Socialist Economies Unit. Washington, D.C.

Reforming Property Rights in China's Industry

Gary H. Jefferson, Lu Mai, and John Z. Q. Zhao

Reforming property rights is a cornerstone of the transition from a centrally planned economy to a market economy. Among the formerly socialist economies three approaches to property rights reform stand out. Privatization, generally the most favored approach among economists, is a central feature of Eastern Europe's transition. In China development of privately owned enterprise has taken place largely through the entry of small start-ups rather than the wholesale conversion of established state enterprises.

A second approach to enterprise reform is corporatization. A rapidly growing number of China's publicly owned enterprises have been corporatized, generally as joint ventures or joint stock companies in which the state remains the majority shareholder. By the end of 1997 more than 400 of China's larger state enterprises had been converted into joint stock companies and listed on public exchanges. During the mid-1990s individualized ownership (gerenhua suoyouzhi) or conversion to joint stock ownership became increasingly popular among rural township and village enterprises.

A third avenue of reform—and the one that was used most extensively by China's established enterprises during the second half of the 1980s and the early 1990s—emphasized management reform without ownership reform. Although the reform of China's state-owned and collective-owned enterprises has relied principally on management reform without privatization or corporatization, by the early 1990s the process of industrial reform had fundamentally altered the allocation of property rights between state and enterprise and among parties within the enterprise.

This chapter addresses three sets of issues. First, it uses the survey data presented in chapter 2 to characterize and contrast the nature of property rights reform within China's two largest ownership forms—state enterprises and township and village enterprises.

Second, it investigates the process of enterprise reform. Most descriptions of enterprise reform begin with the assumption that reform ensues from edicts issued from the center that directly alter the governance and performance of the target enterprises. Although China's central government sets broad parameters for enterprise reform, the pace and character of its implementation are affected by financial and fiscal pressures at the level of the individual enterprise and local jurisdiction. The large variation in reform outcomes reflects a process that is driven by pressures within the industrial system.

Finally, this chapter attempts to characterize the essential flaw of the publicly owned enterprise, namely, the weak incentive to monitor that gives rise to social costs. To remedy this problem of public ownership, application of the Coase theorem, which identifies the benefits of clarifying the allocation of property rights and reducing transactions costs, is proposed.

Property rights in township and village enterprises

The success of China's township and village enterprises has sparked interest in explaining their high rates of productivity growth, which have persisted during the 1980s and into the 1990s at two to three times the rate of state enterprises. Recent studies direct attention to several features that distinguish township and village enterprises from state enterprises:

- Information channels linking (government) principals with (managerial) agents tend to be shorter and simpler for nonstate firms than for state-owned units (Groves and others 1994).
- Local officials and managers of nonstate enterprise focus on financial objectives (profit plus local tax revenues), whereas managers of state enterprises, burdened with the additional responsibilities for housing and other social services, face a more complex set of objectives (Byrd and Gelb 1990).
- Because localities lack the center's borrowing capacity, enterprises under local jurisdiction face harder budget constraints than state enterprises and often fall into bankruptcy (Qian and Xu 1992).

Several researchers have also suggested that, despite the absence of well-specified property rights, the demographic stability of China's rural communities promotes the emergence of "invisible institutions" to provide a "moral framework for rights" or a "cooperative culture" that serves to reduce problems of shirking and monitoring found in most public enterprises (Byrd and Lin 1990; Weitzman and Xu 1994; Yusuf 1993a, 1993b). Other researchers see the dramatic productivity gains of township and village enterprises during the 1980s as largely a matter of the rapid marketization of township and village enterprises relative to state enterprises (Zou and Wang 1994) or as a reflection of catch-up to the more technologically sophisticated state enterprises (see chapter 4).

Alchian and Demsetz (1972), Jensen and Meckling (1976), and Jefferson (1998) emphasize the critical role of a central contracting agent with the authority and incentive to monitor. Within the context of the Chinese state enterprise—and public ownership generally—absent an effective central contracting agent the firm assumes the two properties of a public good—nonexcludability and nondiminishability. The "owners" of the firm are unable and/or unmotivated to exclude a wide set of actors from extracting more value from the firm than they put in. These avenues of plunder include shirking, "stripping" physical and financial assets, and engaging in predatory taxation.

Nonexcludability by itself leads to diminishing returns to rent-seeking behavior as resources are diminished. But in combination with nondiminishability—a property that arises from ubiquitous soft budget constraints—persistent losses are replenished through fiscal or financial subsidies or both. These subsidies are ultimately financed by money creation or taxation; in either case they create an externality in the form of inflation or the diversion of resources from more socially productive expenditures, including employment growth.

From Coase's perspective part of the solution to this public good externality problem entails the clear assignment of property rights in order to improve the incentive to monitor and curtail rent-seeking behavior. A key question for China's industrial reforms is the extent to which in the absence of an outright change in ownership, managerial reform has created a structure in which a central contracting agent has the authority and incentive to monitor the firm effectively.

This chapter examines whether township and village enterprises in China are more evolved than state enterprises in terms of establishing a central contracting agent with the authority and incentive to monitor. It measures changes in the nature of property rights within state enterprises and township and village enterprises, examines the impact of property rights on enterprise performance, and looks at the conditions that give rise to the reform of property rights within the enterprise.

The conceptual framework that Alchian and Demsetz (1972) use to analyze the nature of property rights characterizes ownership as a "bundle of rights" and the firm as a "nexus of contracts" that specify the assignment of these rights. The fact that in Chinese industry the individual enterprise contract, not a uniform legal or regulatory code, has become the pervasive instrument for specifying the distribution of authority, risk, and rewards between the supervisory body and the enterprise makes this contract approach particularly useful for analyzing changes in enterprise governance in China's publicly owned enterprises.

The literature on the impact of reform on performance

Numerous studies examine the impact of China's industrial enterprise reform on enterprise performance. Most of these studies find evidence of improved performance (usually productivity) and attribute the improvement to the reform without linking improvement to any specific structural change. (For a review of the extensive literature on the productivity performance of Chinese industry during the reform period, see chapter 6 and Wu 1996.)

More recent literature, based on enterprise surveys, examines specific avenues of causation through which individual reform instruments affect performance. This approach is important, because it helps to clarify whether improvement in enterprise performance arises from reforms that are specific to the enterprise, such as the reassignment of property rights, or from general environmental reforms, such as the liberalization of product and factor markets and trade.

One theoretical treatment of the subject is presented by Zhang (1997). Modeling the reassignment of decision rights from the central agent (government) to inside members of the firm results in a bargaining solution between the central agent and the firm that is preferred to a one-sided solution. Zhang demonstrates that managerial discretion of state enterprises can substantially improve efficiency, both through its direct incentive effect and by indirectly hardening budget constraints.

One early test of the impact of property rights reform on enterprise performance is reported by Lee (1991). Testing for the individual and interactive effects of various external and internal contracting arrangements, he concludes that "an isolated adoption of any single reform measure, ceteris paribus, has no significant effect on enterprise outputs ... (but) some combinations of reform measures are shown to have positive output effects" (p. 79).

Another early attempt to unbundle the reforms and examine the impact of specific measures (Jefferson and Xu 1991) focuses on the link between changes in structure, conduct, and performance in state industry. They find that "three reforms, the optimal labor combination program, reinvestment out of retained profits, and outside plan purchases of intermediate inputs, have motivated economizing behavior and raise factor efficiency" (p. 62).

Using a larger sample of enterprises, Groves and others (1994) investigate the impact of production autonomy and profit retention on the tendency for managers to create worker incentives, namely, to increase the bonus share of total wage income and to put workers on fixed-term contracts rather than grant permanent employment. Finding a modest association between reform measures and incentive structure, they conclude that incentive reforms within the enterprise are associated with higher levels of productivity.

A growing number of empirical studies (Hay and others 1994; Yao 1997; Wang 1997; Huang and Duncan 1997) confirms the view that specific enterprise reforms—involving the reassignment of property rights between the state and the enterprise or between the state and individual parties within the enterprise—are resulting in measurable, if not always robust, gains in efficiency.

This chapter views the performance of Chinese industry as both driven by and driving reform (an approach first developed by Jefferson and Rawski 1994). The idea that financial distress within the enterprise and fiscal distress at various levels of jurisdiction motivate reform, while reform motivates improved competitiveness and efficiency that in turn heighten competition and financial pressure, complicates the analysis. This view of a circular reform process implies simultaneity bias, in particular a tendency to reject the hypothesis of performance-enhancing reform or to underestimate its impact where reform is the outcome of failing performance. A tendency to implement reform in the most successful enterprises can lead to bias in the opposite direction, with researchers inadvertently attributing too great an impact to reform.

The congruence of property rights

Data from the World Bank Enterprise Surveys (1992) are used to identify the extent to which property rights have been transferred to the enterprise, the ways in which intrafirm decision rights have been allocated, and ways in which risk and reward have been distributed in state enterprises and township and village enterprises. In chapter 2 these data are used to contrast the reassignment of control rights along three dimensions—the assignment of rights to the enterprise (table 2.1), the intraenterprise assignment of rights (table 2.4), and control of the residual (table 2.6). On average, town and village enterprises enjoy greater autonomy and exhibit a greater concentration of managerial authority within the enterprise. These rights are summarized in table 5.1. Control of the residual by the enterprise is not so strikingly dissimilar among state-owned and township and village–owned enterprises.

In chapter 2 the three categories of property rights reform are examined in isolation. In this chapter the potential for ineffective or even perverse outcomes resulting from uncoordinated property rights reform is recognized. Examples of uncoordinated reform include assignment of decision-making rights to the firm without establishing a clearly defined central contracting agent within the firm, assignment of decisionmaking rights to a central contracting agent without establishing the proper set of incentives, and creation of incentives without the assignment of decisionmaking rights. These examples suggest that important complementarities exist among these rights. Unless the reallocation of these rights is congruent—that is, they are transferred to a well-defined central contracting agent and a consistent set of incentives is created—property rights reform may be ineffective or even counterproductive.

The degree of intersection among the three key dimensions of property reform is shown by computing a mean for each dimension of reform (table 5.2) from a pooled sample of state enterprises and township and village enterprises. The intersection of highly reformed enterprises along the three dimensions is shown in figure 5.1. The results show a substantially more congruent assignment of rights for township

TABLE 5.1
Allocation of property rights
(percentage of respondents)

Property right	State-owned enterprises	Township and village enterprises
Decision autonomy		
Enterprise decides	45	81
Enterprise and supervisor jointly decide	36	9
Supervisor decides	18	9
Internal allocation of rights		
Management decides	66	100
Party committee decides	22	0
Employees' council decides	11	0
Incentive structure		
Retention rate (share of gross profit, average 1989–90)	35	35
Bonus as share of total wage and bonus	55	80
Amount of collateral required	20	30
Average amount (yuan)	13,200	38,800
Type of contract (contract for profit)		
Fixed quota (100 percent of extra retained)	15	18
Contract basic quota (progressive share of extra retained)	28	36
Contract basic quota (extra shared at fixed rate)	29	9
Contract/reward for reducing losses	9	17
Other	30[a]	18

a. "Two guarantees and one link" (19 percent) and "second stage tax for profit" (11 percent).
Source: World Bank 1992 (Enterprise Survey).

TABLE 5.2
Means of property rights indexes, 1991
(percentage of expenditures)

Property right	State-owned enterprises	Township and village enterprises
External autonomy	3.69	6.85
	(0.40)	(0.30)
Internal control	4.90	7.30
	(0.75)	(0.28)
Incentive structure	1.50	1.52
	(0.36)	(0.53)

Note: Figures in parentheses are coefficients of variation.
Source: World Bank 1992 (Enterprise Survey).

FIGURE 5.1
Property rights reform by ownership type in three areas

State-owned enterprises (sample size = 482)
Highly reformed: 9.5%

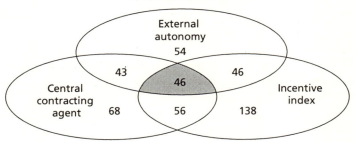

Township and village enterprises (sample size = 211)
Highly reformed: 36.5%

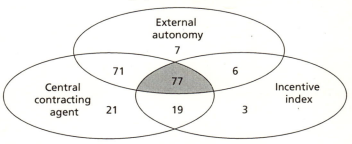

Source: Based on data in tables 2.1, 2.4, 2.7, and 5.2.

and village enterprises (36.5 percent) than for state-owned enterprises (9.5 percent; table 5.3).

Modeling the relationship between property rights and enterprise performance

Has the devolution of control rights to enterprises substantially affected performance? A composite measure of reform is constructed to test the hypothesis. The composite property rights index measures the three dimensions of property rights reform—autonomy, coherent internal authority, and incentives—as complementary components of a reform bundle. To capture complementarity the composite measure of property rights is constructed as a multiplicative combination of the three independent measures, each of which is rescaled along a continuum of 1 to 10. The multiplicative composite index is zero where no reform has taken place along a particular dimension.

An index of total factor productivity (which captures enterprise efficiency) is also constructed, using separate estimates of Cobb-Douglas production functions for state enterprises and township and village enterprises. The estimates of the weights on capital, labor, and intermediate inputs are used to construct total factor productivity indexes for each enterprise.

Using the total factor productivity series, the following relationship is estimated:

$$(5.1) \quad \ln\text{TFP90}_i = a_0 + a_1\text{INDEX0} + a_3\text{INDEX}_i + a_4\ln Q_i + a_5\ln\text{TFP87}_i + \varepsilon_i$$

where Q is gross output in current prices (intended to control for scale effects). All the variables are in natural logs, including ε, which is assumed to have a log normal distribution.

Enterprises with a composite index of zero are assigned a dummy variable INDEX0 which captures the effect of negligible or incongruent

TABLE 5.3
Congruence of property rights reform
(percentage of enterprises)

Type of enterprise	Extensive reform	Limited reform
Based on means derived from own samples		
State-owned enterprise	13.9	12.5
Township and village enterprise	16.1	19.0
Based on means derived from the pooled sample		
State-owned enterprise	9.5	6.4
Township and village enterprise	36.5	3.3

Source: World Bank 1992 (Enterprise Survey).

reform. Equation 5.1 also includes the measure of total factor productivity in 1987. By controlling for total factor productivity in 1987, enterprise performance in 1990 can be assessed relative to performance in 1987. If, for example, the coefficient a_5 were constrained to unity and TFP87 were transposed to the left-hand side of the equation, the estimate of a_3 would measure the impact of reform on the three-year rate of growth of total factor productivity. If a_5 is not constrained and the estimate is less than unity, levels of productivity across enterprises within the sample will have converged during 1987–90.

The fact that the measure of property rights is based on observations from 1991–92 complicates this interpretation of property rights reform causing improved performance as measured in 1990. This issue is addressed later in the chapter. Here the measure of property rights in 1991–92 is assumed to be highly correlated with either the level or the rate of improvement of property rights in 1987–90.

The equation is estimated using three sets of data: the state enterprise sample, the township and village enterprise sample, and a sample that pools the state enterprise and township and village enterprise data. The results for the state enterprise sample reveal a negative association between performance and reform (table 5.4). The estimate of the INDEX coefficient is negative and statistically significant in the state sector, implying that property rights reform depressed rather than enhanced enterprise performance. For the township and village sector the association between reform and performance is positive but not statistically significant. The pooled sample suggests a weaker, but still negative, association between reform and performance than that found in the state sector. Two hypotheses—the capture hypothesis and the endogenous reform hypothesis—have been put forth to explain this negative or neutral association between performance and property rights reform.

The capture hypothesis

During 1984–85 the central government substantially expanded enterprise reform that had previously been carried out only on a limited experimental basis. Enterprises that enjoyed the greatest autonomy during the mid- and late 1980s may have used this authority to expand labor's share of income. Expansion of the wage bill would have eroded profitability; by diverting funds from investment and new product development, autonomy would also have eroded investment and labor productivity.

If the capture hypothesis is correct, there should be an association between enterprises that enjoyed the most extensive rights in 1991 and those for which labor's income share was either large in 1990 or had grown rapidly during the late 1980s. Using the structure of property

TABLE 5.4
Impact of reform on productivity

Item	State-owned enterprise	Township and village enterprise	Pooled
Constant	0.186	−0.980	−0.238
	(2.357)	(4.715)	(2.550)
INDEXO	−0.287	0.012	0.231
	(2.712)	(0.034)	(1.768)
INDEX	−0.199	0.018	−0.016
	(2.554)	(0.639)	(1.598)
SCALE	0.036	0.265	0.552
	(4.400)	(3.709)	(17.798)
TFP87	0.579	0.256	0.552
	(16.971)	(3.709)	(17.798)
Township and village enterprises/ INDEX dummy			−0.231
			(2.730)
Township and village enterprises ownership dummy			0.189
			(4.722)
Adjusted R²	0.557	0.663	0.591
Number of observations	461	155	616

Note: Dependent variable = total factor productivity in 1990. Numbers in parentheses are t-statistics.
Source: World Bank 1992 (Enterprise Survey).

rights reform in 1991 as a proxy for autonomy and incentives in the mid–1980s reflects the implicit assumption of relative stability in the distribution of property rights reform before 1991. The impact of reform on labor's income share (*LS*) is estimated as follows:

$$(5.2) \qquad LS_i = a + \beta INDEX_i + \varepsilon_i$$

Equation 5.2 is estimated in two forms. The first, *LS*, is the absolute level of the income share in 1990 (*WL/PQ*); the second, *gls*, is the rate of growth of labor's income share during 1986–90. Both forms are also estimated for the proportion (NPK) and rate of growth (*gnpk*) of nonproduction capital (NPFA) used for investment in housing, schools, and other facilities that provide in-kind compensation to employees. In both the level and growth versions of the capture hypothesis, the delegation of property rights appears to have had little effect on labor's income share or the accumulation of nonproduction assets (table 5.5). No evidence to support the capture hypothesis is thus found.

A second possible explanation of why reform may not have affected performance is the presence of simultaneity. If the reform and perfor-

TABLE 5.5
Test of the capture hypothesis for the state-owned enterprise sample

Item	(LS) 90	gls 86–90	(NPK) 90	gnpk 86–90
Constant	0.113	0.118	0.178	0.288
	(8.119)	(0.904)	(10.941)	(1.900)
INDEX	–0.010	–0.013	–0.004	0.014
	(0.989)	(0.131)	(0.348)	(0.121)
R²	0.002	0.000	0.000	0.000
Number of observations	429	437	432	416

Note: Variables are defined in text. Numbers in parentheses are t-statistics.
Source: World Bank 1992 (Enterprise Survey).

mance data were from the same period, equation 5.1 could suffer from simultaneity bias. If poor performance motivated an enterprise reform, then equation 5.1—which posits that reform drives performance—would underestimate the positive impact of reform on performance.

The problem may be even more serious than the classic within-period simultaneity problem in that the time structure may not be consistent with that required to test the hypothesis that reform drives performance. While productivity performance is measured for the 1987–90 period, the reform variable INDEX is constructed from data collected in 1991 and 1992, after firms revealed their performance.

If firms with above-average property rights in 1991–92 also enjoyed above-average rights during 1987–90 or experienced improvement in these rights before 1990, a high property rights index in 1991–92 should be associated with rising productivity during 1987–90. This may not be the case, however. The reform variables in 1991–92 may effectively proxy the reform variables during the earlier period, which are responsible for motivating performance in the late 1980s. Reform may be an unstable process, particularly during 1989–91, when the Chinese economy was experiencing severe austerity, which may have magnified pressures for new reform initiatives at the local level. The fact that most state enterprises entered into the second round of responsibility contracts during 1990–91 may also have substantially altered the assignments of property rights after 1990. In this case the time structure of the data makes it impossible to test the impact of reform on performance, since the state of reform in the mid- to late 1980s that was relevant to measured performance in 1989–90 was not measured by the survey.

The endogenous reform hypothesis

Jefferson and Rawski have suggested that enterprise reform is an endogenous process brought about by growing competition, which erodes financial and fixed surpluses (see chapter 3). If the hypothesis is correct, competition, enterprise performance, and enterprise size would be expected to drive property rights reform. Competition places more pressure on enterprises to use their resources efficiently in order to minimize costs. Competition also tends to drive economic profits to zero. Low or declining profits, in turn, reinforce the resolve of managers to seek more autonomy while legitimizing their claim for the enterprise to capture a larger share of total profit. Poor enterprise performance is likely to motivate enterprise managers and their supervisors to more aggressively seek to strengthen enterprise governance.

Enterprise size may affect reform for several reasons. First, smaller state enterprises are typically subject to more intense competition, as reflected in relatively low rates of profit. These conditions are captured by competition and performance measures. Second, smaller enterprises are typically supervised at lower levels of government. These local, municipal, county, and even provincial governments are more susceptible to fiscal pressures arising from financially strapped enterprises, since unlike the central government they are unable to print money or issue debt. Faced with poorly performing enterprises and sagging revenue growth, lower-level supervisory bodies are more likely to press for enterprise reform. Finally, smaller enterprises own fewer assets. China's largest enterprises are commonly viewed as the patrimony of the state. It is not surprising that, wishing to maintain the semblance of a "socialist" market economy, China's central government has formulated a different reform agenda for the largest state enterprises, embodied in the slogan "retain the large, release the small" (juada, fangxiao).

The size of the enterprise should thus affect the extent of reform of its property rights. In general, for both state enterprises and township and village enterprises, reform should be greatest among enterprises that are small, that face competitive pressures and declining profits, that are supervised by lower levels of government facing tighter budget constraints, and that are not affected by the central government's more measured reform agenda. Reform should be most limited among large enterprises, those most directly under the control of the center, and those best able to benefit from the largest of policy loans and other subsidies.

The hypothesis of endogenous property rights reform is tested using the following equation:

(5.3) $\text{INDEX}_i = b + \text{INDEXO} + b_1\text{COMP}_i + b_2\text{PRO8990}_i + b_3\text{TFP8990}_i$
$+ b_4\text{SIZE}_i + \varepsilon_i$

COMP is a composite measure of two separate measures of the degree of competitiveness of the enterprise's market environment. The first asks respondents to rank the intensity of competition within the industry in which the enterprise operates on a scale of 1 to 3. The second asks the respondent to estimate the demand elasticity for the principal product of the enterprise. The variable COMP combines these measures along a scale of 2 to 6. The variable PRO8990 is the pretax profit to–sales-ratio averaged over 1989–90; total TFP8990 is a similar average for total factory productivity; SIZE is a categorical variable for the official size classification of the enterprise (1 = large size, 3 = small size), and INDEX0 is a dummy that isolates the effect of the special case. Where there is no reform along one or more dimensions INDEX = 0.

Equation 5.3 is estimated independently for the samples of state enterprises and township and village enterprises and for the pooled sample of both types of enterprises (table 5.6). For the state sector, the estimates on the coefficients of all four explanatory variables are of the predicted sign and statistically significant. For the township and village enterprise sector each of the estimates exhibits the predicted sign, but the fit of the relationship is not nearly as statistically robust as it is for the state sector.

These results provide strong support for the endogenous reform hypothesis. The extent to which endogenous reform improves enterprise performance cannot be determined, however, because of the time structure of our data and simultaneity issues that made the results presented in table 5.4 unreliable.

TABLE 5.6
Impact of performance on reform

Item	State-owned enterprise	Township and village enterprise	Pooled
Constant	4.015	3.629	1.457
	(11.232)	(5.521)	(11.291)
INDEX0	−13.314	−12.798	
	(99.568)	(26.871)	
COMP	0.164	0.293	−0.495
	(2.344)	(0.235)	(1.704)
PRO8990	−2.320	−0.035	0.043
	(2.635)	(0.769)	(1.977)
TFP8990	−0.583	−0.254	−0.032
	(2.692)	(1.206)	(2.540)
SIZE	0.146		
	(1.863)		
Township and village enterprise ownership dummy			0.539
			(7.922)
Adjusted R^2	0.957	0.791	0.334
Number of observations	467	210	596

Note: Dependent variable = INDEX. Numbers in parentheses are t-statistics.
Source: World Bank 1992 (Enterprise Survey).

Implications: the commons, Coase, and a property rights market

The finding of an endogenous reform process in which competition and poor financial and productivity performance motivate new rounds of reform raises the question "What are the avenues through which these pressures can translate into improved corporate governance?" The monitoring problem is the central problem of the Chinese state enterprise. In the absence of owners and managers who possess the authority and face the incentives to monitor the input of key factors of production and their formal and informal compensation, opportunistic behavior will motivate workers, managers, and officials to take more from the enterprise than they give. The result will be persistent losses and an enterprise structure characterized by soft budget constraints, persistent subsidies, the accumulation of nonperforming debt, and a weak financial system.

Coase (1960) argued that the means to remedying the inefficient use of public goods is to assign property rights clearly and eliminate transactions costs so that assets can be traded to the individuals or groups that can most efficiently use them. In effect, Coase argued for solving the public goods problem by creating a property rights market. Jefferson (1998) investigates how to apply the logic of the Coase Theorem— assigning property rights and reducing transaction costs to create a market in the scarce resource. Chinese industry has begun to implement the essential elements of a property rights market, by adopting the contract responsibility system, corporatizing, and privatizing enterprises, and creating property rights transaction centers.

The contract responsibility system. The principal instrument for implementing change in the effective control over productive resources, in both the agricultural and the industrial sectors in China, has been the contract. Since 1978 the ease and efficacy of contracting has been substantially enhanced through the relaxation of direct controls over production and the development of the household and enterprise contract responsibility systems.

Within the industrial sector, officials at all levels of government and current and potential enterprise managers expect to gain through the assignment of monitoring authority to managers in exchange for the guarantee, or at least anticipation, of enhanced revenues. Transactions costs associated with contracting have been reduced not only by the sanctioning of this administrative practice but also by the emergence of a managerial market that allows for a measure of contestability and the use of collateral, which facilitates contract enforcement.

Coase's second requirement, that of zero transactions costs, is sometimes interpreted as simply the right to bargain.[1] Such an interpretation is too narrow. Within the context of China's enterprise system the requirement must be more broadly interpreted to encompass competition as well as low negotiating costs.

In order for a robust property rights market to exist, bureaucratic ownership cannot be concentrated in a centralized state agency. To avoid monopolistic power, a large number of agents must compete as both buyers and sellers. The very large number of owners of enterprises in China, spread over tens of thousands of subnational jurisdictions, facilitates the emergence of a property rights market.

Low negotiation costs are also necessary. In particular, a high degree of transparency—principally, a regulated auditing process that provides prospective owners with a clear view of the enterprise's performance— and a legal system that allows for low-cost contract negotiation and enforcement are needed.

In a transition economy such as China, public ownership gives rise to ineffective monitoring, particularly at the state level. As a result, public enterprise becomes a commons, in which agents extract resources, which are replenished through a softening of the budget constraint. Enterprise reform, which improves the assignment of property rights, increases competition, lowers transactions costs, and creates conditions that cause jurisdictions and their public officials to incur the costs of inefficient monitoring. Under these conditions, in the absence of substantially improved monitoring, owners will engage in negotiations with other jurisdictions, enterprises, and/or individual entrepreneurs who can use the assets more efficiently. The resulting sales, joint ventures, or mergers and acquisitions result in a shift in the composition of ownership toward agents who can use the assets more efficiently (see Howson 1997). In an economy with well-specified property rights, perfect competition, and zero transactions costs, the allocation of assets and property rights will be Pareto efficient: assets will end up in the hands of those who can use them most efficiently. As in the Coase theorem, this efficient outcome occurs regardless of the initial allocation of property rights.

Given these results, the objective of China's reform program should be to establish the institutional requirements needed for an effectively functioning property rights market. Widespread privatization is neither a necessary nor a sufficient precondition for effective reform; effective reform simply requires that property rights be well specified initially, whether they are assigned to a public agency, an enterprise, or an individual. This approach, at least in its initial conception, is consistent with a socialist market economy, since a substantial portion of assets may continue to be assigned to jurisdictions, public agencies, pension programs, and other forms of public ownership. The important condition is that owners, whether public or private, be subject to market conditions.

Jefferson and Rawski (1997) assess the progress of Chinese industry in terms of clarifying ownership, improving competition, and reducing transactions costs. Their results show substantial progress in some areas, such as entry, and only modest progress in others, such as the exit of state enterprises and the transparency of township and village enterprises (table 5.7).

Coase distinguished his approach to resolving the problem of externalities from that of Pigou (1920), whose approach he criticized. According to Coase, Pigou's approach, which involved the design and

TABLE 5.7
Levels of institutional development of Chinese enterprises, selected years, 1980–97
(1 is low; 5 is high)

Area	1980	1989	1997
Competition			
Entry	1	3	4
Factor mobility			
Capital	1	2	3
Labor			
Unskilled	1	3	4
Management/technical	1	2	4
Production			
State-owned enterprises	1	2	3
Township and village enterprises	1	3	4
Exit			
State-owned enterprises	1	1	2
Township and village enterprises	1	3	3
Clarification of decentralized property rights			
Managerial control rights			
State-owned enterprises	1	2	3
Township and village enterprises	1	3	4
Right to sell			
State-owned enterprises	1	2	2
Township and village enterprises	1	3	3
Transactions costs			
Transparency			
State-owned enterprises	1	2	3
Township and village enterprises	1	1	1
Transactions resources			
Market	1	2	3
Government/official	1	2	2
Law/enforcement			
Contract	1	3	3
Shareholder	1	1	2

Note: Dependent variable = INDEX.
Source: Jefferson and Rawski 1997 (table 4).

imposition of a tax to fill the void between private and social marginal costs, was inherently flawed, since the information required to evaluate private and social costs was generally unavailable. In contrast, the Coasian approach recognized that the reciprocal nature of externalities would lead to an efficient exchange of rights between those with rights to the resource who accrue little benefit from its use and those without rights who anticipate much benefit from its use.

China's current reforms represent a combination of Pigouvian and Coasian approaches. The Thousand-Firm Reinvigoration Program, under which the central government plans to "grab and reinvigorate" the largest firms through technical renovation, interest payment exemptions, debt forgiveness, and redundancy payments for idled workers, represents a Pigouvian approach. Establishment of some 150 property rights transaction centers, which seek to facilitate and mediate the exchange of rights and asset ownership among state enterprises, township and village enterprises, and other ownership types, represents a Coasian approach. The Chinese government should encourage the institutional innovations and improvements needed to strengthen the effectiveness of these centers, which represent an important component in China's formative property rights market.

Conclusions

As Coase has shown, the existence of a property rights market is critical to ensuring enterprise efficiency. The very large number of industrial enterprises in China and the high level of decentralization of ownership and management of these enterprises are facilitating development of what may be the country's most valuable transition institution—an emerging property rights market. Significant reallocation of property rights has already taken place, particularly among township and village enterprises, which typically enjoy more autonomy than state enterprises. Managers of rural enterprises possess more authority and bear more risk and reward than do their counterparts in the state sector.

Although reform of property rights would be expected intuitively to be positively correlated with increases in enterprise performance, regression results yield a neutral or (in the case of the state sector) negative association. The explanation for this seemingly anomalous finding may be that reform is an endogenous process and that problems of simultaneity and the time structure of the data confound regression results. While the effect of reform on enterprise performance remains impossible to gauge given the limitations of the data, the result that competition and enterprise performance drive reform is robust.

This result gives support to the industrial innovation ladder thesis outlined in chapter 3. Rising competition and lagging enterprise performance motivate the search for improved profit and efficiency through two avenues of innovation—new product innovation and new forms of corporate governance.

Notes

This research was supported by the World Bank, the U.S. Department of Education, and the Brandeis University Mazer Fund. The authors appreciate the helpful comments and suggestions provided by Joseph Berliner, Fang Xinhai, Alan Gelb, Arthur Lewbel, Thomas Rawski, Wing Thye Woo, and participants in the International Conference on Property Rights of Township and Village Enterprises in China, held in Hangzhou, Zhejiang, China, August 7–9, 1994.

1. According to Frank (1994, p. 669), for example, "When the parties affected by externalities can negotiate costlessly with one another, an efficient outcome results no matter how the law assigns responsibility for damages."

References

Alchian, Armen, and Harold Demsetz. 1972. "Production, Information Costs, and Economic Organization." *American Economic Review* 62: 777–95.

Byrd, William A., and Alan Gelb. 1990. "Why Industrialize? The Incentives for Rural Community Governments." In William A. Byrd and Lin Qingsong, eds., *China's Rural Industry: Structure, Development, and Reform.* New York: Oxford University Press.

Byrd, William A., and Qingsong Lin. 1990. "China's Rural Industry: An Introduction." In William A. Byrd and Lin Qingsong, eds., *China's Rural Industry: Structure, Development, and Reform.* New York: Oxford University Press.

Coase, Ronald H. 1960. "The Problem of Social Cost." *Journal of Law and Economics* 3: 1–44.

Frank, Robert H. 1994. *Microeconomics and Behavior.* 2nd ed. New York: McGraw Hill.

Groves, Theodore, Yongmiao Hong, John McMillan, and Barry Naughton. 1994. "Autonomy and Incentives in Chinese State Enterprises." *Quarterly Journal of Economics* 109(1):183–209.

Hay, Donald, Derek Morris, Guy Liu, and Shujie Yao. 1994. *Economic Reform and State-Owned Enterprises in China, 1979–1987.* Oxford: Clarendon Press.

Howson, Nicholas C. 1997. *New Acquisition Structures in China: M&A Comes to the Middle Kingdom.* New York: Paul, Weiss, Rifkind, Wharton & Garrison.

Huang, Yiping, and Ron Duncan. 1997. "How Successful Were China's State Sector Reforms?" *Journal of Comparative Economics* 24(1): 65–78.

Jefferson, Gary H. 1998. "China's State-Owned Enterprises, Public Goods and Coase." *American Economic Review* 88(2): 428–32.

Jefferson, Gary H., and Thomas G. Rawski. 1994. "How Industrial Reform Worked in China: The Role of Innovation, Competition, and Property Rights." In Joseph E. Stiglitz and Boris Pleskovic, eds., *Proceedings of the World Bank Annual Conference on Development Economics.* Washington, D.C.: The World Bank.

Jefferson, Gary H., and Xu Wenyi. 1994. "The Impact of Reform on Socialist Enterprises in Transitions: Structure, Conduct, and Performance in Chinese Industry." *Journal of Comparative Economics* 15: 45–64.

Jensen, Michael, and William Meckling. 1976. "Theory of the Firm: Managerial Behavior, Agency Costs, and Ownership Structure." *Journal of Financial Economics* 3:305–60.

Lee, Kuen. 1991. *Chinese Firms and the State in Transition: Property Rights and Agency Problems in the Reform Era.* Armonk, N.Y.: M.E. Sharpe.

Pigou, A. C. 1920. *The Economics of Welfare.* London: Macmillan & Co.

Qian, Yingyi, and Chengang Xu. 1992. *Why China's Economic Reforms Differ: The M-form Hierarchy and Entry/Expansion of the Non-State Sector.* CEPR Publication 319. Stanford University, Stanford, Calif.

Wang, Andrew. 1997. "Economic Reforms and State Enterprise Productivity in China: An Application of Robust Estimation and Latent Variable Measurement Methods." Ph.D. dissertation, Harvard University, Cambridge, Mass.

Weitzman, Martin, and Chenggang Xu. 1994. "Chinese Township and Village Enterprises as Vaguely Defined Cooperatives." *Journal of Comparative Economics* 18(2): 121–45.

World Bank. 1992. "Enterprise Surveys." China and Mongolia Department and the Socialist Economies Unit. Washington, D.C.

Wu, Yanrui. 1996. *Productive Performance in Chinese Industry.* New York: St. Martin's Press.

Yao, Shujie. 1997. "Profit Sharing, Bonus Payment and Productivity: A Case Study of Chinese State-Owned Enterprises." *Journal of Comparative Economics* 24(3): 281–96.

Yusuf, Shahid. 1993a. "Property Rights and Non-State Sector Development in China." World Bank, Washington, D.C.

———. 1993b. "The Rise of China's Non-State Sector." World Bank, Washington, D.C.

Zhang, Weiying. 1997. "Decision Rights, Residual Claims and Performance: A Theory of How the Chinese State Enterprise Reform Works." *China Economic Review* 8(1): 67–82.

Zou, Gang, and Zhigang Wang. 1994. "Marketization and Productivity Change in Chinese Industry." University of Southern California, Los Angeles.

China's Industrial Performance: A Review of Recent Findings

6

Gary H. Jefferson, Inderjit Singh, Xing Junling, and Zhang Shouqing

The comparatively gradual reform of China's state industry, combined with the rapid entry of several million new industrial enterprises of varying ownership types, has raised interest in both the overall performance of industry and the comparative performance of enterprises within different ownership classifications in China. This chapter is based principally on a review of the growing literature that evaluates the performance of Chinese industry. It also includes some statistical analyses of a large sample of large and medium-size industrial enterprises.

The performance of various ownership types is analyzed against the background of an extended version of the structure–conduct–performance (S–C–P) paradigm, a central model in the field of industrial organization.[1] According to this approach, an industry's performance depends on the conduct, or behavior, of firms, which, in turn, depends on the structure of the market within which they operate. The S–C–P paradigm is modified and extended here in order to examine firms within the same ownership classification (state enterprises, township and village enterprises, or foreign-invested enterprises). Each of these ownership types is distinguished by a structure that relates both to the market structure within which the firm operates—the focus of the conventional S–C–P approach—and the governance structure of the firm.

Chapters 1, 2, and 5 describe the different property rights and market structures of China's key ownership types; chapters 4 and 8–12 describe the conduct of China's industrial enterprises along alternative ownership lines. This chapter and chapter 8 evaluate the comparative performance of China's key ownership types. Together these chapters draw connections between the structure, conduct, and performance of each of these ownership types.

Preceding chapters have documented a change in structure, including a strengthening of incentives through performance contracts and increased market competition, and a change in conduct, involving a closer alignment of wages with productivity and of bonuses and investment with pretax profits. Some observers dismiss this evidence, arguing that significant improvement in the performance of publicly owned enterprises is not possible (see, for example, World Bank 1995). According to this view, noncommercial objectives, political interference, lack of incentives for performance, and severe principal agent problems conspire to confound efforts to improve efficiency. Before significant improvement can take place, certain political preconditions, which have not yet been satisfied in China, must be met. Short of privatization, ameliorative or partial reform measures do little to improve performance by state enterprises. Where improvements do occur, they are small, likely to be short-lived, and unsustainable.

State enterprises are not likely to perform as efficiently as their privately owned counterparts. But the weak incentives and lack of efficiency that characterized these enterprises before reform imply substantial scope for efficiency gains under state ownership. Moreover, firms operating under decentralized public ownership in competitive product and factor markets, such as some of China's township and village enterprises, may approach the efficiency standards of private enterprise. The focus here is not on the performance of Chinese industry relative to an international frontier but on the improvement in performance since reform.

Three performance measures are used as benchmarks. The first is a simple measure of levels and rates of growth of labor productivity. Although this measure ignores differences in factor intensities, it provides a useful starting point for the analysis. The second is total factor productivity, which is used to compare overall efficiency. The third is profitability, which is used to capture economic, rather than technical, efficiency. Profit is a more complex and comprehensive measure of economic performance than productivity, because it measures cost in relation to both demand and competition. Each of these performance measures is reviewed below.

Labor productivity

Labor productivity over time and across ownership types is examined based on data on employment and the current value of gross output (table 6.1). Using output in current prices limits the analytical value of measured trends within ownership types, but it is useful in comparing labor productivity across ownership types over time. Several findings emerge from these data. Data from the full population of enterprises show state enterprises with a substantial advantage over collective enterprises but lagging far behind the other category. Controlling for size, however, the sample of large and medium-size enterprises shows state

TABLE 6.1
Labor productivity by ownership, selected years, 1985–96
(yuan per worker)

Type of enterprise	1985	1988	1990	1993	1996
All enterprises					
State enterprise	15,309	24,477	29,933	50,522	66,295
Collective enterprise	5,042	8,721	11,444	22,581	42,234
Other	32,636	63,018	76,297	120,888	223,176
Sample of large and medium-size enterprises					
State enterprise	—	30,935	35,231	43,758	57,383
		(3,010)	(3,628)	(4,528)	(4,627)
Collective enterprise	—	34,058	35,998	52,572	67,125
		(258)	(482)	(924)	(682)
Domestic joint venture	—	36,255	45,890	58,805	78,910
		(58)	(88)	(96)	(61)
Joint stock company	—	—	—	—	135,896
					(176)
Foreign joint venture	—	123,618	148,252	228,768	289,773
		(31)	(69)	(100)	(101)
Foreign wholly owned enterprise	—	—	133,154	219,975	139,783
			(1)	(4)	(3)
Overseas joint venture	—	121,707	130,160	163,654	201,558
		(9)	(52)	(106)	(95)
Overseas wholly owned enterprise	—	—	—	130,345	220,175
				(9)	(1)
Other	—	60,045	116,466	99,386	136,149
		(2)	(3)	(16)	(3)
Sample size	—	3,368	4,323	5,783	5,749

— Not available.
Note: Numbers in parentheses are the number of enterprises in the China State Statistical Bureau enterprise data set.
Source: China State Statistical Bureau 1986, 1989, 1991, 1994, 1997; *China Labor Statistics Yearbook 1993* (pp. 193, 349, 413); *China Industrial Economy Statistical Yearbook 1988* (p. 27); China State Statistical Bureau enterprise data set.

industry with the lowest productivity and foreign–funded joint ventures enjoying the highest productivity.

The disparity between labor productivity in state and nonstate enterprises may be smaller than these figures suggest, for several reasons. First, larger firms that are converted from state to nonstate status are generally the most successful enterprises (table 6.2), as Jefferson, Rawski, and Zheng (1996) have shown. State enterprises converted by 1992 exhibited levels of labor productivity that were nearly 50 percent higher in 1988 than the overall level of labor productivity among state enterprises. This

TABLE 6.2
**Productivity of converted and loss-making state enterprises,
1988 and 1992**

| Year | Gross value of industrial output in current prices as a ratio of | | |
	Unadjusted year-end employment	Net fixed assets at year end	Expenditures on materials, fuel, and power
Balanced sample of large and medium-size state enterprises			
1988	29,079	2.08	1.65
1992	43,380	2.14	1.63
Percentage change	11.56	0.93	−0.27
Firms exiting state enterprise classification during 1989–92 and entering new classification involving state enterprises			
1988	44,701	3.35	1.62
Firms incurring losses throughout 1989–92			
1988	15,800	1.49	1.49
1992	13,464	0.98	1.48
Percentage change	−3.98	−10.50	−0.21

Note: Fixed assets and expenditures are undeflated.
Source: Jefferson, Rawski, and Zheng 1996.

selectivity bias has two consequences. One is that the performance measures of state enterprises that have been privatized or converted to joint ventures or joint stock companies are typically more robust than those of enterprises remaining in the state sector. A second consequence is to depress measures of state industry performance. The China State Statistical Bureau data, therefore, compare the most dynamic and successful of the nonstate enterprises with a comparatively static population of state enterprises. This tendency for the best firms to exit to other ownership classifications and for chronic loss-makers to be retained shifts the distribution of state enterprise performance.

Because firms employ capital, materials, and energy as well as labor in the production of goods, measures of labor productivity are an imperfect, and sometimes misleading, measure of overall enterprise efficiency. In China state enterprises are typically more capital-intensive than are collective-owned enterprises, particularly township and village enterprises. In addition, foreign and overseas-funded enterprises that are engaged in substantial reexport operations are likely to exhibit comparatively low value added ratios. Both capital intensity and intermediate input intensity inflate measures of labor productivity. Total factor productivity, a comprehensive measure of technical efficiency that is a composite of single factor productivities, may therefore provide a more meaningful measure of productivity.

Total factor productivity

Most of the studies reviewed in this chapter use a simple Cobb–Douglas index to construct measures of total factor productivity (TFP), which can be represented as:

$$(6.1) \qquad\qquad TFP = (Q/L)^{\alpha}(Q/K)^{\beta}(Q/M)^{1-\alpha-\beta}$$

where Q represents the gross value of industrial output, L is end-of-year employment, K is the net value of fixed assets, M is the value of intermediate inputs, α is the output elasticity of labor, β is the output elasticity of capital, and $1 - \alpha - \beta$ is the output elasticity of intermediate inputs. For sectoral studies, in which the researcher seeks to estimate average total factor productivity or the total factor productivity of an "average" enterprise, the Cobb–Douglas function will generally yield output elasticities (weights) that adequately approximate the underlying elasticities. For the aggregate study, the advantage of using a flexible functional form or frontier estimation method is likely to be small.

A large body of literature exists on total factor productivity growth in China's industry. Since an assessment of total factor productivity growth over time requires comparing the growth of inputs relative to the growth of output, measured in physical or constant price units, the accuracy of these studies depends critically on the quality of the relevant measures of inputs and output.

Analytical pitfalls

Studies of total factor productivity in China often suffer from one or more of the following shortcomings: gross output value deflators are used to deflate net output or value added, the capital stock is not deflated, output bias is ignored, nonproduction inputs are included, and aggregate performance is inferred from sample data.

Output deflators. One difficulty with formulating value added (or net output) measures of total factor productivity growth is that there is no direct way to calculate deflators for value added. As a result most researchers simply use the gross output deflator to deflate value added. In principle, this is incorrect, since the gross output deflator is a weighted combination of an implicit value added deflator and an intermediate input deflator. Only if value added prices (driven principally by changes in the unit costs of capital and labor) and intermediate input prices rise at similar rates will the gross output deflator serve as a suitable proxy for the value added deflator.

During the 1980s rates of inflation of gross output and intermediate inputs differed significantly in China. In general, the intermediate input deflator (p_m) rose more rapidly than the gross output deflator (p_g), creating a wedge between the gross output deflator and the value added deflator (p_v). This wedge between the gross output deflator and the value added deflator is caused by two factors. First, the gross output deflator is based on ex-factory prices, while the intermediate input deflator is based on purchase prices. As the administered distribution system was replaced by market distribution arrangements, the spread between the ex-factory and the purchase price of intermediate inputs increased. Introduction of this market markup caused intermediate input prices to rise more quickly than ex-factory output prices. Second, before price liberalization, raw material and industrial goods prices were generally more depressed relative to their underlying market values than were prices of consumer and final goods, which were sometimes not controlled at all. Under central planning this practice was maintained, in part to create surpluses in the industrial sector that could be captured easily by government to finance its operations and capital investment. Price liberalization, therefore, resulted in a more rapid rise in raw materials and intermediate prices than in overall output prices. It thus seems likely that $p_m > p_g > p_v$.

This ordering of price deflators troubled Woo and others (1993) and Sachs and Woo (1994), because it contributed to estimates of productivity growth in state industry that they believed were unrealistically high. Using data from a now regularly reported urban price survey administered by the State Statistical Commission, Jefferson, Rawski, and Zheng (1996) found that p_m had risen 2.877; p_g, 1.962; and, given the relative weights of value added and intermediate inputs, p_v just 1.085 (table 6.3). The differential pace of adjustment in gross output prices and intermediate inputs prices was most pronounced during 1984–85, causing the value added deflator to fall in those years.

Using the gross output deflator to deflate value added during periods of price liberalization and market formation is, then, likely to bias measures of total factor productivity growth in two ways. Since the intermediate input deflator is likely to rise more rapidly than the gross output deflator during the transition, using the gross output deflator as a proxy for the value added deflator will tend to overdeflate the growth of value added and create a downward bias in estimates of value added or net output total factor productivity growth.

Using the gross output value deflator to deflate intermediate inputs will tend to correct intermediate inputs insufficiently for inflation, since

TABLE 6.3
Derivation of implicit price index for value added, 1984–92

Year	Output at current prices (billion yuan)		Net value of output/gross value of output at current prices	Deflators (1990 = 100)		
	Gross value	Net value		Gross output	Intermediate input	Value added[a]
1984	505.5	172.1	0.340	0.578	0.421	0.975
1985	611.5	205.8	0.337	0.629	0.497	0.916
1986	687.8	220.7	0.320	0.652	0.545	0.865
1987	799.4	252.9	0.316	0.704	0.604	0.893
1988	994.7	306.3	0.308	0.810	0.749	0.923
1989	1,187.3	346.0	0.291	0.960	0.947	0.989
1990	1,257.0	356.9	0.284	1.000	1.000	1.000
1991	1,437.2	401.9	0.280	1.062	1.091	1.023
1992	1,709.1	483.1	0.283	1.134	1.211	1.058

a. $P_v = mP_gP_m/[P_m - 1(1 - m) P_g]$.
Source: Jefferson, Rawski, and Zheng 1996.

it understates the rise in prices. Because a key input is not deflated sufficiently, estimates of total factor productivity growth will tend to be biased downward.

Capital stock deflators. Using measures of the capital stock reported in standard statistical sources may bias estimates. Careful analysis requires reconstructing the capital stock so that all vintages of capital are priced using a constant price base, which may be current market value. The construction of capital stock deflators, discussed at length in Chen and others (1988a), in turn requires an accurate set of price deflators for investment goods. Naughton (1991) and Jefferson, Rawski, and Zheng (1992) have devised various ways of using Chinese price data to construct such price deflators. Because of price controls before 1980, failure to deflate the capital stock probably gave rise to minimal bias in productivity measures before the reform period. During the 1980s and 1990s, however, investment goods prices have risen substantially, tending to overstate rates of capital accumulation and understate total factor productivity growth when compared with the growth of output measured in constant prices.

Output bias. Two sources of bias exist in reports of Chinese industrial output. New product bias is most frequent in state industry. Falsification occurs more often in collective industry.

In the state sector new product bias artificially inflated measures of real output growth during the late 1980s (Field 1992; Jefferson 1992), especially in the machinery industry. Such bias has had the effect of inflating estimates of real output growth and total factor productivity, although the distortion of total factor productivity is partially offset when equipment and intermediate inputs become inputs to industrial production.

Distortions arise from the frequent misassignment of current costs or prices to represent the constant price of new goods. This practice may arise because there is no comparable product in the relevant base year or from an intent to create an upward bias in reported real output growth. The reckoning of the constant price gross value of output using current prices therefore overinflated the constant price gross output value estimate, which led to an underestimate of the implicit price deflator. When the elapsed time since the creation of constant prices included periods of inflation, constant prices assigned to new products may have been substantially upwardly biased. This occurred during the second half of the 1980s, when inflation drove a wedge between current prices and the 1980 constant prices used to construct industrial price deflators. A combination of price controls and excess demand during the late 1980s exacerbated the measurement problem, as enterprises sought to reclassify standard items as new products in order to escape price controls. When they succeeded, the substitution of current for constant prices in reported output contributed to a downward bias in industrial price deflators.

The impact of new product bias on total factor productivity measurement appears to be an episodic phenomenon the quantitative impact of which is greatest in the presence of inflation, price controls, and an outdated set of constant prices. Furthermore, new product bias affects only the measurement of industrial output at constant prices. The problem was probably most acute during the late 1980s, with the phase out of the dual price system; it has become less important during the 1990s.

It is possible to avoid these problems altogether by using price survey data collected by the Urban Survey Team of the State Statistical Bureau. Collected on a quarterly basis since 1984, these data, which include a composite price index for urban industrial goods and for intermediate goods, are published in various issues of the journal *China Price* (*Zhongguo wujia*).

Falsification of output statistics is a serious problem in some sectors in China. Statistical work in China's state sector is conducted under relatively tight official supervision. No comparable controls exist for the freewheeling collective sector, especially in rural areas, where industries have come to dominate collective production. As Jefferson, Rawski, and Zheng (1996) report, falsification by local administrators of output statistics, particularly in rural areas, has attracted considerable publicity. During the past decade more than 20,000 court cases have been brought against local officials for presenting false statistics about local economic development (*China Daily* 7 December 1993, p. 3). The director of China's State Statistics Bureau complains that ambitious local officials "want to boast of their achievements, so they force officials at the next level to change statistics, especially because promotion of [local] government officers ... depends to a great extent on local economic achievement" (*China Daily* 15 July 1995, p. 27).

This opportunistic behavior affects productivity measures for collective industry because "fiddling with industrial output figures has become rampant among township enterprises," so much so that statistical officials declined to comment on the veracity of "staggering" increases in the output of rural industry reported for 1993/94.

One county reported a 100 percent increase in industrial output value for 1991/92, even though industrial power consumption rose by only 14 percent (*China Daily* 15 January 1994, p. 4). Since provincial and national data for collective industry are derived by aggregating locally reported statistics, local overreporting can lead to inflated output totals and exaggerated total factor productivity results in China's collective industry. Survey data are not available for rural industry. Jefferson, Rawski, and Zheng (1996) show that using price deflators based on the urban industry surveys in lieu of conventional deflators based on self-reported measures of current and constant gross output substantially reduces estimates of total factor productivity growth for both collective and township and village enterprises.

Nonproduction inputs. Consistent with the socialist practice of establishing the enterprise as a social and political unit as well as a unit of production, state enterprises and many collective-owned enterprises in China provide a range of services for their employees and their families, including housing, schooling, and health care. These services often require substantial commitments of fixed assets and labor. Standard measures of capital and labor reported by Chinese enterprises do not usually distinguish between factor inputs used for industrial production and those used for nonproduction use.

This bundling of industrial and nonindustrial inputs raises an obvious problem for measuring levels of total factor productivity; if the proportions change over time, it also creates a problem for measures of total factor productivity growth, as well as for levels of total factor productivity and single factor productivity. Bundling of inputs also complicates cross-ownership comparisons, since these social assets and the services they provide are most prevalent in the state sector, less prevalent in the collective sector, and all but nonexistent in the "other" sector. Most measures indicate that as a result of the neglect of housing production during the

Cultural Revolution, the rise of retained earnings, and the increase in enterprise autonomy, the proportion of nonindustrial to industrial inputs rose during the 1980s. During the 1990s the new emphasis on housing reform—in some cases involving the sale of enterprise housing—and the gradual assumption by local and provincial governments of a range of social services appears to have caused the share of nonindustrial inputs to fall. Proportions of nonproduction fixed assets in the state sector rose from 16.5 percent in 1980 to 20.0 percent in 1988, then fell to 17.8 percent in 1992, according to Jefferson, Rawski, and Zheng (1996).

The alternative to dropping nonproduction capital and labor from measures of total factor productivity is to account for the value of services produced by these inputs, thereby expanding the enterprise's gross output value.[2] In either case, inputs and output must be symmetric.

Aggregate versus sample data. Virtually all samples of China's enterprises are nonrandom and may therefore not be representative of the population of enterprises they presume to represent. Sample selection, generally administered by local officials, tends to be biased toward larger and more successful enterprises.

If enterprise performance demonstrates a tendency to revert to the mean, the choice of large and successful firms at the beginning of the sample period may bias estimates of total factor productivity growth downward. Conversely, selecting successful enterprises at the end of the sample period will yield upwardly biased estimates of total factor productivity growth, since the enterprises in the sample will tend to have performed well en route to becoming large and successful enterprises. For this reason, more credibility is assigned here to estimates of total factor productivity growth based on populations of enterprise data. Sample data are valuable for analyzing the comparative performance and behavior of enterprises in cross-sections and over time, but the overall measure of total factor productivity growth generated by them is no substitute for studies based on the population of enterprises.

Review of literature on total factor productivity

A range of studies have estimated total factor productivity growth in Chinese industry (table 6.4). These studies can be separated into three groups. The first consists of studies that focus on net output measures of total factor productivity growth, including those using aggregations of data and sample survey data. The second consists of studies of gross output total factor productivity, also at the aggregate and survey levels. The third consists of analyses of total factor productivity growth within specific industrial branches. Results of two studies by Jefferson, Rawski, and

Zheng (1992, 1996) are shown separately (table 6.5), because the data cover the longest period, 1980–92, and the studies attempted to address many of the issues raised here in an internally consistent and transparent fashion.

Conclusions about total factor productivity performance

Four conclusions emerge from the analytical studies of productivity growth within China's industrial sector during the first decade of reform:

- Productivity in China's state sector was about 2–4 percent during the period 1980–92. Including intermediate inputs, estimates of total factor productivity growth may be somewhat lower because of material deepening.
- Total factor productivity growth within the nonstate sector is about twice that of the state sector.
- Problems with the accuracy of deflators reduce the reliability of these estimates. Official estimates of real output growth in collective-owned industry may substantially overreport actual growth rates. Reported rates of growth in state industry may have been somewhat upwardly biased during the 1980s.
- Productivity growth differs widely across industries. Productivity growth is typically lowest in the extractive industries and highest in light industry, particularly in the electronics industry. As suggested earlier, some of this spread may reflect biased estimates of output associated with rapid rates of new product innovation in light industry.

Chinese industry enjoyed sustained total factor productivity growth during the reform period. Trend total factor productivity growth in state industry was somewhat higher than 2 percent during the 1980s, and it may have fallen to less than 2 percent in the early 1990s (table 6.5). This slowdown in productivity growth in state industry during 1988–92 most likely reflects the persistent weakness of China's state banking system, as well as business cycle effects and conversions (Jefferson, Rawski, and Zheng 1996).

Sources of total factor productivity growth

The preceding review demonstrates that estimates of total factor productivity are sensitive to the choice of deflators, the coverage of inputs, the nature of samples, and other factors. If total factor productivity in state industry rose during the 1980s and early 1990s, evidence of the two principal sources of productivity growth—gains in allocative efficiency, including scale economies, and technical change—should be visible. The evidence in support of these sources of productivity change is reviewed below.

TABLE 6.4
Overview of studies of total factor productivity in Chinese industry

Authors	Scope	Data
Studies of net output measures by ownership		
Chen and others (1988)	Net output of state industry	Aggregate
Beck and Bohnet (1988)	Net output of state industry	Same data as Chen and others (1988b)
Gordon and Li (1995)	Net output of state industry	Sample of 400 state enterprises
McMillan and Naughton (1992)	Net output of state industry	Sample of 769 state enterprises in four provinces
Hay, Morris, Liu, and Yao (1994)	Value added by state industry	Sample of 386 state enterprises
Studies of gross output measures		
Jefferson, Rawski, and Zheng (1992)	Gross output of state and collective industry	Aggregate (city level to estimate weights)
Prime (1992)	Gross output of state and collective industry in Jiangxu	Aggregate
Woo and others (1993)	Gross output of state and township and village enterprises	Sample of 300 large and medium-size enterprises
Sectoral studies		
Jefferson (1990)	Gross output of state iron and steel industry	Largest 110 enterprises
Hay, Morris, Liu, and Yao (1994)	Value added by state industry	Sample
Li, Gong, and Zheng (1992)	Gross output of 21 industrial branches for state and collective independent accounting units	Aggregate
Zheng (1993)	Gross output of industrial branches for state and collective independent accounting units	Aggregate

Source: Author's compilations, based on listed sources.

Change in total factor productivity	Description
1947–77: 0.8–1.4% 1978–85: 5.2–5.9%	Uses estimated weights and corrects for inflation of capital and nonproductive inputs to challenge earlier results of Lardy (1987) and Rawski (1986) showing no improvement in total factor productivity
1957–71: No change 1971–77: Decline 1978–85: 3.8% 1983–87: 4.6%	Uses a nonparametric frontier production function technique
1980–89: 3.4%	Adjusts inflation to capital for each individual enterprise
1980–85: Slight increase 1985–87: Decline	Uses gross output deflator rather than a value added deflator; deflates capital stock

State enterprises,
  1980–88: 2.4%
Collective-owned enterprises,
  1980–88: 4.6%
	Constructs deflators for capital stock and intermediate inputs; corrects for nonproductive inputs

State enterprises,
  1979–88: 4.1%
Collective-owned enterprises,
  1979–88: 6.2%
	Deflates capital stock and omits housing capital

State enterprises, 1984–88: No change Township and village enterpirses, 1984–88: Positive but not statistically significant	Directly challenges Jefferson, Rawski, and Zheng (1992), contending that their deflator for intermediate inputs is too high and overestimates total factor productivity growth
1952–57: 9.7% 1957–80: –1.6% 1980–85: 2.5%	Demonstrates the sensitivity of estimates of total factor productivity and capital's output elasticity to deflating capital, excluding nonindustrial capital, and controlling for product mix
	Shows that extractive industries show the least productivity gain, textiles, energy, chemicals, and pharmaceutical the most. Coastal enterprises exhibit higher productivity and lower costs, even after controlling for labor quality and scale.
1981–87: 2.3%	Uses Jorgenson's methods to construct estimates for motor vehicles and machinery (high growth) and natural gas, tobacco, and mining (low growth)
1980–90: 1.9%	Estimates total factor productivity growth as follows: electronics and communication 6.6%, home electronic appliances 5.7%, pharmaceuticals 7.5%, machinery other than for daily use 3.8%

TABLE 6.5

Annual rates of growth of total factor productivity (in constant price) in state and collective industry, 1980–92
(percentage)

Year	Gross output (dgv)	Net fixed assets ($a_k dnpf$)	Labor ($a_l lab$)	Intermediate inputs ($a_m dint$)	(tfp)
INITIAL CALCULATIONS					
State enterprises					
1980–92	6.90	1.38	0.33	2.69	2.50
		(6.73)	(2.73)	(3.98)	
1980–84	7.06	0.72	0.35	3.73	2.24
		(3.53)	(2.93)	(5.55)	
1984–88	7.52	1.67	0.44	2.73	3.68
		(7.13)	(3.64)	(4.05)	
1988–92	5.11	1.75	0.20	1.59	1.58
		(7.53)	(1.64)	(2.35)	
Collective-owned enterprises					
1980–92	16.08	1.36	0.37	7.19	7.15
		(10.20)	(3.19)	(9.60)	
1980–84	14.03	1.14	0.53	9.06	3.29
		(7.54)	(4.54)	(12.10)	
1984–88	19.86	1.92	0.55	7.66	7.73
		(14.36)	(4.73)	(11.55)	
1988–92	14.37	1.03	0.03	3.86	9.44
		(7.71)	(0.29)	(5.15)	
REVISED CALCULATIONS[a]					
Collective-owned enterprises					
1980–92	12.36	1.36	0.37	7.19	3.43
		(10.20)	(3.19)	(9.60)	
1980–84	13.54	1.14	0.53	9.06	2.80
		(7.54)	(4.54)	12.10)	
1984–88	15.65	1.92	0.55	7.66	4.52
		(14.36)	(4.73)	(11.55)	
1988–92	7.90	1.03	0.03	3.86	2.98
		(7.71)	(0.29)	(5.15)	

Note: Numbers in parentheses are growth rates for factor inputs. The normalized values of a_k, a_l, and a_m used in these calculations are 0.205, 0.120, and 0.675 for the state sector and 0.134, 0.117, and 0.749 for collective industry
a. The revised figures result from recalculating real output for collective industry by applying the price index for state sector industrial output used in Jefferson, Rawski, and Zheng (1996) to the official figures for nominal output of collective industry.
Source: Jefferson, Rawski, and Zheng 1992.

Gains in allocative efficiency. Gains in allocative efficiency may arise from the tendency of factor returns to equalize across firms as factor and product markets develop and become more competitive. Several studies have examined the convergence of factor returns within Chinese industry.

Gains in allocative efficiency were found in a sample of 20 state and collective-owned enterprises in Wuhan (Jefferson and Xu 1991). Using a more extensive sample, Jefferson and Xu (1992) evaluate gains in allocative efficiency among 226 large and medium-size state enterprises at the core of the state system. Their study concludes that during 1980–89 average productivities for labor, capital, and, to a lesser degree, materials showed patterns of convergence. To address the problem of heterogeneous branch technologies, Jefferson and Xu look for patterns of convergence among enterprises within the same industries, where homogeneous technologies allow average products to be suitable proxies for marginal products. They find that for both 1980–85 and 1985–89, 8 of 10 industries show a convergence of total factor productivity measured in current prices. The pattern of convergence is most notable among enterprises that operate under similar price regimes. The results (partially reproduced in table 6.6) show that convergence is most rapid and most complete among enterprises that are most exposed to market forces. Firms operating 100 percent within the plan experience the lowest convergence of total factor productivity, enterprises operating only partially within the plan demonstrate greater convergence, and those operating entirely outside the plan show the greatest convergence.

Using provincial data for rural and urban industry spanning 1986–90, Wu (1996) reports finding convergence from below of total

TABLE 6.6
Coefficients of variation for average products and total factor productivity, selected years, 1980–89

Item	Gross value of industrial output in current prices as ratio of			Total factor productivity[a]
	Wage bill	Net value of fixed assets	Intermediate inputs	
Sales 100 percent within plan (n = 74)				
1980	0.883	0.998	0.314	0.363
1985	0.832	0.904	0.307	0.332
1989	0.749	0.701	0.294	0.271
Sales partially within plan (n = 105)				
1980	0.800	1.044	0.206	0.265
1985	0.737	0.693	0.201	0.194
1989	0.662	0.574	0.217	0.153
Sales entirely outside plan (n = 44)				
1980	0.834	0.800	0.272	0.221
1985	0.506	0.614	0.206	0.144
1989	0.452	0.490	0.220	0.123

a. Calculated using variables in current prices.
Source: Jefferson and Xu 1994.

factor productivity in rural industry toward higher levels of productivity in urban industry. Estimating that by 1990 Chinese enterprises had on average achieved only 50–70 of their potential output, Wu concludes that "there is scope for further improvement in performance ... even in the absence of technical change" (p. 141).

Cao (1992) finds improvement in allocative efficiency among his sample of 99 state steel plants. Estimating a frontier production function, he finds that average technical efficiency rose from 0.46 in 1980 to 0.53 in 1987. Contributing to this improvement was a decline from a factor of 2.2 to a factor of 1.9 in the spread between the average total factor productivity level of the more efficient (large-scale) plants and the less productive (small-scale) plants.

Xiao (1990) also finds evidence of convergence. In his sample of 903 state enterprises, the total factor productivity gap between his subsets of "good" firms and "bad" firms fell during 1980–85; average total factor productivity among the "good" firms declined from 1.6 to 1.1 times that of "bad" firms by 1985.

Allocative efficiency may also arise from the realization of scale economies. Jefferson, Rawski, and Zheng (1992) estimate 1987 scale parameters of 1.03 for the state sector and 1.02 for the collective sector. These estimates are somewhat smaller than their 1984 estimates (1988). Since the average scale of state enterprises grew (in constant prices) from 4.5 million yuan of gross output in 1980 to 7.5 million yuan in 1988, increasing scale efficiencies in state industry contributed 0.36 percent annually to total factor productivity growth during this period. Using enterprise data from the coal and steel industries, Wu (1996) finds that medium-size enterprises are the most efficient, with efficiency declining at the extremities of size.

Innovation and technical change. Gains in allocative efficiency arise only where disparities in factor returns exist. In the absence of innovation that creates disparities in factor returns, gains in allocative efficiency will become exhausted. In the long run, gains in allocative efficiency require continuous innovation; in this sense, innovation and gains in allocative efficiency are, to use a Chinese aphorism, "like lips and teeth."

Using enterprise survey data, Jefferson, Rawski, and Zheng investigate the incidence of innovation and the extent to which resources for innovation are distributed efficiently between state industry and township and village enterprise industry (see chapter 4). Their sample of 254 enterprises is drawn from the three types of ownership (state enterprises, urban cooperatives, and township and village enterprises) and from three industrial branches (cotton textiles, electronic components, and machine building). In their 1990 survey they find evidence of innovative activity becoming substantially more profit oriented than in the past. They also find relatively high returns to R&D effort in all three ownership types, measured in terms of either R&D expenditure or number of technicians.

The strongest evidence in support of rising rates of technical change and profitable innovation in Chinese industry is the rising rate of export activity. Perkins (chapter 11) describes the rapid rise in exports by Chinese industry as a whole. Virtually all Chinese exports are of products that are new to Chinese industry: very few of the goods China exported in the second half of the 1990s were produced in China in the mid-1980s.

In summary, a range of studies provide consistent evidence of advances in allocative efficiency and technical change in Chinese industry. The existence of more than 7 million industrial enterprises in China (almost 25 times as many as in the United States) suggests that vast opportunities remain for substantial gains in allocative efficiency through factor reallocation and the realization of economies of scale and scope. The existence of more than 6 million small individual, private, and collective-owned industrial enterprises combined with extensive direct foreign investment along China's coast indicates the enormous potential for technical change through innovation, imitation, and factor reallocation.

Profitability

As product and factor markets increasingly reflect underlying scarcities in Chinese industry, accounting profit rates are becoming increasingly representative of economic profit and therefore more meaningful as measures of economic performance.

Profit rates
Profit performance varies across ownership types, although profit rates have declined for all ownership types since 1988 (tables 1.9 and 1.10).[3] Overseas-funded joint ventures reported the lowest profit rates, while shareholding enterprises reported the highest. Surprisingly, measured in terms of output, pretax profit rates in the state sector appear to be higher than profit rates in the collective and foreign sectors.

This aggregate measure of state enterprise profit performance masks substantial losses. State enterprises incurred losses of approximately 0.6 percent of FDP over the 1986–88 period (table 6.7). The macroeconomic stabilization program of 1988 aggravated losses, which reached nearly 2 percent of GDP in 1990. These losses fell to 1.1 percent in 1994. Since the late 1980s the share of industrial state enterprises incurring losses has increased, from just 13 percent in 1986 to more than 30 percent in 1991 (Hwa 1992). More than a third of these losses were concentrated in the coal and oil sectors.

Reasons for declining profitability

Productivity and profitability would not be expected to move together over long periods. Capturing a stylized fact of growth and capital, the neoclassical growth model predicts a stable return on capital even as total factor productivity rises. The technical change that shifts an economy's production function, outward not only raises capital's marginal product, it also increases society's savings, which are then converted into investment to take advantage of higher returns. Investment and enlargement of the capital stock cause movement along the production function, which drives the return to investment back to its "normal" level. Why, then, does industrial productivity in Chinese industry appear to have declined?

Naughton (1992) investigates the hypothesis that growing competition has eroded the state's monopoly, causing profit rates to decline in the state sector. Three findings support his hypothesis. First, the sum of remitted enterprise profits and indirect taxes, which represented 24.7 percent of GDP in 1978, fell to just 10.7 percent of GNP in 1989. Second, profits have tended to equalize across state industrial branches. In 1980 profit rates ([profit + tax]/total capital) across China's 38 industrial branches varied considerably. (The coefficient of variation of profit rates was 0.78.) During the 1980s rates of profit tended to converge

TABLE 6.7
Losses by state-owned enterprises, selected years, 1986–94
(100 million yuan)

Industry	1986	1988	1991	1994
Coal	21.8	37.0	75.1	—
Oil	—	13.1	57.0	—
Iron and steel	0.6	0.6	12.1	—
Chemical fertilizer	7.4	2.4	13.1	—
Textiles	1.7	1.3	33.7	—
Light industry	4.1	4.6	37.9	—
Tobacco	0.1	1.3	14.8	—
Total	54.4	81.9	367.0	482.0
Percentage of losses incurred in state industry	67.5	73.6	66.4	
As a percentage of GDP	0.6	0.6	1.9	1.1

— Not available.
Source: Personal communication from Hwa Ehr-Eheng to Peter Harrold, both of the World Bank, China and Mongolia Country Department (September 19, 1992); China State Statistical Bureau 1995.

across industrial branches: by 1989 the coefficient of variation of branch profit rates declined to just 0.44.

Third, and most important for explaining the secular decline in profitability, the superprofits earned in the nonstate sector after initial entry declined over time, falling from 40 percent in 1978 to about 13 percent in 1990. Naughton argues that the ability of the nonstate sector to bid away superprofits within the state sector has reduced profitability both within state industry and within the nonstate sector, where opportunities to exploit monopoly profits have diminished.

If declining profitability in the state sector has resulted from increasing competition, we would expect to observe that state-owned enterprise profitability, initially inflated by extensive barriers to entry, has fallen most rapidly in those regions and industrial branches in which the entry of nonstate producers during recent years has been most rapid. To test the competition hypothesis, we examine two sets of results, both shown in table 6.8. The first of these, reported by Singh, Ratha, and Xiao (1993), who use provincial data, supports the competition hypothesis. Their results indicate that a single percentage point rise in the share of nonstate output causes a 0.29 percentage point decline in state enterprise profitability (measured as profit plus taxes to gross fixed assets; see table 6.8).

The impact of a change in shares of industrial branch output on state enterprise profitability was estimated for the 1987–95 period. The observations are drawn from the 39-industry classification system, for which 27 observations were complete for both the early and later years. The results (table 6.8) are consistent with those of Singh, Ratha, and Xiao (1993), reported above. In those industries in which nonstate industry captured the largest share of output growth during 1987–95, state industry experienced the greatest erosion of profitability, with a 1 percent increase in the share of nonstate output associated with more than a 1 percent decline in state industry profitability. These findings strongly support the hypothesis that competition is driving down profits throughout Chinese industry. Why, then, are profits in state industry falling faster than elsewhere?

The paradox of rising productivity and falling profits in state industry

The paradox of rising productivity and falling profitability is an industrywide phenomenon in China, not a condition limited to state industry. Although productivity has risen in the collective-owned sector, profit rates have fallen there, too (Jefferson, Rawski, and Zheng 1992, 1996; Prime 1992).

Bai, Li, and Wang (1997) demonstrate that when the manager of a firm is biased toward increasing output, high productivity may induce

TABLE 6.8
Tests of the competition hypothesis

Results	Number of observations
Provincial data[a]	
$PK = 0.01 - 0.29*GNS - 0.58*SH + e$	
$\quad$ (7.42) (2.51) $\quad$ (5.4)	
Adjusted $R^2 = 0.49$	30
Industrial branch data	
$\ln(PK\_95/PK\_87) = -0.337 + 1.258*\ln(GNS\_95/GNS\_87) + e$	
$\quad\quad\quad\quad\quad$ (1.720) (3.543)	
$R^2 = 0.334$	27

Note: PK = (state-owned enterprise profit rate measure as profit + taxes/net fixed assets + average balance circulating funds), GNS = nonstate share of gross value of industrial output; SH = share of heavy industry in gross value of industrial output; PK_95 = (state enterprise profit rate measured as profit + taxes/net value of fixed assets + average balance circulating funds); PK_87 = same as PK_95 using 1987 data; GNS_95 = nonstate share of gross value of industrial output in 1995; and GNS_87 = same as GNS_95 using 1987 data.
Source: Singh, Ratha, and Xiao 1993.

the manager to deviate from the profit-maximizing level of output; if a firm's output bias is sufficiently strong, an increase in productivity can lead to lower profit and, with additional qualification, lower efficiency.

Resolving the apparent paradox may be more straightforward, and it need not rely on certain implausible parameter values, as do Bai, Li, and Wang. Although profitability has declined throughout Chinese industry, Bai, Li, and Wang limit their argument to state industry. Yet survey results reported in chapter 2 indicate that managers of state enterprises appear to be more preoccupied with financial variables than managers of township and village enterprises, who report focusing on expanding the scale and productivity of their enterprise.

A more likely explanation of the relative decline in the profitability of state industry is that its productivity, while growing, appears to be lagging behind that of the nonstate sector. From an industry perspective, while the long-run average cost curve of the representative state enterprise is shifting down over time, that of the representative nonstate enterprise is shifting down more rapidly, causing nonstate enterprises to becoming increasingly competitive over time.

In addition to positive but lagging productivity growth, in virtually all industries state enterprises are commanding a declining market share (see table 1.4). This declining market share generally reflects the rapid influx of township and village enterprises, foreign-invested enterprises, and individual and private firms. The sheer growth in the number of firms within each industry and product group erodes the residual demand faced by state enterprises. As the number of competitors increases, industrial demand becomes more price-elastic, making it increasingly difficult for state industry to sustain prices in excess of those charged by their expanding nonstate competitors. As prices fall, reflecting the comparatively rapid growth of nonstate productivity and business formation, profits in state industry decline, even as total factor productivity rises.

A further reason for declining profit rates in the state sector can be seen in patterns of capital productivity (table 6.9). Between 1980 and 1992 capital productivity first rose and then fell. From 1980 to 1984 capital productivity rose by an annual rate of 3.53 percent. During the next four-year period it remained virtually flat at 0.39 percent, while it declined at an annual rate of 3.42 percent between 1988 and 1992. Continued weaknesses in China's system of industrial finance must account not only for part of the decline in productivity growth but also for the decline in state enterprise profitability.

Profit performance among large and medium-size enterprises

Analysis of a sample of large and medium-size enterprises spanning four ownership types shows significant differences across ownership categories in rates of profit reported (table 6.10). Several regressions were run to try to explain the causes of these profit disparities. The first regression (table 6.11), incorporating only ownership dummies, confirms the profit differences shown in table 6.8. In 1988 the foreign and collective sectors were less profitable than the state sector (the reference); by 1992 the state sector had become the least profitable. What explains these differences in profit rates across ownership and over time?

Industry and regional effects appear to have played an important role. In 1988 all but one of the industrial branches demonstrates a significant industry effect, and three of the seven regional dummies show significant regional effects. If anything, however, the addition of these industry and regional effects strengthens the profit advantage of the collective-owned and foreign sectors over the state sector in 1992.

TABLE 6.9
Annual rates of growth of capital productivity for state-owned and collective-owned enterprises, 1980–92
(percent)

Years	State-owned enterprises	Collective-owned enterprises
1980–92	0.16	2.16
1980–84	3.53	4.99
1984–88	0.39	1.29
1988–92	−3.42	0.19

Source: Jefferson, Rawski, and Zheng 1996.

TABLE 6.10
Profit rates (pretax profit/revenues) for large and medium-size enterprises, by ownership type, 1988 and 1993
(percent)

Type of enterprise	1988	1993
State-owned	14.9	6.2
Collective-owned	13.9	7.4
Foreign-funded	7.1	6.4
Other	15.1	9.2

Source: China State Statistical Bureau data set.

TABLE 6.11
Profitability in large and medium-size enterprises, 1988 and 1992

Item	Regression 1 1988	Regression 1 1992	Regression 2 1988	Regression 2 1992	Regression 3 1988	Regression 3 1992
Constant	0.149 (72.697)	0.062 (22.347)	0.134 (17.594)	0.062 (7.292)	0.147 (17.422)	0.051 (5.369)
COE	−0.010 (1.415)	0.012 (1.780)	−0.001 (0.168)	0.013 (1.874)	−0.005 (0.760)	0.009 (1.247)
FOR	−0.078 (4.365)	0.003 (0.224)	−0.077 (4.359)	−0.001 (0.046)	−0.080 (4.517)	−0.007 (0.534)
OTH	0.001 (0.098)	0.030 (1.705)	0.010 (0.726)	0.031 (1.800)	0.006 (0.449)	0.028 (1.571)
TEX			−0.010 (2.165)	−0.021 (3.484)	−0.014 (3.106)	−0.024 (3.997)
CLO			−0.036 (2.108)	0.028 (1.886)	−0.033 (1.940)	0.022 (1.480)
CHE			0.052 (6.005)	0.045 (4.025)	0.048 (5.617)	0.046 (4.104)
PHA			0.043 (5.612)	0.065 (6.856)	0.035 (4.504)	0.058 (6.062)
FIB			0.018 (1.536)	0.067 (4.622)	0.012 (0.990)	0.071 (4.869)
CONS			0.114 (9.167)	0.132 (12.328)	0.116 (9.351)	0.137 (12.769)
FER			0.039 (4.330)	0.062 (5.423)	0.035 (3.908)	0.071 (3.862)
AUTO			−0.018 (2.339)	0.046 (4.240)	−0.018 (2.247)	0.036 (3.379)
BIGCITY[a]			0.034 (4.169)	0.009 (0.864)	0.031 (3.800)	0.004 (0.379)
NE[b]			−0.021 (2.486)	−0.065 (6.555)	−0.016 (1.939)	−0.059 (5.916)
NECENTRAL[c]			−0.000 (0.028)	−0.020 (1.708)	0.004 (0.368)	−0.015 (1.300)

(Table continues on next page.)

TABLE 6.11 (CONTINUED)

Profitability in large and medium-size enterprises, 1988 and 1992

Item	Regression 1 1988	Regression 1 1992	Regression 2 1988	Regression 2 1992	Regression 3 1988	Regression 3 1992
CENTRAL[d]			0.008 (0.907)	−0.010 (0.871)	0.012 (1.384)	−0.004 (0.425)
SW[e]			0.024 (2.602)	−0.042 (3.645)	0.029 (3.124)	−0.037 (3.163)
NW[f]			−0.001 (0.083)	−0.046 (3.501)	0.004 (0.400)	−0.037 (2.838)
ECOAST[g]			0.008 (1.096)	−0.004 (0.471)	0.009 (1.112)	−0.005 (0.596)
K-Q					−0.002 (2.176)	−0.006 (7.752)
PEN					−0.002 (5.828)	−0.001 (2.361)
SERV					−0.084 (5.039)	−0.037 (1.926)
Adjusted R^2	0.005	0.001	0.073	0.061	0.090	0.072
Number of observations	3,368	5,782	3,368	5,782	3,361	5,749

Note: Dependent variable = (profit plus tax)industrial sales. Each pair of columns represents a different regression specification. Regression 1 omits the industry and regional dummies, as well as the effect of capital intensity (k-Q), pension obligation (PEN), and the portion of the capital stock used in services (SER), housing, schools, and so forth. Regression 1 thus shows differences in profitability by ownership without controlling for other enterprise differences. Regression 2 controls for industry and regional differences. Regression 3 includes all of the control variables.
a. Includes Beijing, Tianjin, and Shanghai.
b. Includes Liaoning, Jilin, and Heilongjiang.
c. Includes Inner Mongolia, Hegel, Shaanxi, and Menan.
d. Includes Anhui, Jiangxi, Hubei, and Munan.
e. Includes Sichuan, Guizhou, Yunan, and Tibet.
f. Includes Xinjiang, Ninxia, Qinghai, Gansu, and Shaanxi.
g. Includes Guangdong, Guangxi, Hainan, and Fijian.
Source: Based on enterprise data from China State Statistical Bureau.

Investigation of three institutional variables—the capital–output ratio, pension obligations per employee, and the proportion of the capital stock dedicated to the provision of services—shows that all are of the expected negative sign and are statistically significant. Capital intensity, pensions, and housing and social services, all of which are most extensive in the state sector, tend to depress reported profit rates. Inclusion of these variables also weakens the effect of ownership on profitability. While the ownership dummies are statistically significant when industry branches and regional dummies are included, they become less significant when capital intensity, pension obligations, and the provision of social services are controlled for.

Conclusions

This chapter has examined the performance of various ownership forms of Chinese industrial enterprises and identified problems in research methodology that often distort efforts to measure productivity growth. Its central findings include the following:

- Productivity throughout Chinese industry rose between 1980 and 1992.
- The rate of increase in state enterprises appears to have been lower than in the collective/township and village enterprise sector, although the data in that sector are generally less complete and less accurate than for state industry.
- This acceleration of productivity is associated both with gains in allocative efficiency, even in the larger state enterprises, and an intensification of market-oriented innovative activity.
- As productivity has risen throughout Chinese industry, profitability has fallen. This apparent paradox can be explained by the relatively free entry of new firms and the decline in trade restrictions.
- Profitability has fallen most in those sectors experiencing the least productivity growth, the greatest increase in competition, and the most extensive social obligations, most notably the state sector.

This combination of rising efficiency and falling profitability is a measure of the increasingly competitive nature of Chinese industry. Firms that are not effectively restructuring are increasingly vulnerable to financial pressures; financial pressure, in turn, is motivating resource reallocation, gains in allocative efficiency, and innovative activity. State enterprises are, on average, raising productivity, but the pace of efficiency gain lags behind that in other sectors, subjecting state enterprises to falling profits and a rising incidence of chronic loss-making enterprises.

Notes

1. The structure-conduct-performance approach was developed by Edward S. Mason (1939) and his colleagues and students at Harvard University, notably Joe S. Bain (1959).

2. Jefferson and Xu (1991) adopted this approach in their survey and analysis of 20 industrial enterprises in Wuhan.

3. Some researchers, including Naughton (1992) and official statistical sources, use a ratio of profit to capital to assess profitability. Because of ambiguities over the economic meaning of reported measures of fixed assets in Chinese industry, the profit-sales ratio is used here as the measure of profitability.

References

Bai, Chong-en, David D. Li, and Yijiang Wang. 1997. "Enterprise Productivity and Efficiency: When Is Up Really Down?" *Journal of Comparative Economics* 24(3): 265–80.

Bain, Joe S. 1959. *Barriers to New Competition*. Cambridge, Mass.: Harvard University Press.

Beck, Martin, and Armin Bohnet. 1988. "Productivity Change in Chinese Industry: 1953–85: Some Further Estimations." Working paper. University of Biessen, Giessen, Germany.

Cao, Yong. 1992. "Chinese Iron and Steel Industry in Transition: Toward Market Mechanisms and Economic Efficiency." Ph.D. dissertation. Australia National University. Canberra, Australia.

Chen, Kuan, Gary H. Jefferson, Thomas G. Rawski, H.C. Wang, and Y.X. Zheng. 1988a. "New Estimates of Fixed Investment and Capital Stock for Chinese State Industry." *China Quarterly* 114: 243–66.

———. 1988b. "Productivity Change in Chinese Industry." *Journal of Comparative Economics* 12 (December): 570–91.

China State Statistical Bureau. 1988. *China Industrial Economy Statistical Yearbook (Zhongguo gongye jingji tongji nianjian)* (in Chinese). Beijing: China Statistical Publications Office.

———. 1993. *China Labor Statistics Yearbook (Zhongguo laodong tongji nianjian)* (in Chinese). Beijing: China Statistical Publications Office.

———. Various years. *China Statistical Yearbook (Zhongguo tongji nianjian)* (in Chinese). Beijing: China Statistical Publications Office.

Field, Robert Michael. 1992. "China's Industrial Performance Since 1978." *China Quarterly* 131: 577–607.

Gordon, Roger, and Wei Li. 1995. "The Change in Productivity of Chinese State Enterprises, 1983–87." *Journal of Productivity Analysis* 6(1): 5–26.

Grossman, Gene M., and Elhanan Helpman. 1991. "Quality Ladders and Product Cycles." *Quarterly Journal of Economics* 106:557–86.

Hay, Donald, Derek Morris, Guy Liu, and Shujie Yao. 1994. *Economic Reform and State-Owned Enterprises in China, 1979–87*. Oxford, U.K.: Clarendon Press.

Hwa, Erh-Cheng. 1992. "Enterprise Reform in China." Background paper prepared for the World Bank, China and Mongolia Department, Washington, D.C.

Jefferson, Gary H. 1990. "China's Iron and Steel Industry: Sources of Enterprise Efficiency and the Impact of Reform." *Journal of Development Economics* 33: 329–55.

———. 1992. "Growth and Productivity Change in Chinese Industry: Problems of Measurement." In M.J. Dutta, ed., *Asian Economic Regimes: An Adaptive Innovation Paradigm*. Research in Asian Economic Studies. Greenwich, Conn.: JAI Press.

Jefferson, Gary H., and Wenyi Y. Xu. 1991. "The Impact of Reform on Socialist Enterprises in Transition: Structure, Conduct and Performance in Chinese Industry." *Journal of Comparative Economics* 15: 45–64.

———. 1994. "Assessing Gains in Efficient Production among China's Industrial Enterprises." *Economic Development and Cultural Change* 42(3): 597–616.

Jefferson, Gary H., Thomas G. Rawski, and Zheng Yuxin. 1992. "Growth, Efficiency, and Convergence in China's State and Collective Industry." *Economic Development and Cultural Change* 40(2): 239–66.

———. 1996. "Chinese Industrial Productivity: Trends, Measurement Issues, and Recent Developments." *Journal of Comparative Economics* 23(2): 146–80.

Jorgenson, Dale W. 1995. *International Comparisons of Economic Growth*. Cambridge, Mass.: MIT Press.

Lardy, Nicholas R. 1987. "Technical Change and Economic Reform in China: A Tale of Two Sectors." Unpublished manuscript. Yale University, New Haven Ct.

Li, Jingwen, Gong Feihong, and Zheng Yisheng. 1992. "Productivity and China's Economic Growth, 1953–1990." Paper presented at the conference on productivity, efficiency, and reform in China, August 3–6, Chinese University of Hong Kong.

Mason, Edward S. 1939. "Price and Product Policies of Large-Scale Enterprise." *American Economic Review* 29:61–74.

McMillan, John, and Barry Naughton. 1992. "How to Reform a Planned Economy: Lessons from China." *Oxford Review of Economic Policy* 18(1): 130–43.

Naughton, Barry. 1991. "Prices of Machinery Used for Industrial Investment." University of California at San Diego.

———. 1992. "Implications of the State Monopoly over Industry and its Relaxation." *Modern China* 18 (January): 14–41.

Prime, Penelope. 1992. "Industry's Response to Market Liberalization in China: Evidence from Jiangsu Province." *Economic Development and Cultural Change* 41(1): 27–50.

Rawski, Thomas G. 1986. "Productivity Change in Chinese Industry: Problems of Measurement." Unpublished manuscript. University of Pittsburgh.

———. 1991. *How Fast Has Chinese Industry Grown?* Research Paper Series 7, World Bank, Country Economics Department, Socialist Economies Reform Unit, Washington, D.C.

Sachs, Jeffrey, and Woo, Wing Thye. 1994. "Structural Reforms in the Economic Reforms of China, Eastern Europe, and the Former Soviet Union." *Economic Policy* 18:101–45.

Singh, Inderjit, Dilip Ratha, and Geng Xiao. 1993. *Non-State Enterprises as an Engine of Growth: An Analysis of Provincial Industrial Growth in Post-Reform China.* World Bank Research Paper Series, China CH-RPS#20, Washington, D.C.

Woo, Wing Thye, Gang Fan, Wen Hai, and Yibiao Jin. 1993. "The Efficiency and Macroeconomic Consequences of Chinese Enterprise Reform." *China Economic Review* 4(2):153–68.

World Bank. 1995. *Bureaucrats in Business: The Economics and Politics of Government Ownership.* New York: Oxford University Press.

Wu, Yanrui. 1996. *Productivity Performance in Chinese Enterprises: An Empirical Study.* New York: St. Martin's Press.

Xiao, Geng. 1990. *The Impact of Property Rights Structure on Productivity, Capital Allocation and Labor Income in Chinese State and Collective Enterprises,* Research Paper Series 24. World Bank, Socialist Economies Reform Unit, Washington, D.C.

Zheng, Yuxin. 1993. "Change in Productivity of China's Manufacturing Sector and Its Sources in the 1980s." In Zheng Yuxin and Thomas G. Rawski, eds., *Productivity and Reform in Chinese Industry.* Beijing: Social Science Literature Press.

Zou, Gang. 1992. "Enterprise Behavior Under the Two-Tier Plan/Market System." Unpublished manuscript, University of Southern California, Los Angeles.

Are China's Rural Enterprises Outperforming State Enterprises? Estimating the Pure Ownership Effect

7

Gary H. Jefferson

One of the most striking results of economic reform in China has been the relative increase in productivity by the country's township and village enterprises. Total factor productivity by the collective sector, which included township and village enterprises, rose at an estimated annual average rate of 3.43 percent between 1980 and 1992, approximately 40 percent higher than the 2.50 percent rate of productivity growth in the state sector (table 7.1). Although productivity grew more rapidly in the collective sector than in the state sector, however, it is not clear that the level of productivity was higher in the sector by the end of the decade.

The causes of the higher productivity growth by township and village enterprises remains unclear. One hypothesis, the catch–up hypothesis, posits that rapid productivity gains in the sector reflect the low base from which it began relative to the state sector. According to this view, average productivity growth by township and village enterprises will slow as the sector approaches the productivity envelope defined by the state sector.

A second hypothesis, the overtaking hypothesis, suggests that the differences in productivity reflect pure differences in ownership or other

TABLE 7.1
Annual growth of productivity by state-owned and collective-owned enterprises, 1980–92
(percent)

Period	State-owned enterprises	Collective-owned enterprises
1980–92	2.00	3.43
1980–84	2.24	2.80
1984–88	3.68	4.52
1988–92	1.58	2.98

Source: Jefferson, Rawski, and Zheng 1996.

153

factors, such as enterprise-specific characteristics or policy differences. Pure ownership differences include production scale effects or effects of different levels of social service provision by enterprises.[1] Policy differences include the level of government to which the firm is subordinate, the extent to which the enterprise can self-market goods, the kind of management systems and contractors used, and related incentives, such as the presence or absence of collateral provided by the contractor. In principle, to the extent that performance differences reflect policy, one or more levels of government can modify these policies to create more equal conditions between the state and nonstate sectors. To the extent that performance differences reflect enterprise-specific differences, policy changes alone will not be sufficient to close the productivity gap; scale and social service functions will have to be examined to explain productivity differences. If controlling for policy and enterprise-specific conditions leaves significant unexplained productivity differences, pure ownership differences may be assumed to be critical, suggesting that ownership reform belongs at the center of the ref orm agenda. The fact that during the 1980s and early 1990s the Chinese government chose to concentrate on reforming enterprise management systems rather than ownership reform makes investigation of the nature of these differences in productivity particularly important.

Are township and village enterprises catching up or surpassing state enterprises in their levels of technical efficiency? Do differences in efficiency reflect differences in policy or conditions embodied in ownership? Whatever the relative levels of efficiency, can policy reforms improve the performance of state-owned and township and village enterprises? To answer these questions, this chapter uses two sets of panel data drawn from the World Bank Enterprise Surveys (World Bank 1992; table 7.2). One data

TABLE 7.2
Number of state and collective-owned enterprises in sample, by industry branch

Industry	State-owned enterprises	Township and village enterprises
Coal (81)	39	15
Apparel (241)	25	23
Papermaking (282)	37	9
Daily-use chemicals (377)	34	23
Cement (451)	37	25
Daily-use metal products (519)	24	22
Home appliances (586)	8	15
Total	204	132

Note: Numbers in parentheses are Standard Industrial Codes.
Source: World Bank 1992 (Enterprise Surveys).

set consists of 204 state enterprises, the other consists of 132 township and village enterprises. Both data sets are distributed over seven three-digit industrial branches and cover 1984, 1988, and 1990.[2] Differences in policy and enterprise-specific variables by ownership are examined (table 7.3).

Differences in ownership

Popular accounts of Chinese industry often mistakenly assume that rural industry is predominantly privately owned. In fact, most of China's rural

TABLE 7.3

Differences between state-owned and township and village enterprises, 1991

Characteristic	State-owned enterprises	Township and village enterprises
Size of enterprise (percentage of total)		
Large	15.7	0
Medium	30.9	0
Small	53.4	100
Average annual sales (billion yuan)	40.02	3.91
Nonindustrial fixed assets	0.21	0.07
Supervision (percentage of total)		
Central	22.1	0
Province	33.8	0
City	44.1	0
District (county)	0	12.7
Township	0	77.6
Village	0	9.0
No subordination	0	6.7
Other	0	3.0
Self-market (percentage of total)	48.0	100.0
Management system (percentage of total)		
Lease	0.4	3.3
Contract	82.6	54.3
Capital	7.3	0
Share	1.5	0
Other	8.1	42.4
Signatory to contract (percentage of total)		
Director	60.7	21.6
Group	27.3	65.7
All employees	11.5	7.8
Other	0.6	4.9
Collateral requirement (percentage of total)		
No	44.2	53.3
Yes	55.8	46.7

Source: World Bank 1992 (Enterprise Surveys).

industry is publicly owned by local township and village governments. Within the township and village enterprise sample analyzed here, the average date of establishment was 1976. At that time rural enterprises were typically part of the widespread system of people's communes (*gongshe*). Following the dissolution of the communes in the late 1970s and early 1980s, ownership of these enterprises was transferred to newly established units of local township and village government.

Township and village enterprises are often assumed to perform more efficiently than their state enterprise counterparts. Three reasons are commonly cited.

Greater autonomy

State enterprises typically produce and sell some output within their plans, whereas township and village enterprises do not. All township and village enterprises in the sample self-market all of their sales; fewer than half of state owned enterprises fully self-market (table 7.3). This and other evidence indicates that township and village enterprises enjoy greater production autonomy and market exposure than do state enterprises, thereby exposing them to greater market competition and discipline. The pattern of greater autonomy among township and village enterprises is also confirmed by the results of the World Bank Enterprise Survey (see figure 5.1).

Harder budget constraints

Local township and village governments operate under harder budget constraints than does the central government. Unlike the state government, local governments cannot print money to finance the deficits of the enterprises they own. Moreover, community governments cannot directly engage in deficit financing. Hence enterprises supervised at lower levels of government are likely to face harder budget constraints and therefore to be more efficient.

Cooperative culture

Byrd and Lin (1990, p. 4) suggest that "the most important characteristic of China's rural communities has been their stable population." This characteristic and the relatively small scale of township, village, and rural enterprises have prompted Weitzman and Xu (1994, p.16) to argue that township and village enterprises embody a kind of "cooperative culture" within which members "resolve prisoner's dilemma–type free-riding problems internally, without the imposition of explicit legalistic rules of behavior." This cooperative culture permits enterprises to operate as if there were well-defined property rights. In contrast, state enterprises are owned by "all the people" *(quanmin)* of China, which means that no one is assigned central authority or has the incentive to monitor enterprise performance. Jefferson, Lu, and Zhao suggest that, in combination with a soft budget constraint, the absence of effective monitoring causes the state enterprise—and to a lesser extent, the township and village enterprise—to exhibit the qualities of a quasi-public good (see chapter 5).

These conditions suggest that China's township and village enterprises might be more efficient than state enterprises. Some evidence suggests that the opposite is true, however. In their survey of the innovative capacity of industrial enterprises under different types of ownership, Jefferson, Rawski, and Zheng (1992) found no significant differences between state enterprises and township and village enterprises in terms of the importance of the profit motive; if anything, township and village enterprises appeared to focus more on expanding their scale and sales than on increasing profits. Moreover, in 1991 it was state enterprises, not township and village enterprises, that typically operated at the frontier of new product development. Asked about the ownership type of the frontier innovators within their product line, more than 90 percent of all state enterprises and township and village enterprises indicated that state enterprises are more innovative. New products of state enterprises also commanded the highest initial profit rates. In short, even if incentives and autonomy are weaker in state enterprises than in township and village enterprises in China, the concentration of resources for innovation (technicians and R&D spending) in these enterprises may be enabling many, if not most, state enterprises to maintain a technological edge over their rural industrial counterparts.

The model

This analysis uses a two-step procedure for investigating the impact of policy, firm-specific, and ownership differences on total factor productivity. The first step consists of using a fixed-effects procedure to estimate a production function in order to obtain the relevant output elasticities required to construct measures of total factor productivity. Output elasticities are used as weights to construct estimates of total factor productivity, and estimates of the determinants of total factor productivity are modeled using the relevant policy, enterprise-specific, and ownership variables.

To estimate the output elasticities for capital and labor, the following production function is used:

(7.1) $\ln Q_{jt} = A_o + \Sigma A_j + \Sigma A_t + \gamma_{tve} + \Sigma_i \alpha_i \ln X_{ijt} + \varepsilon_{jt}$

where α_K and α_L may exhibit increasing, constant, or decreasing returns to scale; t covers the years 1984, 1988, and 1990; Q represents value added measured in constant prices; and the i in X_{ijt} includes K, the net value of fixed assets, and L, the end-of-year total employment. The dummy variable, γ_{tve}, captures the average productivity differential between township and village enterprises and state enterprises during the sample period.[3] A_o is a constant, and A_j is a fixed effect for each individual enterprise that remains constant over time. These enterprise-specific characteristics include the usual considerations of uneven techniques and managerial capabilities relative to other state enterprises or township and village enterprises. In the context of China, the fixed effect may also capture differences in pricing regimes, the production of nonindustrial outputs (employee housing and social services), problems with systematic measurement error, and other factors. A_t represents period effects that capture industrywide change in productivity and other time-specific factors.

Converting equation 7.1 into the intensive form yields:

$$(7.2) \qquad \ln(Q/L)_{jt} = A_o + \Sigma A_j + \Sigma A_t + \gamma_{tve} + a_K \ln(K/L)_{jt} + \beta \ln Q_{jt} + \varepsilon_{jt}$$

where the term in Q arises as a result of constraining $a_K + a_L = 1$ so that the parameter β captures the scale effect. The parameter a_K is the weight used to assess capital's contribution to output growth; $1 - a_K$ is labor's weight.

The estimator

Two different estimators can be used to estimate equation 7.2, a frontier production function estimator and a fixed-effects estimator. In principle, a frontier estimator is preferable because it identifies the shape of the relevant technology frontier, not just its position. As Schmidt, Lovell, and Knox (1979, p. 343) point out, "If the [production frontier] is a neutrally scaled transform of the [fitted average function], then the shape, but not the placement, of the frontier can be inferred from the fitted average function. But if the former is not a neutrally scaled transform of the latter, then virtually nothing can be learned about the frontier from estimation of the 'average' function."

Given the occasionally large errors associated with measuring Chinese enterprise data, results from a frontier estimator may incorrectly suggest that the fitted frontier is not a rescale of the "average" function; large and possibly systematic measurement errors may distort the shape and position of the fitted frontier. Because this analysis focuses on average and individual levels of total factor productivity, not the distribution of technical efficiency revealed by a frontier estimator, a frontier estimator is not used here.

The fixed-effects estimator allows fixed differences among individual enterprises to be captured. The wide range of potential individual effects, including systematic measurement error, in the data make the fixed-effects estimator preferable to both the frontier estimator and the standard least-squares estimator.

The estimation results show that estimates of the capital coefficient based on the pooled data and the branch data are positive (table 7.4). Only in the papermaking industry is the estimate not statistically significant at the 95 percent level. In all but one case (coal), significant economies of scale (GVIO) are exhibited. The pooled data show a significant increase in the 1988 efficiency dummy over 1984 and no significant change from 1988 to 1990. These estimates on the time dummies are difficult to interpret. While they capture technical change, they also capture time-dependent changes in relative input and output prices, measurement error, and other systematic changes that may have a time-dependent component. Nonetheless, the economic retrenchment from 1989–91 is likely to account for some of the apparent stagnation in efficiency during 1988–90. In the pooled data and in data in each of the branch industries, the township and village enterprise dummy is positive and significant.

Total factor productivity estimates

The factor weights for capital shown in table 7.4, the imputed weights for labor $(1 - a_K)$, and the standard Solow accounting equation are used to evaluate the levels of total factor productivity to compute a total factor productivity index for each type of enterprise in 1984 and 1990:

$$(7.3) \qquad \text{TFP}_{jt} = \exp(\ln Q_{jt} - \Sigma a_i \ln X_{ijt})$$

where output is measured as value added in current prices (in contrast to the constant price measure used to estimate the production function in equation 7.2).

Within the pooled sample, total factor productivity was higher in the township and village enterprise sector than in the state sector in 1984 (table 7.5). Although the relatively small number of observations available for the township and village enterprise sector in 1984 limits the usefulness of branch-level comparisons, the data show that township and village enterprise sector productivity was higher in five of the six branches for which results are available. By 1990 a large disparity in productivity emerges, with total factor productivity in the township and village enterprise sector rising well above total factor productivity in the state sector. Across all seven industrial branches, the productivity of township and village enterprises in 1990 was equal to or higher than that of state enterprises.

Notwithstanding the scale advantages of the comparatively large state enterprises, the pooled raw total factor productivity data support the overtaking hypothesis. Starting from a lower level in the 1970s, total factor productivity within the township and village enterprise sector exceeded total factor productivity in the state sector by 1990 (see table 7.5). The source(s) of the productivity advantage of the township and village enterprise sector is not revealed by these data, however.

Sources of differences in enterprise performance

Total factor productivity is assumed to be generated through the following process:

(7.4) $$\ln TFP_{jt} = a + \partial \mathbf{Z}_{jt} + \mu_{jt}$$

where $\mathbf{Z}$ is a vector of policy, enterprise-specific, and ownership variables that affect the firm's productivity.

Policy variables. Policy variables represent conditions that could be changed in the short term by administrative edict. They include the level

TABLE 7.4
Estimation results, by industry

Item	Pooled data	Coal	Apparel	Papermaking
Constant	−3.00	−1.68	−2.51	−3.35
	(14.95)	(5.24)	(5.19)	(6.43)
1988	0.33	0.02	0.39	0.43
	(4.22)	(0.28)	(1.76)	(2.80)
1990	0.29	−0.08	0.24	0.23
	(3.63)	(0.56)	(1.05)	(1.46)
Township and village enterprise dummy	2.28	1.15	1.97	1.65
	(11.68)	(3.95)	(4.66)	(3.23)
a_K	0.29	0.43	0.26	0.13
	(8.96)	(5.38)	(3.24)	(1.13)
GVIO	0.27	0.03	0.27	0.31
	(10.10)	(0.77)	(4.36)	(4.51)
R^2	0.58	0.85	0.59	0.72
D-W				

Note: GVIO is economics of scale. Numbers in parentheses are t-statistics.
Source: Based on data from World Bank 1992 (Enterprise Surveys).

of supervising the share of outside-plan sales, the type of management system used, the signatory to contracts, and the need to commit collateral to guarantee performance (see table 7.3).

Data on the type of management system in force within the enterprise sample suggest no dramatic differences by type of ownership. Although state enterprises exhibit a broader variety of management systems—notably, the share system and the capital responsibility systems—the majority of both types of enterprise management operate under the basic contract system (*chengbao*).

Directors of state enterprises typically contract for the enterprise, whereas a group of employees typically contracts for township and village enterprises. Within the sample a majority of the contractors within state enterprises put up collateral, while most of their township and village enterprise counterparts do not.

Enterprise-specific variables. Enterprise-specific factors are variables that cannot be modified by policy in the short term. They include scale effects and use of nonproduction inputs to support a range of social services. If scale effects (measured as the log of the gross value of industrial output in current prices) are significant, then, other things equal, smaller firms will reveal lower levels of total factor productivity than larger firms. The scale variable shows

Daily-use chemicals	Cement	Daily-use metal products	Home appliances
-3.56 (6.09)	-4.21 (11.63)	-1.71 (3.06)	-3.17 (4.53)
-0.03 (0.14)	0.55 (3.46)	0.11 (0.70)	-0.09 (0.31)
0.03 (0.17)	0.27 (1.68)	0.21 (1.30)	0.03 (0.10)
3.71 (6.33)	2.92 (7.95)	1.50 (2.75)	3.83 (5.55)
0.24 (3.70)	0.71 (10.62)	0.53 (7.730)	0.53 (3.60)
0.43 (6.71)	0.37 (7.20)	0.16 (2.04)	0.40 (4.12)
0.37	0.80	0.77	0.59
1.46	1.52	1.67	1.57

that all of the township and village enterprises are designated as "small scale," whereas nearly half of the state enterprises are "large" or "medium scale."

Provision of social services will reduce measured total factor productivity, since capital and labor inputs are used to produce services that do not appear in output. The variable "house" is the proportion of fixed assets used for purposes other than industrial production. The "house" variable shows that state enterprises dedicate a substantial portion of their capital stock to nonindustrial investment. Township and village enterprises reserve a smaller, but still significant, portion of their capital stock for nonindustrial activities.

Ownership. A sharp dichotomy in the level of subordination exists between state enterprises and township and village enterprises. Whereas all state enterprises are managed at or above the county level, by definition all

TABLE 7.5

Mean total factor productivity in state-owned and township and village enterprises, 1984 and 1990
(value added in current prices)

	1984	
Item	State-owned enterprises	Township and village enterprises
Pooled data		
Total factor productivity	0.52	0.65
Number of observations	193	40
Coal		
Total factor productivity	0.30	0.93
Number of observations	35	14
Apparel		
Total factor productivity	0.60	0.54
Number of observations	23	4
Papermaking		
Total factor productivity	0.44	1.19
Number of observations	36	8
Daily-use chemicals		
Total factor productivity	0.77	—
Number of observations	34	0
Cement		
Total factor productivity	0.23	0.78
Number of observations	35	6
Daily-use metal products		
Total factor productivity	0.55	0.92
Number of observations	23	4
Home appliances		
Total factor productivity	0.45	2.79
Number of observations	7	4

— Not available.
Source: Based on data from World Bank 1992 (Enterprise Surveys).

township and village enterprises are managed at lower levels of government. Within the sample the majority of state enterprises are managed at the municipal level, and the vast majority of township and village enterprises are owned by townships. In principle, ownership and the level of subordination are distinguishable. The level of subordination is treated as a policy variable.

Estimation results

The total factor productivity data based on enterprise performance measures in 1990 and the institutional and policy data reported in the management questionnaire administered in 1991 are used to estimate equation 7.4 (table 7.6).

1990		Annual growth 1984–90 (percent)	
State-owned enterprises	Township and village enterprises	State-owned enterprises	Township and village enterprises
1.15	1.50	14.0	17.1
199	124		
0.50	1.37	8.4	6.5
39	15		
1.13	1.83	10.6	20.4
23	19		
1.00	1.00	13.8	27.6
36	8		
1.83	3.23	14.4	—
34	22		
0.93	1.11	17.9	5.9
36	24		
1.31	2.08	14.4	13.6
23	21		
1.34	2.50	18.2	−1.1
8	15		

TABLE 7.6
Determinants of differentials in total factor productivity, 1990

	Regression					
Item	1	2	3	4	5	6
Ownership (township and village enterprise)	0.24 (2.14)*	1.02 (8.20)*	0.84 (3.90)*		0.90 (5.19)*	0.77 (2.81)*
Scale		0.33 (10.21)*	0.35 (9.65)*	0.20 (9.28)*	0.31 (7.39)*	0.33 (6.98)*
House			0.04 (0.12)			−0.34 (0.65)
Subordination			0.08 (1.17)			0.09 (1.00)
Self-marketing		−0.13 (0.93)	0.32 (3.49)*			−0.12 (−.68)
Management system						0.39 (2.28)*
Contract system					0.69 (1.28)	
Lease system					1.22 (1.440)	
Share system					1.83 (1.70)**	
Other					1.09 (1.82)**	
Contractor						0.13 (1.48)
Director					0.05 (0.38)	
All employees					0.23 (1.27)	
Collateral requirement					0.23 (1.67)**	1.24
(1.78)**						
Adjusted R^2	0.13	0.35	0.35	0.23	0.32	0.33

* Significant at the 5 percent level.
** Significant at the 10 percent level.
Note: Constant and individual branch dummies are not reported. The constant represents the capital management responsibility system, group contracting, and no collateral. Numbers in parentheses represent t-statistics.
Source: Based on data from World Bank 1992 (Enterprise Surveys).

Pooled data

The results based on pooled data indicate the relatively high level of total factor productivity within the township and village enterprise sector. Addition of scale alone creates the largest productivity disparity in the ownership variable. These results demonstrate the presence of substantial economies of scale; by realizing these economies township and village enterprises would operate at considerably higher levels of efficiency.

The "house" variable is not statistically significant. As a simple accounting matter, dedication of measured inputs to nonindustrial activities should depress measured productivity. It may be that controlling for ownership and scale, more successful enterprises dedicate more of their investment to in-kind services for their work force. The use of nonindustrial capital as a proxy for the diversion of resources to social services is also fraught with measurement error, given that labor, which is also included in the standard measure of the work force, is also used in the provision of child care, education, health, and other services. The combination of the simultaneous relationship between total factor productivity and nonindustrial capital and serious mismeasurement would bias the estimate of the coefficient toward zero, thus underestimating the negative impact of housing expenditure on enterprise productivity.

Among the policy variables, the subordination variable, although not highly statistically significant, suggests that the decentralized supervision of state enterprises further enhances their productivity. In regressions 3 and 6 self-marketing does not show the expected impact, but regression 4 suggests that these weak results may be a result of multicollinearity with the ownership and subordination variables, making it difficult to disentangle the impact of self-marketing from ownership and subordination. This ambiguous result suggests that it may be difficult to establish categorical distinctions between ownership and other characteristics, such as the level of subordination, the degree of self-marketing, or the provision of social services. Given that over the past three decades these variables have been altered at the policy or enterprise level, they are assumed to be modifiable without changing the basic ownership classification.

Regression 5 allows the impact of individual management systems, the choice of contractor, and the practice of guaranteeing collateral on performance to be analyzed. The results for the management systems are reported in ascending order of the magnitude of their point estimates. At the 10 percent significance level, the share and "other" systems are associated more closely with high total factor productivity performance than is the standard capital responsibility system embodied in the regression's (unreported) constant.

Although these results suggest that the capital responsibility system is the least effective management system, it may or may not be intrinsically less effective than the others. By specifying investment and product innovation targets, the capital responsibility system attempts to compensate for the short-term horizon implicit in the standard three-year management contract. Although these quantitative targets tend to distort resource allocation, it may be that such provisions are waived only for the more successful managers and enterprises.

In regression 5 the contractor variables show weak evidence that enterprises in which all employees are party to the contract are more productive than those in which a management group holds the contracts. The results show stronger support for the proposition that the guarantee of collateral enhances performance.

In regression 6 the management system and contractor variables are consolidated on the basis of their empirical rankings in regression 5, and are then combined with the full list of institutional and policy variables. The point estimate township and village enterprise dummy (0.77) indicates that controlling for these variables increases the relative

TABLE 7.7
Determinants of differentials in total factor productivity, by industry, 1990

Item	Coal	Apparel	Papermaking
Own	1.02	−0.10	−0.26
	(4.97)*	(0.32)	(0.78)
Adjusted R^2	0.31	−0.02	−0.01
Own	1.50	−1.74	1.58
	(3.37)*	(1.82)**	(2.24)*
Scale	0.09	0.56	0.64
	(0.79)	(5.61)*	(5.91)*
House	−0.54	−4.40	0.99
	(0.64)	(4.16)*	(0.66)
Subordination	−0.11	0.17	0.06
	(0.52)	(1.14)	(0.41)
Self-marketing	−0.02	1.19	0.17
	(0.09)	(1.60)	(0.52)
Marketing system	1.00	0.67	1.88
	(1.79)**	(1.81)**	(2.52)*
Contractor	0.52	−0.46	−0.12
	(3.20)*	(2.14)*	(0.49)
Collateral requirement	0.72	0.23	0.56
	(2.67)*	(0.69)	(1.89)**
Adjusted R^2	0.56	0.53	0.58

* Significant at the 5 percent level.
** Significant at the 10 percent level.
Note: Numbers in parentheses are t-statistics.
Source: Based on data from World Bank 1992 (Enterprise Surveys).

efficiency of the township and village enterprise sector relative to regression 1, in which no controls are imposed. But comparison of regressions 2 and 6 demonstrates that the variable most responsible for this result is scale. Adding the other control variables weakens the demonstrated performance advantage of the township and village enterprise sector.

Industrial branch data

Analyzing each industry individually allows for relaxing the assumptions that technology is uniform across industries and that the impacts of policy, enterprise, and ownership differences are uniform across industries. Because of space limitations, only regressions 1 and 6 are presented here (table 7.7).

Daily-use chemicals	Cement	Daily-use metal products	Home appliances
0.35	0.18	0.31	0.81
(1.27)	(0.70)	(1.56)	(2.61)*
0.01	0.01	0.06	0.24
	−0.01	0.03	0.21
0.54	0.36	−0.37	−0.48
(0.70)	(0.57)	(0.53)	(0.20)
0.38	0.52	0.33	0.00
(3.21)*	(3.86)*	(2.91)*	(0.02)
−1.90	1.74	−1.81	3.36
(1.51)	(1.09)	(1.40)	(1.24)
0.20	0.22	0.38	0.14
(0.88)	(1.30)	(1.38)	(0.29)
−0.88	−0.19	0.40	3.38
(1.74)**	(0.44)	(0.92)	(1.46)
0.41	−0.15	0.17	0.00
(1.45)	(0.29)	(0.92)	(0.00)
−0.10	−0.04	0.06	1.01
(0.52)	(0.21)	(0.32)	(1.40)
−0.43	0.12	0.65	−0.76
(1.38)	(0.39)	(0.30)	(1.23)
0.25	0.46	0.40	0.75
	0.32	0.21	0.41

Analysis of the determinants of productivity differentials at the industry level provides a somewhat richer picture of productivity comparisons between state-owned and township and village enterprises than do the pooled data. Branch-level estimates for the basic regression that incorporates only the township and village enterprise ownership dummy reveal substantially more variation than suggested by regression 1 using the pooled data. Among the seven industries only coal and home appliances reveal a more efficient township and village enterprise sector. Among the other five industries three of the point estimates of the township and village enterprise ownership variable are positive and two are negative, but none of these five is statistically significant at even the 10 percent level.

When the control variables are incorporated, substantial variation in the pure ownership effect persists. Only township and village enterprises within the coal industry maintain their productivity advantage. The advantage of home appliance township and village enterprises vanishes, but productivity advantage in papermaking becomes apparent. Within the apparel sector, state industry productivity exceeds that of the township and village enterprises at the 10 percent significance level.

Coefficient estimates for all of the individual control variables have the expected sign in a majority of the branches. For only two of the control variables, however—scale and management system—are the estimates significant at the 10 percent level or better in three or more of the branches.

Conclusions

Virtually all productivity studies of state-owned and township and village enterprises (or collective-owned enterprises) during the 1980s and 1990s conclude that the growth of productivity in the rural collective sector has outpaced that of state industry. These studies have not, however, attempted to compare levels of productivity between state and rural collective industry. Moreover, they have not attempted to control for various conditions that are likely to bias comparisons of unadjusted productivity data. Controlling for various policy variables, including the level of supervision, marketization, management system, contractors, and the commitment of collateral, and enterprise-specific conditions, including scale and nonindustrial inputs, allows for a more accurate calibration of the pure ownership effect of state and collective ownership. The principal results of this analysis include the following:

- Not controlling for the above conditions, productivity in all but one of the seven industrial branches was higher in the town and village sector than in the state sector.

- Disaggregated analysis at the industry-branch level indicates that, controlling for policy and enterprise-specific factors, in 1990 neither ownership type performed at an unambiguously higher level of productivity.
- In coal and papermaking, township and village enterprises outperformed their state counterparts; in the apparel sector, state enterprises outperformed their town and village counterparts. Ranked in terms of relative statistical importance, factors that explain differences in productivity across enterprises are scale, management system, collateral requirement, choice of contractor, level of subordination, and share of nonindustrial inputs. In the most inclusive of the regressions, all except the degree of self-marketization yield the predicted sign.

Some important considerations fall outside the scope of this study. One of these is quality comparisons. Although the state-owned and township and village enterprises in the sample are in the same industries, product mix and product quality differ considerably within each three-digit sector (see chapter 4). Moreover, quality advantages that are typically found in the state sector may not be reflected in measures of productivity based on current prices. In both the textile and apparel industries, for example, export prices are often lower than domestic prices. Nevertheless, enterprises often choose to export at discounted prices because they receive payment on delivery; domestic customers often withhold payment. Future studies on this subject should attempt to control for systematic differences in product quality, although these differences are likely to become narrow and to be increasingly reflected in price differences.

Notes

1. State enterprises provide significant social services, including housing, medical services, and education.
2. The industries included coal, apparel, papermaking, chemicals, cement, metal products, and home appliances.
3. The township and village enterprise dummy variable is created after the data are differenced to eliminate the fixed effects. Within the differenced data set, a series of ones is created for the township and village enterprises.

References

Byrd, William A., and Qingsong Lin. 1990. "China's Rural Industry: An Introduction." In William A. Byrd and Lin Qingsong, eds., *China's Rural Industry: Structure, Development, and Reform.* New York: Oxford University Press.

Jefferson, Gary H., and Wenyi Xu. 1991. "The Impact of Reform on Socialist Enterprises in Transition: Structure, Conduct and Performance in Chinese Industry." *Journal of Comparative Economics* 15(March): 45–64.

Jefferson, Gary H., Thomas G. Rawski, and Yuxin Zheng. 1992. "Growth, Efficiency, and Convergence in China's State and Collective Industry." *Economic Development and Cultural Change* 40(2): 239–66.

———. 1996, "Chinese Industrial Productivity: Trends, Issues and Recent Developments." *Journal of Comparative Economics* 23(2): 146–80.

Schmidt, Peter, C. Lovell, and A. Knox. 1979. "Estimating Technical and Allocative Inefficiency Relative to Stochastic Production and Cost Functions." *Journal of Econometrics* 9: 343–66.

Weitzman, Martin L., and Chenggang Xu. 1994. "Chinese Township and Village Enterprises as Vaguely Defined Cooperatives." *Journal of Comparative Economics* 18(2) 121–45.

World Bank. 1992. "Enterprise Surveys." China and Mongolia Department and the Socialist Economies Unit. Washington, D.C.

Wage and Employment Behavior in Chinese Industry

8

Gary H. Jefferson, Inderjit Singh, Albert G. Z. Hu,
and Wang Benzhou

Profitable enterprises must hire an efficient mix of labor services and deliver a package of compensation and incentives that sustains high levels of productivity while leaving sufficient residual surplus to allow the firm to invest in the fixed capital and innovation needed to compete successfully in the future. Under China's system of central planning, performance of these essential functions by industrial enterprises was severely compromised by government authority that assigned workers to jobs for life, fixed basic wages, and prohibited bonuses. The arrogation of wage and employment decisions to government attenuated the link between compensation, productivity, and profitability; limited the hiring and firing needed for enterprise restructuring; undermined work incentives; and stifled productivity.

From 1965 to 1977 labor productivity in state industry remained more or less stagnant, while real wages declined about 11 percent. During the 1980s the Chinese government initiated a set of labor market reforms that allowed greater enterprise autonomy and labor incentives. The effect on labor productivity has been explosive (figure 8.1). Between 1980 and 1992 labor productivity in state industry rose at an annual rate of nearly 4 percent, rising in 1990 prices from 24,390 yuan per worker to 38,800 yuan per worker (Jefferson, Rawski, and Zheng 1996).

This chapter uses enterprise data collected by the World Bank and the China State Statistical Bureau to investigate the following questions:

- As reform proceeds are the relationships between wages and productivity, bonuses and productivity, and bonuses and profitability significant and increasingly robust?
- Within a formal model that allows for the simultaneou͏   ͏f employment, wages, productivity, and bonuses at the there evidence of profit-seeking behavior?
- To what extent do these behaviors and relationships ͏ ership types?

171

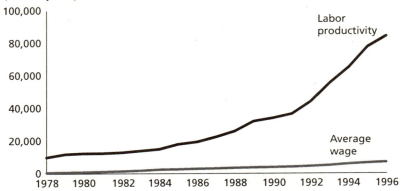

FIGURE 8.1

Labor productivity and nominal wage in Chinese state industry, 1978–96
(current yuan per worker)

Note: 1996 labor productivity was calculated using output as measured by the accounting system in effect through 1995.
Source: China Labor Statistics Yearbook 1993, 1997; *China Statistical Yearbook* 1994, 1997.

The first half of the chapter uses a wide range of data sources to investigate these issues. In recognition of the extensive opportunities for simultaneity within the industrial wage employment system, including the possibility of incentive effects of wages and bonuses, the second half of the chapter formulates and estimates a five-equation model that attempts to capture both neoclassical and institutional conditions that bear on important labor market outcomes.

In their study of state enterprises, Hay and others (1994) estimate a four-equation model. They conclude that "the most surprising feature of the results is how well the standard neoclassical model seems to fit these firms, even though imperfect adjustment and/or lags are clearly evident" (p. 143). Their model does not include an equation for productivity (incentive effect), and it looks only at state enterprises. It does not investigate differences in wage and employment behavior across enterprise types. Where possible, the results reported by Hay and others and those generated by the five-equation model examined here are compared.

Labor market regulation and reform

Since the late 1970s China has adopted several key labor market reforms. As a result of these reforms nominal and real wages have risen; managers have been granted discretion to establish internal wage systems, including piecework, and to set wage differentials within the firm; workers have been given the right to retain profits and receive bonus payments: d enterprises have been given greater autonomy in hiring and firing workers. In addition, in setting guidelines that fix wage bills and bonus limitations, central and local supervisory bodies have become more responsive to enterprise performance.

Although the degree of control varies across ownership types and the discretion at the level of the firm has been expanded, government institutions continue to play an active role in employment and wage decisions in industry. The three institutions most involved in setting guidelines for wage and employment decisions are the Central Labor Bureau in Beijing, the local labor bureau, and the enterprise. The Central Labor Bureau determines labor policy at the macroeconomic level. It fixes a total planned quota for the wage bill, with a view toward regulating overall consumption, the level of employment in the state industrial sector, and the basic wage rate of industrial workers. Wage quotas, based on anticipated levels of employment, are then allocated among lower-level labor bureaus, whose task is to implement national policy locally within the enterprises under their jurisdictions.

Hu and Li (1993) describe how the current "floating" wage system evolved from pilot experiments carried out in various provinces between 1981 and 1984 in the construction and coal mining industries. Based on those experiments local governments and state industrial enterprises now link the wage bill, directly or indirectly, to an index of enterprise performance. The wage bill, which includes the bonus, is linked to one or more of the following: gross value of output, average labor productivity, total amount of profit and taxes remitted, or, occasionally, some other performance index. Hu and Li report that by 1989 most large industrial enterprises had adopted some type of fully floating wage system in which total compensation is responsive to enterprise performance.

In the World Bank Enterprise Surveys (see chapter 2 and World Bank 1992) conducted between 1991 and 1992, nearly 77 percent of state enterprises reported operating under compensation schemes in which "total income is tied to profit and tax payment (as well as other possible performance measures)." Among urban cooperatives and township and village enterprises, less than half this percentage reported being constrained to link their wage bill to profit and taxes.

The Central Labor Bureau also establishes national policy concerning occupational wage rates. The basic wage formally includes wage scales, which are uniform across all firms, and a wage allowance. Variations from the guidelines consist mainly of supplements to the scales, granted by industry and region. Although the differentials are supposed to be determined nationally, in practice the local labor bureau uses its discretion to introduce additional local variation (Hay and others 1994). In practice compliance with national guidelines is uneven, reflecting variation in local economic conditions and differences in bureaucratic relations between local officials and enterprises. Many managers also have authority to establish wage differentials between workers within the enterprise.

Notwithstanding these national wage guidelines, many industrial enterprises have the authority to establish internal wage systems in which the enterprise chooses the type of wage system (time-based, piece rate, or combination) and compensation schedules for various classifications of employees. Within the World Bank sample, 74 percent of township and village enterprises established an internal wage system, about twice the proportion of state enterprises and urban cooperatives.

Within the World Bank sample township and village enterprises enjoy substantially greater autonomy than state enterprises in recruiting employees and setting wage differentials, somewhat more autonomy in dismissing employees, and somewhat less authority in setting the overall bonus and individual bonus differentials within the firm (table 8.1).

Before the early 1980s enterprises in China had virtually no autonomy in wage and employment decisionmaking. By 1991, when the surveys were conducted, both township and village enterprises and state enterprises had substantial authority in these areas.[1] Between two-thirds

TABLE 8.1
Enterprise autonomy, 1991
(percentage of respondents)

Area of authority	State-owned enterprises	Township and village enterprises
Dismiss employees		
Enterprises	62.8	72.2
Consultation	26.4	23.6
Supervisory agency	10.8	4.2
Recruit employees		
Enterprises	22.6	66.7
Consultation	50.0	29.8
Supervisory agency	27.4	3.5
Set wage differentials		
Enterprises	43.6	79.2
Consultation	19.8	11.7
Supervisory agency	43.6	9.2
Set bonus levels		
Enterprise	62.8	54.4
Consultation	18.2	27.0
Supervisory agency	18.9	18.6
Set bonus differentials		
Enterprise	93.3	86.9
Consultation	4.4	8.2
Supervisory agency	2.3	5.0

Source: World Bank 1992 (Enterprise Surveys).

and three-quarters of township and village enterprises report exercising autonomy in dismissing and recruiting workers. While the majority of state enterprises also report the authority to dismiss workers, less than one-quarter report having the authority to recruit new workers without consultation with their supervisory body.

Productivity, wages, and bonuses

Analysis of the data from the World Bank and China State Statistical Bureau surveys reveals various differences in productivity, wages, and bonuses across ownership types.

Labor productivity has risen in all sectors since 1984. The World Bank data indicate that labor productivity is highest among state enterprises; the State Statistical Bureau sample indicates that collective enterprises enjoyed higher rates of labor productivity (table 8.2). The difference in the two findings may reflect the fact that the State Statistical Bureau data set consists only of large and medium-size enterprises, virtually all of which were state-owned in the mid-1980s. By 1993 about a fourth of China's larger enterprises were nonstate enterprises. The new entrants to this elite group of large enterprises are generally the most successful of the enterprises in the collective and joint venture categories; the large increases in output that these firms experienced are likely to have been associated with high productivity. The comparatively high levels of productivity among collective-owned enterprises and joint ventures in the State Statistical Bureau sample are therefore likely to reflect some selectivity bias.

Differences in labor productivity may reflect differences in efficiency. Differences in single-factor productivity may also result from differences in relative factor intensity. In particular, foreign joint ventures that specialize in assembling imported components typically exhibit low value added ratios, and large state enterprises enjoy more capital per worker than smaller collectives.

Both the full population and the State Statistical Bureau sample reveal that enterprises in the "other" and joint venture sectors (which overlap substantially) pay considerably higher compensation than state enterprises (table 8.3). In 1992 the average wage paid by foreign-invested enterprises was nearly twice that of the state enterprise sector.

After bonuses were reintroduced in 1977 and 1978, the share of bonuses in total compensation rose by the mid-1980s to about 20 percent for all enterprise types (table 8.4). During the early 1990s the bonus share in the total money compensation was fairly uniform across ownership types, registering the lowest in urban collectives and township and village enterprises and highest in joint ventures.

TABLE 8.2
Average labor productivity, selected years, 1984–92
(yuan per worker)

Item	1984	1988	1990	1992
Full population				
State enterprises	14,396	24,477	29,933	39,425
Collective enterprises	4,195	8,721	11,444	14,802
Ratio of state enterprises to				
collective enterprises	3.43	2.81	2.62	2.66
Other enterprises	29,091	63,018	76,297	112,941
Ratio of state enterprises				
to other enterprises	0.49	0.39	0.39	3.35

	1984	1986	1988	1990
World Bank survey				
State enterprises	—	26,968	36,512	42,990
Urban cooperatives	—	16,970	23,863	25,018
Ratio of state enterprises				
to urban cooperatives	—	1.59	1.53	1.72
Township and village enterprises	8,688	11,328	17,988	20,193
Ratio of state enterprises				
to township and village enterprises	—	2.38	2.03	2.13

	1988	1990	1992
State Statistical Bureau survey			
State enterprises	30,953	35,231	43,758
Collective enterprise	34,058	35,998	52,572
Joint ventures	71,504	101,030	149,585
Foreign-invested enterprises	123,188	140,417	245,318
Ratio of state enterprises			
to joint ventures	0.43	0.35	0.29
Ratio of state enterprises			
to collective enterprises	0.91	0.98	0.83
Ratio of state enterprises			
to foreign-invested enterprises	0.25	0.25	0.23

— Not available.
Note: Data are in current prices except for 1984 figures, which are in constant 1980 prices.
Source: China State Statistical Bureau 1985, 1989, 1991, and 1996.

Have reform of the national wage and employment system and expanded enterprise autonomy strengthened the link between wages and productivity? Are bonuses and productivity or bonuses and profitability positively correlated? Have these relationships strengthened over time? Do they vary significantly by ownership type?

Across all ownership groups the relationship between productivity and wages has generally become more robust over time (table 8.5). The point estimates are higher for urban cooperatives than for state enterprises, higher for township and village enterprises than for urban cooperatives, and highest for the joint venture sector. The difference

TABLE 8.3

Average wage, selected years, 1984–92

(current yuan)

Item	1984	1988	1990	1992
Full population				
State enterprises	1,213	1,853	2,284	2,878
Collective enterprises	967	1,426	1,681	2,109
Ratio of state enterprises				
to collective enterprises	1.25	1.30	1.36	1.36
Other enterprises	1,436	2,382	2,987	3,966
Ratio of state enterprises				
to other enterprises	0.84	0.78	0.76	0.73
	1984	**1986**	**1988**	**1990**
World Bank survey				
State enterprises	—	1,453	2,043	2,642
Urban cooperatives	—	1,302	1,639	2,045
Ratio of state enterprises				
to urban cooperatives		1.17	1.25	1.29
Township and village enterprises	885	1,082	1,844	1,599
Ratio of state enterprises				
to township and village enterprises	—	1.34	1.11	1.65
		1988	**1990**	**1992**
State Statistical Bureau survey				
State enterprises		2,004	2,451	3,039
Collective enterprises		1,906	2,242	2,780
Joint ventures		2,579	3,452	5,049
Foreign-invested enterprises		3,442	4,365	5,847
Ratio of state enterprises				
to joint ventures		0.78	0.71	0.60
Ratio of state enterprises				
to collective enterprises		1.05	1.09	1.09
Ratio of state enterprises				
to foreign-invested enterprises		0.58	0.56	0.52

— Not available.

Source: China State Statistical Bureau 1993 (pp. 130, 136–8); World Bank 1992 (Enterprise Surveys).

in the R^2 statistics suggests that wage-setting behavior is less dispersed in the joint venture sector than in the other sectors. Wage responsiveness to productivity appears to be greatest and most uniform among joint ventures.

Within the state sector, bonuses have become increasingly responsive to labor productivity. Trends in the other sectors are mixed. All the estimates cluster in the range of 0.4–0.6. During the most recent period, estimates using the State Statistical Bureau sample suggest that workers in collectives capture the largest proportion of incremental productivity through bonus payments; workers in joint ventures

TABLE 8.4
Share of bonus in total wage, selected years, 1986–90
(percent)

Type of enterprise	1986	1988	1990
World Bank survey			
State enterprise	0.19	0.23	0.21
Urban collective	0.18	0.19	0.17
Township and village enterprise	0.17	0.21	0.1

	1988	1990	1992
State Statistical Bureau survey			
State enterprise	0.23	0.20	0.22
Collective enterprise	0.25	0.20	0.21
Joint venture	0.23	0.23	0.26
Foreign-invested enterprise	0.23	0.23	0.24

Source: World Bank 1992 (Enterprise Surveys); China State Statistical Bureau various years.

TABLE 8.5
Responsiveness of wages and bonuses to performance, 1984–93

Type of enterprise	1984–87	1988–90	1991–93
Effect of a 1 percent increase in labor productivity on the basic wage			
State enterprise (1)	0.070[a]	0.113	
	(8.054)	(15.062)	
R^2	0.038	0.088	
Collective-owned enterprise (1)	0.146[a]	0.126	
	(9.199)	(9.022)	
R^2	0.148	0.099	
Township and village enterprise	0.172	0.191	
	(6.372)	(5.760)	
R^2	0.096	0.083	
State enterprise (2)	0.192	0.251	
		(20.921)	(23.408)
R^2		0.047	0.075
Collective-owned enterprise (2)		0.261	0.287
		(10.401)	(12.168)
R^2		0.100	0.106
Joint venture		0.361	0.385
		(9.395)	(11.733)
R^2		0.214	0.250
Effect of a 1 percent increase in labor productivity on per capita bonus			
State enterprise (1)	0.421[a]	0.519	
	(21.801)	(30.113)	
R^2	0.223	0.279	
Collective-owned enterprise (1)	0.505[a]	0.469	
	(12.307)	(14.700)	
R^2	0.237	0.225	
Township and village enterprise	0.567	0.601	
	(10.922)	(9.614)	

(Table continues on next page.)

TABLE 8.5 (CONTINUED)
Responsiveness of wages and bonuses to performance, 1984–93

Type of enterprise	1984–87	1988–90	1991–93
R^2		0.238	0.202
State enterprise (2)		0.504	0.634
		(48.073)	(41.251)
R^2		0.208	0.202
Collective-owned enterprise (2)		0.569	0.650
		(14.114)	(16.313)
R^2		0.171	0.175
Joint venture		0.444	0.390
		(9.846)	(8.675)
R^2		0.230	0.154
Effect of a 1 percent increase in gross profit per capita on per capita bonus			
State enterprise (1)	0.344[a]	0.245	
	(30.310)	(25.760)	
R^2	0.356	0.221	
Collective-owned enterprise (1)	0.324[a]	0.238	
	(12.715)	(13.036)	
R^2	0.249	0.184	
Township and village enterprise	0.452	0.386	
	(11.589)	(9.759)	
R^2	0.260	0.207	
State enterprise (2)		0.344	0.342
		(52.792)	(38.268)
R^2		0.241	0.179
Collective-owned enterprise (2)		0.371	0.372
		(14.702)	(15.223)
R^2		0.183	0.156
Joint venture		0.306	0.262
		(10.045)	(9.490)
R^2		0.238	0.179

Note: The estimation equation is $\ln Y = a + \beta \ln X + e$. Data for state enterprises (1), collective-owned enterprises (1), and township and village enterprises are from the World Bank data set; data for state enterprises (2), collective-owned enterprises (2), and joint ventures are from the State Statistical Bureau data set. Numbers in parentheses are t-statistics.
a. 1986–87 only.
Source: Based on enterprise data from World Bank 1992 (Enterprise Surveys) and China State Statistical Bureau various years.

appear to capture the smallest share of productivity gains. In the state and collective sectors current changes in productivity tend to be captured by bonus payments; in joint ventures the basic wage is relatively more responsive to productivity.

Within both samples bonuses in state and collective enterprises, both urban and rural, are most responsive to changes in profitability. During 1988–90, when government controls were reimposed as part of the austerity program, all three sectors in the World Bank sample show reductions in the responsiveness of bonuses to gross profitability.

The model

A model of Chinese industrial enterprise wage and employment behavior should satisfy three conditions. First, the model should account for the simultaneous nature of wage and employment decisionmaking. Individual enterprises in China make decisions that explicitly determine or indirectly influence wages, bonuses, employment, and productivity simultaneously. Although wages are assumed to be determined exogenously in market economies, in practice, firms—particularly firms in which management believes that compensation imparts incentive effects—exercise some discretion.

Second, the model should incorporate salient institutional characteristics of the wage and employment system. A distinguishing feature of Chinese industry is the role of the state, including provincial and local governments, in setting constraints on enterprise compensation and employment behavior. China's wage and employment system substantially reduces the direction of industrial enterprises, particularly in state enterprises but also in other ownership types.

Finally, the model should attempt to incorporate the flexibility needed to capture differences in the relative importance of unfettered optimizing behavior and binding institutional constraints across different ownership types. The model attempts to estimate and compare the wage and employment behavior of several distinct types of firms: state enterprises, collective-owned enterprises, and other firms, principally domestic joint ventures and foreign-invested enterprises. Each of these categories of firms operates within a different institutional setting. Each outcome is assumed to be determined by optimizing behavior that is constrained by a common set of institutional conditions. Across different ownership groups, however, these institutional conditions effectively constrain enterprise behavior to different degrees, with state enterprises generally the most constrained and joint ventures generally enjoying the most autonomy.

Firms are assumed to maximize the present discounted net worth of their key stakeholders: government, which derives tax revenue from the enterprise; managers and workers, who receive wages and bonuses; and shareholders of joint ventures and joint stock companies, who receive dividends. Distributions from profits—in the form of bonuses, dividends, and profit remittances—generate utility in the current period for managers, workers, and owners; spending on innovation and investment contributes to future profits, compensation, and utility. Independent of the role of the pure discount rate in allocating resources between present and future compensation, within China's regulatory setting the intertemporal allocation of distributions and investment resources is affected by the following institutional arrangements.

The basic wage

The basic wage rate, which is based on nationwide standards and local conditions, is an important component of unit labor costs and a major determinant of gross profit. The wage rate affects the size of the surplus. The bonus policy determines how the surplus is allocated between distributions and investment.

The bonus

Bonus payments are expected not to exceed the equivalent of four months of basic wages. Although enterprises can and frequently do make payments in excess of this cap, excess bonus payments are subject to a steeply increasing bonus tax. Both the rising opportunity cost of bonus payments, in terms of lower growth of future output and profits, and the progressive tax motivate managers to allocate some share of retained earnings to future growth and production.

The manager responsibility contract

Manager responsibility contracts, negotiated for multiyear intervals, always specify a minimum level of profit remittance and provision for management bonuses. They often also specify targets for new product development and investment. Falling short of these targets can jeopardize management's bonus.

In principle, these institutional arrangements are strictly applied to state enterprises. In practice, they serve as guidelines that are applied with a declining degree of rigor and consistency in state, urban collective, township and village, and joint venture enterprises. As suggested by table 8.1, even within ownership categories, the impact of enterprise regulation and guidelines on the effective decision authority of individual enterprises is uneven. Nonetheless, systematic differences are assumed to exist across ownership types in terms of the degree to which these institutional arrangements restrict enterprise behavior. These anticipated differences allow predictions to be made with respect to the relative magnitude and sign on various coefficients in the model formally specified below.

Five equations—describing the wage bill, the basic wage, employment, bonuses, and productivity—comprise the model. (All variables are defined in box 8.1) For each of the equations the underlying technology is represented by a stochastic Cobb-Douglas production technology with inputs of capital (K) and labor (N), that may exhibit nonconstant returns to scale:

$$(8.1) \qquad VA = A_o e^{A(Z,t)} K^{\alpha} N^{\beta} \varepsilon$$

The productivity variable is modeled as follows:

(8.2) $$A(Z,t) = \partial_0 + \partial_1 wr + \partial_2 br + \Sigma \partial t \text{YEAR} + \Sigma \partial_i \text{IND} + \Sigma \partial_j \text{LOC} + \Sigma \partial_k \text{TYPE} + \mu$$

The *A* function is intended to capture variations in performance across firms and time that arise from the incentive effects of wages *(wr)* and bonuses *(br)*, changes in productivity and prices across *t* years, differences in production technologies across *i* industries, productivity differences across *j* regions, and differences in human capital across *k* occupational types. The individual estimation equations that make up the model are described in the following sections.

The wage bill

The total wage bill in China's state industrial enterprises is generally set by a quota. Under the floating wage system, described earlier, the total wage bill (including the bonus of the enterprise) is linked, in principle, to the total amount of profit and taxes remitted, to average labor productivity, and/or to the gross value of output.

To capture the impact of these performance measures on the wage bill, the equation specifies that the wage bill is affected by three prior-period variables: profit plus taxes (pro_{t-1}), labor productivity (gvn_{t-1}), and last period's expectation of output growth in the current period, which is assumed to be realized in the current period (that is, $E_{t-1}[dgv^r]$). The employment level (n) in the last period is independent of labor productivity. Rigidity in adjustment to the wage bill is represented by the lagged value of the wage bill. The log-log form is written as follows:

$$(8.3) wb_t = a_0 + a_1 pro_{t-1} + a_2 gvn_{t-1} + a_3 dgv_t + a_4 n_{t-1} + a_5 wb_{t-1} + \Sigma_t a_t \text{YEAR}_t + a_{f1} \text{FIE} + \varepsilon_{1t}$$

This and the other four equations are estimated separately for state enterprises, collective-owned enterprises, and joint ventures. The joint venture equation, which covers both domestic and foreign joint ventures, includes a dummy for foreign-invested joint ventures (FIE)

The expected signs on a_1 through a_4 are positive. The estimate of a_5 is expected to be nonnegative, with the magnitude depending on the degree of institutional rigidity, as determined by the weight assigned by the labor bureau to the enterprise's last-period quota as compared with its current and expected performance. Because collectives and joint ventures enjoy more autonomy in setting their total wage bill, these enterprises should be expected to exhibit less institutional rigidity than the enterprises in the state sector. The estimate of a_5 is thus expected to be largest for the state sector. Because the wage bill equation is designed to emphasize the institutional constraints that determine the wage bills of individual enterprises, the estimated equation should yield a better fit than the equations for the other ownership types.

The basic wage rate

The basic wage in state industry is based on wage scales, which are uniform across all firms, and a wage allowance, which consists mainly of supplements that reflect local working conditions and labor markets. Although rates are nationally determined, some discretion is exercised by local authorities to adjust national standards to account for local conditions and individual enterprise performance.

Because nationally determined wage rates exist for different categories of workers, the variable TYPE in equation 8.4 represents the share of managers, technicians, production workers, and apprentices in the total work force. Reflecting national wage policy, more uniformity of wages is expected within occupations for state industry than for the collective and joint venture sectors.

The wage is hypothesized to be responsive to differences in industry and regional differences as well as to firm-level labor productivity. Wage-setting behavior is likely to be more responsive to firm-specific labor productivity in the collective sector than in the state sector and more responsive to enterprise productivity in the joint venture sector than in the collective sector.

Incorporating these arguments yields the regression equation for the average basic wage:

$$(8.4) \quad wrt = b_0 + b_1 van_{t-1} + b_2 wr_{t-1} + \Sigma_k b_k \text{TYPE}_k + \Sigma_t b_t \text{YEAR}_t + \Sigma_i b_i \text{IND}_i + \Sigma_j b_j \text{LOC}_j + b_f \text{FIE} + \varepsilon_{2t}$$

Because the basic wage is a function of lagged values of productivity (van_{t-1}) and the wage rate (wr_{t-1}) and various fixed effects, it enters the model as a predetermined variable. This allows the firm to determine its optimal employment level in a setting in which the wage is more or less exogenous. Because collective-owned enterprises and joint ventures are relatively unconstrained by supervisory bodies, estimates of the coefficient on labor productivity (b_1) should be relatively large. In contrast, institutional rigidities within state industry suggest that the estimate of b_2 will be more robust for state enterprises than for collective-owned enterprises and joint ventures.

Employment

The labor supply in China's formal enterprise sector is assumed to be highly elastic (that is, the slope of labor's supply schedule is close to horizontal). This assumption is based on the observation that China's labor market embodies the essential characteristics of the Lewis (1955) and Fei and Ranis (1964) two-sector models, in which surplus labor in the agrarian sector gives rise to a highly elastic supply of labor in the industrial sector. Moreover, given the redundancy of labor within many Chinese enterprises, small increases in incentives may effectively induce a significant labor response.

In the standard neoclassical formulation, firms optimize by setting the employment level such that labor's marginal product, $\partial \text{VA}/\partial \text{N}$, equals the real wage, WR/p. The following employment function can be derived:

$$(8.5) \quad N = \beta(p\text{VA}/\text{WR})$$

where p represents the price of the firm's output.

In a neoclassical world, employment demand would be explained by value added and wages; in a world with adjustment costs, lagged values of these variables affect demand. In China's state industry, where the bonus is generally limited to four months of wages and is normally expected by workers when retained earnings are sufficiently large, the level of employment may also be affected by the "obligation" to pay a bonus. The model assumes that the firm predicts the bonus–wage ratio on the basis of the previous year's ratio, that is, $(\text{B}/\text{W})_{t-1}$. If the bonus is viewed as a wage markup, a high bonus–wage ratio will tend to depress employment demand. Furthermore, by imposing limits on the firm's wage bill, WB, the labor bureau can limit employment demand, particularly to the extent that the enterprise uses standardized wage rates.

Representing the value added–wage ratio (pVA/WR) as *vaw* and and incorporating the bonus–wage ratio and wage-bill quota into equation 8.5 yields the following equation in logarithmic form:

(8.6) $n_t = c_0 + c_1 vaw_t + c_2 (B/W)_{t-1} + c_3 wb_t + c_4 n_{t-1} + \Sigma c_5 \text{YEAR} + c_f \text{FIE} + \varepsilon_{3t}$

The lagged measure of employment reflects the presence of institutional rigidities within all employment systems, which are assumed to be particularly acute within China's state sector. The YEAR variable measures the employment trend, which may be interpreted as a systematic shedding or accumulation of redundant labor. Because institutional constraints bear more heavily on state enterprises than on collective-owned enterprises or joint ventures, the estimates of c_1 are expected to be smaller, the estimates of c_2 more negative, and the estimates of c_3 larger for state enterprises.

The bonus rate

Some analysts (Wiemer and Li 1994) argue that China's state enterprises retain an excess supply of labor that can be motivated by an efficiency wage. They argue that the principal task for many enterprises is not to evaluate the cost-minimizing labor requirement but rather to employ or motivate many "extra" workers in each workshop. Under this assumption that the incentive structure can affect efficiency, production and productivity are endogenous. Another view, advanced by Walder (1989), argues that because state enterprise workers cannot be motivated by the negative threat of lay-off, incentives must take the form of cash reward, principally bonuses.

Because bonuses are paid out of retained earnings, the bonus rate is constrained by retained earnings per worker. Bonuses in excess of the four-month cap are discouraged through the imposition of a progressive tax that rises to a maximum rate of 300 percent when the average bonus exceeds six months of basic wages.

To capture these institutionally determined conditions, the bonus equation is specified as:

(8.7) $br_t = d_0 + d_1 retn_t + d_2 wr_t + d_3 br_{t-1} + \Sigma d_4 \text{YEAR} + d_f \text{FIE} + \varepsilon_{4t}$

where the variable *retn* represents per worker retained earnings.

Since bonuses are paid out of retained earnings, they should be responsive to retained earnings, so that $d_1 > 0$. Because state enterprises cap the bonus based on a fraction of the basic wage, d_2 should be positive for state enterprises. For other ownership types, which are not subject to a uniform bonus guideline, the relationship between the bonus and the wage rate is ambiguous. Higher wages imply higher labor productivity. If productivity shocks, on which variations in bonuses are based, are proportional to labor's marginal product and hence to labor's wage, d_2 should be positive. Alternatively, higher wages may imply lower retained earnings and lower bonuses. For the nonstate sector, therefore, the sign on the wage coefficient is ambiguous.

The productivity-incentive equation

A productivity function is derived by substituting the productivity equation 8.2 into the production function 8.1. Dividing both sides by n to convert the expanded production function to intensive form yields:

$$(8.8) \quad van_t = e_0 + e_1 wr_t + e_2 br_t + e_3(k - n)_t + e_4 n_2 + \Sigma e_k \text{TYPE} \\ + \Sigma e_t \text{YEAR}_t + \Sigma e_i \text{IND} + \Sigma e_j \text{LOC}_j + e_f \text{FIE} + \varepsilon_{5t}$$

where $(k - n)$ is the capital-labor ratio.

A positive value of e_4 is evidence of increasing returns; $e_4 = 0$ infers constant returns to scale. The dummy variable TYPE, representing five different occupational types, is intended to capture productivity differences across occupations. A positive value for either e_1 or e_2 implies the presence of incentive effects. Because the negative threat of layoff is less in state industry than in the joint venture sector, the positive incentive of wages and bonuses would be expected to be larger in state industry than elsewhere. If wages and bonuses are linked—with, say, bonuses constrained by wages—the magnitude of the two coefficients should be similar.

To address the obvious simultaneity among wages, employment, bonuses, and labor productivity, the system of five equations is estimated with a two-stage least squares (2SLS) estimator:

Wage quota
$$(8.9) \quad wb_t = a_0 + a_1 pro_{t-1} + a_2 gvn_{t-1} + a_3 dgv_t + a_4 n_{t-1} + a_5 wb_{t-1} + \Sigma a_t \text{YEAR}_t + a_f \text{FIE} \\ + \varepsilon_{1t}$$

Basic wage
$$(8.10) \quad wr_t = b_0 + b_1 van_{t-1} + b_2 wr_{t-1} + \Sigma_k b_k \text{TYPE}_k + \Sigma_t b_t \text{YEAR}_t + \Sigma_i b_i \text{IND}_i \\ + \Sigma_j b_j \text{LOC}_j + b_f \text{FIE} + \varepsilon_{2t}$$

Employment
$$(8.11) \quad n_t = c_0 + c_1 vaw_t + c_2 (B/W)_{t-1} + c_3 wb_t + c_4 n_{t-1} + \Sigma c_5 \text{YEAR} + c_f \text{FIE} + \varepsilon_{3t}$$

Bonus rate
$$(8.12) \quad br_t = d_0 + d_1 wr_t + d_2 retn_t + d_3 br_{t-1} + \Sigma d_4 \text{YEAR} + d_f \text{FIE} + \varepsilon_{4t}$$

Production

$$(8.13) \quad van_t = e_0 + e_1 wr_t + e_2 br_t + e_3(k - n)_t + e_4 n_t + \Sigma e_k \text{TYPE}$$
$$+ \Sigma e_t \text{YEAR}_t + \Sigma e_i \text{IND} + \Sigma e_j \text{LOC}_j + e_f \text{FIE} + \varepsilon_{5t}$$

Results and interpretation

The regression results are shown in tables 8.6–8.10. Key results are summarized below.

Wage bill equation

The state enterprise sample provides a substantially better fit with the wage bill equation than either the collective or joint venture sectors (table 8.6). This is to be expected given that the estimation equation was formulated with a view toward capturing the institutionally determined wage quota in the state sector.

TABLE 8.6
Estimates of wage bill equation

Item	State-owned enterprises	Collective-owned enterprises	Joint ventures
Intercept	0.263	2.757	2.333
	(3.178)	(6.223)	(3.103)
pro_{-1}	0.034	0.042	0.089
	(4.827)	(1.869	(1.592)
gvn_{-1}	0.299	0.190	0.182
	(23.385)	(4.070)	(1.859)
dgv	0.727	0.406	0.417
	(64.452)	(7.718)	(5.856)
n_{-1}	0.388	0.320	0.557
	(19.006)	(4.607)	(3.932)
wb_{-1}	0.467	0.228	0.077
	(25.303)	(4.188)	(0.615)
1992[a]	0.050	0.092	–0.073
	(2.992)	(1.566)	(0.571)
Foreign-invested enterprise	n.a.	n.a.	–0.181
			(1.730)
Adjusted R^2	0.727	0.279	0.459
D-W	1.849	1.592	1.430
Number of observations	4,817	486	121

n.a. Not applicable.
Note: Numbers in parentheses are t-statistics.
a. The dummy intercepts for 1990 and 1991 are not reported.
Source: Based on enterprise data from Enterprise World Bank 1992 (Enterprise Surveys) and China State Statistical Bureau various years.

In all three sectors past levels of productivity affect the wage bill, but the effect is weaker for collectives and joint ventures than for state enterprises. Past levels of profits plus taxes contribute to a higher wage bill, but the statistical relationship is only marginally significant for collectives and joint ventures. As expected for the state sector, the current period's wage bill is significantly constrained by the previous period's wage bill. The constraint is less restrictive for the collective sector, and it appears to be unimportant in the joint venture sector.

Basic wage equation

In all three sectors the basic wage is responsive to labor productivity, although the state sector demonstrates less responsiveness than the two nonstate sectors (table 8.7). The estimation results indicate that within state industry, the basic wage is largely set outside the firm. As demonstrated by the comparatively large t-statistics on the occupational dum-

TABLE 8.7
Estimates of basic wage equation

Item	State-owned enterprises	Collective-owned enterprises	Joint ventures
Intercept	−0.603	0.056	−1.547
	(3.388)	(0.108)	(1.372)
van_{-1}	0.092	0.324	0.277
	(2.818)	(3.821)	(2.485)
wr_{-1}	0.282	0.105	0.273
	(20.832)	(2.787)	(3.363)
Production workers	0.907	0.327	1.058
	(4.676)	(0.650)	(0.826)
Apprentices	0.340	0.058	2.043
	(1.269)	(0.095)	(1.334)
Technicians	−0.704	−1.429	−0.948
	(2.318)	(1.557)	(0.517)
Managers	0.839	0.259	3.535
	(2.932)	(0.305)	(1.530)
1992[a]	0.509	0.325	0.346
	(19.587)	(4.915)	(2.324)
Foreign-invested enterprise	n.a.	n.a.	0.245
			(1.403)
Adjusted R^2	0.251	0.404	0.587
D-W	1.904	1.565	1.753
Number of observations	4,817	486	121

n.a. Not applicable.
Note: Numbers in parentheses are t-statistics.
a. Estimates of dummy variables for 1990 and 1991 and the industry and location dummies are not reported.
Source: Based on enterprise data from China State Statistical Bureau various years.

mies, state enterprises exhibit more wage uniformity by occupation. All ownership types show a pattern in which technicians receive the lowest wage and managers the highest. The spread among occupational wage differences is most pronounced in the joint venture sector, where managers are relatively well compensated; moreover, the relatively high t-statistics for state industry imply higher wage uniformity within each occupational category. As with the wage bill, the state sector demonstrates the greatest wage rigidity, as shown by the relatively large and statistically robust estimate of the coefficient on the lagged value of the wage rate. Finally, the results show a rise in the basic wage for all enterprise types in 1992 relative to 1989, with the increase most substantial in the state sector.

Employment equation

In all three sectors employment is constrained by the wage bill, although as anticipated, the constraint is substantially more binding in the state sector, where the basic wage is more uniform (table 8.8). Although the significance of the estimate of the elasticity of employment demand with

TABLE 8.8
Estimates of employment equation

Item	State-owned enterprises	Collective-owned enterprises	Joint ventures
Intercept	−0.025	2.004	0.275
	(0.413)	(4.553)	(0.042)
vaw	0.054	0.067	0.111
	(3.912)	(1.237)	(1.819)
$(B/W)_{-1}$	−0.042	−0.068	−0.116
	(5.613)	(2.803)	(1.770)
wb	0.780	0.431	0.594
	(44.144)	(6.330)	(5.803)
n_{-1}	0.074	0.160	0.180
	(8.526)	(5.174)	(2.654)
1992[a]	−0.276	−0.149	−0.222
	(17.332)	(2.809)	(2.086)
Foreign-invested enterprise	n.a.	n.a.	−0.220
			(2.868)
Adjusted R^2	0.778	0.321	0.684
D-W	1.490	1.326	1.732
Number of observations	4,817	486	121

n.a. Not applicable.
Note: Numbers in parentheses are t-statistics.
a. Estimates of dummy variables for 1989–91 are not reported.
Source: Based on enterprise data from China State Statistical Bureau various years.

respect to the value added–wage ratio is greatest in the joint venture sector, as anticipated, the magnitude of the elasticity is substantially smaller than unity, the long-run equilibrium expectation. The negative estimate on the bonus–wage ratio suggests that the bonus is viewed as a markup over the basic wage. This result holds across all three sectors. Moreover, the magnitude of the estimate on the bonus–wage ratio is virtually identical (with opposite sign) to the coefficient on the value added–wage ratio. This result suggests that throughout Chinese industry the bonus is viewed as a wage cost and that wage and bonus outlays enter symmetrically into calculations of employment demand. This result is consistent with that reported by Hay and others (1994).

Holding all the control variables constant, the estimates show a decline in employment demand relative to 1989. The decline is largest and most statistically robust in state industry. Everything else equal, foreign-invested enterprises tend to retain less labor than their domestic counterparts.

Bonus equation

Estimates of the coefficients on per worker retained earnings lie in the vicinity of 0.2 for each of the three ownership categories (table 8.9). These

TABLE 8.9
Estimates of bonus equation

Item	State-owned enterprises	Collective-owned enterprises	Joint ventures
Intercept	−0.440	−0.239	−0.491
	(18.428)	(1.673)	(2.764)
retn	0.185	0.244	0.179
	(11.471)	(3.878)	(2.931)
wr	0.099	0.002	0.364
	(2.802)	(0.016)	(2.831)
br_{-1}	0.313	0.338	0.203
	(25.170)	(7.573)	(3.159)
1992[a]	0.407	0.143	0.368
	(11.834)	(1.033)	(1.684)
Foreign-invested enterprise	n.a.	n.a.	−0.492
			(2.574)
Adjusted R^2	0.218	0.173	0.302
D-W	1.744	1.788	1.364
Number of observations	4,817	486	121

n.a. Not applicable.
Note: Numbers in parentheses are t-statistics.
a. Estimates of dummy variables for 1989–91 are not reported.
Source: Based on enterprise data from China State Statistical Bureau various years.

results indicate a universal tendency to distribute a declining fraction of retained earnings in the form of bonus payments. This finding is consistent with the permanent income hypothesis, under which profits can be viewed as a form of temporary income, a substantial portion of which is reinvested to generate future compensation.

Because bonuses in state enterprises are intended not to exceed four months of the basic wage, the bonus rate should rise with the wage. The regression results show that a 1 percent increase in the basic wage yields only a 0.1 percent increase in the bonus. The relationship may be weaker than expected because a rise in the wage may reduce the profits from which bonuses are distributed.

As with the other equations, the state sector shows a relatively large and statistically robust estimate of the coefficient on the lagged dependent variable. This implies a comparatively high level of rigidity in the state sector, in which the bonus remains relatively stable from one year to the next. In light of the fact that the basic wage demonstrates a relatively high degree of rigidity in state industry and the bonus is tied to the basic wage, it is not surprising that the bonus rate demonstrates a similar degree of rigidity.

After controlling for the basic wage and profit from 1989 to 1992, state enterprises are found to have increased bonus payments relative to their counterparts in other sectors. These increases, combined with the estimate of the wage bill coefficient suggesting proportional increases in wages and bonuses in that sector, imply that state industry should also demonstrate the largest increases in the basic wage—which it does.

Productivity-incentive equation

Estimates on the labor variable are statistically insignificant, suggesting that all three of the production technologies exhibit constant returns to scale (table 8.10). As a result, the output elasticity of capital, ak, is that reported for the capital-labor ratio; the output elasticity of labor is just $a_1 = 1 - a_k$. Under this interpretation $a_k = 0.352$ for the state sector, 0.272 for the collective sector, and 0.646 for the joint venture sector.

The results also show substantially higher levels of productivity for managers in the joint venture sector than in either the state or collective sectors. Presumably, these higher productivities justify the relatively high wages paid in these sectors.

The incentive effects of wages and bonuses vary substantially across enterprise types. The largest incentive effect is shown in the collective sector, where a 1 percent rise in the wage rate is associated with 0.73 percent increase in labor productivity. The incentive effects of a 1 yuan rise in the wage can be estimated using the elasticity estimates shown in table 8.11 and measures of labor productivity.

TABLE 8.10
Estimates of productivity/incentive equation

Item	State-owned enterprises	Collective-owned enterprises	Joint ventures
Intercept	0.624	0.084	-2.123
	(2.229)	(0.075)	(1.102)
wr	0.376	0.726	0.293
	(10.970)	(5.004)	(1.437)
br	0.286	0.186	-0.036
	(10.059)	(2.746)	(0.186)
k–n	0.352	0.272	0.646
	(23.675)	(6.828)	(6.121)
n	0.004	0.029	0.049
	(0.207)	(0.239)	(0.247)
Production workers	0.540	0.522	2.081
	(3.159)	(1.080)	(1.769)
Apprentices	0.953	0.736	3.082
	(4.092)	(1.141)	(2.119)
Technicians	0.730	2.142	3.257
	(2.844)	(2.540)	(1.965)
Managers	0.439	1.906	8.432
	(1.566)	(2.096)	(3.521)
1992[a]	-0.185	-0.184	-0.931
	(7.981)	(2.453)	(0.526)
Foreign-invested enterprises	n.a.	n.a.	-0.218
			(1.167)
Adjusted R^2	0.447	0.597	0.717
D-W	1.389	1.492	1.450
Number of observations	4,817	486	121

n.a. Not applicable.
Note: Numbers in parentheses are t-statistics.
a. Estimates of dummy variables for 1990 and 1991 and the industry and location dummies are not reported.
Source: Based on enterprise data from China State Statistical Bureau various years.

In the state sector a 1 yuan increase in the wage or bonus yields about a 1.2–1.3 yuan rise in labor productivity. The estimates of the employment demand equation suggest that wages and bonuses enter symmetrically: it is reassuring that they also demonstrate similar incentive effects. In the collective sector a 1 yuan increase in the wage or bonus yields a 2.1–2.3 yuan increase in labor productivity. Curiously, in the joint venture sector neither the wage nor the bonus demonstrates a statistically significant incentive effect. High wages in the joint venture sector reflect high levels of productivity the previous

TABLE 8.11
Estimates of labor's income share in value added
(average 1988–92)

Item	State-owned enterprises	Collective-owned enterprises	Joint ventures
Labor's income share[a]	0.538	0.460	0.435
Labor's income share, excluding bonus[b]	0.298	0.340	0.286
Labor's output elasticity (A)	0.648	0.728	0.354
Wage incentive effect (A/2)	1.262	2.135	1.025
Bonus incentive effect [A/(1–2)]	1.192	2.267	0.000

a. Includes all cash components of income (wage, welfare, and bonus).
b. Includes wage and welfare cash components of income.
Source: Based on enterprise data from the China State Statistical Bureau various years.

year. They do not appear to generate higher productivity in the current period, however.

One possible explanation for this apparent anomaly is that the joint venture sector does not possess a large supply of redundant labor, operates within a highly competitive labor market, and expects and receives maximum effort of its new hires. Once workers are in the joint venture sector, additions to the capital stock, rather than increases in wages or bonuses, appear to have the strongest effect on productivity.

Struck by the rapid increase in wages, bonuses, and benefits in the state sector, some observers believe that "excessive compensation paid to state enterprise personnel has weakened the financial performance of industrial state enterprises" (Woo and others 1993). From 1980 to 1993 labor's total wage bill as a share of gross output in state industry rose from 7.04 percent to 7.15 percent (China State Statistical Bureau 1994). This increase does not in itself support the view that labor is increasingly capturing the revenues of state industry.

Labor's income share may not be warranted by its technical contribution to production. Under the conditions that motivate Euler's theorem—constant returns to scale and perfectly competitive product and factor markets—factor payments are expected to just exhaust revenues. If these conditions are satisfied and Cobb–Douglas technology is assumed, factor income shares should be identical to the relevant output elasticities.

To examine the relative magnitudes of labor's income share and its output elasticity, output elasticities derived from estimates of the value added production function are used. Whether measured with or without bonuses, labor's income share in value added is less than its output elasticity for both the state and collective sectors. Only in the joint venture sector does the measure of labor's income share, inclusive of bonus, exceed the estimated output elasticity, although the difference is unlikely to be statistically significant.

The inclusion of in-kind services, which inflates labor's effective income share, may or may not alter the picture. Particularly in state enterprises, which often provide subsidized housing, health care, and educational services, services inflate labor's income share. When the market value of these services is computed, the value of those services produced should also be included in the value added of the enterprise, as Jefferson and Xu note (1991). Hence both the numerator and denominator of labor's income share should be adjusted by the same magnitude.

Letting labor's total cash compensation $= X$, value added $= Y$, and the value of noncash services $= Z$, then labor's total compensation share is $(X + Z)/(Y + Z)$, where the value of Z is added to the numerator and denominator. The empirical question is whether this share exceeds labor's output elasticity (0.648), which we assume to represent labor's output elasticity in the firm's total production of goods and services. Since we know that $X/Y = 0.538$, inclusive of bonus, we can compute the permissable share of noncash compensation in value added (Z/Y) as 0.313. Provided that the total annual value of noncash services to labor does not exceed approximately one-third of value added, then labor's total compensation does not exceed its technical contribution to production.

Within the collective sector, labor's income share is less than its estimated output elasticity. This result is consistent with the finding that payments to labor do not fully reflect labor's technical contribution to production, reported by Pitt and Putterman in chapter 9.

Conclusions

Several key findings emerge from this analysis:

- State enterprises are more constrained than other enterprises by past values of the wage bill, the basic wage, past levels of employment, and prior bonuses. Collectives demonstrate more flexibility, and joint ventures generally exhibit the most wage and employment flexibility. In particular, the wage bill in the state sector is substantially constrained by past levels of profit, productivity, employment, and the wage bill itself. The basic wage structure of the state sector shows more uniform occupational stratification but less responsiveness to differences in enterprise productivity.
- The intention of reformers to raise wages and reintroduce bonuses in order to strengthen incentives appears to have worked in the state sector. Incentive effects are even more pronounced in the collective sector. Such effects are hardly noticeable in the joint venture sector.
- Across the three sectors wages and bonuses appear to enter symmetrically in their effect on employment behavior, implying that bonus-

es are viewed as a kind of production cost. This result is most statistically significant within the state sector.

- After controlling for the expected determinants of wages and bonuses, wages and bonuses are found to have risen more rapidly in the state sector than elsewhere. Employment, however, has also fallen more rapidly within the state sector, so that there has been little effect on labor's income share.

China's wage and employment reforms have caused industrial enterprises there to become more responsive to both productivity and profitability in setting employment, wage, and bonus levels. In their study of wage and employment behavior in state industry, Hay and others (1994, p. 143) conclude that "the standard neoclassical model seems to fit these firms, even though imperfect adjustment and/or lags are clearly evident." They find that although enterprises appear to exercise little discretion over the basic wage, bonuses respond to efficiency and employment demand responds to wage costs. The results obtained here for state enterprises confirm these results. They also show, however, that relative to collective and joint venture enterprises, state enterprises exhibit more rigidity and somewhat less responsiveness to performance, particularly in basic wage-setting behavior.

Both wages and bonuses have incentive effects in the state and the collective sectors; in the joint venture sector the wage incentive effect is weak, and there is no effect of bonuses on incentives. Confirming the Wiemer-Li hypothesis (1994), these results indicate that the rise of labor productivity in China's state and collective enterprises was motivated in part by rising wages and the introduction of bonuses.

Notes

The authors appreciate the invaluable collaboration with China's State Statistical Bureau, which provided the data set on large and medium-size enterprises, and the support and assistance of Li Qiming, Xing Junling, and Zhang Shouqing. The helpful comments and suggestions of Louis Putterman and Calla Wiemer are also gratefully acknowledged.

1. A large portion of town and village enterprises within the sample may appear to operate under the authority of supervisory bodies. These decentralized authorities may be significantly more responsive than the municipal or provincial bodies responsible for making decisions for state enterprises.

References

China State Statistical Bureau. Various years. *China Statistical Yearbook (Zhongguo tongji nianjian)* (in Chinese). Beijing: China Statistical Publications Office.

Fei, J.C., and Gustav Ranis. 1964. *Development of Labor Surplus Economy.* Homewood, Ill.: Irwin.

Hay, Donald, Derek Morris, Guy Liu, and Shujie Yao. 1994. *Economic Reform and State-Owned Enterprises in China, 1979–1987.* Oxford: Clarendon Press.

Hu, Tei-Wei, and Elizabeth Li. 1993. "The Labor Market." In W. Galenson, ed., *China's Economic Reform.* The 1990 Institute. Ann Arbor: University of Michigan Press.

Jefferson, Gary H., and Thomas G. Rawski. 1994. "Enterprise Reform in Chinese Industry." *Journal of Economic Perspectives* 8(2): 47–70.

Jefferson, Gary H., and Xu Wenyi. 1991. "The Impact of Reform on Socialist Enterprises in Transition: Structure, Conduct and Performance in Chinese Industry." *Journal of Comparative Economics* 15(1): 45–64.

Jefferson, Gary H., Thomas G. Rawski, and Yuxin Zheng. 1996. "Chinese Industrial Productivity: Trends, Measurement Issues, and Record Developments." *Journal of Comparable Economics* 23(2): 146–80.

Lewis, W. Arthur. 1955. *The Theory of Economic Growth.* Homewood, Ill.: Irwin.

Singh, Inderjit, and Dilip Ratha. 1994. "Ownership, Wages and Efficiency in Chinese Industry." Working paper. World Bank, Washington, D.C.

Walder, Andrew. 1989. "Factory and Manager in an Era of Reform." *China Quarterly* 118(June): 242–64.

Wiemer, Calla, and Binsheng Li. 1994. "Wage Reform and Work Effects in China's State Enterprises." Working paper. University of Hawaii, Honolulu.

Woo, Wing Thye, Gang Fan, Wen Hai, and Yibiao Jin. 1993. "The Efficiency and Economic Consequences of Economic Reform." *China Economic Review* 4(2):153–68.

World Bank. 1992. "Enterprise Surveys." China and Mongolia Department and the Socialist Economies Unit. Washington, D.C.

Employment and Wages in Township, Village, and Other Rural Enterprises 9
Mark M. Pitt and Louis Putterman

Rural nonagricultural production has been the fastest-growing sector of China's economy since 1978. By 1989 rural industry accounted for 26 percent of China's industrial output and employed 56 million people, about 25 percent more than the state sector.[1] Exports by rural industrial enterprises also grew rapidly during the late 1980s, both in absolute terms and as a share of total exports. Both employment and total factor productivity grew more rapidly in rural than in urban state and collective industry (Jefferson, Rawski, and Zheng 1992). Most observers would agree that during the late 1980s and early 1990s, rural industry was the most dynamic sector in China's economy, contributing significantly to the success of the country's economic reforms.

This chapter examines the behavior of rural industrial enterprises in order to determine how those enterprises set employment and wage levels and how those levels affect technical efficiency. The analysis is based on panel data collected between 1984 and 1989 from 200 enterprises located in 10 Chinese provinces.

The results suggest that employment in township and village enterprises is below the profit-maximizing levels and that these enterprises may be sharing with their workers some of the rents generated from scarce capital goods. No relationship between enterprise type and technical efficiency is found.

Theory and review of the literature

Although township and village-owned enterprises have proved viable in a market or semimarket environment, it is unclear whether they are primarily profit-seeking firms. As Weitzman and Xu (1992) point out, the property rights of these enterprises are vaguely defined. In principle, township and village enterprises are collectively owned by the permanent residents of their jurisdictions, but disbursements of profits or of the proceeds of sales of assets to their nominal owners are rare. Moreover, control of township or village governments, which exercise substantial control over rural enterprises, is not democratic. The officials in charge of these governments and their enterprises are elected under local Communist Party auspices, and standard economic theory provides no basis for predicting their objectives.[2]

Chinese enterprises are often assumed to be founded to create employment (Byrd and Lin 1990), but local governments also have an interest in generating tax revenues and are probably interested in fostering economic development in their jurisdictions (Walder 1995). Paternalistic or populist officials may wish to create jobs paying high wages. If incumbent workers or their family members influence the manner in which enterprises are managed, they may also seek to set high wages, possibly at the cost of expanded employment (Bonin and Putterman 1987).

Standard microeconomic theory assumes that firms maximize profits subject only to technological and market constraints. By requiring entrepreneurs to pay suppliers of required inputs their opportunity earnings, competitive markets make maximum attainable profit zero for firms operating under constant returns to scale. Operation by an owner, who presumably values profits as a source of income, also helps to justify the profit-maximization assumption, although as Demsetz (1983) points out, owner-operators might indulge private nonpecuniary preferences in running their firms. With imperfect competition in product markets and nonowner managers, the profit-maximization assumption is less easily justified, but competitive pressures in capital, managerial compensation, and corporate control markets are assumed to maintain profit seeking as a primary objective (Demsetz 1983; Jensen and Meckling 1976; Putterman 1993).

If supplier markets are noncompetitive, the outcome may be different. McDonald and Solow (1981) model a firm that bargains over employment and wages with a monopoly labor union assumed to value both wages and employment. Equilibrium is found on a contract curve consisting of tangencies between "isoprofit curves" of the firm and indifference curves of the union, with the outcome, which depends on relative bargaining powers, always lying at wage and employment levels higher that are higher than the profit-maximizing point when the union holds some power.

Wage and employment outcomes may also deviate from profit-maximizing outcomes as a result of control arrangements within the firm. In his classic article Ward (1958) models a labor-managed firm that is assumed to select variable worker membership in order to maximize profit per worker member. When the labor-managed firm and a capitalist twin use the same technology and operate in the same product market, the labor-managed firm hires fewer workers and produces less output than the twin, provided that the twin earns positive profits.[3] Although subsequent and more realistic models, including some that model the rights of incumbent members, find that cooperatives are not quick to dismiss members to raise the incomes of those that remain employed, Ward's qualitative result continues to hold in the long run, when membership adjusts through attrition, provided that memberships are not salable and nonmember workers cannot be hired at a market wage (Bonin and Putterman 1987).[4]

All of these models assume that firms minimize the cost of producing a given amount of output—that is, that they are technically efficient. Managers who are not owners, however, may shun the psychic and other costs of maximizing the productivity of the inputs they use. Socialist state-owned firms are widely believed to suffer from technical inefficiency because their bureaucratic superiors are unable to extract full information about their technologies and resources and because their managers expect that losses will be made up by state subsidies. Township and village enterprises could conceivably share a degree of inefficiency with their state-owned counterparts. Social constraints against laying off local resident employees, for example, could make it more difficult for township and village enterprises to discipline them, thereby reducing work effort among employees of such firms.

Some cooperatives in market economies reportedly enjoy superior incentives, in part because of mutual monitoring by worker-owners (Bonin, Jones, and Putterman 1993); the possibility that at least some township and village enterprises also benefit from such incentives cannot be ruled out (see Gelb and Svejnar 1990). Weitzman and Xu (1992), for example, conjecture that there is a culture of cooperation in the township and village enterprises that sustains a high effort level in a repeated game model of effort choice.

Demands by local authorities that weight be placed on employment or other objectives could be consistent with an ideological environment in which discipline by township and village enterprise managers is lax. If managers are required to earn profits and if product and input markets are highly competitive, however, imposing constraints that would otherwise reduce profits could, at least in theory, prompt managers to make supernormal efforts to raise technical efficiency as the only way to remain profitable.

Several studies of China's rural enterprises have been undertaken. The study by Svejnar (1990) appears to be unique in using statistical methods to obtain evidence on the nature of rural enterprise objectives.[5] Svejnar assumes that the enterprise chooses variable labor input and wages to maximize an objective function that is a weighted geometric average of profits, employment, and the difference between the internal wage and that available to workers in the external labor market. To obtain information on the weights placed on each argument of this function, Svejnar takes the first-order condition of the assumed objective function with respect to labor and solves for the optimal employment level. He then estimates the parameters of this labor demand function on a panel of data from 122 rural enterprises located in four widely separated and economically distinctive rural counties during the period 1980–86. Although the large majority of the enterprises are township and village enterprises, various private and joint venture enterprises are also included. When the regression equation controls for location and ownership, Svejnar interprets the results as showing that enterprises in two of the four counties placed positive weight on employment creation during the full seven-year period but not during the last four years as a subperiod. When the controls are not included, he finds no evidence that weight is placed on employment creation. The hypothesis of profit-maximizing behavior cannot therefore be unambiguously rejected. To the extent that evidence that deviation from profit-maximizing behavior is found, it suggests a bias toward employment generation.[6]

The model

Like Svejnar's (1990) model, the model presented here considers the possibility that enterprises may seek to ensure employment and maintain wages at a particular level relative to some market or reservation wage. The objective function of an enterprise of ownership type k is given by:

$$(9.1) \qquad U_{it} = U_k(L_{it}, \Pi_{it}, w_{it} - w_{mit})$$

where L_{it} is employment in enterprise i in year t, Π_{it} is enterprise profit, w_{it} is the wage paid by the firm, and w_{mit} is the "market" wage.[7] All arguments in equation 9.1 have nonnegative partial derivatives. Enterprises maximize the objective function subject to the technology:

$$(9.2) \qquad Y_{it} = F(K_{it}, L_{it}, \mu_i)$$

where Y_{it} is output of enterprise i in year t, K_{it} is a measure of the flow of capital services, and μ_i is firm-specific technical efficiency.

A special case of equation 9.1 is profit maximization, in which case the weights assigned to employment and the wage differential are zero. Treating capital as fixed in the short run and assuming that the firm is a price taker in the market for (homogeneous) labor, the usual first-order condition for profit maximization applies, and the enterprises' demand for labor, L_{it}^{π}, can be derived straightforwardly:

$$(9.3) \qquad L_{it}^{\pi} = \pi^L(K_{it}, P_{it}, w_{mit}, \mu_i)$$

where P_{it} is the price of enterprise i's product in year t.

The general model of maximizing equation 9.1 subject to equation 9.2 yields two demand equations:

$$(9.4) \qquad L_{it}^* = g^L(K_{it}, P_{it}, w_{mit}, \mu_i)$$

and

$$(9.5) \qquad w_{it} - w_{mit} = g^w(K_{it}, P_{it}, w_{mit}, \mu_i)$$

Profit maximization takes place if the difference $(L_{it}^* - L_{it}^{\pi})$ is unrelated to the arguments of equation (9.4). Under the hypothesis of profit-maximizing behavior, the estimates of the differenced demand equations for L_{it}^* and L_{it}^{π} (imputed from equation 9.2 and the market wage) should not be statistically different from zero.[8] In particular, the determinants of deviations from profit-maximizing employment across ownership types are examined.

Barring incentive considerations of the type raised in efficiency wage theories in a competitive labor market with homogeneous labor, profit-maximizing firms would be expected to pay their workers wages equal to those in the local labor market. Given that the local wage itself is the wage analogue to the profit-maximizing employment level given by equation 9.3, a test of profit maximization in the choice of wages is a test of whether the difference between the actual wage and the local wage, given by equation 9.5, is unrelated to the arguments of the latter demand equation.

A measure of enterprise-specific technical efficiency, μ_{it}, is obtained from the panel data. Technical efficiency is a direct determinant of both L_{it}^{π} and L_{it}^* through its effect on the marginal product of labor. A more general model of enterprise behavior might include management effort as an argument in equation 9.1 but with a negative marginal utility to reflect the fact that effort is costly in psychic or other ways, and with another "technology" that describes how technical efficiency is produced by management effort. In this way, the level of technical efficiency depends on preferences. It seems likely, however, that the substitutability of effort for other goods in equation 9.1 would depend on ownership characteristics and unobserved attributes of the managers of each enterprise, which are unlikely to change much over a short period of time. Thus the treatment of (enterprise-specific differences in) technical efficiency as a fixed (time-invariant) effect in a short panel seems reasonable.[9]

The data

The data consist of annual observations for the period 1984–89 on 200 rural enterprises located in the provinces of Anhui, Gansu, Guangdong, Hebei, Hubei, Jiangsu, Liaoning, Shanxi, Sichuan, and Zhejiang. The data, collected by the Research Center for Rural Development (RCRD), in Beijing, cover a large number of variables, although information on many items is missing. The RCRD data are supplemented with province-level data obtained from the *China Statistical Yearbook*.

The first step in the analysis—estimation of a production function with fixed-effects methods—requires enterprise-level panel data on output and inputs (table 9.1). The RCRD data include information on gross value of output, value of current inputs (consumed raw materials and energy), number of employees at year end, and various measures relating to capital stock.[10] The current inputs measure is subtracted from an output measure in order to allow value added to be used as the dependent variable in equation 9.2. Given that both output and current inputs are provided in nominal terms and that reliable price deflators for either

TABLE 9.1
Descriptive statistics
(mean and standard deviation)

Variable	All enterprises	Township enterprises	Village enterprises	Private enterprises[a]
Value added	323.8	337.40	321.83	102.50
(10,000 yuan)	(805.48)	(860.97)	(459.37)	(166.28)
Employment	387.14	402.46	346.88	219.84
(number of workers)	(393.56)	(411.17)	(295.85)	(189.47)
Capital assets	142.73	149.80	116.45	83.76
(10,000 yuan)	(237.18)	(250.82)	(163.68)	(77.65)
Wage paid	1,424.37	1,494.24	1,116.63	954.97
(yuan per worker)	(6,226.82)	(6,799.08)	(729.86)	(456.37)
Market wage[b] (yuan per	869.96	876.81	866.05	765.58
number of enterprises[c])	(316.40)	(319.28)	(329.83)	(204.70)
Number of enterprises	200	166	22	12

Note: Sample sizes for the data differ slightly. Observations were included if they provided valid data on employment, capital assets, and (when different) the variable in question. All financial data are in current yuan. See text for discussion of assets variable. Numbers in parentheses are standard deviations.
a. Includes household associations, individually owned enterprises, and "other" ownership types.
b. The market wage is defined at the province level; differences among ownership types result from differing incidences of each type by province and year only.
c. Refers to the number of enterprises in the full sample. The actual number of observations used in these and other regressions reported in the chapter may be lower.
Source: Based on data from World Bank 1992 (Enterprise Surveys).

variable are not available, year dummies had to be used to control for price changes with respect to both inputs and outputs.

The primary measures of capital stock in the data set are the net and original values of fixed assets (where the difference between the two reflects depreciation). Because newly acquired capital goods enter even the net value of fixed assets series in nominal terms, that measure is influenced by changes in their prices. In an effort to account for depreciation and price changes, the net value of fixed assets is used as the measure of capital and the year dummies in the production function are interpreted as capturing average changes in investment goods prices as well.

Two wage variables are used. For the average wage of an enterprise's workers, "total wage actually paid" (including the basic or per piece wage rate, bonus, and other payments) divided by the number of year-end employees is used. For the opportunity cost of labor, the average wage of township and village enterprise employees, by province, is used.[11] Although not specific to the locality, this series has the advantage of being generated from a source completely independent of the other data and is thus free of contamination by any common computational elements.[12] The analysis uses dummy variables for the 10 provinces and for township and village ownership type.

Specification and econometric issues

Any econometric specification of the technology and demand for labor must take into account the possibility that unobserved fixed effects, the μ_i, are determinants of the enterprise's choice of inputs, as in equations 9.3 and 9.4. Fixed-effects estimation not only eliminates this correlation between regressor and error as a source of estimation bias, it also captures information on all time-invariant enterprise attributes that directly affect firm output, including the technical efficiency of the enterprise.

A Cobb-Douglas technology is estimated:

$$(9.6) \qquad \ln(Y_{it}) = \alpha\ln(K_{it}) + \beta\ln(L_{it}) + \mu_i + \varepsilon_{it}$$

where ε_{it} is a nonsystematic shock to the production process that is assumed to be unknown to firm managers at the time employment decisions are made and uncorrelated with μ_i and the inputs.

The fixed effects, which contain information on the efficiency of enterprises, are identifiable and become "data" in the estimation of the demand equations for employment and relative wage rates (equations 9.4 and 9.5). The demand equations (9.3 and 9.4) are linearized and subtracted, so that the estimated equation takes the following form:

$$(9.7) \quad \ln(L^*)_{it} - \ln(L^\tau)_{it} = \gamma_o + \gamma_w \ln(w_{mit}) + \gamma_p \ln(P_{it}) + \gamma_k \ln(K_{it}) + \gamma_\mu \mu_i + \gamma_d d_i + \eta_{it}$$

where μ_i is the estimated fixed effect, η_{it} is an error term that is not necessarily independently and identically distributed; and the γs are parameters to be estimated. The equations for the demand for relative wage payments take an identical linear form. Because complete information on the value added deflator P_{it} is unavailable, these price-level effects are captured by a set of year dummy variables. The variables d_i are firm attributes that are not structural determinants of a firm's output—that is, they are not arguments of the technology, but they are factors that might affect the allocation decisions of firms. These attributes are dummy variables for firm ownership and province location.

The possibility of measurement error and its implications for estimation must always be taken into account in analyzing enterprise-level data. The issue is dealt with in two ways. First, contamination of the employment and wage analyses by measurement errors affecting measured enterprise technical efficiency is avoided by substituting for each enterprise's estimate of average technical efficiency a period-specific estimate that, for each period t, is based on the enterprise's data for all years except t (see appendix). Second, the employment and wage deviation equations are estimated using two methods. The White (1980) (or Huber) method estimates robust standard errors using the asymptotic bootstrap, or jackknife, technique. The robust regression estimates parameters by assigning weights to absolute residuals in order to reduce the influence of outliers. These parameters were estimated because of concerns that coding or keypunch measurement error might give rise to significant outliers, which might unduly influence ordinary least squares parameter estimates.

Results and interpretation

Ordinary least squares, random effects, and fixed-effects estimates of the production function were calculated (table 9.2). A Lagrange multiplier (Breusch-Pagan) test of the null hypothesis that enterprise error components do not exist is firmly rejected ($\chi^2(1) = 107.5$). The Hausman specification test rejects the hypothesis that the random effects model is the correct specification in favor of the fixed-effects specification. In the fixed-effects estimate, coefficients for both labor and capital and those on most of the year dummies are statistically significant. The unconstrained estimate of returns to scale is 0.86, a result that could reflect downward bias as a result of measurement error, a problem that unfortunately is magnified in fixed-effects estimation (see Griliches and Hausman 1986).

TABLE 9.2

Fixed effects, random effects, and least square estimates of enterprise production functions

Item	Fixed effects	Random effects	Ordinary least squares
Log (employment)	0.6144504	0.758001	0.766965
	(4.2741)	(7.842)	(9.744)
Log (assets)	0.2489348	0.281332	0.303610
	(2.755)	(4.286)	(5.586)
1985	0.2785451	0.224592	0.197650
	(1.697)	(1.290)	(1.019)
1987	0.5143209	0.359751	0.319767
	(3.130)	(2.043)	(1.649)
1988	0.3506106	0.249973	0.226690
	(2.019)	(1.385)	(1.148)
1989	0.3382114	0.211499	0.168553
	(1.8930	(1.158)	(0.847)
Intercept		−1.062947	−1.173696
		(−2.3742)	(−3.202)
R^2	0.515		0.252
Number of observations	1,033	1,033	1,033

Note: Numbers in parentheses are t-statistics. Lagrange multiplier (Breusch-Pagan) test Chi (1) = 107.50. Hausman test Chi (7) = 65.66.
Source: Based on data from World Bank 1992 (Enterprise Surveys).

Enterprise efficiency is calculated as described by equation 9.12 (in the appendix) based on the same estimates.

Using the first-order condition that sets the value of the marginal product (VMP) of labor equal to the market wage, the equation for L_{it}^{π} is:

(9.8) $$L_{it}^{\pi} = \frac{\beta Y_{it}}{w_{mit}}$$

where the firm's actual (reported) output and the market wage for the relevant province and year are used. Estimates of the equation for actual levels of enterprise employment relative to profit-maximizing levels (and estimates of the identically specified equation for wage payments relative to market wages are calculated (table 9.3). The ratios of actual to profit-maximizing levels of employment and actual to the market wages are shown in table 9.4.

Two estimates of each relationship are given: one uses the White (or Huber) method, the other uses the robust regression method (table 9.3). The two regression estimates are qualitatively similar. The discussion here focuses on the White estimates.[13]

The full set of intercept and slope dummy variables are jointly significant in the estimates presented in column 1 of table 9.3 [$F_{(8,1065)} = 4.25$], as are the intercept and slope dummy variables for each enterprise type [township $F_{(4,1065)} = 4.34$; village $F_{(4,1065)} = 6.63$]. However, the dummy variables for township enterprises differ from those for village enterprises at only the 0.12 level of significance [$F_{(4,1065)} = 1.82$]. In

TABLE 9.3
Deviations from profit-maximizing employment and market wages

Item	Log difference in employment		Log difference in wages	
	Ordinary least squares	Robust	Ordinary least squares	Robust
Log (assets)[a]	−0.0880538 (1.166)	0.0774386 (0.869)	−0.0339574 (−0.933)	−0.0194678 (−0.412)
Log (assets) x township	−0.2198894 (−2.291)	−0.322334 (−3.499)	−0.1303073 (3.303)	0.1210295 (2.481)
Log (assets) x village	−0.2909224 (−2.251)	−0.351805 (−3.4250	0.1076681 (2.067)	0.122746 (2.262)
Log (market wage)	0.0079133 (0.011)	0.3017273 (0.619)	−0.6496401 (−2.248)	−0.4305172 (−1.667)
Log (wage) x township	0.0516722 (0.080)	0.2896946 (0.629)	−0.2838471 (−1.217)	−0.4431379 (−1.998)
Log (wage) x village	0.0609034 (0.092)	0.2525446 (0.551)	−0.0123369 (−0.047)	−0.2675805 (−1.104)
Efficiency	0.0662927 (0.225)	−0.2199843 (−0.804)	0.0573128 (0.402)	0.04874 (0.347)
Efficiency x township	−0.5590052 (−1.837)	−0.1178414 (−0.429)	0.102661 (−0.714)	0.0920674 (0.653)
Efficiency x village	−0.8162184 (−2.033)	−0.3417138 (−1.229)	0.1530065 (0.978)	0.0954337 (0.668)
Township	0.4476127 (−0.107)	−0.734219 (0.266)	1.319156 (0.824)	2.393275 (1.634)
Village	0.5676589 (0.134)	−0.3020266 (−0.100)	−0.4654428 (−0.263)	1.203801 (0.754)
1985	0.1181658 (0.638)	0.0576556 (0.518)	0.0795231 (1.094)	0.0492486 (0.835)
1986	0.127886 (0.552)	0.0778077 (0.558)	0.0940481 (1.0140)	0.0229971 (0.311)
1987	0.1669358 (0.709)	0.1276276 (0.805)	0.2165132 (2.074)	0.1551238 (1.844)
1988	0.3538512 (1.136)	−0.1399862 (−0.742)	0.3866719 (2.980)	0.2935587 (2.934)
1989	0.5386137 (1.552)	−0.1030404 (−0.456)	0.4413609 (2.789)	0.3378396 (2.826)

(Table continues on next page.)

· TABLE 9.3 (CONTINUED)
Deviations from profit-maximizing employment and market wages

Item	Log difference in employment		Log difference in wages	
	Ordinary least squares	Robust	Ordinary least squares	Robust
Hubei	−0.0570316	0.036938	−0.0663726	−0.1131916
	(−0.260)	(0.329)	(−0.741)	(−1.919)
Sichuan	−0.1108792	0.0455511	−0.435705	−0.417912
	(−0.579)	(0.392)	(−6.151)	(−6.823)
Guangdong	0.1891605	0.1359216	0.2355047	0.2002341
	(0.820)	(0.901)	(2.324)	(2.504)
Zhejiang	0.1868459	−0.2299163	0.139049	−0.1039421
	(0.658)	(−1.908)	(1.841)	(−1.633)
Jiangsu	0.5763	−0.1165858	−0.228659	−0.2332635
	(0.219)	(−0.990)	(−3.048)	(−3.736)
Anhui	−0.1922847	−0.042985	−0.2965387	−0.2332635
	(−1.094)	(−0.380)	(−4.028)	(−3.736)
Hebei	−0.0553654	−0.1842417	0.0847431	−0.00025
	(−0.253)	(−1.667)	(1.064)	(−0.004)
Liaoning	0.1744766	−0.0754783	−0.0641664	−0.0798952
	(0.632)	(−0.580)	(−0.762)	(−1.158)
Shanxi	0.2560651	−0.0852956	0.0603189	0.0797312
	(0.995)	(−0.666)	(0.698)	(1.169)
Intercept	7.556339	5.695788	4.599715	3.154723
	(1.615)	(1.805)	(2.407)	(1.886)
R^2	0.1438		0.3246	
Number of observations	1,091	1,091	1,097	1,097

Note: Numbers in parentheses are t-statistics.
a. Parameter for private enterprises.
Source: Based on data from World Bank 1992 (Enterprise Surveys).

TABLE 9.4
Average ratios of actual to profit-maximizing employment and of internal to market wages

Enterprise type	Ratio of actual to profit-maximizing employment[a]	Ratio of internal to market wages[b]
All	0.3687	1.637
Township	0.3719	1.704
Village	0.3578	1.289
Private	0.3415	1.247

a. For computation of profit-maximizing employment ($L*$), see text. Appropriate unit corrections have been incorporated.
b. Derived from data shown in table 9.1.
Source: Based on data from World Bank 1992 (Enterprise Surveys).

short—and with the caveat that the small sample of "private" enterprises could be unrepresentative—there is stronger evidence that private enterprises respond differently from village and township enterprises and weaker evidence of a difference between township and village enterprises. The value of assets is jointly significant in this equation [$F(3,1065) = 3.39$], as is the level of technical efficiency [$F(3,1065) = 15.94$]; the market wage [$F(3,1065) = 0.02$] is not significant.

For township and village enterprises, larger values of capital assets and higher levels of technical efficiency are associated with lower ratios of actual to profit-maximizing employment. A possible interpretation of the results with respect to assets is that the access of township and village enterprises to capital was rationed, and that those that succeeded in obtaining more tended to substitute it, to some degree, for labor. With respect to technical efficiency, the profit-maximizing level of employment was constructed using first-order conditions that incorporate the level of technical efficiency, insofar as it is reflected in actual output. Thus, under profit-maximization conditional on the level of technical efficiency, the level of efficiency should not be a determinant of the employment ratio. Furthermore, there is no automatic relationship between a tendency to pad employment (should such a tendency exist) and enterprise efficiency: the employees added could still be producing in a technically efficient manner. Nor is the negative correlation between efficiency and the employment ratio likely to be the result of systematic measurement error, given the technique used to estimate the fixed effect. It is possible that it is more difficult to monitor enterprise managers' effort to achieve technical efficiency when they are expected to be allocatively inefficient, because of the difficulty of distinguishing inefficiency that stems from inadequate performance by managers from other sources of inefficiency. The fact that the employment ratio and (in)efficiency are correlated for township and village but not private firms is consistent with such a possibility. However, the fact that most enterprises appeared to have been underemploying rather than overemploying labor makes even this interpretation problematic. The employment ratio is not related to the market wage, province, or year, suggesting that the relationships held more or less constant over the sample period and among differing Chinese regions and that price and technology differences were well controlled for in equation 9.6.

The full effect of ownership type on employment is estimated by calculating the derivative of the ratio of actual employment to profit-maximizing employment based on the parameter estimates of column 1 with respect to enterprise type. Evaluated at the mean values of the independent variables, this derivative is −0.0002 for township enterprises and

−0.02 for village enterprises. These negative values, even though small and probably not significantly different from zero, are not inconsistent with the fact that on average township and village enterprises have higher employment ratios than private firms (see table 9.4). Compared with township enterprises, private firms have, on average, lower asset values and lower technical efficiency, both of which are associated with lower levels of actual relative to profit-maximizing levels of employment.

The suggestion that the relative employment proneness of township and village enterprises confirms the proemployment bias conjectured by Svejnar is thrown into sharp doubt, however, by the values in the left-hand column of table 9.4. These values show not only that the difference in the employment ratios by ownership type is fairly small, but more importantly that all three enterprise types tend to employ barely more than a third of the number of workers that standard theory and the estimated parameters imply would be profit maximizing. Although the large discrepancy is unsettling and suggests the need for further work (with alternative specifications of the technology, for example), the same tendency has been identified in other recent studies both of China's township and village enterprises and of state-owned enterprises, suggesting the existence of a real phenomenon that calls for an economic explanation.[14] An attempt to offer such an explanation is beyond the scope of this chapter. The hypothesis of a proemployment bias by these enterprises can be firmly rejected, however.

Estimates of an equation explaining the difference between actual wage payments and the provincial market wage are presented in the last two columns of table 9.3. The set of intercept and slope dummy variables are jointly statistically significant [$F_{(8,1071)} = 3.00$], but township and village enterprises do not differ significantly [$F_{(4,1071)} = 1.24$]. The log ratio of actual to market wages is negatively correlated with the market wage. As this coefficient is less than −1 for all enterprise types, a 1 percent increase in market wage yields less than a 1 percent increase in actual wage payments. One interpretation is that rent-sharing with workers is reduced when market conditions require that enterprises pay higher wages, in part because those wages may have reduced rents themselves. Wages paid to workers are positively associated with capital assets only for township and village-owned enterprises. The magnitude of this effect is slightly larger for township enterprises than for village enterprises, but the difference is not significant ($t = 0.57$), suggesting that township and village enterprises indeed engage in some rent sharing with their employees. The same inference is suggested by the finding that the ratio of internal to market wages is highest among township enterprises, followed by village enterprises, although the difference between village and private enterprises appears to be slight according to this measure.[15] Although none of the individual parameters on measured technical efficiency is significantly different from zero, they are significant as a group ($F(3,1071) = 25.21$). Higher wage payments are associated with higher levels of technical efficiency. The province dummies are significantly correlated with the dependent variable, with the highest values found in Guangdong and Zhejiang.

Although equation 9.1 treats the wage differential as a direct argument in the enterprise objective function, several alternative explanations are consistent with the observed association between wages and assets for township and village enterprises. Enterprise decisionmakers can indeed treat high wages as an end in themselves, because of paternalism by the authorities, or worker influence within the firms. Alternatively, in attempting to sustain the long-term employment of their workers under politico-ideological constraints or an efficiency-wage motive, township and village enterprises may have been adopting a rent-sharing strategy to elicit more effort from their workers (Weitzman and Xu 1992).

Some simple tests of whether township and village enterprises behave as pure wage maximizers were run. According to the simple theory of Ward (1958), a labor-managed firm that takes wage maximization as its objective will be completely insensitive to the level of external market wages in choosing both its internal wage and its employment. To test whether the township and village enterprises in the sample behave as predicted, the log of employment and the log of the enterprise wage were separately regressed on the independent variables included in the employment and wage difference equations. An F-test rejects the hypothesis that the effect of the market wage on employment is zero for village but not for township enterprises.[16] The signs for all point estimates of the wage effect are normal. These results do not allow rejection of the hypothesis that township enterprises, but not village enterprises, behave like labor-managed firms. However, little weight should be placed on the results, because the same equation shows no significant effect of local wages on employment or internal wage of the private enterprises in the sample (that is, they do not support rejection of the hypothesis that the firms behave like labor-managed firms). Moreover, the estimated coefficient on wage for private enterprises is low (0.35) in the internal wage equation, and it is of the wrong sign in the employment equation.

Finally, correlates with the measured fixed effect were sought (table 9.5). These results demonstrate that none of the exogenous variables, with the exception of the asset variable, is significantly correlated with

TABLE 9.5
Alternate specifications of technical efficiency correlates

Item	Regression 1	Regression 2	Regression 3
Township	0.2109897	0.1571157	0.1265167
	(0.605)	(0.456)	(0.359)
Village	0.2685932	0.3064539	0.2821462
	(0.642)	(0.743)	(0.677)
Assets		0.161646	0.1581222
		(2.541)	(2.461)
Market wage			0.2143936
			(0.442)
Intercept	−0.4310261	−1.053075	−2.445032
	(−1.274)	(−2.545)	(0.769)
R^2	.002	.004	0.004

Note: Each column reports results based on a different set of independent right-hand side variables. Numbers in parentheses are t-statistics; $n = 188$.
Source: Based on data from World Bank 1992 (Enterprise Surveys).

technical efficiency as measured by the enterprise fixed effect. Regression specifications not displayed in table 9.5 reveal that the full set of ownership intercept and slope dummies is not jointly significant [$F(6,171) = 0.61$] nor is the set of provincial dummy variables [$F(9,171) = 1.04$]. The result suggests that enterprise efficiency is not systematically related to the type or location of the enterprise or the market wage.

Conclusions

Analysis of panel data on township, village, and privately owned rural enterprises suggests that all three ownership types employ substantially less than the estimated profit-maximizing number of workers, with weak evidence that private enterprises are even more conservative in their employment behavior than public township and village enterprises. These results are inconsistent with Svejnar's conclusion that township and village enterprises value employment at the potential expense of profits.

Identification problems prevented Svejnar from identifying objectives or behavior with regard to wage setting. This study finds that township and village enterprises, but not their private counterparts, share rents with workers. This result could reflect the paternalism of local officials or the influence of workers within publicly owned firms. Although township enterprises set wages and employment levels in a manner consistent with Ward's (1958) labor-managed firm model, strong conclusions are unwarranted given the counterintuitive results of those tests with regard to the private enterprises in the sample. Alternatively, town and village collective enterprises may be adopting a rent-sharing strategy to elicit more effort from their workers, as Weitzman and Xu (1992) have suggested. Given that no productivity differences are found between township and village enterprises and their private counterparts, this strategy may indeed be meeting with success.

The fact that only 12 private enterprises are included in the panel— and that those firms may not be representative—suggests that results based on comparison with private firms must be treated with caution.

Follow-up work on wage and employment behavior by township and village enterprises, including private enterprises, deserves high priority for future research.

Appendix

Ordinary least squares parameter estimates are biased toward zero under the classical assumption that measurement error in the independent variables is uncorrelated with the regression residual. In this case the ordinary least squares parameters are lower bounds of their true (absolute) values. In the estimation of equation 9.7, however, the problem is more severe, because it is unlikely that measurement error in μ_i is uncorrelated with the error μ_{it}. Consider the case of measurement error in employment. Measured employment L_{it}^* is a noisy measure of actual employment L_{it}:

$$(9.9) \qquad\qquad L_{it}^* = L_{it} + v_{it}$$

where v_{it} is an independently and identically distributed error. In the case of keypunch and coding errors, v_{it} could have a skewed distribution with a relatively high probability of large errors. Regression estimates of fixed effects μ_{it} are nothing more than the means of the residuals for each enterprise:

$$(9.10) \qquad\qquad \hat{\mu} = \Sigma_t(Y_{it} - \alpha K_{it} - \beta L_{it}^*)/T_i$$

where T_i is the number of time periods of data of enterprise i in the panel, (fewer than seven for these data). Consider a regression such as equation 9.7, in which observed employment, L_{it}^*, is regressed on an estimate of μ_{it}:

$$(9.11) \qquad\qquad L_{it}^* = \gamma_\mu \hat{\mu} + v_{it} + \eta_{it}$$

Because measurement error in employment contaminates the measure of the fixed effect, the fixed effect estimate equation (9.11), which contains the measurement error v_{it}, will be negatively correlated with the residual (which also contains the measurement error v_{it}) in a subsequent regression of employment on the measured fixed effect. This systematic measurement error problem is dealt with by constructing separate estimates of the fixed effect for each year t by dropping year t from equation 9.10:

$$(9.12) \qquad \tilde{\mu}_{it} = \Sigma_{t \neq 1}(Y_{i\tau} - \alpha K_{i\tau} - \beta L_{it}^*)/(T_i - 1)$$

Under the assumption that v^{it} is independently and identically distributed, there is no longer systematic measurement error.

Notes

The authors wish to thank Rekha Menon for her assistance and Gary Jefferson for his extensive comments and suggestions.

1. Urban collective enterprises accounted for an additional 18 million industrial jobs (China State Statistical Bureau 1990).

2. Rozelle (1991) attempts to recover the objective functions of local government officials from their behavior.

3. When the twin loses money, the labor-managed firm tries to employ more workers than the capitalist firm; when the twin just breaks even, employment is identical to that in the capitalist firm.

4. Differences between labor-managed firms and capitalist firms also vanish in the long run, as long as free entry and exit are allowed.

5. Other studies that warrant mention include Byrd and Lin, eds. (1990) and Ody (1992). Wiemer (1992) obtains some evidence on township and village enterprise resource allocation using data from a township in Hebei Province. See also Dong and Putterman (1995) and Xu (1995).

6. Under a certain set of assumptions, one of the four counties appears to have restricted employment during 1980–86, something that Svejnar does not mention.

7. With the market wage exogenous to the enterprises, the third argument of equation 9.1 could be written simply as w_{it}.

8. Differences between the actual employment levels of profit-maximizing firms and the levels indicated by equation 9.3 could be attributable to measurement error, unobserved variables, or misspecified technology. These factors are assumed to be uncorrelated with the arguments of equation 9.4. Equation 9.4 is not solved for explicit models of nonprofit-maximizing enterprise behavior. Instead, any effects of the arguments of equation 9.4 that are uncovered are provided by less formal explanations. While judicious specification of functional forms for equations 9.1 and 9.2 might permit the identification of the structural parameters of both the objective and the production function (see Svejnar), an aversion to relying too heavily on functional form for parameter identification, as well as limitations in the data—particularly the lack of appropriate deflators—demand that the more agnostic approach outlined above be taken.

9. The specification allows the average technical efficiency of all enterprises in the sample to change by the same proportion in each year, since all estimated relationships include year dummy variables. Thus, fixed-effects estimates of technical efficiency can be interpreted to represent enterprises' deviations from period-specific levels of average efficiency for all enterprises.

10. Both nominal variables (output, inputs, capital) and physical variables (labor) are used in the analysis. Interpretation of output elasticities is made difficult by the fact that physical units are fixed, while value units are changing over time (see Nerlove 1965).

11. Data are from the *China Statistical Yearbook*. The 1986, 1987, 1988, and 1990 issues contain data on the total number of employees in township and village enterprises, and on the total wage bill of those enterprises by province for the previous year. Values for 1984, 1988, and 1989 were calculated by extrapolating from a linear trend regression equation for each province.

12. Average earnings per agricultural or per rural worker were not computed because the results are subject to errors introduced by assumptions about the size and allocation of each province's rural labor force. Although township and village enterprise wages may be higher than the opportunity wage for many job seekers, they do show marked variation by province and year, suggesting that they reflect local labor market conditions, at least to the extent that the province is an approximate local unit.

13. It is worth noting that when ordinary fixed effects rather than those that exclude the contemporaneous period are used to estimate the same (ordinary least squares) regression, thereby reducing systematic errors in variables bias, "biased" estimates are obtained, as feared. The coefficient on efficiency is -0.83 ($t = 2.96$), rather than the 0.066 obtained with the amended measure. The method used to treat measurement error turns out to be important.

14. Using province-level data for 1982–87, Xu (1995) finds a large gap between the estimated value of labor's marginal product and the full wage in township and village enterprises, implying that hiring additional workers would have increased profits. Hay and others (1994) also find a large gap between labor compensation and value of marginal product in state-owned enterprises during the mid-1980s. Jefferson and Rawski (1994, 54–55) conclude that in that sector "labor's effective income share is unlikely to exceed 0.15, the figure around which estimates of labor's (gross) output elasticity appear to cluster." Interestingly, direct estimates of labor's marginal product in the township and village enterprise data set studies by Svejnar also show a large gap with the full wage paid, implying underemployment, despite the partial overemployment finding suggested by Svejnar's approach.

15. The payment of wages that exceed average market wages is not inconsistent with the fact that estimated values of the marginal product of labor exceed wages paid, consistent with the results of the left-hand column of table 9.4. On the whole, $\text{VMPL} > w_{it} > wm_{it}$.

16. $F(1, 1077) = 1.25$ for township and 3.16 for village enterprises; only the village figure is significant at the 10 percent level. F-tests are required because the net effect for each enterprise type is the sum of the coefficient for the default type (private enterprises) and the coefficient on the variable interacted with a type dummy.

References

Bonin, John P., and Louis Putterman. 1987. *Economics of Cooperation and the Labor-Managed Economy* (Fundamentals of Pure and Applied Economics, volume 14). London: Harwood Academic Publishers.

Bonin, John P., Derek C. Jones, and Louis Putterman. 1993. "Theoretical and Empirical Studies of Producer Cooperatives: Will Ever the Twain Meet?" *Journal of Economic Literature* 31(3): 1290–320.

Byrd, William A., and Lin Qingsong, eds. 1990. *China's Rural Industry: Structure, Development, and Reform.* New York: Oxford University Press.

China State Statistical Bureau. 1990. *China Statistical Yearbook.* Beijing: State Statistical Publication Office.

Demsetz, Harold. 1983. "The Structure of Ownership and the Theory of the Firm." *Journal of Law and Economics* 26: 375–90.

Dong, Xiao-Yuan, and Louis Putterman. 1995. "Productivity and Organization in China's Rural Industries: An Efficiency Frontier Analysis." University of Winnipeg, Manitoba, and Brown University, Providence, R.I.

Gelb, Alan, and Jan Svejnar. 1990. "Chinese TVPs in an International Perspective." In William A. Byrd and Lin Qingsong, eds., *China's Rural Industry: Structure, Development, and Reform*. New York: Oxford University Press.

Griliches, Zvi, and Jerry Hausman. 1986. "Errors in Variables in Panel Data." *Journal of Econometrics* 31: 93–118.

Hay, Donald, Derek Morris, Guy Liu, and Shujie Yao. 1994. *Economic Reform and State-Owned Enterprises in China 1979–1987*. Oxford: Clarendon Press.

Jefferson, Gary H., and Thomas Rawski. 1994. "Enterprise Reform in Chinese Industry." *Journal of Economic Perspectives* 8: 47–70.

Jefferson, Gary H., Thomas G. Rawski, and Yuxin Zheng. 1992. "Growth, Efficiency, and Convergence in China's State and Collective Industry." *Economic Development and Cultural Change* 40: 239–66.

Jensen, Michael, and William Meckling. 1976. "Theory of the Firm: Managerial Behavior, Agency Costs and Ownership Structure." *Journal of Financial Economics* 3: 305–60.

McDonald, Ian, and Robert Solow. 1981. "Wage Bargaining and Employment." *American Economic Review* 71: 896–908.

Nerlove, Marc. 1965. *Estimation and Identification of Cobb-Douglas Production Functions*. Chicago: Rand-McNally.

Ody, Anthony. 1992. *Rural Enterprise Development in China, 1986–90*. World Bank Discussion Paper 162. Washington, D.C.

Putterman, Louis. 1993. "Ownership and the Nature of the Firm." *Journal of Comparative Economics* 17: 243–63.

Rozelle, Scott. 1991. "The Economic Behavior of Village Leaders in China's Reform Economy." Ph.D. diss. Cornell University.

Svejnar, Jan. 1990. "Productive Efficiency and Employment." In William A. Byrd and Lin Qingsong, eds., *China's Rural Industry: Structure, Development, and Reform*. New York: Oxford University Press.

Walder, Andrew. 1995. "Local Governments as Industrial Firms: An Organizational Analysis of China's Transitional Economy." *American Journal of Sociology* 101: 263–301.

Ward, Benjamin. 1958. "The Firm in Illyria: Market Syndicalism." *American Economic Review* 48: 566–89.

Weitzman, Martin, and Xu Chenggang. 1992. "Chinese Township-Village Enterprises as Vaguely Defined Cooperatives." *Journal of Comparative Economics* 18: 121–45.

White, Halbert. 1980. "A Heteroskedasticity-Consistent Covariance Matrix Estimator and a Direct Test for Heteroskedasticity." *Econometrica* 48: 817–38.

Wiemer, Calla. 1992. "State Policy and Rural Resource Allocation in China as Seen through a Hebei Province Township, 1970–1985." University of Hawaii at Manoa.

World Bank. 1992. "Enterprise Surveys." China and Mongolia Department and the Socialist Economies Unit. Washington, D.C.

Xu, Chenggang. 1995. *A Different Transition Path: Ownership, Performances, and Influence of China's Rural Industrial Enterprises*. New York: Garland Publishers.

Industrial Investment, Finance, and Enterprise Performance in Chinese Industry

10

Gary H. Jefferson, Albert G. Z. Hu, and Inderjit Singh

Investment spending is a key element of any nation's economic activity. In the short run it is the most volatile component of national product; in the long run it is a basic determinant of economic growth. Investment spending is particularly important in transitional economies that are attempting to achieve several objectives simultaneously. At the macroeconomic level these objectives include price stability and economic growth; at the microeconomic level they include sectoral adjustment and enterprise restructuring. All of these objectives critically depend on closely aligning investment activity with enterprises that can use investment resources most efficiently.

Before reform, investment in China was determined largely by central and provincial authorities. Since reform China's investment system has been substantially decentralized, and enterprises and local jurisdictions have taken on more decisionmaking authority. With the introduction of retained earnings, rising rates of private savings, and new channels of intermediation, investment decisions and the ability to finance them increasingly fall within the domain of the firm. In 1995 half of total fixed investment in state enterprises, both industrial and nonindustrial, was financed by self-raised funds, principally retained earnings. Just 28 percent originated from state appropriations and domestic loans, with the balance provided by foreign investment and other sources (China State Statistical Bureau 1994). Widespread concern remains, however, over whether soft budget constraints, underdeveloped capital markets, and official interference in the allocation of scarce investment resources are leading to vast misallocations of capital.

This chapter examines several questions about the investment behavior of enterprises:

- Is there evidence that reform has motivated a more efficient allocation of industrial capital?

- Are patterns of investment activity in China's industry—in both the state and nonstate sectors—consistent with those expected of a neoclassical profit-seeking firm?
- To what extent are the best-performing enterprises capturing scarce investment resources in order to expand capacity where it is most needed?
- How, if at all, do patterns of investment behavior and activity differ across ownership types?

A central phenomenon of China's industrial reforms has been the rapid entry and growth of nonstate enterprises, particularly rural township and village enterprises and foreign-invested enterprises. This dramatic growth of production at the periphery of China's state industrial system has required extensive investment, even as state industry has continued to grow rapidly and capture most of the capital invested in China's industrial sector. The investment behavior of these new entrants and of traditional state enterprises is therefore central to understanding the apparent success of China's new industrialization. This chapter draws on the World Bank Enterprise Surveys (World Bank 1992), which include data on state enterprises, urban cooperatives, and township and village enterprises, and the China State Statistical Bureau data set, which covers state enterprises, collective-owned enterprises, and joint ventures, to investigate various formulations of investment behavior.

Background

Several empirical studies examine the investment behavior of state enterprises. Hay and others (1994) derive a neoclassical investment demand function that they use to investigate the behavior of state enterprises. They estimate their model using a sample of 769 enterprises in four provinces spanning the period 1980–89.[1] After finding a remarkably close fit with the data, the authors conclude, "While we can say relatively little about external constraints, and nothing about externally provided subsidies, we are able to infer that investment behavior on the part of the enterprises involved is reasonably predictable and in large measure consistent with profit-maximizing principles" (p. 298).

If China's transition is to be successful, investment decisions must be dominated by commercially based calculations that link enterprise profitability and investment. Two studies investigate the strength of the relationship between rates of profit and rates of capacity growth. Using a small sample of 20 enterprises in Wuhan City and a national sample of 110 steel mills, Jefferson and Xu (1991) find a statistically significant relationship between profit rates, lagged one year, and rates of capacity growth. Drawing on the sample of 900 state enterprises in the World Bank data set, Jefferson and Rawski (1994) find strong associations between current and lagged retained earnings and investment activity. Their results show that over the current and lagged periods, a 1 percent increase in retained earnings yields a cumulative 0.73 percent increase in investment spending.

These findings, which imply the commercialization of investment behavior within China's state industry, are particularly interesting in light of earlier research by Kornai and Matits (1984). They found no evidence of a relationship between profitability and investment activity in Hungary during 1975–84, the period of "goulash communism" with which China's reform program is sometimes compared.

If investment activity in China's state sector has become more responsive to differences in capital's marginal product across enterprises, the variation of returns to capital would be expected to decline as the reforms progress. A prediction of the neoclassical model—characterized by profit-maximizing behavior and perfectly competitive product and factor markets—is that as competitive conditions become more pervasive, returns to factors will become more equal across firms. Starting with this paradigm, Jefferson and Xu (1994) postulate that if market activity and profit-seeking behavior significantly infused China's state industry during the 1980s, factor returns should tend to converge. Furthermore, the more enterprises are exposed to market forces, the more complete the convergence of factor returns should be.

The results of the Jefferson and Xu study are reproduced in table 10.1, which shows the coefficients of variation for the average product for funds spent on labor, capital, and materials by 226 large and medium-size state enterprises, all measured in current prices. Coefficients of variation for total factor productivity in current prices are also reported.

The results for the full sample show a monotonic decline from 1980 to 1985 and 1985 to 1989 for the coefficient of variation of returns to capital, labor, and materials. Levels of total factor productivity also converge. The level of market exposure significantly affects the pattern of convergence: among enterprises that operate entirely within the market, convergence is most rapid during the decade and most complete by the end of the decade. Rates and levels of convergence are less striking for enterprises that operate within the plan and in the market; convergence is least in evidence, although still notable, for enterprises operating entirely within the plan. These results imply that at the core of state industry, investment capital in the industrial

TABLE 10.1
Coefficient of variation for factor returns

Year	Gross output/ wage	Gross output/ net fixed assets	Gross output/ intermediate inputs	Total factor productivity
Full sample (n = 226)				
1980	0.86	1.04	0.29	0.32
1985	0.80	0.82	0.26	0.26
1989	0.73	0.64	0.25	0.21
Sales 100% within plan (n = 74)				
1980	0.88	1.00	0.31	0.36
1985	0.83	0.90	0.31	0.33
1989	0.75	0.70	0.29	0.27
Sales partially within plan (n = 105)				
1980	0.80	1.04	0.21	0.27
1985	0.74	0.69	0.20	0.19
1989	0.66	0.57	0.22	0.15
Sales not within plan (n = 44)				
1980	0.83	0.80	0.27	0.22
1985	0.51	0.61	0.21	0.14
1989	0.45	0.49	0.22	0.12

Note: All variables are measured in current prices.
Source: Jefferson and Xu 1994 (tables 2 and 4) .

sector has gravitated to enterprises that enjoy the highest return on capital, thereby driving down capital productivity in the most profitable enterprises and generating increasingly uniform returns across enterprises.

This chapter extends these investment studies in several ways. After reviewing national statistics that describe changes in the sources and allocation of investment finance, it extends the neoclassical investment model used by Hay and others (1994), with minor variations, to new sets of state enterprise data. It also uses the model to investigate investment behavior in the nonstate sector. It relaxes a restrictive assumption in the model used by Hay and others, namely, that desired investment fully materializes in each period, so that the actual measured capital stock is equal to the desired capital stock. Since adjustment is not instantaneous, the model of Hay and others is, strictly speaking, a model of the desired capital stock rather than a model of investment. An attempt to remedy this shortcoming is made by adding a simple adjustment mechanism. Finally, a neoclassical relationship between investment and gross profit is desired, which allows the statistical association between profitability and investment found in earlier studies to be investigated within a behavioral context.

Sources and allocation of investment funds

As in other transition economies, both the source of investment resources and decisions regarding their use have shifted away from the state since 1978.

Sources of funds

The source of investment for state enterprises has shifted away from grants from the state budget toward domestic loans and other sources, particularly self-raised funds and foreign investment (table 10.2). The share of industrial state enterprise funds that came from state grants fell from 41 percent in 1983 to just 5 percent in 1995. In that year more than 70 percent of all funds were secured from outside the state budget and the state banking system, with 48 percent self-raised.

Collective-owned enterprises obtain more than a fourth of their investment finance from the state budget and domestic loans. Self-raised funds provide 55 percent of total investment finance. For the "other" sector, which includes firms ranging from small individual enterprises to large

TABLE 10.2
Sources of investment finance, selected years, 1983–95
(percent)

Type of enterprise and year	State budget	Domestic loans	Foreign investment	Self-raised funds	Other
State enterprises					
1983	40.6	14.3	1.7	43.4	..
1985	26.4	23.1	2.8	40.4	7.3
1988	14.7	24.2	9.0	40.5	11.7
1992	6.3	30.4	8.0	46.5	8.7
1995	4.9	23.4	7.8	48.2	15.7
Collective enterprises (including township and village enterprises)					
1983	—	—	—	—	—
1985	1.5	37.6	0.9	..	60.0[a]
1988	0.7	36.3	1.6	41.6	19.8
1992	0.1	36.7	2.6	39.8	20.8
1995	1.7	25.3	6.2	54.8	12.0
Other					
1983	..	..	..	100.0	..
1985	..	..	..	100.0	..
1988	..	..	..	100.0	..
1992	..	..	4.2	84.1	11.7
1995	0.3	12.5	20.0	57.0	10.2

.. Zero or negligible.
— Not available
Note: Data for 1995 have been corrected for rounding errors.
a. Includes self-raised funds.
Source: China State Statistical Bureau various years.

foreign-invested enterprises, just 13 percent of funds originate from the state budget or domestic loans. Self-raised funds provide 57 percent of the total for the other sector, with foreign investment contributing 20 percent.

These differences across ownership are further magnified by the level of supervision. In the World Bank sample large state enterprises that are supervised from the center rely heavily on state funds, while township and village enterprises, which are supervised at the local level, depend most heavily on their own funds for investment. The decentralization of investment resources reflects two trends: the shift away from state-controlled investment funds within state industry, and the rapid expansion of the nonstate sector, which relies less on state resources, within industry as a whole.

Allocation of funds

At the beginning of the reform period, in 1978, industry accounted for nearly 80 percent of industrial output in China. In 1980 the state sector held more than 90 percent of the stock of industrial and fixed assets. Collective enterprises accounted for virtually all of the balance of fixed assets.

As reform accelerated, investment funds initially shifted rapidly toward the nonstate sector (table 10.3). By 1983 just two-thirds of investment in fixed assets was controlled by state enterprises. By 1995 that figure had fallen to 54 percent, with collective-owned enterprises accounting for 16 percent and foreign-invested enterprises, individual businesses, and shareholding enterprises accounting for 29 percent of total fixed investment.

The institutional setting

Changes in China's industrial investment system after 1978 can be understood in terms of the shifting authority of key institutions involved in the investment process. These include government agencies, the banking system, nonbank financial institutions, and the enterprises themselves.

TABLE 10.3
Allocation of investment in fixed assets, selected years, 1983–95
(percentage of total investment)

Year	State enterprises	Collective-owned enterprises	Other enterprises
1983	66.6	10.9	22.5
1984	64.7	13.0	22.3
1988	61.4	15.8	22.8
1992	65.6	11.9	22.5
1994	57.0	16.3	26.7
1995	54.4	16.4	29.2

Source: China State Statistical Bureau 1993 (p. 145), 1995 (p. 137), 1996 (p. 140).

Before 1979 fixed capital investment had to be approved by the planning agencies; once approved, it was allocated through the Ministry of Finance. The large majority of investment funds allocated by the state took the form of grants financed directly by the budget rather than by loans. A monobank system, led by the People's Bank of China, played a limited role in "policy lending."

Beginning in 1979 a series of changes in the investment approval and investment financing system were gradually introduced. The role of the central government was reduced, a banking system was developed, and enterprise autonomy was increased. In addition to phasing out budgetary grants, the central government devolved authority for approving decisions for investments below certain amounts to lower levels of government. At the same time, the central government began to waive the need for approval, if enterprises were able to raise their own investment resources.

The new banking system created a more open financial environment in four ways. First, direct budgetary grants for investment were reduced, and loans through the banking system began to replace grants. Second, the monobank system was divided into a central bank, the People's Bank of China, and four specialized banks, including the Bank of Industry and Commerce. Third, although the operations of specialized banks were heavily restricted by the state credit plan, they were granted some autonomy over selecting borrowers and projects and thus began to undertake a combination of policy and commercial lending. Finally, the financial system was expanded to accommodate new lending institutions that did not undertake policy lending. These included new state banks and urban and rural credit cooperatives, which provided a significant amount of commercial lending to rural township and village enterprises. In the mid-1990s "full-service" branches of foreign commercial banks were introduced.

Two major changes in the state enterprise system affected the investment decisions of enterprises. First, profits were separated from taxes, thereby permitting enterprises to retain a part of their profits to be used—with some discretion—as a source of investment funds. Second, a contract responsibility system was introduced, allowing local governments to transfer revenues from enterprises to extrabudgetary funds that were not required to be transferred to the central government. These extrabudgetary funds provided another source of financing for investment, particularly for townships and villages.

Under the contract responsibility system, decisionmaking authority along several dimensions was shifted away from government supervision to the enterprise (table 10.4). On average, township and village enterprises enjoy substantially more autonomy than do state enterprises, as

TABLE 10.4
Locus of decisionmaking autonomy
(percentage of all enterprises)

Decision/decisionmaker	State enterprises	Township and village enterprises
Overall measure of managerial autonomy		
Enterprise	45	64
Joint	30	22
Supervisory agency	25	14
Investment decision		
Enterprise	14	25
Joint	57	60
Supervisory agency	29	16

Source: World Bank 1992 (Enterprise Surveys).

Jefferson, Zhang, and Zhao show in chapter 2. Along the 11 dimensions of decisionmaking authority, 69 percent of the township and village enterprises report that the enterprise is the locus of authority; just 37 percent of the state enterprise sample enjoy a similar level of autonomy. For both state enterprises and township and village enterprises, however, autonomy over investment decisions is relatively limited. Although a higher proportion of township and village enterprises enjoy investment autonomy for both types of ownership, the majority of enterprises report that investment decisions are made jointly by the enterprise and its supervisory agency. Nonetheless, relative to the prereform era, when China's industrial enterprises exercised virtually no autonomy over investment decisions (in part because they did not have the retained earnings needed to finance them), enterprise control over investment activity has grown substantially.

The models

This chapter formulates, estimates, and interprets three models of investment behavior. The first neoclassical model of investment demand has the advantage of being comparable to that used by Hay and others (1994). While this allows the results of the two models to be compared, the model has the distinct disadvantage of assuming an instantaneous speed of adjustment. The second model relaxes this rigid assumption, which may be unrealistic in the Chinese setting, in which underdeveloped capital markets and institutional constraints weigh heavily. The third model, also derived from neoclassical principles, features expected profit as a determinant of investment. This model allows for a more direct test of the role of profit in driving investment behavior.

Model 1: Desired capital stock

The formulation of an investment demand equation starts with the approach of Hay and others (1994), who derive their investment model from a standard Cobb-Douglas production function ($Q = AK^\alpha L^\beta$) that permits nonconstant returns to scale. The standard first-order condition derived from profit maximization requires that firms add to the capital stock until the marginal revenue of capital equals the marginal cost of capital:

$$(10.1) \qquad \partial Q / \partial K = \alpha Q / K = rc / P$$

where rc is the user cost of capital, and P is the price level of output.

Solving equation 10.1 for the optimal capital stock K^* yields the standard neoclassical results:

$$(10.2) \qquad K* = \alpha Q(P/rc)$$

For purposes of empirical investigation, the assumption of a unitary restriction on the elasticity of the optimal capital stock with respect to both output and relative prices is relaxed:

$$(10.3) \qquad K* = (\alpha Q)^{s_1}[(P/rc)]^{s_2}$$

where $s_1 > 0$ and $s_2 > 0$. The user cost of capital is defined as:

$$(10.4) \qquad rc = P_k^{\beta_1}(i + \delta)^{\beta_2}(1 - t)^{\beta_3}\text{IF}\beta^{\beta_3}e^g$$

where P_k is the price of capital goods, i is the interest rate, δ is the depreciation rate, and t is the tax rate. The rental cost of capital includes $g = a_t \text{YR} + a_j \text{IND} + a_q \text{REG}$, which captures time, industry, and regional differences. The dummy variables represent the costs of capital, which vary systematically from year to year as well as across industries and regions.[2]

The term IF is a measure of available internal funds—the sum of retained earnings and the depreciation fund. Given that imperfect capital markets may cause enterprises to be constrained in their access to external funds, following Hay and others (1994), equation 10.4 distinguishes between external and internal funds. A negative value of β_3 implies that an increase in the availability of internal funds effectively relaxes the constraint on available funds and lowers capital's user cost.

Hay and others (1994) model the investment process as a partial adjustment process in which a fraction, γ, of the difference between the net capital stock and the optimal capital stock is invested in each period:

$$(10.5) \qquad I = \gamma (K* - K_{-1})$$

where $0 < \gamma \leq 1$.

The estimation equation can be derived in logarithmic form by substituting the rental cost equation 10.4 into equation 10.3, the equation for the desired capital stock; substituting it into equation 10.5, the partial adjustment process; and rearranging and lagging the right-hand side of the equation one period.

$$(10.6)\ \ln[I + K_{-1}] = a_0 + a_1 \ln Q_{-1} - a_2 \ln(P^k/P)_{-1} - a_3 \ln(i + \partial)_{-1} + a_4 \ln(1 - t)_{-1}$$
$$- a_5 \ln IF_{-1} + a_t YR + a_i IND + a_j REG + \varepsilon$$

To derive this estimation equation, Hay and his colleagues make the very strong assumption that γ, the adjustment parameter, is unity and adjustment occurs fully within one year. They do not address the possible implications of this strong assumption, which implies that the right-hand side of the equation measures the firm's desired capital stock while the dependent variable measures the firm's actual capital stock. If γ is nonunity—as it will be if there are lags in the investment process—equation 10.6 will be misspecified. For purposes of obtaining comparable results, the assumption of instantaneous adjustment in the investment process is retained here. Later the implications of relaxing this assumption are examined. This model is designated as the "neoclassical model," because it is derived from a pure model of investment behavior that assumes complete adjustment within a short period.

Equation 10.6 is estimated using the World Bank data set, which covers state enterprises, urban cooperatives, and township and village enterprises for the 1986–90 period. The variables are defined and constructed according to the definitions that appear in box 10.1. Separate estimation results for the state, collective, and township and village enterprise sectors (reported in table 10.5) allow the investment behavior of these three types of enterprises in China's public sector to be compared.

Investigation of the township and village enterprise database reveals many omissions for gross output measured in constant 1980 prices, which is used to construct the real price of capital series. Within the township and village sector these data are unevenly and often inaccurately reported, thereby creating a classic measurement error problem, which will cause the estimate of the price coefficient column to be biased toward zero. Because the estimate on the real price of capital for the township and village sector is statistically insignificant and many observations are lost for the price variables, the results omitting this variable from the investment equation are also reported.

With the exception of the estimate on the capital price deflator in the township and village sector, the signs on all the coefficients reported in table 10.5 are as predicted. Because the time, industry, and regional

Box 10.1 Definition of variables and parameters

Variables

K = net value of fixed assets (NVFA)

NI = net investment (newly installed fixed assets completed) [NVFA − NVFA (−1)]

$K*$ = optimal capital stock (NVFA*)

Q = gross value of industrial output (GVIO)

P = output price index (GVIO/GVIO80)

P_k = price of capital goods

rc = user cost of capital

t = tax rate

    World Bank: income tax/gross profit

    China State Statistical Bureau: 1 − (retained earnings/gross profit)

IF = available internal funds (retained earnings + depreciation)/Pk

i = effective interest rate

    World Bank: interest payment/total borrowed funds

    China State Statistical Bureau: interest payment/$(NI+NI(-1)$

    − retained earnings − retained earnings (−1)

∂ = depreciation rate (depreciation fund/original value of fixed assets)

π = gross profit (profit + taxes)

π^e = expected gross profit

YR = year (dummy variable)

IND = industry (dummy variable)

REG = region

Coefficients

α = output elasticity of capital

β = output elasticity of labor

Γ = elasticity of the user cost of capital with respect to the availability of internal funds

γ = speed-of-adjustment coefficient

dummy variables capture differences in productivity and product prices as well as financial variables, they are not reported. Somewhat surprisingly, the robustness of the fit, measured by the adjusted R^2, is lower in the state enterprise sector than in the urban cooperative sector, and it is lower still in the township and village sector.

The results show that investment demand is responsive to output across all three ownership types. All ownership types also demonstrate substantial responsiveness to capital's rental cost. State enterprises and urban cooperatives are responsive to the real price of capital and to the income tax; estimates of these variables are not statistically significant for township and village enterprises. Overall, the estimation results suggest that township and village enterprises appear to be more responsive to output and state enterprises more responsive to price variables. The

TABLE 10.5
Estimates of neoclassical investment model using World Bank data

Item	Hay and others data State enterprises	World Bank data			
		State enterprises	Urban collectives	Township and village enterprises (1)	Township and village enterprises (2)
Constant (a_0)	1.232	7.413	6.452	−0.668	−0.556
	(8.2)	(34.747)	(11.115)	(0.987)	(2.820)
Gross output (a_1)	0.591	0.450	0.529	0.520	0.785
	(16.7)	(27.556)	(12.060)	(7.989)	(26.936)
Real price of capital (a_2)	−0.692	−0.440	0.364	−0.107	
	(5.4)	(10.809)	(3.281)	(1.143)	
Rental cost (a_3)	−0.503	−0.217	−0.168	−0.142	−0.105
	(6.2)	(9.816)	(4.702)	(3.045)	(3.814)
Tax (a_4)	0.028	0.154	0.175	0.007	0.025
	(0.5)	(8.645)	(3.750)	(0.073)	(0.371)
Available funds (a_5)	0.196	0.440	0.457	0.250	0.074
	(7.8)	(28.257)	(10.989)	(3.880)	(4.446)
Adjusted R^2	0.69	0.846	0.835	0.612	0.621
Number of observations	448	2,573	557	244	812

Note: Because of the large number of missing observations for gross output in constant prices, the regressions for township and village enterprises were run with (1) and without (2) the real price of capital. Estimates of the dummy variables for years, industries, and regions are not reported. Numbers in parentheses are t-statistics.
Source: Based on Hay and others 1994 (table 8.4, p. 300) and World Bank 1992 (Enterprise Surveys).

investment behavior of urban cooperatives falls in between, but like state enterprises their investment demand demonstrates substantial price responsiveness. The finding that investment behavior by state enterprises appears to be comparatively responsive to prices while township and village enterprise investment is responsive to output is consistent with the finding of Jefferson, Zhang, and Zhao (see chapter 2) regarding the greater emphasis of state enterprise managers on profits and that of township and village enterprise managers on growth.

The positive estimates of the internal funds coefficients indicate that access to retained earnings and depreciation funds spurs investment demand by effectively reducing the rental cost of capital. The smaller estimate of this coefficient for township and village enterprises relative to state enterprises and collective-owned enterprises suggests that within China's townships and villages, rural enterprises enjoy substantial access to external finance. The result may also reflect the requirement that for most state-owned enterprises, a certain proportion of retained earnings should be set aside for investment and that a minimum fraction of investment costs should be financed out of retained earnings.

Estimates of the neoclassical investment model using the State Statistical Bureau data are consistent with those obtained from the World Bank data (table 10.6). All three ownership types show significant responsiveness of investment demand to output, although the point estimates for the sample of large and medium-size enterprises are somewhat smaller than for the enterprises covered in the World Bank sample. The estimates on the tax variable are somewhat larger, while estimates of the capital price and rental cost variables are generally smaller. The smaller estimates for the rental cost variable may reflect a downward bias resulting from measurement error associated with imputing an interest rate from the ratio of interest payments to borrowing using available data for only the current and past years. For each of the ownership types, the estimate on the real price of capital is positive. This puzzling result might be explained by another simplification, in which the capital price variable is constructed as the inverse of the implicit price deflator. Changes in the nominal cost of capital, assumed to be uniform across all enterprises, are intended to be captured by the year dummies. Finally, investment demand among enterprises in all three ownership groups shows similar levels of responsiveness to available internal funds.

TABLE 10.6
Estimates of neoclassical investment model using China State Statistical Bureau data

Item	State enterprises	Collective-owned enterprises	Joint ventures
Constant (a_0)	3.761	5.667	4.119
	(24.029)	(8.221)	(6.376)
Gross output (a_1)	0.398	0.289	0.371
	(24.644)	(5.484)	(5.088)
Real price of capital (a_2)	0.177	0.066	0.307
	(7.106)	(1.029)	(2.131)
Rental cost (a_3)	−0.034	0.009	−0.063
	(4.649)	(0.451)	(1.748)
Tax (a_4)	0.234	0.942	0.673
	(6.414)	(4.813)	(3.727)
Available funds (a_5)	0.345	0.344	0.358
	(26.332)	(8.448)	(5.400)
Foreign joint ventures	n.a.	n.a.	0.397
			(3.102)
Adjusted R^2	0.769	0.696	0.835
Number of observations	2,682	246	88

n.a. Not applicable.
Note: Estimates of the dummy variables for years, industries, and regions are not reported. Numbers in parentheses are t-statistics.
Source: Based on data from China State Statistical Bureau various years.

Overall, the enterprise data are consistent with the neoclassical investment model. Across both data sets the fit is best for state enterprises. Some of the price variables do not fit as well for the other ownership groups.

Because of difficulties using the conventional Durbin-Watson statistic to diagnose problems of autocorrelation, the model is also estimated using between (ordinary least squares on means) estimates. Estimating the model using a mean value of each variable for each enterprise, computed over the relevant number of years, restricts the analysis to a cross-section, thereby eliminating the effect of autocorrelation in the time series. The results (table 10.7) are consistent with the ordinary least squares results shown in tables 10.5 and 10.6. Within the World Bank data set every estimate that is of statistical significance and of the predicted sign in the regular ordinary least squares estimates maintains the sign and significance in the between estimates. This is also true for the state enterprises in the State Statistical Bureau data set, but it is not true for estimates of the tax variable for collective-owned enterprises and joint ventures in the State Statistical Bureau data set or for the output variable for the joint venture sample.

TABLE 10.7
Between (ordinary least squares on means) estimates of neoclassical model

| Variable | World Bank data | | |
	State enterprises	Urban cooperatives	Township and village enterprises
Constant (a_0)[a]	7.869	7.227	0.044
	(21.112)	(7.161)	(0.059)
Gross output (a_1)	0.400	0.469	0.513
	(14.579)	(6.329)	(6.582)
Real price of capital (a_2)	−0.522	−0.475	0.086
	(7.641)	(2.504)	(0.653)
Rental cost (a_3)	−0.244	−0.231	−0.227
	(6.391)	(3.480)	(2.970)
Tax (a_4)	0.200	0.209	0.114
	(5.772)	(2.185)	(0.728)
Available funds (a_5)	0.506	0.541	0.358
	(19.142)	(7.686)	(5.400)
Foreign joint venture	n.a.	n.a.	n.a.
Adjusted R^2	0.869	0.859	0.648
Number of observations	2,682	246	88

n.a. Not applicable.
Note: Figures in parentheses are t-statistics.
a. Estimates of the dummy variables for years, industries, and regions are not reported.

The robustness of the estimates using the between estimator, combined with the significant decline in the goodness of fit of the fixed-effect estimators (not reported), suggest that most of the robustness of the fit comes from the cross-sectional data. In general, investment activity is sensitive to output and available internal funds over time. Prices demonstrate little effect. The neoclassical investment function thus performs well, particularly for state enterprises, in explaining differences in the stock of capital across enterprises, but it is unable to capture dynamic lags in responsiveness to prices.

Model 2: Investment demand

A drawback of the specification used by Hay and others (1994) is its untenable assumption of a unitary speed-of-adjustment coefficient.[3] In its place, the following flexible functional form, which allows for a speed-of-adjustment coefficient that is less than unity, is used:

(10.7) $$K = A(K* / K_{-1})^{\gamma*} K_{-1}$$

According to this partial adjustment specification, the increase in the capital stock from the last period to the current period is proportional

China State Statistical Bureau data		
State enterprises	Collective-owned enterprises	Township and village enterprises
2.951	3.540	4.549
(9.486)	(1.843)	(3.402)
0.321	0.430	0.278
(7.024)	(1.983)	(1.464)
0.060	0.163	−0.529
(1.058)	(0.867)	(1.768)
−0.044	−0.048	−0.349
(3.811)	(0.877)	(2.403)
0.360	0.376	0.529
(5.791)	(0.437)	(0.693)
0.426	0.265	0.392
(20.065)	(1.662)	(2.041)
n.a.	n.a.	0.320
		(3.421)
0.747	0.416	0.781
1,126	79	55

Source: Based on data from World Bank 1992 (Enterprise Surveys) and China State Statistical Bureau various years.

to the ratio of desired capital stock in this period to last period's actual stock. If, as assumed in the specification used in the previous section, the speed-of-adjustment coefficient is unity, then $K = K*$—that is, the actual stock equals the desired stock—and the specification collapses to the neoclassical specification.

Transforming equation 10.7 to log-linear form, substituting equation 10.6, and rearranging yields:

$$(10.8) \quad \ln K = b_0 + b_1 \ln Q_{-1} - b_2 \ln(P_k/P)_{-1} - b_3 \ln(i + \partial)_{-1} + b_4 \ln(1 - t)_{-1} \\ - b_5 \ln \text{IF}_{-1} + b_6 \ln K_{-1} + b_t \text{YR} + b_i \text{IND} + b_j \text{REG} + \varepsilon$$

From equation 10.6, in which $K = K^*$, and equation 10.7 it can be shown that $b_6 = 1 - \gamma$ and that each of the other b_k coefficients (that is, $k = 1...5, t, i, j) = \gamma a_k$. If adjustment is instantaneous, then $\gamma = 1$; b_6, the coefficient on the lagged dependent variable, is zero; and each of the other coefficients assumes the same interpretation as in equation 10.6.

Estimates of equation 10.8 for both the World Bank and State Statistical Bureau data sets are shown in table 10.8. Within both data

TABLE 10.8
Ordinary least squares estimates with a lagged dependent variable

	World Bank data		
Item	State enterprises	Urban cooperatives	Township and village enterprises
Constant (b_0)	1.151	0.571	−0.508
	(9.169)	(1.700)	(1.130)
Gross output (b_1)	0.085	0.144	0.272
	(9.460)	(5.741)	(4.680)
Real price of capital (b_2)	−0.070	−0.002	0.115
	(3.425)	(0.029)	(1.734)
Rental cost (b_3)	0.008	−0.027	−0.052
	(0.645)	(1.319)	(1.525)
Tax (b_4)	0.049	−0.005	0.018
	(3.000)	(0.111)	(0.252)
Available funds (b_5)	0.046	0.035	0.239
	(5.352)	(1.447)	(4.745)
Net capital stock (−1) (b_6)	0.860	0.839	0.434
	(89.708)	(38.628)	(9.807)
Foreign joint venture	n.a.	n.a.	n.a.
Adjusted R^2	0.963	0.959	0.587
Number of observations	2,538	534	366

n.a. Not applicable.
Note: Estimates of the dummy variables for years, industries, and regions are not reported. Figures in parentheses are t-statistics.

sets, nonstate enterprises, particularly township and village enterprises and joint ventures, exhibit larger adjustment coefficients $(1 - b_6)$ than state enterprises. A corollary of this result is that the estimated short-run responsiveness of investment demand to output and the price variables in the township and village enterprise and joint venture sectors is generally greater than the short-run investment responsiveness within the state sector. These results suggest that short-run investment activity is more responsive to quantity and price signals in the nonstate sector but that stock adjustment is as great or greater in the state sector in the long run. While this result of rapid adjustment is important, neither the neoclassical model nor the investment model with a lagged dependent variable performs well in capturing the dynamic time structure of investment activity in Chinese industry.

Model 3: Investment demand II

If Chinese industry and China's economy are to grow out of the plan—in the sense of replacing government-mediated transactions with market-

China State Statistical Bureau data		
State enterprises	Urban cooperatives	Joint ventures
2.486	4.000	3.246
(19.598)	(6.427)	(5.586)
0.014	0.038	0.167
(0.868)	(0.704)	(2.208)
0.070	−0.007	0.138
(3.546)	(0.118)	(1.076)
0.022	0.022	0.000
(3.829)	(1.323)	(0.003)
0.177	0.671	0.496
(5.962)	(3.921)	(3.129)
0.240	0.296	0.271
(22.396)	(8.354)	(4.560)
0.597	0.412	0.374
(40.608)	(8.744)	(4.783)
n.a.	n.a.	0.233
		(2.030)
0.856	0.776	0.880
2,668	246	88

Source: Based on data from World Bank 1992 (Enterprise Surveys) and China State Statistical Bureau various years.

based activity and rigid forms of enterprise management with innovative and efficient forms of corporate governance—investment resources at the margin must flow to firms engaged in innovative, efficient market activity. Preliminary evidence suggests that by the end of the 1980s a substantial link between profitability and investment activity had been established in industry (Jefferson and Rawski 1994), with the effect of creating more uniform returns to capital. These results demonstrate a statistical relationship between profitability and investment but do not investigate the behavioral content of this relationship. If the firm's investment demand is linked to profit, it should be responsive to after-tax profit (that is, profit and taxes), as well as to the set of prices that bear on the cost of capital.

To derive a model of investment that explicitly incorporates profit, a production technology of the standard Cobb-Douglas form is used. From the standard first-order condition (equation 10.1), the optimal capital stock is determined (equation 10.2). Gross profit per unit of capital is now defined as the excess of capital's marginal revenue product over the rental cost of capital:

$$(10.12) \qquad\qquad \pi/K_{-1} = [\, aPQ/K_{-1} - rc \,]$$

where K_{-1} is measured as the end-of-year net value of fixed assets. Equation 10.12 carries the straightforward interpretation that the rate of profit on capital equals its marginal revenue product net of unit user cost. Multiplying both sides by K_{-1}/rc and substituting $K*$ from equation 10.2 yields:

$$(10.13) \qquad\qquad K* - K_{-1} = \pi/rc$$

Substituting equation 10.13 in the partial adjustment process shown in equation 10.5 yields:

$$(10.14) \qquad\qquad I = \gamma(\pi/\mathrm{rc})$$

To derive an estimation equation, the same definition of the rental cost of capital shown in equation 10.4 is used, except that the term for internal funds (IF) is dropped (to reflect the fact that a substantial portion of these funds is embodied in profit net of taxes).

Because investment behavior depends not on current profit but on the expectation of a future stream of profits, expected long-run gross profit, π^e, is defined as an adaptive-expectations process driven by current and previous levels of gross profit:

$$(10.15) \qquad\qquad \pi^e = M_0 e^{pt} \pi^{d0} \pi^{d1}$$

where $d_0 + d_1 = 1$, and e^{pt} represents an exponential trend rate of change in expected gross profit as determined by a combination of real growth and inflation. Substituting equation 10.6 and equation 10.12 into equation 10.15 and taking logs yields:

$$(10.16) \quad \ln NI = c_0 + c_1 \ln \pi + c_2 \ln \pi_{-1} + c_3 \ln(i + \eta)_{-1} + c_4 \ln(P_k/P_q)$$
$$+ c_t YR + c_i IND + c_j REG + \varepsilon$$

where $c_0 = \ln \gamma + \ln M_0 + pt$.

Estimates using the World Bank data demonstrate that investment behavior is generally responsive to profitability (table 10.9). State enterprises and urban cooperatives exhibit the most robust response to profit, although the time structure of the response varies across ownership types. Township and village enterprises and joint ventures exhibit greater responsiveness to the three price components. The model performs poorly with respect to capturing the effect of real and anticipated price changes on investment behavior, except in the township and village enterprise and joint venture sectors.

One possible explanation of the relatively insignificant estimates of the impact of the price variables on investment demand in the state enterprise and urban cooperative sectors is that much of their variation may be captured by the time, industry, and regional dummies. To the extent that the relevant prices and taxes are administered or mediated by industry and regional authorities, one would expect that these variables would be relatively stable over time, that changes would occur across-the-board when they do occur, and that changes would be relatively uniform within a given industry or region. Because these circumstances may draw explanatory power from the price variables to the dummies (as well as problems of measurement error for the State Statistical Bureau data set), the price variables are restricted to equal zero, and equation 10.16 is reestimated without the price variables but with the dummies. For some of the samples, the restrictions permit a substantial expansion of enterprise observations that had suffered from missing price observations.

The results reveal a substantially more robust link between investment demand and profitability, particularly for the data from the State Statistical Bureau data set (table 10.10). For all six samples the relationship between profit and investment is statistically robust for at least one year; in four of these cases both current and lagged profit performance drive investment behavior. For these four sets of estimates, including both state industry samples, $d_0 + d_1$ falls in the range of 0.58–0.77; for the remaining two, the sum of the elasticities is 0.26 for the collective-owned enterprises and 0.31 for joint ventures in the State Statistical Bureau data set. The comparatively large response of state enterprises to profit performance may be explained in part by their substantial reliance on self-raised funds and by their comparative attention to profitability (chapter 2).

TABLE 10.9
Estimates of investment model with profit expectations

Item	World Bank data		
	State enterprises	Urban cooperatives	Township and village enterprises
Constant (c_0)	3.588	1.626	4.655
	(6.824)	(1.217)	(12.430)
Profit (c_1)	0.375	0.449	0.239
	(14.402)	(6.764)	(0.993)
Profit (−1) (c_2)	0.327	0.204	0.365
	(11.732)	(2.811)	(1.490)
Real price of capital (c_3)	0.045	0.173	−0.574
	(0.409)	(0.628)	(1.824)
Rental cost of capital (c_4)	0.078	−0.063	−0.572
	(1.093)	(0.619)	(1.711)
Tax (c_5)	0.221	0.003	0.402
	(2.124)	(0.010)	(1.360)
Foreign joint venture	n.a.	n.a.	n.a.
Adjusted R²	0.458	0.413	0.492
Number of observations	2,171	434	39

n.a. Not applicable.
Note: Estimates of the dummy variables for years, industries, and regions are not reported.
Figures in parentheses are t-statistics.

TABLE 10.10
Estimates after placing restrictions on the price variables

Item	World Bank data		
	State enterprises	Urban cooperatives	Township and village enterprises
Constant	1.026	3.298	0.003
	(8.385)	(3.983)	(0.007)
Profit	0.383	0.397	0.206
	(16.687)	(8.794)	(2.433)
Profit (−1)	0.319	0.267	0.561
	(13.142)	(5.601)	(5.896)
Foreign joint venture	n.a.	n.a.	n.a.
Adjusted R²	0.447	0.471	0.482
Number of observations	3,087	988	182

n.a. Not applicable.
Note: Estimates of the dummy variables for years, industries, and regions are not reported.
Figures in parentheses are t-statistics.

| China State Statistical Bureau data | | |
State enterprises	Urban cooperatives	Joint ventures
4.601	7.391	−1.209
(9.878)	(4.995)	(0.526)
0.465	0.282	1.104
(11.024)	(1.426)	(3.453)
0.073	−0.070	−0.177
(1.484)	(0.338)	(0.543)
0.266	0.104	−1.264
(2.723)	(0.316)	(1.745)
−0.013	0.101	−0.252
(0.499)	(1.157)	(0.974)
−0.040	−1.554	0.796
(0.298)	(1.301)	(0.760)
n.a.	n.a.	−0.400
		(0.745)
0.363	0.416	0.418
1,497	100	54

Source: Based on data from World Bank 1992 (Enterprise Surveys) and China State Statistical Bureau various years.

| China State Statistical Bureau data | | |
State enterprises	Urban cooperatives	Joint ventures
2.916	6.307	3.246
(12.565)	(3.567)	(5.586)
0.385	0.424	0.167
(12.296)	(3.409)	(2.208)
0.195	−0.162	0.138
(5.691)	(1.188)	(1.076)
n.a.	n.a.	0.233
		(2.030)
0.288	0.160	0.880
3,420	269	88

Source: Based on data from World Bank 1992 (Enterprise Surveys) and China State Statistical Bureau various years.

Conclusions

In 1983 more than 40 percent of state sector investment was financed by state grants; by 1995 that figure had fallen to just 5 percent, while funds from other sources, including retained earnings, foreign investment, and other commercial sources represented nearly 72 percent of investment in fixed state sector assets. For the collective sector these other sources supplied 73 percent of investment finance in 1995, with the balance coming from domestic loans. This dramatic shift in resource allocation away from state agencies and state-controlled banks, combined with the growth of managerial control in China's industrial enterprises, demonstrates that the enterprise has become an important, and probably the dominant, locus of investment decisionmaking initiative and authority in Chinese industry.

All three of the specifications of the investment process examined provide evidence that capital's marginal revenue product, enterprise profitability, and relative prices are significantly affecting patterns of capital accumulation. With some differences in emphasis, this pattern appears to be as much in evidence in state industry as it is among urban cooperatives, township and village enterprises, and joint ventures.

Considerable evidence was found that capital's marginal product, the price of capital, the rental cost, and tax rates significantly influence the allocation of investment capital across enterprises in the long run. Across all ownership types, investment resources are being captured by the most profitable industrial enterprises. A related finding is that enterprises are constrained in their investments by the supply of available funds on hand, including retained earnings. The shift in resources to enterprises has strengthened incentives to align investment with performance.

Output, profit, and available internal funds substantially affect both short-run investment decisions and long-term decisions regarding capital allocation. Although prices and taxes play a substantial role in determining and motivating optimal capital allocations over the long run, the simple models with one-period lags do not reveal that prices consistently affect short-run investment behavior.

Across ownership types the speed of adjustment to investment demand tends to be higher in the nonstate sectors than in the state sector. Short-run price responsiveness also appears to be somewhat higher in township and village enterprises and joint ventures than in state enterprises, although in the long run investment responsiveness is just as great, if not greater, in state industry. All enterprise types exhibit considerable responsiveness to profitability and internal funds, although the robustness of these estimates is greater in the state sector. The overall picture obtained is one of a system of industrial investment that is providing a far more efficient allocation of capital than is typical in a centrally planned economy.

Notes

1. Because of missing observations, the pooled analysis of Hay and others (1994) typically included a smaller number (300–330) of enterprises. They required that the firms included in their sample have levels of investment that were both positive and less than 40 million yuan.

2. Differences across time, industries, and regions may reflect differences in one or more elements of the user cost of capital. They may also arise from productivity and/or product price changes.

3. See, for example, Nickell (1978) for a careful and comprehensive discussion of conditions giving rise to adjustment lags and ways of modeling them.

References

China State Statistical Bureau.Various years. *China Statistical Yearbook (Zhongguo tongji nianjian)* (in Chinese). Beijing: China Statistical Publications Office.

Hay, Donald, Derek Morris, Guy Liu, and Shuie Yao. 1994. *Economic Reform and State-Owned Enterprises in China, 1979–1987*. Oxford: Clarendon Press.

Jefferson, Gary H., and Thomas Rawski. 1994. "Enterprise Reform in Chinese Industry." *Journal of Economic Perspectives* 8(2): 47–70.

Jefferson, Gary H., and Wenyi Xu. 1991. "The Impact of Reform on Socialist Enterprises in Transition: Structure, Conduct, and Performance in Chinese Industry." *Journal of Comparative Economics* 15:45–64.

———. 1994. "Assessing Gains in Efficient Production among China's Industrial Enterprises." *Economic Development and Cultural Change* 42(3): 595–615.

Jefferson, Gary H., Mai Lu, and John Z. Zhao. 1994. "Reforming Property Rights in Chinese Industry." Department of Economics, Brandeis University, Waltham, Mass.

Kornai, Janos, and A. Matits. 1984. "Softness of the Budget Constraint—An Analysis Relying on Data of Firms." *Acta Oeconomica* 32(3–4): 223–48.

Krugman, Paul. 1994. "The Myth of Asia's Miracle." *Foreign Affairs* (November–December) 62–78.

Nickell, S. 1978. *The Investment Decisions of Firms*. Cambridge Economic Handbooks. Cambridge University Press.

World Bank. 1992. "Enterprise Surveys." China and Mongolia Department and the Socialist Economies Unit. Washington, D.C.

Export Performance and Enterprise Reform in China's Coastal Provinces *11*

Frances C. Perkins

China's exports grew at an average annual rate of 13 percent between 1978 and 1993, a rate equal to that of the most successful Asian economies. The pace of export growth increased during the first half of the 1990s to about 20 percent a year. China's export performance has not been uniform across provinces or enterprise ownership type, however. Just six coastal provinces—Guangdong, Shanghai, Jiangsu, Shandong, Zhejiang, and Fujian—accounted for 74 percent of China's exports in 1994 (table 11.1); more than two-thirds of China's export growth has come from the dynamic nonstate sector.

A number of excellent studies have examined the trade policy reforms that moved China from near autarchy before 1978 to an increasing export orientation in the 1980s and 1990s (for example, Lardy 1992; World Bank 1994). This chapter examines several specific issues related to those reforms. First, it examines the impact of export orientation on

TABLE 11.1
Exports by selected provinces, 1994

Province	Exports (millions of dollars)	Share of China's total exports (percent)
Guangdong	53,274	44.0
Shenzhen	9,506	7.9
Shanghai	9,937	8.2
Jiangsu	6,957	5.7
Shandong	6,507	5.4
Zhejiang	6,482	5.4
Fujian	6,079	5.0
Xiamen	2,618	2.2
Liaoning	6,161	4.3
Qingdao	3,065	2.5
Tianjin	3,025	2.5
Total	121,038	100.0

Source: General Administration of Customs 1994.

enterprise productivity performance.[1] Second, it compares the domestic resource cost ratios of exporting enterprises, a measure of the financial benefit of export activity, by province and by ownership type. Third, it formulates and estimates a regression model to explain the impact of reform policy on export performance and to describe the characteristics of ownership and provincial setting independent of reform policy. The chapter is based on a 1993 survey of 300 enterprises in four cities—Guangzhou, Shenzhen, Xiamen, and Shanghai—and across nine industrial branches.[2]

Impact of economic and trade reform on export performance

One of the major reform successes in the Chinese economy has been the growth of its foreign trade. This is one crucial difference between the economic performance of China and that of most transition economies in Eastern Europe. Between 1978 and 1993 China grew from the world's 32nd largest trading nation to its 11th; over the same period trade (imports plus exports) grew from 9.7 to 38.6 percent of gross national product (GNP).[3] Total exports rose from $18.1 billion in 1980 to $121 billion in 1994.

The relative importance of the state sector in export performance has been diminishing. In 1985 the state sector accounted for 92 percent of exports; by 1992 its share of exports had fallen to about 58 percent. Only a third of the growth in exports between 1985 and 1992 came from the state sector, with the remainder coming from joint ventures and foreign-funded, collective, and private enterprises. The share of exports from township and village enterprises increased fivefold, from 5 to 25 percent, over this period, while the contribution from private enterprises and joint ventures rose from 1 to 20 percent. Since 1992 the export share of foreign-funded and other nonstate enterprises in total exports has continued to grow, with foreign-funded enterprises generating 29 percent of total exports in 1994 (General Administration of Customs 1994). Early that year more than 90 percent of the exports from nonstate enterprises were manufactured goods, and 94 percent were produced in the coastal provinces (World Bank 1994).

What has accounted for this dramatic and uneven export growth over the past two decades? Four hypotheses are tested. First, the effect of special economic zones is examined. The earliest trade reforms included the establishment of special economic zones and open cities in several coastal provinces. Policymakers hoped the zones' superior infrastructure and more liberal trade, foreign investment, taxation, and foreign exchange regulations would attract export-oriented foreign firms, and they expected that firms located in these zones would achieve more rapid productivity and export growth than firms outside the zones. The empirical sections of this chapter examine whether these zones actually boosted productivity and export growth.

Second, the effect of the creation of a competitive system of 3,600 dispersed foreign trade corporations (in place of the prereform system of 12 centralized foreign trade corporations) is examined. By 1987 Guangdong Province alone counted 900 foreign trade corporations. Large exporters were given permission to export on their own account, and by 1992 half of China's 10,000 large and medium-size state enterprises were given this right (*China Daily* 1 August 1992). In Guangdong, enterprises exporting as little as $1 million a year were allowed to export on their own account; in other provinces annual exports had to be at least $3 million before firms could export on their own account, and in practice this minimum was often much higher (Lardy 1992). Firms trading on their own account had the opportunity to search out international customers and respond to their needs, which should have allowed them to expand exports relative to firms trading through foreign trade corporations. Whether these firms did enjoy stronger export performance is tested in the empirical section. By 1996, as the number of foreign joint ventures expanded, more than 200,000 enterprises had acquired foreign trading rights (letter from Ministry of Finance, Trade and Economic Cooperation, to the Australian Department of Foreign Affairs and Trade, 24 October 1996).

Third, the effect of the abolition of export subsidies for the foreign trade sector is examined. Under the new policies foreign trade corporations were, in principle, made responsible for their own profits and losses.[4] This reform was expected to strengthen the incentive for foreign trade corporations to adjust their product mix and expand the export of goods that could secure the greatest premium on international markets while restricting the export of commodities with high domestic resource cost ratios. The success of the policy is tested by monitoring movements in the domestic resource cost ratios of the surveyed enterprises over the reform period.

Fourth, the effect of increased exposure of industries to international competition is examined. Until 1994 China's tariff and nontariff barriers remained among the highest of all large developing countries, and they provided a significant level of protection for Chinese industry. Although barriers were high, import duties represented only 5.6 percent of the value of imports in China in 1992 because of the extensive regime of duty drawbacks for exporting enterprises and possibly because of the widespread use of nontariff barriers that prevent the entry of many categories of imports without generating tariff revenue for the government (World Bank 1994). Given the extensive use of duty drawbacks in China, as well as the heavy use of nontariff barriers, effective protection is highly uneven across industries and is difficult to measure from published tariff rates. The hypothesis that exposure to international trade has increased and has raised efficiency and export competitiveness in Chinese industry is considered in the empirical section of the chapter.

Performance in Guangdong and Shanghai

Before the early 1990s the economic performances of China's two premier exporting regions, Guangdong and Shanghai, contrasted sharply. Between 1981 and 1990 Guangdong's real GDP growth of almost 17 percent a year was the fastest in China, while Shanghai's 6 percent annual growth was the country's slowest.

Before reforms began in 1978, Shanghai, as the center of China's traditional industrial heartland, was the most important exporting province, producing 30 percent of total exports. By 1986, however, Guangdong had replaced Shanghai as the country's leading exporter. By 1990 Shanghai produced only 10 percent of total exports; the city's share had fallen to 8 percent by 1994.

Guangdong's growth has been driven largely by exports originating in its three special economic zones. Between 1978 and 1993 nominal exports rose by 29 percent a year, more than twice the rate of the province's output growth. Exports as a percentage of GDP in Guangdong jumped from 13 percent in 1978 to 34 percent in 1990. In 1993 exports reached 67 percent, 50 percentage points higher than the national average of 17 percent. Guangdong's superior export performance alone accounts for about 80 percent of the difference between its economic performance and that of the rest of China.

Guangdong has undoubtedly benefited from its close geographical and cultural proximity to Hong Kong and Macao. During the early 1990s the province received about two-thirds of the foreign direct investment in China from Hong Kong and Macao and one-third of the country's total foreign direct investment (China State Statistical Bureau various years). Hong Kong provides vital marketing services for southern Guangdong's manufacturers. The province has also enjoyed relatively low fiscal transfers to the central government compared with Shanghai. These geographic and fiscal advantages existed before 1978, however.

The main reason for Guangdong's success has been the rapid pace of reform and liberalization there. Three of China's four original special economic zones were located in Guangdong, and the Pearl River Delta Economic Development zone was established there in the mid-1980s. In 1988 the entire province was made a reform experiment zone, which allowed it to introduce reforms in 10 major areas, including the financial sector. Stock exchanges, joint stock companies, and foreign exchange swap centers were established, trade policy was relaxed, and fiscal management was introduced. Trade reforms that included more flexible import licensing and export marketing regimes further exposed the region's economy to international trade and investment. Guangdong also led China in price reform and the removal of mandatory planning. It was given greater freedom to invest in infrastructure and other projects that exceeded centrally set limits, and it has, in turn, given county and municipal governments greater freedom to undertake necessary investments (World Bank 1994).

Shanghai has remained one of the most centrally controlled provincial-level governments in China. It was late in introducing reforms needed to facilitate the entry of nonstate firms, encourage foreign direct investment, deregulate trade and prices, liberalize labor and capital markets, and expand enterprise autonomy. The proportion of output produced by nonstate enterprises was well below the national average, as was the proportion of output sold at market prices (Shanghai Statistical Bureau 1993). Consequently, between 1979 and 1990 Shanghai attracted only a small proportion of China's total foreign direct investment—just one-fifth the value received by Guangdong.[5] The poor growth performance of Shanghai during the 1980s was a direct result of these central government policies.

Recognizing that Shanghai's growth was lagging behind the southern provinces and responding to local pressures to allow faster reform, in 1990 the government opened Pudong, an area east of the city center, as a free-trade and investment zone. Belatedly, Beijing also authorized Shanghai's authorities to tackle problems in the state sector by merging smaller, loss-making enterprises with larger, more successful firms and converting or merging loss-making enterprises with collective groups and joint ventures. Substantial public sector infrastructure investment was approved, focused largely on the new Pudong development, and the flow of foreign direct investment into Shanghai increased significantly. Between 1991 and 1993 foreign direct investment grew more than fourfold, increasing from 6.8 billion yuan to almost 30 billion yuan (Shanghai Statistical Bureau 1991, 1993). As a result of these policy reforms and capital inflows, Shanghai's growth rate has been accelerating rapidly and has virtually caught up with the national average. In 1992 and 1993, for example, Shanghai's real GDP grew by 14.9 percent, nearly equal to the national average of 15.1 percent during the same period. Real growth still lagged behind the 22 percent rate posted in Guangdong during the same period, however (China State Statistical Bureau 1994).

This chapter tests the hypothesis that the divergent policy regimes operating in Shanghai and Guangdong in the 1980s influenced the productivity growth and export performance of their enterprises. It also examines the impact of policy reforms in Shanghai in the early 1990s.

Export orientation and the growth of enterprise total factor productivity

Rates of productivity growth of the industrial enterprises surveyed are estimated using an unconstrained Cobb-Douglas production function. This functional form was selected after constrained and unconstrained versions of Cobb-Douglas and translog functions were estimated and the relevant restrictions were tested.

Taking logs, the estimation equation can be expressed as:

(11.1) $$\ln Q = \sum_{i=1}^{3} \alpha_i \ln X_i + T(X,t) + \varepsilon$$

where α_i are the output elasticities of input factors X (labor, capital, and materials) and $T(X,t)$ is technical progress or the total factor productivity growth coefficient. The α_i coefficients from equation 11.1 are used to construct estimates of total factor productivity growth using the following geometric weighting of the factor inputs:

(11.2) $\quad tfp = (\ln Q - \ln Q_{-1}) - \alpha_L(\ln L - \ln L_{-1}) - \alpha_K(\ln K - \ln K_{-1}) - \alpha_M(\ln M - \ln M_{-1})$

where $\alpha_L + \alpha_K + \alpha_M = 1$, tfp is total factor productivity growth, and the terms in parentheses are the first differences of the logs of labor, capital, and materials.

The capital stock series has been corrected for distortions arising from China's practice of aggregating current valuations of new investment to form a capital stock series (see Chen and others 1988a, 1988b). Using ordinary least squares, equation 11.1 was estimated to obtain the output elasticities for labor, capital, and material inputs for each of the six principal industrial branches covered by the survey.[6]

These elasticities were used to calculate a total factor productivity growth rate for each firm, using equation 11.2. Indexes of total factor productivity growth were formed by normalizing the 1980 value of total factor productivity to unity. The association between export orientation and total factor productivity growth is consistently strong and positive. In all industries in which there were both exporting and nonexporting enterprises, total factor productivity growth is 22–34 percent higher in the exporting enterprises than in nonexporting enterprises in both the state and nonstate sectors (table 11.2).

In every city in which both exporting and nonexporting enterprises are surveyed, export-oriented firms experience consistently higher productivity growth over the 12-year period than do non–export-oriented firms (table 11.3). The difference between the two sectors is particularly large in the economic zones of Shenzhen and Xiamen.

Causation between total factor productivity growth and export orientation could run in either (or both) directions. That is, exposure to international competition may encourage systemic improvements in management, resource allocation, and marketing (sometimes called X-efficiency gains) that generate increases in total factor productivity. Alternatively, firms that achieve higher total factor productivity growth could be better able to compete in international markets, so that rising productivity fuels exports.

Following Granger (1969) causality is tested by running two regressions. The first regresses export orientation (X/Q) lagged three periods and total factor productivity lagged three periods on total factor productivity. The second regresses export orientation (X/Q) lagged three periods and total factor productivity lagged three periods on X/Q. Unidirectional causality from export orientation to total factor productivity can be demonstrated if the sum of the coefficients on lagged X/Q in the first regression are significantly different from zero and the sum of the coefficients on lagged total factor productivity in the second regression are equal to zero. This is found to be the case, indicating that greater export orientation induces higher total factor productivity growth.

Domestic resource cost ratios in different policy environments

The Bruno Ratio provides a measure of the financial benefit that an enterprise can generate from its exports (Bruno 1967; Perkins 1994). Domestic resource cost ratios can be compared for enterprises operating in different policy environments (in different provinces and inside or outside special economic zones), with different ownership structures, and in different industries to assess their relative cost-effectiveness as exporters.

The numerator of a nondiscounted domestic resource cost ratio includes the cost of all inputs the enterprise purchases in the local economy minus the revenue from any domestic sales, all valued in domestic prices and denominated in local currency. The denominator is the value of the enterprise's exports minus any import costs, all valued in foreign exchange. The formula for a nondiscounted domestic resource cost ratio is

TABLE 11.2

Total factor productivity growth indexes of exporting and nonexporting enterprises by ownership and industry, 1980–92
(1980 = 1)

Type of firm	1981	1982	1983	1984	1985	1986	1987
STATE-OWNED FIRMS							
Exporting enterprises							
Textiles	1.030	1.084	1.150	1.233	1.442	1.451	1.516
Garments	1.086	1.143	1.197	1.224	1.171	1.159	1.147
Electrical appliances	0.946	0.969	0.982	1.010	0.903	0.908	1.074
Machine tools	1.039	1.016	1.030	1.060	1.151	1.235	1.358
Iron and steel	0.999	1.027	1.064	1.086	1.358	1.326	1.361
Metal products	—	—	—	—	—	—	—
Total	1.012	1.041	1.079	1.126	1.212	1.220	1.310
Nonexporting enterprises							
Textiles	1.062	1.144	1.119	1.177	1.344	1.398	1.446
Garments	0.886	0.688	0.673	0.585	0.592	0.632	0.748
Electrical appliances	—	—	—	—	—	—	—
Machine tools	—	—	—	—	—	—	—
Iron and steel	0.963	0.988	1.026	1.055	0.876	0.949	1.017
Metal products	1.000	1.010	0.983	0.990	0.968	0.988	1.021
Total	0.999	1.023	1.820	1.080	1.842	1.162	1.160
NON-STATE-OWNED FIRMS							
Exporting enterprises							
Textiles	—	—	—	—	—	—	—
Garments	1.101	1.158	1.206	1.214	1.260	1.312	1.371
Electrical appliances	1.109	1.120	1.630	1.633	1.293	1.354	1.696
Machine tools	—	—	—	—	—	—	—
Iron and steel	1.039	1.085	1.308	1.474	1.597	1.650	1.667
Metal products	—	—	—	—	—	—	—
Total	1.097	1.196	1.292	1.390	1.457	1.555	1.682
Nonexporting enterprise							
Textiles	1.090	1.137	1.189	1.259	1.280	1.320	1.444
Garments	—	—	—	—	—	—	—
Electrical appliances	1.198	0.954	0.625	0.587	0.657	0.603	0.712
Machine tools	—	—	—	—	—	—	—
Iron and steel	—	—	—	—	—	—	—
Metal products	1.047	1.060	1.087	1.157	1.034	1.060	1.084
Total	1.112	1.050	1.029	1.083	1.091	1.097	1.121

— Not available.

Note: Number of observations is the number of panel data observations employed to estimate production function coefficients used to calculate total factor productivity. The number

$$(11.3) \qquad \text{DRCR} = [(C^L - B^L)(\$L)]/[B^F - C^F)(\$US)]$$

where C^L is the domestic input costs of the enterprise measured in local currency, \$L; B^L is the local sales made by the enterprise, measured in local currency, \$L; B^F is the export earnings of the enterprise, measured

1988	1989	1990	1991	1992	Number of observations	Percentage difference export over nonexports
1.596	1.348	1.406	1.380	1.441		29.05
1.183	1.243	1.095	1.105	1.299		23.83
1.178	1.186	0.644	1.140	1.222		—
1.482	1.119	1.626	1.666	1.807		—
1.341	1.300	1.490	1.501	1.531		34.19
—	—	—	—	—		—
1.384	1.293	1.170	1.330	1.435		16.89
1.498	1.170	1.145	1.189	1.117	311	
0.797	0.955	1.023	1.017	1.049	426	
—	—	—	—	—	300	
—	—	—	—	—	70	
0.896	0.842	1.064	1.016	1.141	165	
0.978	0.950	1.210	1.449	1.398	60	
1.140	1.838	1.024	1.173	1.227	1,332	
—	—	—	—	—		—
1.391	1.563	1.601	1.668	1.713		—
1.777	1.889	1.488	1.896	1.989		21.75
—	—	—	—	—		—
1.845	1.920	1.909	1.969	2.023		—
—	—	—	—	—		—
1.779	1.877	1.974	2,072	2.169		47.39
1.469	1.540	1.535	1.618	1.606		
—	—	—	—	—		
1.321	1.466	1.525	1.407	1.634		
—	—	—	—	—		
—	—	—	—	—		
1.230	1.262	1.208	1.161	1.668		
1.264	1.347	1.238	1.459	1.472		

of observations is the same for each industry, as only one production function was estimated for all firms in each industry in order to obtain the output elasticities of factors in each industry.
Source: China Academy of Social Sciences 1993.

in foreign exchange, $US; and C^F is the import costs of the enterprise, measured in foreign exchange, $US.

According to the Bruno Ratio, for exports to be financially profitable, the domestic resource cost ratio, DRCR, must be less than or equal to the

TABLE 11.3

Total factor productivity growth indexes of exporting and nonexporting enterprises by city, 1980–92
(1980 = 1)

Year	Guangzhou		Shenzhen	
	Non-exporting enterprises	Exporting enterprises	Non-exporting enterprises	Exporting enterprises
1981	0.994	1.021	—	1.201
1982	0.995	1.060	—	1.295
1983	1.020	1.115	—	1.665
1984	1.051	1.171	—	1.673
1985	1.028	1.336	1.211	1.129
1986	1.082	1.300	1.169	1.265
1987	1.173	1.374	0.782	1.507
1988	1.226	1.453	0.823	1.509
1989	1.211	1.356	0.978	1.535
1990	1.249	1.342	0.578	1.313
1991	1.275	1.514	1.046	1.461
1992	1.426	1.634	1.085	1.515
Ratio of indexes in export and nonexport sectors in 1992	1.15		1.40	
Number of observations	105	154	61	107

n.a. Not available.
a. Only export-oriented enterprises were surveyed in Shanghai.

effective exchange rate, EER, confronting the firm. The requirements for profitability can be expressed as:

(11.4) $DRCR = [(S - M - p) - (S - X)](yuan)/(X - M)(\$US) < EER(yuan/\$US)$

or, in terms of the Bruno Ratio,

(11.5) $DRCR/EER = (X - M - p)(yuan)/[(X - M)(\$US)*EER (\$US/yuan)] < 1$

where, for each enterprise in each year, S is total sales, M is the import costs of the enterprise, p is pretax profit, and X is export sales, all measured in local currency.

A Bruno Ratio for each enterprise is calculated using equation 11.5. Enterprises are then grouped by ownership type, sector, and location to determine whether their Bruno Ratios are systematically higher or lower than unity (table 11.4). These ratios are also used in estimating equation 11.6 below. Ratios of less than unity imply that the domestic cost of producing a unit of exports is less than the relevant effective exchange rate, so that enterprises export at a profit.

Bruno Ratios are calculated using the actual reported costs of enterprises rather than the true economic domestic costs of production. In the

Xiamen		Shanghai		Total (excluding Shanghai)	
Non-exporting enterprises	Exporting enterprises	Non-exporting enterprises[a]	Exporting enterprises	Non-exporting enterprises	Exporting enterprises
1.244	1.105	—	1.017	1.1186	1.0632
1.193	1.040	—	1.044	1.094	1.6971
1.117	0.981	—	1.082	1.0685	1.8803
1.179	0.885	—	1.112	1.1152	1.8647
1.199	1.191	—	1.122	1.719	1.828
1.208	1.300	—	1.165	1.7293	1.9326
1.271	1.333	—	1.210	1.6132	2.1072
1.386	1.527	—	1.255	1.7175	2.2444
1.383	1.896	—	1.273	1.786	2.3936
1.286	1.971	—	1.157	1.5566	2.3133
1.494	2.130	—	1.232	1.90791	2.551
1.369	1.973	—	1.324	1.93965	2.56093
1.44				1.32	
79	50	—	85	245	396

Source: China Academy of Social Sciences 1993.

early 1980s the capital assets of most state enterprises had been installed under the plan, and no capital charges were paid for their use. Furthermore, most raw materials and energy were supplied at plan prices that were substantially below free market prices. Consequently, the reported costs of state enterprises would have been significantly less than their true economic costs of production. This expectation is confirmed by the low values of the ratios for state enterprises in the early and mid-1980s, when the cost of earning 1 yuan of export income was only 0.58–0.76 yuan. By the early 1990s state enterprises were securing a higher proportion of their investment finance from loans, and they were paying free market prices for most of their production inputs. Furthermore, export subsidies were abandoned in January 1991. During the 1990s the domestic cost of earning 1 yuan of export income increased significantly for state enterprises, rising from 0.65 yuan in 1980 to 1.14 yuan in 1991 (see table 11.4).

The Bruno Ratios for collective enterprises were more stable than those for state enterprises over the period 1980–92. They also rose slightly during the 1990s relative to the 1980s, although the increase was smaller than it was in state enterprises. The ratios of township and village enterprises were the

TABLE 11.4

Average Bruno Ratios by type of ownership, selected years, 1980–92

Year	State enterprises	Collective enterprises	Township and village enterprises	Joint ventures	Wholly foreign-owned
1980	0.65	0.89	0.96	—	—
1982	0.65	0.75	—	—	—
1984	0.62	0.79	—	—	—
1985	0.76	0.57	0.78	0.61	—
1987	0.58	0.89	—	0.92	—
1988	0.65	0.92	—	0.66	—
1990	0.95	0.97	0.90	1.00	0.91
1991	1.14	0.89	0.92	0.87	0.95
1992	0.82	0.94	0.85	0.95	0.93
Number of observations in 1992	85	14	11	55	13

— Not available.
Source: Survey data.

lowest of all the enterprise types in the 1990s. Township and village enterprises enjoyed these low ratios despite the fact that, like joint ventures and wholly foreign-owned firms, they secured the majority of their capital, raw materials, and energy at market prices. Compared with township and village enterprises, the ratios of the joint ventures and wholly foreign-owned enterprises were generally higher during the early 1990s and about the same or slightly lower than those of state and collective enterprises.

In most industrial sectors the measured ratios of domestic resource cost ratios to effective exchange rates rose during 1980–92 (table 11.5).

TABLE 11.5

Average Bruno Ratios by industry sector, selected years, 1980–92

Year	Cotton textiles	Noncotton textiles	Garments	Electrical appliances
1980	0.61	0.54	0.93	1.05
1984	0.62	—	0.79	0.64
1985	0.68	0.51	0.81	0.71
1986	0.96	—	0.91	0.81
1988	0.84	—	0.86	0.88
1989	0.76	—	0.96	0.66
1990	0.96	0.76	0.94	1.06
1991	0.91	0.92	1.07	0.80
1992	0.95	0.96	0.95	0.90
Number of observations in 1992	15	10	51	25

— Not available.
Note: Bruno Ratios are computed using the effective exchange rate confronting enterprises,

The increased exposure of enterprises to market forces throughout this period is the most likely explanation for the phenomenon. Input prices, which had been widely suppressed, were allowed to rise, while output prices for finished consumer goods tended to fall as a result of competition from nonstate enterprises. In contrast, the Bruno Ratio for the iron and steel industry fell over this period, reflecting the rise toward international prices of artificially low output prices of iron and steel products.

By 1992 the ratios of most of the included industrial sectors had narrowed (0.77–0.97 yuan versus 0.54–1.05 yuan in 1980), suggesting that exporting enterprises in different sectors were subject to an increasingly uniform policy regime. The electronic instruments branch, which reported the lowest Bruno Ratios in 1992, is classified as "high tech" and consequently enjoys preferential treatment, including access to duty drawbacks, bank credit, and subsidized inputs. These policies should be expected to reduce the financial cost of domestic resources and the estimated Bruno Ratio. The high tariff protection these products enjoy also raises the price they can charge for their output, lowering the measured ratios.

The average Bruno Ratios varied across the four coastal cities (table 11.6). The ratios of surveyed enterprises in Guangzhou were significantly lower than those in Shanghai. This finding is consistent with the expectation that the more liberal policy regime in Guangzhou reduces production costs. In addition, the close marketing ties with Hong Kong and international markets and the greater flexibility given to firms to trade on their own account should have increased the export revenues of Guangzhou firms. The ratios of Shenzhen enterprises are somewhat higher than those of Guangzhou and rose during the 1990s. This result

Machine tools	Iron and steel	Heavy metal products	Nonelectrical appliances	Electronic instruments	Other
—	—	—	0.75	—	1.01
—	—	—	—	—	—
—	—	—	0.69	—	0.56
0.45	1.00	—	—	—	—
0.53	1.02	—	—	—	0.81
0.71	0.89	1.83	—	—	—
0.91	0.77	1.17	0.90	0.79	1.03
0.85	0.82	1.00	0.86	0.61	0.98
0.89	0.97	0.80	0.87	0.77	0.84
4	8	2	20	5	29

which changed significantly over the sample period.
Source: China Academy of Social Sciences 1993.

TABLE 11.6
Average Bruno Ratios by city, selected years, 1980–92

Year	Guangzhou	Shenzhen	Xiamen	Shanghai
1980	0.76	—	—	0.80
1982	0.75	—	0.65	—
1984	0.79	0.64	0.62	—
1985	0.59	0.71	—	0.80
1986	0.66	0.89	—	—
1987	0.71	0.95	0.73	—
1988	0.76	0.81	0.87	—
1989	0.76	0.83	1.12	—
1990	0.89	0.87	1.15	1.10
1991	0.69	0.89	1.04	1.17
1992	0.68	0.94	0.90	1.10
Number of observations in 1992	41	50	24	64

— Not available.
Note: Bruno Ratios are computed using the effective exchange rate confronting enterprises, which changed significantly over the sample period.
Source: China Academy of Social Sciences 1993.

mirrors the falling total factor productivity growth in Shenzhen in the late 1980s and early 1990s (table 11.7), which in turn may reflect rising labor and land costs in Shenzhen.

The ratios of Xiamen enterprises were also higher than those of Guangzhou but lower than the Shanghai enterprises in the sample. After peaking in 1990, the Bruno Ratios of Xiamen enterprises have been falling steadily, perhaps reflecting the greater competitiveness of the many new export–oriented Taiwanese joint ventures and wholly foreign-owned firms in Xiamen (many of which were surveyed and had begun production only in the late 1980s and early 1990s).

TABLE 11.7
Indexes of total factor productivity growth by city, 1980–92

Year	Guangzhou	Shenzhen	Xiamen	Shanghai
1980	1.000	1.000	1.000	1.000
1981	1.012	1.201	1.188	1.015
1982	1.039	1.295	1.131	1.041
1983	1.084	1.665	1.060	1.073
1984	1.132	1.673	1.183	1.101
1985	1.234	1.223	1.188	1.108
1986	1.228	1.330	1.227	1.150
1987	1.308	1.488	1.280	1.194
1988	1.377	1.494	1.430	1.235
1989	1.309	1.537	1.604	1.251
1990	1.313	1.288	1.598	1.150
1991	1.435	1.488	1.770	1.233
1992	1.566	1.540	1.632	1.334

Source: China Academy of Social Sciences 1993.

The finding that ratios of Shanghai enterprises are higher than Guangzhou firms is consistent with a study of aggregate data from the two cities. That suggests that the high domestic cost of earning export income in Shanghai resulted from the skewing of Shanghai's industrial structure toward less competitive, capital-intensive heavy industry cities (Sung Yun-Wing and China Ministry of Foreign Trade and Economic Cooperation 1994). Although this may provide part of the explanation, the fact that the average ratios of the exporting enterprises in all the major heavy and light industrial sectors covered in the survey had fallen below 1.0 by 1992 whereas that of Shanghai stood at 1.1 that year may suggest that the full explanation lies elsewhere. The lower productivity performance of Shanghai enterprises—the result of the slower pace of enterprise and industrial policy reform in Shanghai—may account for the higher ratios.

Determinants of enterprise export performance

In a market economy firms export if it is profitable to do so. A country's export performance will be enhanced by policies that increase the capacity and incentive for enterprises to export. This section employs panel data on firm characteristics and export behavior to test hypotheses related to these policy prescriptions. It attempts to determine whether enterprises achieve superior export performance (measured by the ratio of exports to sales) if they operate in a policy environment that includes the following components:

- *Exposure to international markets.* Low average rates of protection should increase the profitability of production for export markets relative to domestic markets.
- *Planning and production autonomy.* A low ratio of planned to total production indicates autonomy in setting product mix and output levels on the basis of market signals and profit-maximization criteria.
- *Decisionmaking autonomy.* Internal decision autonomy enables firms to secure, allocate, and monitor inputs in order to maximize profits.
- *Trade autonomy.* Firms that are able to trade internationally on their own account or can use competitive export trading corporations can be expected to give exporters access to higher prices for their exported products and increase their profits from exporting.
- *Profit retention.* Firms with higher profit retention rates will have more incentive to exploit profit-making opportunities abroad.
- *Hard budget constraints.* Enterprises' reliance on bank loan finance rather than on plan-allocated investment funds serves as a proxy for

the presence of hard budget constraints, which should increase the incentives for enterprises to maximize profits.

- *Liberal provincial trade regimes.* Provinces with more liberal trade regimes—that is, provinces that are subject to fewer import, export, and foreign exchange controls—have greater incentive and capacity to maximize profits.

In addition to these policy variables, the impact of international comparative advantage and ownership is examined. Once policy parameters are controlled for, differences in domestic resource cost ratios may be attributable to differences in the enterprise's underlying comparative advantage. Independent of policy, intrinsic ownership characteristics may affect incentives or organization in such a way as to encourage or inhibit export activity.

In addition, China's macroeconomic developments may influence export performance. When the domestic economy is overheated and domestic demand grows rapidly, the quantity of goods available for export may decline, and export performance may deteriorate.[7]

To test the effect of these policy, location, ownership, and macroeconomic variables, an expanded export supply function is estimated using ordinary least squares (the variables are defined in box 11.1):

Box 11.1 Definition of variables

RXQ = ratio of the value of exports to total output, valued in local currency

BR = ratio of the DRCR to the effective exchange rate

ATP = weighted average rate of protection on output. atp is used instead of the preferred effective rate of protection because many of the relevant sectors exhibit negative value added at international prices, making it impossible to calculate their effective rates of protection (World Bank 1994)

RPP = ratio of planned to total production

RPR = ratio of profits retained by the enterprise to total profits

LFI = proportion of total investment funded by bank loans

DMA = dummy indicating whether the firm controls its own decisionmaking or whether supervisory authorities are wholly or partially responsible for decisionmaking

DET = dummy indicating whether the enterprise can trade directly on its own account

DO = ownership dummies for collective (DOC), township and village (DOV), and foreign-funded (DOF) enterprises. dof also indicates access to and attractiveness for foreign direct investment.

DL = locational dummies for Guangdong (DLG), Xiamen (DLX), and Shenzhen (DLS) intended to capture the effect of different provincial policy environments

dY = rate of change in gross domestic product.

$$(11.6) \; RXQ = c + \alpha_1 BR + \alpha_2 ATP + \alpha_3 RPP + \alpha_4 RPR + \alpha_5 LFI + \alpha_6 DMA$$
$$+ \alpha_7 DET + \alpha_8 DO + \alpha_9 DL + \alpha_{10} dY$$

Several alternative regressions based on equation 11.6 were run using ordinary least squares to explain enterprise export performance, measured by the ratio of exports to total output.

For all firms, decisionmaking autonomy, DMA, was the most important factor in explaining export performance (table 11.8). Firms that suffered less interference in their decisionmaking by bureaucratic supervisors appeared better able to compete in export markets. The ratio of planned to total output of enterprises, RPP, was also significant in explaining export performance; as could be expected, it was negatively correlated with the export achievement of enterprises. As enterprises were given more freedom to sell their output in the market, they appeared to increase their capacity to export. This improvement in export performance may well reflect the skills and attributes that such firms acquired in competing in the domestic market, including improved marketing, product quality, and presentation.

The Bruno Ratio was significant in explaining export performance but had a positive sign (firms with a higher ratio exported more). In a market economy firms with lower Bruno Ratios would be expected to export more. The financial domestic resource cost ratio of all enterprises, particularly state enterprises, rose during the reform period, probably as a result of their increasing exposure to market forces. At the same time—and probably for similar reasons—the export performance of Chinese enterprises improved. The regression thus appears to have found a positive relationship between export performance and financial ratios. This association is probably spurious, however, and merely reflects the fact that both were correlated with increased exposure to market forces.

The inclusive ordinary least squares regression was run for state enterprises in Shanghai. Ownership dummies were included for collective (DOC) township and village (DOV), and foreign-funded (DOF) enterprises. The positive and significant coefficients on the collective, township and village, and foreign-funded enterprise dummies indicate that all were significantly more successful exporters than state enterprises, even after controlling for the various policy variables. This result supports findings cited previously based on aggregate data that show that the bulk of export growth has been generated by the nonstate sector. These more dynamic sectors appear to have been better able to take advantage of export opportunities.

Locational dummies were included for Guangzhou (DLG), Shenzhen (DLS), and Xiamen (DLX). Enterprises located in the two special economic zones, Shenzhen and Xiamen, were significantly more successful exporters than those situated outside the zones, in Guangzhou and Shanghai. More detailed analysis would be necessary to determine which aspect of the special economic zones' policies (superior infrastructure, preferential tax, foreign-exchange retention policies) encouraged exports. A full cost-benefit analysis would be needed to determine whether the benefits of exports generated exceeded the costs of preferential policies provided to zone

TABLE 11.8

Enterprise-level determinants of export performance

Item	Total-1	Total-2	State-owned enterprises	Nonstate enterprises
BR	0.249	0.251	0.126	0.377
	(5.151)	(5.26)	(2.48)	(4.633)
ATP	0.273	0.292	0.304	0.364
	(4.659)	(5.141)	(4.65)	(4.397)
RPP	−0.094	−0.085		−0.207
	(2.110)	(1.944)		(2.248)
RPR	−0.001			
	(0.055)			
LFI	0.001			
	(0.057)			
DMA	0.299	0.291	0.266	0.5
	(10.113)	(10.089)	(10.246)	(0.391)
DET	−0.037			0.141
	(1.141)			(2.454)
DOC	0.168	0.13		
	(3.575)	(3.283)		
DOV	0.126	0.146		
	(2.334)	(2.809)		
DOF	0.074	0.064		
	(2.13)	(1.902)		
DLG	−0.031			0.067
	(0.974)			(0.925)
DLS	0.105	0.107	0.046	0.157
	(2.816)	(3.473)	(1.072)	(2.746)
DLX	0.178	0.179	0.097	0.229
	(3.927)	(4.402)	(1.632)	(3.576)
dY	−0.003			
	(1.072)			
C	0.214	−0.141	−0.09	−0.318
	(0.698)	(2.459)	(1.857)	(2.566)
R^2	0.523	0.525	0.47	0.441
Number of observations	512	512	238	274

Note: Numbers in parentheses are t-statistics.
Source: China Academy of Social Sciences 1993.

firms (see Lin 1994). The mix of policies pursued in the zones, however, does appear to have stimulated exports.

The capacity of firms to export on their own account, DET, had a positive impact on export performance but was significant only at the 12 percent level. Gross national product growth rates, dy, had a small negative impact on export performance (in years with a more rapid growth in domestic demand the availability of goods for export declined somewhat) but were not highly significant.

The coefficient on the average rate of tariff protection, ATP, was found to be significant in explaining export orientation but had a positive sign. This result may indicate that some unnecessary protection in import tariffs is imposed by China on imports competing with export-oriented garments and electronic appliances. High tariffs have been applied to many product categories to prevent the "waste" of foreign exchange on luxury items; at the lower-quality end China is now a very competitive exporter. Quantitative barriers and import licensing are also at least as important as tariffs in China in determining the overall level of protection. The average rate of tariff protection is therefore a very imperfect proxy for aggregate nominal protection. Given that no account is taken of protection on inputs, ATP is an even poorer measure of the effective rate of protection.

The proportion of profits retained by enterprises, RPR, and the proportion of loans in total investment, LFI, were not found to be significant determinants of export performance in the original model and were therefore dropped from the final model (total-2). A separate study found that the proportion of loans in total investment and the percentage of retained profits both have a positive impact on total factor productivity growth (World Bank 1994).

The ability to export on their own account was more significantly related to export orientation for nonstate firms than for state enterprises. This may reflect the greater ability of nonstate firms to exploit their right to trade on their own account to promote the sale of their exports. Location in the special economic zones, Shenzhen and Xiamen, was also much more likely to be associated with export orientation for nonstate firms than for state enterprises. This probably indicates that nonstate firms have been able to exploit the preferential policy environment in special economic zones more effectively to enhance their export competitiveness.

Conclusions

The Bruno Ratios of enterprises in Guangzhou—and to a lesser extent Shenzhen and Xiamen, where the pace of reform and marketization has been more rapid—are considerably lower than those in Shanghai. These differences imply that exporters in south China are more cost efficient and profitable than those in Shanghai.

Among the different ownership forms, the market-oriented township and village enterprises have the lowest Bruno Ratios. These ratios rose rapidly for state enterprises throughout the reform period, reflecting their increased exposure to market forces.

The major determinants of export success at the enterprise level appear to be enterprise decisionmaking autonomy and exposure to freer domestic markets. For nonstate firms the right of firms to export on their own account also has a positive impact on export success. Even controlling for policy differences, collective, township and village, and foreign-funded enterprises are all significantly more successful exporters than state enterprises. Enterprises located in the two special economic zones, Shenzhen and Xiamen, enjoy a substantial export advantage.

Several policy conclusions can be drawn from these results. Export performance can be enhanced by withdrawing supervisory authorities from decisionmaking within enterprises, by revoking any remaining obligations for firms to produce under the plan, and by granting firms the right to trade on their own account. Extending 100 percent duty drawbacks, tax, and other privileges enjoyed by firms in the special economic zones to all enterprises or, preferably, dismantling China's heavy protection regime and achieving a fully convertible yuan are likely to improve China's industrial export performance. The continuing growth of the nonstate sector is likely to be one of the most important factors in improving China's export performance. Consequently, policies that encourage this sector, including capital market reform, should be given high priority.

Notes

1. The positive relationship between trade liberalization and growth, through mechanisms such as increased productivity of the traded and nontraded goods sectors, was first tested by Krueger (1978), Feder (1983), and others. Some of the literature linking export orientation to higher productivity growth, including studies by Harrison (1991), Dollar (1992), and Thomas and Wang (1993), is summarized in World Bank (1993). Other studies, including those by Krugman (1994), challenge the relationship between export orientation and growth and claim that old-fashioned factor accumulation accounts for the growth of East Asian economies.

2. The industries are cotton textiles, noncotton textiles, garments, electrical appliances, machine tools, iron and steel, heavy metal products, nonelectrical appliances, and electronic instruments.

3. Accurate estimates of the ratio of trade to GNP are complicated by the difficulty of obtaining reliable calculations of GNP. Purchasing power parity estimates of China's GNP may be several times higher than official GNP data. Although using exchange rate–adjusted measures of income in lieu of purchasing power parity estimates will pro-

vide an upward bias to these ratios, it will do so for both 1978 and 1993 data and should thus not substantially affect the conclusion that the Chinese economy has become significantly more integrated into the world economy over the reform period. As the purchasing power parity estimates of virtually all developing countries exceed their official GNP data, this bias also exists in ratios of exports to GNP of most of the industrializing economies in Asia with which China is compared.

4. Although foreign trade corporations continued to subsidize trade in planned imports, efforts were made to pare back the rate of these companies by raising domestic prices for many important imported commodities, such as iron and steel, nonferrous metals, and grains, to the point where many came to approximate international prices. As a result of these reforms and the abolition of export subsidies, the losses of the foreign trade corporations subsidized through the plan fell from a peak of 33.6 billion yuan in 1989 to 17.6 billion yuan in 1991. In 1989 these losses represented 2.1 percent of GDP and 85 percent of the central government's deficit; by 1991 foreign trade corporations' losses had fallen to 0.9 percent of GDP and 25 percent of the deficit (World Bank 1994).

5. Between 1979 and 1990 Shanghai received $1.3 billion of foreign direct investment, while Guangdong attracted $6.5 billion. Including loans and processing investments, Shanghai received only $4.5 billion over this period, just over a third of the $12.4 billion invested in Guangdong (see Sung Yun-Wing and Ministry of Foreign Trade and Economic Cooperation 1996).

6. The estimated factor output elasticities are reported in Perkins (1996). The robustness of these estimates was checked using an F-statistic to test for heteroscedasticity across time and across enterprises within each industry. The results reported in Perkins and Raiser (1994) demonstrate that for all but one industry the hypothesis of homoscedasticity over time could not be rejected. However, across enterprises within each industry, heteroscedasticity could not be rejected in most cases. Because this finding suggests that there were significant differences in the technologies employed by different firms within the same industry, the production functions were reestimated allowing for fixed and random effects. A Hausman specification test was then employed to test for the dominance of fixed over random effects. Although the null hypothesis of the dominance of fixed effects could not be rejected in two industries (the P-statistic was significant at the 5 percent level), in only one case (heavy metal products) did the labor and capital output elasticity coefficients significantly differ from those produced by the ordinary least squares estimates. Because a uniform estimation technique should be used across all industry production functions to estimate and compare total factor productivity growth, the ordinary least squares estimates were retained in equation 11.1.

7. All of these hypotheses assume that supply-side factors rather than demand factors, such as the level of world income growth, dominate China's export performance (see Yang 1993).

References

Bell, Michael, Hoe Ee Khor, Jun Ma, Simon N'guiamba, and Rajiv Lall. 1993. "China at the Threshold of a Market Economy." Occasional Paper 107, International Monetary Fund, Washington, D.C.

Bruno, Michael. 1967. "The Optimal Selection of Export-Promoting and Import-Substituting Projects." *Planning the External Sector: Techniques, Problems and Policies.* New York: United Nations.

Chen, Kuan, Gary H. Jefferson, Thomas G. Rawski, Hongchang Wang, and Yuxin Zheng. 1988a. "New Estimates of Fixed Investment and Capital Stock for Chinese State Industry." *China Quarterly* (June): 243–66.

———. 1988b. "Productivity Changes in Chinese Industry: 1953–1985." *Journal of Comparative Economics* 12: 570–91.

China State Statistical Bureau. Various years. *China Statistical Yearbook. (Zhongguo tongji nianjian)* (in Chinese). Beijing: China Statistical Publications Office.

Chinese Academy of Social Sciences. 1993. "Enterprise Survey." Beijing.

Dollar, David. 1992. "Outward Oriented Developing Countries Really Do Grow More Rapidly: Evidence from 92 LDCs, 1976–1985." *Economic Development and Cultural Change* 40(3): 523–24.

Feder, Gershon. 1983. "On Exports and Economic Growth." *Journal of Development Economics* 12: 59–73.

General Administration of Customs. 1994. *China's Customs Statistics.* Beijing: General Administration of Customs.

Granger, C. W. J. 1969. "Investigating Causal Relations by Econometric Models and Cross-Spectral Methods." *Econometrica* 37: 424–38.

Harrison, Anne. 1991. "Openness and Growth." PRE Working Paper 809. World Bank, Washington, D.C.

International Monetary Fund. 1993. *Annual Report.* Washington, D.C.

Kalirajan, K. P., and R. T. Shand. 1991. "Causality between Technical and Allocative Efficiencies: An Empirical Testing." *Journal of Economic Studies* 2: 3–17.

Krueger, Anne O. 1978. "Alternative Trade Strategies and Employment in LDCs." *American Economic Review* 68(2): 270–74.

Krugman, Paul. 1994. "The Myth of Asia's Miracle." *Foreign Affairs* (November–December) 62–78.

Lardy, N. 1992. *Foreign Trade and Economic Reform in China, 1978–1990.* New York: Cambridge University Press.

Lin, Shujuan. 1994. "Application of Cost-Benefit Analysis in China: A Case Study of the Xiamen Special Economic Zone." In Frances C. Perkins, ed. 1994. *Practical Cost Benefit Analysis.* Melbourne: MacMillian.

Perkins, F. C., ed. 1994. *Practical Cost Benefit Analysis.* Melbourne: MacMillian.

———. 1996. "Productivity Performance and Priorities for the Reform of China's State Owned Enterprises." *Journal of Development Studies* 32(3): 414–44.

Perkins, Frances C., and M. Raiser. 1994. "State Enterprise Reform and Macroeconomic Stability in Transition Economies." Working Paper 665. Institute of World Economics, Kiel.

Shanghai Statistical Bureau. 1993. *Shanghai Pudong.* New Area, Statistical Annual Report. Shanghai.

———. Various years. *Statistical Yearbook of Shanghai.* Shanghai.

Sung, Yun-Wing, and China Ministry of Foreign Trade and Economic Cooperation. 1994. *Almanac of MOFTEC.* Beijing: Ministry of Foreign Trade and Economic Cooperation.

Thomas, Vinod, and Yan Wang. 1993. "Government Policy and Productivity Growth: Is East Asia an Exception?" Background paper for *The East Asian Miracle.* World Bank, Policy Research Department, Washington, D.C.

World Bank. 1992. *China: Reform and the Role of the Plan in the 1990s.* Washington, D.C.

———. 1993. *The East Asian Miracle*. New York: Oxford University Press.

———. 1994. *China: Foreign Trade Reform*. Washington, D.C.

Yang, Yongzheng. 1993. "China, the New Giant—Is Its Trading Pattern Following?" Festschrift Seminar for Professor Helen Hughes, Australian National University, Canberra.

Appendix A
A Model of Economic Reform
Gary H. Jefferson and Thomas G. Rawski

Discussions of socialist economic reform tend to focus on two opposing policy alternatives. Recommendations for economic reform in the former Soviet Union and Eastern Europe emphasize rapid transition to a market economy. Proponents of this view argue that gradualism only postpones the inevitable costs of restructuring while reducing the likelihood of achieving the desired outcome (see, for example, IMF and others 1990). Proponents of gradualism point to China's rapid growth to demonstrate the "efficacy of gradual and partial reform" (Chen, Jefferson, and Singh 1992, p. 201). They find that "growing out of the plan" rather than abruptly dismantling the planning system can transform the behavior of state and enlarge the role of the nonstate sector while reducing the risk of mass unemployment and other dangers associated with sudden and comprehensive reform (see, for example, Naughton 1994; Gelb, Jefferson, and Singh 1993).

Neither perspective is firmly linked to any body of economic theory. The frequency with which positions are defended with references to a single episode in one country or to simple-minded aphorisms ("leaping a chasm requires a single jump"; "crossing a river requires stepping stones") suggests the need for a unified analytical framework that can help determine whether prescriptions for sweeping or gradual reform represent potentially optimal strategies for all, some, or none of the former socialist states.

One way in which economic analysis progresses is by applying established theories to new topics. Schultz (1961) used the theory of investment to study human capital. The same theory can be used to create a systematic framework for thinking about the process of economic transition.

The model of reform developed here is based on an analogy between factors affecting a firm's investment decision and factors affecting a government's choice of reform policy. Investment decisions and reform efforts share key characteristics. In both cases the agent solves a problem of economic transition—how to get from the current state of the world to a preferred state of the world. In the case of the investment decision the owner-manager maximizes the firm's expected net worth; in the case of economic reform the agent maximizes society's expected welfare. Both seek to understand a set of technical and intertemporal relationships in which current inputs—factors of production in the case of the investor, instruments of reform in the case of the reformer—expand production capabilities and profit or welfare in the future. Both the investment process and the reform process entail costs of adjustment that involve risk and uncertainty.

The central argument presented here is that just as the optimal rate of investment for the firm depends on circumstances that are specific to the firm and its market environment, the socially optimal reform strategy depends on conditions that are specific to each country. For the firm, these conditions include the market environment, the degree of substitutability or complementarity between labor and capital, the costs of adjustment, and the level of uncertainty regarding the capabilities of the new technologies to be installed and the level of future sales demand. The weights assigned to the level of uncertainty will depend on the owner's degree of risk aversion. For economies in transition, analogous conditions include a nation's reform environment, or the initial conditions within which the reform package is formulated; the extent of substitutability or complementarity among reform instruments; the costs of adjustment; the level of uncertainty concerning the effectiveness of alternative reform strategies; and society's vision of a preferred set of post-transition institutions. The consequences of uncertainty for the means and ends of transition will depend on the degree of society's risk aversion. This appendix attempts to give some formal structure to this analogy between the investment and reform decision and to derive various implications for the design and speed of transition programs.

At the outset it is important to clarify a critical distinction between two elements of economic transition—inputs to transition (or reform policy) and the output of transition (or gains in social welfare). For the firm in transition this distinction between inputs and output is also important, since the adjustment of capital, labor, and other inputs gives rise to improved efficiency or profitability. The inputs and outputs of economies in transition are described below.

The reformer's problem

In the model presented here the reformer operates within a larger context involving feedback and experimentation, captured explicitly by parameters in the model that represent uncertainty regarding the vision of the post-transition society and the technique of reform.[1] From the reformer's perspective, the object of reform is to maximize social welfare over a time horizon that begins at $t = 0$ and extends to $t = T$. The basic structure of the reformer's problem is captured by equation A1.1:

$$(A1.1) \qquad \max E(W) = \int_{t=0}^{T} e^{-\delta t} \, Iw_t(\overset{+}{Y_t}, \overset{-}{R_t}, \rho_t \overline{\theta}_T - \theta_t) dt$$

where W is the expected present value of social welfare, δ is the discount rate, and w_t is social welfare in the current period. As the population is assumed to be risk-averse, welfare can increase with either a rise in Y (income per capita) or a decline in R (a measure of risk). The term $\rho_t \theta_T - \theta_t$ represents the distance of society's vision of the optimal set of post-transition and institutional arrangements (θ_T) from its current set of institutional arrangements (θ_t). The parameter $0 \leq \rho \leq 1$ represents the clarity of the post-transition vision, with $\rho = 1$ representing a clear vision and $\rho = 0$ representing a yet-to-be formulated vision. The term $\rho_t \theta_T - \theta_t$ may be small, either because $(\theta_T - \theta_t) \to 0$ or $\rho_t \to 0$. The closer society's institutions are to a clear alternative vision—that is, the smaller the value of $\rho_t \theta_T - \theta_t$—the greater the increase in social welfare. Friedman and Johnson (1996) argue that if initial conditions are poor, countries will want to make the transition to a better state of the world more quickly.

Income per capita grows at rate g, the rate of productivity growth, so that $Y_t = Y_{0e}^{gt}$, where Y_0 represents income per capita at $t = 0$, the beginning of the reform period. The reformer maximizes equation A1.1 subject to the following reform function:

$$(A1.2) \qquad g_t = f_1[A_{t-1}, X_t(\mathbf{M}_t, \mathbf{S}_t), \Omega_t]$$

In equation A1.2 productivity growth arises from three factors: A, a set of predetermined conditions faced by the country at the end of $t - 1$; X, a bundle of reform instruments defined by $X(\mathbf{M,S})$, where $\mathbf{M}$ and $\mathbf{S}$ are vectors that define the mix ($\mathbf{M}$) and intensity or speed ($\mathbf{S}$) of the reform package, and Ω, a random variable that captures the uncertain link between various reform inputs and their outcomes. While $\mathbf{M}$, a list of on-off $(0,1)$ choices for each reform instrument, establishes the mix of reform, $\mathbf{S}$ rises monotonically with the intensity of reform. In equation A1.2, $g_A > 0$ and $g_X > 0$ in the long run; in the short run more reform may result in slower productivity growth. In addition, $\text{var}(g)_\Omega > 0$.

In the long run a reformed system supports a higher rate of productivity growth than an unreformed system. With convex costs of adjustment, over some range of $\mathbf{S}_t$ it is possible that $g_S < 0$, as exhibited by the "J"-curve phenomenon displayed by the transition paths of Eastern European countries and the former Soviet republics.

Risk is determined by the following function:

(A1.3)
$$R_t = f_2[\rho_t, \Omega_t; \text{var}(y_{it})]$$

where

(A1.4)
$$\text{var}(y_{it}) = h_2(A_{t-1}, X_t)$$

and $R_S > 0$ and $R_{s,s} > 0$ for a given **M**.

As reform occurs, individuals are subject to various forms of risk. Within the model risk arises from three sources—end-state risk, means risk, and the risk of fluctuations in household income. End-state risk involves the risk that reformers may move to the wrong state of the world. If ρ is low, reformers may make misguided decisions that will require a second transition. Since transition is costly, rapid transition toward an uncertain state of the world entails risk. Means risk arises from uncertainty over the technique of reform—that is, which reform bundles work and which do not. When Ω is large, reformers lack certainty regarding the impact of bundles of reform; reforms that are expected to raise productivity may in fact slow it through unintended consequences.

The risk of fluctuation in household income arises from two sources. The first is intertemporal or time-series variations in gross domestic product, such as the protracted fall in reported real output in Russia during 1989–97. The second is inequality, or the cross-sectional dispersion of household incomes. An increase in var(y_{it}) may have broad social ramifications, such as a rise in crime or an increase in political instability.

According to equation A1.3, the risk associated with a particular bundle of reforms depends on the mix and intensity of reform. In general, however, risk is convex in **S**, so that increasing the intensity of reform generates more than a proportional increase in risk.

Based on the transition model summarized by equations A1.1 through A1.4, inputs to transition consist of $X(\mathbf{M,S})$—bundles of reform instruments. Transition outputs consist of the variables that directly affect social welfare summarized in equation A.1—living standards that are driven by productivity growth (g), economic stability [ρ, Ω, var(y_{it})], and proximity to society's post-transition vision ($\rho_t\theta_T - \theta_t$). Notice that the parameter ρ affects welfare through two channels. As $\rho \rightarrow 1$ the risk of a misguided transition declines; as $\rho \rightarrow 0$ dissatisfaction regarding the current set of institutions declines.

Reform is approached as a transition problem that involves three stages of analysis. In the first stage the reformer identifies the set of feasible and efficient bundles of reform (X). This set defines the economy's transition possibilities frontier, shown in figure A1.1. A reform bundle is on the frontier if it minimizes risk (maximizes stability) for a given rate of productivity growth (alternatively, for a given level of risk an efficient bundle of reforms maximizes productivity growth). Every point on the frontier is associated with a unique reform bundle. In figure A1.1 only the segment AB is efficient, since to the left of A a reduction in productivity growth leads to less, not more, stability, and below B a reduction in stability leads to less, not more, productivity growth.

The reform function will vary across countries. In equation A1.2, the functional form, f_1, will differ across countries since different reform instruments will have different effects—both independently and in combination with other instruments—because they share different degrees of complementarity. Moreover, significant uncertainty may exist in some societies about the means to reform (that is, Ω will differ across countries).

The second stage of the reform decision involves a description of society's preferences for high living standards, Y; economic stability, R^{-1}, and convergence to a preferred set of social, political, and economic institutions, $\rho_t \theta_T - \theta_t$. At the beginning of the reform period living standards are fixed at Y_0; at time t they are fixed by g, the rate of increase in living standards or productivity.

FIGURE A1.1
Tradeoff between productivity growth and stability

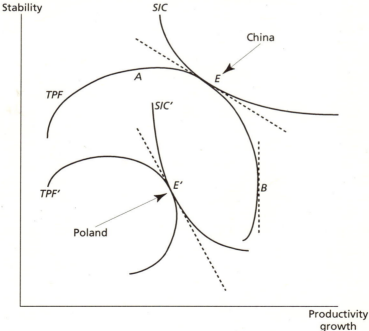

Source: Authors' schematization.

The reformer's last analytical problem involves the choice of a specific welfare-maximizing bundle of reforms. If preferences for income and stability are assumed to be convex, then society's indifference curve (SIC) and transition possibilities curve (TPF) together create a unique intersection at which society's marginal rate of substitution between risk and rising living standards equals its marginal rate of transformation in reform. This unique solution is shown at E in figure A1.1.

This economic model enjoys several advantages. First, construction of the transition possibilities frontier separates consideration of the set of feasible and efficient reform possibilities from society's preferences. Second, the model explicitly takes into account society's preferences for income and risk. Third, by separately identifying reform techniques and social preferences, the model establishes an analytical framework for combining these considerations to allow for systematic comparisons of reform options within a country and comparisons of efficient reform scenarios across countries.

A key conclusion of this analysis is that there is no single recipe for reform. In the investment theory of the firm, differences in technologies, certainties regarding production possibilities and future sales demand, and the degree of risk aversion between two firms will affect their optimal paths of adjustment. For the reformer, similar reform strategies—that is, the same $X(\mathbf{M},\mathbf{S})$—may result in very different outcomes some of which may be optimal for one country but not for another.

The transition possibilities frontier

Like goods production, economic reform can be viewed as a process in which multiple inputs and outputs share an identifiable relationship that can be summarized by a stochastic functional form. The three conditions that determine the set of feasible, technically efficient bundles of reforms that establish the shape and position of the transition possibilities frontier are the degree of substitutability (complementarity) among the instruments of reform, the costs of adjustment, and the productivity or initial conditions parameter, A. Together these conditions determine the combinations of productivity growth and stability that can be achieved with various mixes and intensities of reform.

Imagine that the firm is attempting to maximize profit in the face of growing but uncertain demand that is projected to outstrip capacity. The firm employs two factors, labor and capital, in a stochastic production function. Labor can be hired and fired costlessly; the investment process entails convex costs of adjustment. The following set of propositions and analogies can be derived from this model.

Substitutability and complementarity

For the firm attempting to add capacity in a world of uncertainty and adjustment costs, substitutability is desirable, since in the short run the firm may have more flexibility in adjusting its work force than its capital stock. Many commentators implicitly visualize the reform function from a Leontief perspective, in which inputs are required in fixed proportions. Dhanji (1991), for example, argues that reform is "a 'seamless web' in which every element is intimately related to every other" (p. 327). As a result, "because reforms are all of a piece, countries do not enjoy the luxury of doing one thing at a time. ... it is important to act on ... many fronts at once" (p. 327). This view implies that there is little or no substitutability among policies. The omission of certain "essential" components is predicted to compromise the beneficial consequences of other reform initiatives.

PROPOSITION 1. *When the costs of adjustment for one factor (the reform instrument) are held fixed, the greater the elasticity of substitution among inputs the less comprehensive the adjustment process (reform) and the higher the level of attainable outputs (welfare) in the short run. The greater the degree of substitutability, the longer it takes to achieve the steady state mix of inputs and outputs.*

Given a firm's production technology, such that $\sigma_{K,L} > 1$, the firm can approach its output target Q^* with additions of either labor or capital. If the investment process entails costs of adjustment but the hiring and firing of labor does not, then to produce a level of output that is close to Q^*, the firm will adjust labor input more quickly than its capital stock. Unless σ is infinite, diminishing returns to labor will require the full adjustment of capital and labor to achieve profit maximization in the steady state.

Analogously, for the transition economy substitutability among reform instruments implies unbalanced transition. Reform in some areas will proceed more rapidly than in others. Reforms involving large costs of adjustment will lag, while those for which adjustment costs are small will be rapid. Since substitutability will allow for substantial welfare gains from partial reform and the incremental gains of comprehensive and complete welfare will be small, reforms involving large adjustment costs will be postponed.

Privatization involving substantial layoffs creates large costs of adjustment. Management reform under continuing public ownership, including incentive contracts and layoff constraints, is a less costly avenue for securing short-run productivity gains. The greater the productivity gains of management reform under public ownership, the longer privatization can be postponed.

PROPOSITION 2. *The converse of Proposition 1 is that with a given positive cost of adjustment to one factor (instrument), as σ → 0 the adjustment (reform) process will be increasingly balanced. Relative to the case in which substitutability is high, complementarity will imply a faster rate of adjustment for the factor whose adjustment cost is high and a slower rate of adjustment for the factor whose adjustment cost is low.*

For the transition economy complementarity will imply a more comprehensive and balanced reform program. However, a high degree of jointness among all reform instruments implies that if one instrument is costly, they are all costly. If σ → 0, to take advantage of the benefits of complementarity, the speed of adjustment of the reform with high costs of adjustment will be faster than in the case of high substitutability. Relative to the case of high substitutability, jointness among reforms with high and low adjustment costs will slow the adjustment of the instruments with low intrinsic adjustment costs. As σ → 0 reform proceeds only as fast as the most difficult reform.

Bank reform and enterprise reform are widely understood to be highly complementary. Successfully converting a banking system to commercial practices may entail relatively little cost and substantial benefit. Successful banking reform, however, depends on the ability to harden the soft budget constraints of loss-making enterprises that subsidize overemployment. Tightening the soft budget constraint of enterprises in order to eliminate the requirement for loan subsidies therefore requires substantial layoffs and social cost. The costs of banking reform and the costs of enterprise reform become indistinguishable. If banking reform and enterprise reform were not complements, banking reform by itself would not induce the costs required of enterprise reform. It is the fact of complementarity that requires costs of adjustment to be viewed as the property of a bundle of economic reforms rather than as the consequence of a single reform in isolation.

Costs of adjustment

If reform were costless and easily reversible, transitions would occur instantaneously, since to do otherwise would reduce welfare below its attainable level. In general, however, reform is neither costless nor reversible. Convex costs of adjustment will generally induce firms to spread out the investment process. Investing to alter existing facilities is inherently disruptive since it displaces ongoing production. Rapid reform creates the possibility of brief or even extended reductions in output and declines in productivity growth. Reform erodes or destroys long-standing systems of supply, procurement, and distribution before new arrangements can fully replace them (Murphy, Schleifer, and Vishny 1992). These costs correspond to the "myriad teething troubles experienced with new plant" at the microeconomic level (Nickell 1978, p. 25) and to the "J-curve" phenomenon, in which a country's trade balance may deteriorate in the initial aftermath of currency devaluation because prices shift more rapidly than quantities (Brada and King 1991). By disrupting production, each of these reform measures can cause a decline in productivity and gross national product.

Costs of adjustment affect social welfare by depressing productivity growth (equation A1.2) and living standards (equation A.1) and by increasing risk (equation A1.3). Propositions 1 and 2 are based on comparative statics, which assume fixed costs of adjustment with increasing substitutability (Proposition 1) and increasing complementarity (Proposition 2). Proposition 3 examines the case in which the substitution elasticity is held fixed and adjustment costs are allowed to vary.

PROPOSITION 3. *For any given finite σ, the higher the cost of adjustment for any factor, the slower the adjustment process (reform).*

This phenomenon explains why transitions in socialist economies take years rather than days or months. The high cost of privatization and layoffs retards the rate of privatization. Because privatization shares a complementary relationship with so many other reforms (including establishing a government-financed social insurance system, price stabilization, and banking reform), those reforms, which do not directly involve layoffs, proceed more slowly than they would if they were not jointly linked with privatization.

The productivity parameter

The efficiency parameter, A_{t-1}, affects both the marginal product of individual factors of production and the productivity of the overall bundle of inputs. Imagine two firms that produce the same level of output and are identical in every respect except that firm 1 enjoys a productivity parameter that is twice that of firm 2. Both firms want to double output. With $A_1 = 2A_2$, to achieve $2Q$, firm 1 requires only half the additional quantity of inputs required by firm 2.

PROPOSITION 4. *The larger the productivity parameter, the greater the impact of reform; that is, dg/dX is increasing in A. For the firm, high productivity allows small increments in inputs to have a large impact; for transition economies, a favorable set of initial conditions magnifies the impact of reform initiatives.*

China's Open Door policy had an immediate and dramatic impact on trade and investment. The creation of special economic zones in China's southeastern provinces capitalized on the infrastructure of Hong Kong and the large pool of overseas Chinese investors. The effect was a large flow of overseas investment to the zones—far more than the foreign direct investment Russia was able to attract.

PROPOSITION 5. *The effect of a large productivity parameter on the speed of transition is ambiguous. If the cost of adjustment increases with the magnitude of **S** only, for a given intensity of reform input a larger **A** will increase the returns to reform and speed transition. If, however, the cost of adjustment is increasing in **A** and **X**—that is, it depends on the impact of reform rather than on its intensity alone—then by causing the benefits and costs of reform to rise equally, an increase in **A** may not accelerate the transition process. Instead, it may slow down the rate of reform while achieving a higher rate of productivity growth. Alternatively, if reformers have a target level of productivity (g*) or welfare (W*) in mind, an increase in the productivity parameter may actually slow the process of reform.*

It could be argued that reform has not progressed faster in China because it has not needed to progress faster. For various reasons that can be summarized by the **A** vector, China's gradual reform program has yielded exceptionally high rates of productivity and per capita income growth. A comparatively high rate of productivity growth has been achieved with a bundle of reforms that is modest relative to those adopted in East Europe.

Society's preferences for reform

For a risk-averse population, households may feel worse off even as incomes rise if rising living standards are insufficient to compensate for the risk of unemployment, inflation, and changing relative prices and incomes that are intrinsic to the transition process. As with the firm's investment decision, the introduction of risk and uncertainty fundamentally influences the optimal path of reform. Three types of risk and uncertainty—regarding the end-state of reform, the means or technique of reform, or the stability of individual household income—may affect society's preferences. These costs of reform that arise from society's risk aversion constitute the second leg of reform's costs of adjustment, the first being predictable output or productivity declines arising from disruption to the prereform process of production.

End-state risk

One of the arguments of the social welfare function shown in equation A1.1 is $\rho_t \theta_T - \theta_t$. The interpretation of this equation is similar to that of the Harris-Todaro migration model (1970), in which the incentive for the rural resident to migrate to the city is proportional to the distance between the expected urban wage and the existing wage, which is known with certainty. The expected wage is the urban wage weighted by the employment rate, a proxy for the probability of employment, $0 \leq \rho \leq 1$. In equation A1.1, the distance between the existing set of institutions and the post-transition institutions is determined not only by the difference between the preferred and current institutions $(\theta_T - \theta_t)$ but also by the clarity of society's vision of these post-transition institutions (ρ_t).

PROPOSITION 6. *As $\rho \rightarrow 0$ the risk of undertaking a misguided transition rises. If the firm ends up with useless production capacity or the society has moved to the wrong state of the world, it must subsequently organize a second transition. Because transitions are costly, in a world of learning-by-reforming, uncertainty concerning the post-transition state of the world should delay the reform process. Alternatively, as $\rho \rightarrow 1$ the distance between the existing and preferred states of the world grows. The two conditions—the risk associated with moving too quickly with an unclear vision and the dissatisfaction of the status quo with a clear alternative vision—argue for a faster pace of transition as $\rho \rightarrow 1$.*

Analogies with investment theory are instructive with respect to uncertainty about the preferred end-state. In the rare case in which a firm faces no uncertainty regarding the future state of the world (that is, the level of sales demand and the quality of its product), it should move hastily to invest in the plant and equipment required to achieve this state. If the firm is uncertain about the mix and level of future sales demand, it should proceed more slowly, particularly with those investments that are costly to reverse. Within this context, it is not surprising that eastern Germany, which sought to copy the economic institutions and policies of western Germany, moved rapidly to transform its economy; the other Eastern European nations moved somewhat more slowly; the former Soviet republics generally moved more slowly still; and China pursued the most gradual path of transition.

Means risk

Equation A1.2, the reform productivity function, is modeled as a stochastic function. This represents the uncertainty that is inherent in newly adopted technologies and reforms. Since differences in economic systems are large relative to differences in firms producing the same product line, uncertainty regarding the impact of reform instruments is inherent in the reform process.

PROPOSITION 7. *In the presence of uncertainty about available production technologies, the firm will postpone or slow adoption of new technologies in order to learn about their appropriateness of fit with production objectives. Uncertainty about the means of reform, costly reversal of reform, and learning-by-doing that clarifies the techniques of reform will each slow the transition process.*

Because of their physical and cultural proximity to Western Europe, Eastern Europeans had little doubt that adopting the economic policies and institutions of Western Europe would work in Eastern Europe. In contrast, China's reformers have been more skeptical of the relevance of "Western economics" for China. As a result, China's reformers have made extensive use of reform experiments as a means of testing and learning about the wider impacts of various reform initiatives. This, more than any other feature of China's reform program, marks it with "Chinese characteristics."

Risk of output fluctuations and income variations

If society is risk-averse, the increase in welfare from additional income may not compensate for the welfare loss resulting from increased risk associated with macroeconomic fluctuations or a deteriorating distribution of income.

PROPOSITION 8. *If rapid reform is expected to increase the likelihood of output fluctuations and income inequality (that is, $R_{S,S} > 0$), reformers will progress more slowly.*

The disruption and economic decline in Eastern Europe and Russia following their abrupt abandonment of central planning reinforced the view of many Chinese leaders and intellectuals that a gradual reform program that avoids the risk of sudden declines in output and rising income inequality is superior to shock therapy. Chinese reformers' desire to preserve political stability in the face of economic transition also argued for minimizing economic instability. Eastern European reformers, in contrast, were able to blame economic instability on the inevitable cost of abandoning the old economic regime.

Applications to countries in transition

The key parameters of the model and the eight propositions can be used to rank countries in transition in terms of the speed and comprehensiveness of their transitions. (Because Proposition 2 is a reformulation of Proposition 1 and Proposition 4 does not have an explicit implication for the speed or comprehensiveness of reform, they are omitted from the accounting scheme.) The assigned values for each of the six propositions are arbitrarily assigned values 1 (high) to 3 (low) and summed (table A1.1). The procedure is arbitrary; readers are invited to use the propositions to derive their own relative rankings of the economies shown in table A1.1.

TABLE A1.1
Ranking of countries/regions by key transition parameters
(mean, standard deviation)

Parameter	Eastern Germany	Eastern Europe	Russia	China
Initial conditions	1	1	2	3
Substitutability	2	1	1	2
Cost of adjustment	3	2	1	2
Ends uncertainty	3	3	2	1
Means uncertainty	3	3	2	1
Risk aversion	3	3	2	1
Sum	15	13	10	10

Source: Authors' assessment based on analysis presented in this appendix.

Conclusions

The framework presented here represents a very preliminary investigation into a general approach to the analytics of transition. It suggests a rich set of research issues, including empirical analyses of the reform production function to investigate substitutional elasticities among reforms, output (productivity) elasticities of individual reform instruments, and the importance of various initial conditions. The approach is intended to explain in a systematic manner why different countries should be expected to implement reform and achieve transition at different rates.

Note

1. Jefferson and Rawski (1995) have developed an alternative model of bottom-up reform that emphasizes reform as an endogenous process based on competition, innovation, and learning rather than as an event emanating from the political center.

References

Brada, Josef C., and Arthur E. King. 1991. "Sequencing Measures for the Transformation of Socialist Economies to Capitalism: Is There a J-Curve for Economic Reforms?" Research Paper Series, No. 13. Transition and Macrostabilization Division, World Bank, Washington, D.C.

Chen, Kang, Gary H. Jefferson, and Inderjit Singh. 1992. "Lessons from China's Economic Reform." *Journal of Comparative Economics.*

Dhanji, Farid. 1991. "Transformation Programs: Content and Sequencing." *American Economic Review* 81(2): 323–28.

Gelb, Alan, Gary H. Jefferson, and Inderjit Singh. 1993. "Can Communist Economies Transform Incrementally? A Review of China's Experience." Paper presented at the Eighth Annual Macroeconomics Conference of the NBER, Cambridge, Mass., March 12–13.

Friedman, Eric J., and Simon Johnson. 1996. "Complementarities in Economic Reform." *Economics of Transition* 4(2):319–29.

Harris, John R., and Michael P. Todaro. 1970. "Migration, Unemployment and Development: A Two Sector Analysis." *American Economic Review* 60: 126–42.

International Monetary Fund, International Bank for Reconstruction and Development, Organisation for Economic Co-operation and Development, and the European Bank for Reconstruction and Development. 1990. *The Economy of the USSR: Summary and Recommendations.* Washington, D.C.: International Monetary Fund.

Jefferson, Gary H., and Thomas G. Rawski. 1995. "How Industrial Reform Worked in China: The Role of Innovation, Competition, and Property Rights." In Michael Bruno and Boris Pleskovic, eds., *Proceedings of the World Bank Annual Conference on Development Economics 1994.* Washington, D.C.: World Bank.

Murphy, Kevin M., Andre Shleifer, and Robert W. Vishny. 1992. "The Transition to a Market Economy: Pitfalls of Partial Reform." *Quarterly Journal of Economics* 107(3): 889–906.

Naughton, Barry. 1994. *Growing Out of the Plan.* New York: Cambridge University Press.

Nickell, S.J. 1978. *The Investment Decisions of Firms.* New York: Cambridge University Press.

Perkins, Dwight H. 1992. "China's 'Gradual' Approach to Market Reforms." Paper presented at the conference Comparative Experiences of Economic Reform and Post-Socialist Transformation, July 6–8, El Escorial, Spain.

Schultz, Theodore. 1961. "Investment in Human Capital." *American Economic Review* 51: 1–17.

Appendix B
Development of the Hengdian Township Enterprise Group: A Case Study

Chen Jianbo and Gary H. Jefferson

During the 1980s China's industrial transformation was marked by the flowering of rural township and village enterprises. One of the most successful of these enterprises has been in the township of Hengdian, in Dongyang City, Zhejiang Province. Led by the extraordinary success of the Hengdian (Group) Company (HGC), the township has developed a highly diversified industrial economy that employs world-class technologies and produces goods for export.

This case study describes how this township, with a population of just 63,000, grew from a rural people's commune into a technologically sophisticated industrial conglomerate with extensive international operations in less than 20 years. Several themes of China's rural industrial transformation are highlighted by this case study. These include the key role of entrepreneurial spirit and personal relations in compensating for the absence of managerial and technology markets, the ill-defined nature (in a formal legal sense) of property rights in China's township and village enterprise sector, and the central role of both explicit and implicit contracts in managing business and motivating workers.

Establishment and growth of the Hengdian Company

Much of the success of the Hengdian Company appears to have resulted from the seemingly unbounded entrepreneurial energy of Xu Wenlong, founder of the company's first enterprise and the company's chief executive officer. Having worked in county and township government, as well as in the local supply and marketing cooperative, Xu had broader knowledge of the outside world than other residents of this small rural community. In an economic system based on limited markets and a system of property rights based on social and political relationships, personal relationships were then, and still are, an intangible asset that can form the basis of a successful business career. Xu knew how to establish these personal relationships and how to use them effectively. ·

During the Cultural Revolution many state-run silk factories closed, resulting in severely limited demand for silkworms, the principal crop of the Hengdian People's Commune. To avoid losses, the commune decided to set up a silk factory to process its unsold silkworms. They applied to the Light Industry Bureau of Zhejiang Province in late 1974 to obtain the necessary permit. As party secretary of the Hengdian Brigade, Xu was responsible for securing the permit. He drew on the personal relationships he had developed with officials in the bureau to secure the permit.

In April 1975 the new Dongyang County Silk Factory signed a contract with the brigade for land acquisition. Initially, the factory was not required to pay rent, although it later compensated the brigade for its use of the land. Xu became the factory manager, and the factory rapidly expanded. By 1976 the company employed 238 workers and earned profits of 76,000 yuan, equivalent to all the agricultural tax revenues paid to the township that year.

By exploiting his relationships, Xu persuaded the Zhejiang Province Silk Company to purchase the products of the Dongyang County Silk Factory. Responding to the call of the central government to support industrial development in rural areas, state-owned enterprises dispatched technicians to help peasants start small industrial enterprises such as the Dongyang Factory. The Hangzhou Xinhua Silk Factory offered free training for 120 staff from Dongyang and sent technicians to provide technical assistance for installation of instruments and other technical tasks. Xu continued to develop his network of relationships, anticipating that they might eventually be useful for the factory. When workers and cadres who found work or had been assigned outside Hengdian returned home for vacation, Xu would visit their homes, thus nurturing an ever-expanding circle of personal relationships.

By the end of 1978, its third year of operation, the silk factory had earned 360,000 yuan in profits, allowing it to pay off its loans. The factory's success established Xu's credibility. The following year Xu and the town set up the Hengdian Knitting Factory, which flourished. A major reason for the success of the knitting factory was the technology and training offered by the state-owned Jiangsu Knitting Factory. Two years after it was established, the Hengdian Knitting Factory sold over 3 million yuan worth of output, generating 437,200 yuan in profit. At the same time, the silk factory continued to expand, and several new plants were established. In 1980, 1.4 million yuan was spent to set up an underwear factory, an apparel factory, a print and dye mill, and a magnetic material factory. Not every venture succeeded. Some enterprises, most notably a cement factory and a linen textile plant, failed.

In 1981 another six enterprises began production. Because Xu could not possibly manage all of them, others were appointed as factory directors. Some of the directors clashed with Xu over how factories should be run. Xu lacked the authority to control the directors, who had been appointed by the commune leaders. Only the commune had the authority to override or replace individual factory directors.

To give Xu effective control of the new enterprises, the commune authorized him to establish the Hengdian Textile and Light Industry General Factory. The general factory was given authority to allocate capital, authorize construction, and oversee personnel decisions of the affiliated enterprises. In 1983 the fixed assets of the township and village enterprises under the control of the general factory amounted to 3.6 million yuan, employment stood at 1,924, industrial output reached 12.2 million yuan, and profits exceeded 2.3 million yuan. Xu, the town, and the company were on their way to establishing one of the first major township and village enterprise conglomerates in China's countryside.

By 1997 the Hengdian China Group Company included nearly 1,000 local township and village enterprises and a variety of enterprises in other parts of China and abroad. The company is engaged in industrial production, research and development, and domestic and international marketing and trade. It is the first national township and village enterprise group to have been granted the authority to export and import.

Outside Hengdian, the company controls more than 20 subsidies, which are spread across mainland China, and four ventures, located in Hong Kong, Japan, and the United States. The company's 11 industrial (group) companies include textiles, knitting, industrial dyestuffs, machinery and electronics, electroacoustic materials, magnetic materials, pharmaceuticals, chemical engineering, construction materials, and tourism. The operation also includes 142 enterprises that are directly affiliated with the HGC and with an export-import company.

At the end of June 1995 about 20,000 people worked directly for HGC, and another 12,000 worked in 142 directly affiliated enterprises. The HGC's assets were estimated to be worth 1.63 billion yuan, nearly 10 times the value of its assets in 1990. Sales revenues had reached 1.1 billion yuan and total profit 93 million yuan in 1994; average annual income per worker that year was 7,500 yuan. Exports in 1994—which accounted for 80 percent of the company's magnetic material production and 100 percent of its textile production—included electronics and electroacoustic products.

Dispute over ownership of the company

The 295,800 yuan of fixed assets acquired by the Hengdian Company in its first year was financed from a variety of sources. A portion (50,400 yuan) was borrowed from 39 brigades across the commune (the equivalent of borrowing 2.4 yuan from each member of the commune); the balance was financed by a loan from the local credit cooperative administered by the Bank of Agriculture. Although the permit was granted to the commune, the commune never committed equity directly to the enterprise. The local government nonetheless continues to assert that it invested in the founding enterprise and is now the principal owner of the company.

Further complicating the issue of ownership were various transfers of funds. Xu, for example, borrowed 2,000 yuan from the commune to purchase lunch for visiting technicians. Typically a loan would not be considered as an investment, but in China in the 1970s the inference of ownership might accompany even small loans. One reason for this presumption is the ambiguous status that loans then had in China. Rationed capital seldom covered discount rates, let alone risk, and loans were difficult to recover if the borrower was unable or unwilling to repay. It was thus unclear whether a loan represented a loan in the conventional sense or a kind of equity that was repaid only if it were convenient and feasible for the borrower do so.

The ambiguity of property law in China makes it difficult to specify property rights within the system of township and village enterprises. The charter for the original silk factory was granted to the commune; by law the commune (now the town government) has absolute control over, and responsibility for, the operations of the enterprises. The local government, however, never invested its own equity in the venture; all of the loans it provided were repaid. Moreover, governments at various levels—both commune-level brigades below the commune and the provincial and central governments, including a variety of state-owned enterprises— have contributed funds on noncommercial terms and "sweat equity" to the development of the company.

To resolve these ambiguous property rights, the Hengdian Company put forward its 1994 charter (*chanquan zhidu gangyao*), an eclectic document that stipulates that the company is a mass organization comprising enterprises of different ownership types. It characterizes the company's assets, which include its wholly owned enterprises, as public-owned (*gongyou zhi*) and mass-operated (*minying*). The charter stipulates that the company's property is not claimed by the state, the local government, the village collectives and cooperatives, or any individual. Instead, ownership is assigned to current members of the company. Membership, and hence ownership, means the right to work and share benefits without the right to claim the underlying assets of the company and its affiliates. Loss of membership means the loss of all rights. The company is independent of the government and assumes full responsibility for its profits and losses.

Although the company's charter clarifies certain areas of control and management of its assets, some issues remain unclear. The charter stipulates that the property is owned by the members of the company, but it does not specify how the residual is to be distributed among the members. Moreover, membership in the company apparently does not confer the right to participate in enterprise management, operations, or decisionmaking.

Formally, the company is not a stock company, a limited liability company, or a cooperative enterprise. In practice, Xu Wenlong, the company's CEO and founder, retains residual rights and hence controls the right to make final decisions. However, there is no clear definition of his ownership that is protected by law. In this respect, Hengdian represents the kind of "vaguely defined cooperative," as characterized by Weitzman and Xu (1994), that typified the township and village enterprise sector in the 1980s. By the mid-1990s many of China's township and village enterprises, especially larger enterprises and enterprise groups, were being converted to shareholding cooperative enterprises (*gufen hezuo qiye*) in which a substantial portion of shares is held by individuals, including managers, workers, and members of the community. The balance of the shares is held by the enterprise or by local government. This process of individualizing ownership (*rengehua suoyouzhi*) was not implemented in the Hengdian Company, which remained largely "owned by the public."

Property rights in Hengdian: the role of contracts

The central office of the Hengdian Company retains control over corporate strategy, investment decisions, top-level appointments, and major distribution decisions. Individual industrial (group) companies exercise autonomy over routine management and perform as independent profit centers. Factory managers, in turn, control day-to-day decisions, and their factories operate as independent accounting units. Acting with the consent of the Hengdian town government, the company, in the role of central contracting agent, uses its authority to negotiate and monitor a comprehensive set of contracts, directly or through the industrial groups, with all of its nearly 1,000 enterprises.

A system of property rights can be defined as a set of formal or informal contracts that reflects the distribution of the responsibilities and rewards between contract signatories. Under an economic system in which property is not exclusive, incentives may instead result from the de facto distribution of managerial control and residual rights.

Two kinds of contracts are used by the Hengdian Company. The company signs annual contracts with each of the industrial groups (*chengbao hetong*), the general companies, and the directly affiliated enterprises; these enterprises, in turn, negotiate annual subcontracts with their affiliated enterprises. Some enterprises that either break even or make losses are leased for several years. Whether an annual contract or a lease is signed, the legal entity (*faren*) is required to post collateral, worth either 10 times the sum of the contractor's annual income or 10 percent of the combined assets of the enterprise. Collateral can take the form of cash or private property.

Each contract specifies a rate of profit remittance for the subcontractor. Before 1995 each member enterprise remitted 70 percent of its profit to the company; the rate was reduced to 50 percent in 1995. The company also specifies parameters for the use of retained earnings. Usually, 30 percent of retained earnings can be distributed as bonuses, with the remaining 70 percent dedicated to the enterprise development fund. The share of earnings allocated to bonuses is flexible and can be adjusted according to profit performance. Enterprises exceeding profit expectations can distribute as much as 35 percent of retained earnings; poor performers have sometimes been able to distribute as little as 17 percent of earnings.

During the early 1990s the town, the company, and Xu disagreed over a range of issues concerning both profit remittance and control of the company. Xu and town officials reached an impasse; county leaders came down on the side of Xu and dismissed a number of town officials. Initially, the company promised to turn over an agreed-upon level of profit; later, it contributed more than the town had demanded. In the end, the town agreed not to stipulate a rate of profit, and the company agreed to try to turn over whatever the town government needed. Soon after agreement was reached, the company financed the construction of a new town administration building. Since then it has built roads, schools, a temple, and a movie theater. Hengdian has become a company town in the fullest sense in that civic functions, decision authority, and ownership overlap and merge between the company and the town.

Wages, bonuses, and benefits

In 1984 the company overhauled its employment system, replacing guarantees of lifetime employment with contracts for fixed periods of time.

As part of this reform, salaries were made flexible, based on performance, and an incentive system based on bonus distributions was put in place.

In 1995 the basic wage for workers and ordinary managers consisted of a daily wage of 9–25 yuan. Factory directors and contracted technicians received monthly salaries of 500–1,000 yuan; general managers of general companies and industrial groups were paid 1,400–2,500 yuan a month. The wage and salary schedule is restructured every year on the basis of the performance of the industry groups and average industrywide standards. Each employee's basic pay reflects individual performance; the company maintains substantial wage and salary differentials both within occupational groups and between production workers and general managers.

A second important feature of Hengdian's compensation system is the link between total compensation and the profit generated by the enterprise. At the end of the year the industrial groups determine the total bonus package for each enterprise on the basis of the enterprise's profit performance. Bonuses are substantial, with technicians and factory directors earning about 40 percent of their income from bonuses.

Among factories that have been leased out (usually those with a history of poor profit records), contractors that generate profits in excess of contracted levels can retain 4 percent of the excess as bonus. If the enterprise suffers a loss, the contractor absorbs 10–20 percent of the total loss through deductions from its collateral.

Among the Hengdian Company's 11 industrial groups, two are particularly noteworthy. The Machinery and Electronics Groups (MEG), established in 1992, had within five years built a civil nuclear engineering facility and separate factories that produce condensers, aluminum foil, telecommunication equipment, and film plating. Of the company's enterprises, MEG ranks first in profit-making per capita and second in total profit. Total per capita income of MEG's staff in 1995 averaged 10,000 yuan—a substantial real increase over the previous year's level of 7,000 yuan (the national rate of inflation was less than 20 percent). This income includes a distribution of 19.5 percent of the group's profits. Compensation is closely tied to performance. If the group fails to achieve its production and profit goals, MEG managers are penalized with a 40 percent salary cut. MEG workers are also penalized: If profits fall 10 percent below the company's goal, the daily wage of the workers is cut by 1.2 yuan, about 10 percent of the average wage.

The company has put in place powerful incentives to promote innovation. Since 1992 staff who innovate promising projects have been entitled to bonuses of up to 100,000 yuan. In addition, technicians who develop new products or technology-improving processes are awarded 10 percent of the after-tax profits generated by the project in its first year.

Those who introduce high-tech products are awarded 15 percent of first-year after-tax profits. A technician who brings in a high-tech project can also be promoted to factory director.

The sales staff earn generous bonuses based on their sales. Each salesperson is expected to achieve a minimum of 10 million yuan worth of sales a year. Performance that exceeds the target is rewarded, and shortfalls are penalized. If sales fall short of the target, the salesperson pays a penalty of 15 yuan for every 10,000 yuan shortfall the first month. After the first month, the penalty rises to 30 yuan for every 10,000 yuan shortfall. To minimize arrears, sales staff are largely responsible for securing payment as well as for contracting sales. Consequently, recruiting new customers also entails a thorough check by the sales staff of the new customer's creditworthiness.

Another industrial group, the Dongyang Magnetic Material Group (DMMG), has emerged as one of China's largest electronic components producers. Its profit-sales ratio of nearly 20 percent is based principally on the meteoric growth of its exports of magnetic speaker material.

Ranked third in the world in terms of sales of magnetic steel for speakers, DMMG sells to Phillips, Samsung, and Sharp. In its supplier contracts with Phillips, DMMG agreed to subject itself to competitive monthly evaluations based on price, quality, and service. The provision of monthly figures has provided a powerful incentive to DMMG's management and workers. After having ranked as first among all of Phillips' suppliers in 1994, DMMG subsequently increased its sales to Phillips from 20 tons to 200 tons a month.

The Hengdian Company provides some housing for its employees, principally villas for its engineering staff. Retired staff are usually paid a pension and provided with medical care. Staff who work at Hengdian at least five years receive 100 percent of their medical benefits; those who have been on the payroll for less than five years receive 70 percent of their benefits. Pensions range from 300 to 1,000 yuan a month. Some of the industry groups have developed special programs. Dongyang Magnetic Material Group, for example, has established a staff welfare foundation. Every year the group contributes to the foundation an amount of money equivalent to bonuses paid from profits. Members of the staff who resign or are dismissed lose their claim on welfare benefits.

Rural township and village enterprises have created a new model of property relations in China, as peasants, who were once excluded from China's industrialization, have obtained the right to accumulate and manage industrial assets. The Hengdian Company epitomizes the township and village enterprise as a community asset. Instead of paying a fixed tax rate, Hengdian pays what it can; with annual profits more than doubling every two years, its tax payments more than cover the town's needs. The urgency to define property rights clearly may not exist in Hengdian or other public Chinese firms as long as all parties prosper. When robust growth recedes, however, pressures will emerge for clarifying the implicit and ad hoc contracts that have sufficed until now.

Index

to workers, 177, 179; on workers wages, 175

China Statistical Yearbook, ownership classification in, 24

Coal, price controls effect on, 32

Coase theorem, 108; property rights market and, 120–23; reforms and, 11–12

Cobb-Douglas production function, 225, 234, 246; technology estimate with, 203; technology represented by, 181; total factor productivity and, 114

Collateral, demand for, 54–55

Collective enterprises, autonomy within, 59; described, 39; overemployment of labor in, 15; rapid growth of, 27–28; state-owned enterprises outstripped by, 16; total factor productivity and, 153

Commerce, inconsistent rules restrict, 68

Competition, competition of incipient, 69; on eve of reforms, 75; intensifies in markets for industrial products, 75–76; market environment and, 61–62; profitability and, 35–37

Concentration ratios, on eve of reforms, 76; industrial, 35, 36t

Contract responsibility system, 51–52; decisionmaking authority and, 223–24; described, 120–23; management contracts used with, 52–53

Contracts, enterprise responsible, 47; establishment of central agency for, 47–48; incentives and, 51–52; management responsible, 181–82; managerial objectives and, 56–57; provisions of, 55–58; types of, 51–52

Corporate governance, forms of ownership and, 58; reform of, 44–55

Corporatization, reforming property rights by, 107

Cost ratios, in different policy environments, 247–55

Costs, of reforms, 272–23; importance of lowering transaction, 12; state-owned enterprises retirement, pensions, welfare, 33t, 72

Creative reduction, in state-owned enterprises, 90–91

Crude oil, effect of price controls on, 32

Daqing oilfields, price controls effect on, 32

Decentralization, of investment spending, 217; property rights development and, 30; of public enterprise ownership, 29–30; of supervision, 68–69

Decentralized supervision, industrial reform model and, 68–69

Decision rights, allocation of, 49t; authority and contract responsibility system, 223–24; creation of intrafirm, 47–51; institutional innovation and, 10, 44–47; within enterprises, 50t

Declining profitability, reasons for, 144–45. *See also* Profitability; Profits

Directors, appointment of, 48, 49t

Domestic cost ratios, in different policy environments, 247–55

Domestic quality ladder, hierarchy of, 230

Earnings, bonuses as, 185–86. *See also* Profitability; Profits

Economic reforms, impact of on export performance, 242–44;

model of, 265–77; paradoxes of, 6–7. *See also* Reforms

Employees, state-owned enterprises recruiting of, 46

Employment, average ratios of profit-maximizing, 207t; behavior model, 180–87; deviations from profit-maximizing, 205–08; equation, 186, 189–90; factors effecting, 184–85; model of, 200–01; in township and village enterprises, 197–215

Endogenous reform, 8; equation of endogenous property rights and, 118; hypothesis, 117–20; industrial innovation ladder and, 11; model of, 65–88

Engineers, in the workforce, 93t

Enterprise performance, enterprise specific variables, 161–62; estimation results, 163–68; industrial branch data and, 167–68; ownership and, 172–63; policy variables and, 160–61, 165; relationship of property rights and, 114–23; sources of differences in, 160–63

Enterprise responsible contract, 47. *See also* Contracts

Enterprises, autonomy of, 174–75; distribution of decisionmaking authority within, 50t; governments' reasons for establishing, 198; improving performance within existing, 78–79; innovation and reforms in, 89–106; levels of institutional development of, 122t; model of wages in, 180–87; number of in selected years, 25t; performance of, 30–37, 160–63; property rights in townships and village, 108–10; responses to market pressures, 77–80. *See also* Industry

Export performance, 241–63; Bruno Ratio and, 247–55; determinants of, 255–59; in Guangdong and Shanghai, 244–46; impact of economic and trade reform on, 242–44; ownership total factor productivity and, 246–47

Exports, 241–63; Bruno Ratio and, 247–55; growth of, 241; Guangdong and, 244–46; Hong Kong and, 244; impact of reforms on, 242–44; Macao and, 244; Shanghai and, 244–46; sustainability of grow of, 19; total factor productivity and, 246–47

Feedback, mechanisms to amplify and extend reforms, 83

Fiscal revenues, eroded by competition, 76–77

"Floating" wage system, 173

Foreign-funded enterprises, described, 24; profitability of, 13

Fujian province, exports and, 241

Funds, sources of for investment spending, 221–22

Government policy, effects on enterprises of, 80–83

Government revenues, decline of, 80

Groping reform strategy, 8–9

Gross output deflator, total factor productivity and, 132–33

Guangdong, export performance of, 241; 244–46; foreign trade corporations in, 243

Hausman specification test, random effects model and, 204

Hengdian Company, establishment and growth of, 279–81; ownership dispute, 10, 281–82; property rights in, 282–83; state-owned enterprise contributions to, 37; wages, bonuses, and benefits of, 283–87

Hengdian township, case study of development of, 279–87

Heterogeneity, of industrial firms, 70

Hierarchy, of industrial firms, 70

Hong Kong, export performance of Guangdong and, 244; south China enterprise development and, 74

Incentives, autonomy and, 95–97; bonuses, compensation and, 54, 94–95, 191–94; contracts and, 51–52; demand for collateral and, 54–55; distribution of profits and, 52–54; effect on institutional innovation, 10; labor and, 58–60; managerial, 13; for new product innovation, 95t; structure of, 55; structures effect on institutional innovation, 10. *See also* Bonuses

Incipient competition, description of, 69; on eve of reforms, 75

Individual-owned enterprises, described, 23

Industrial, concentration ratios, 35, 36t

Industrial growth, overview of, 5; paradoxes of, 6

Industrial innovation ladder, 9, 65–88; causality and, 11; measures needed to strengthen, 18; sustainability of reforms and, 19; as transition resource, 11

Industrial output, changes in ownership and, 26–27; selected years gross, 27t

Industrial products, competition intensifies markets for, 75–76

Industrial reform model, 68–72; decentralized supervision and, 68–69; dependence on profits and,

69; heterogeneous enterprise types and, 70–72; incipient competition and, 69

Industry, changes affecting, 27–30; decision rights in, 44–47; dynamics of partial reform in, 72–85; growth of outside state sector, 27–29; as a hierarchy of heterogeneous enterprise types, 70–72; output by sector, 28t; ownership of, 6, 23–27; productivity of, 30–32; profitability of, 32–37; profit-capital ratios, 75t; structure of, 5. *See also* Enterprises

Industry codes of urban enterprises, described, 43

Inflation, of gross output and intermediate inputs, 132

Innovation, activity model of, 98–104; autonomy and, 95–97; bonuses and, 14–15; decisionmaking authority and, 10, 44–47; decision rights and industrial, 44–47; enterprise reforms and, 89–106; factors constraining product, 79; in institutional enterprises, 10; lack of in Socialist countries, 89; measure of, 92t; mismatch hypothesis versus catch-up hypothesis and, 91–98; for new products, 95t; property rights and, 10; resources and, 97–98; total factor productivity gains and, 142–43

Innovation activity model, and catch-up hypothesis, 101–04; and mismatch hypothesis, 98–101

Institutional enterprises, innovation in, 10; persistence of weaknesses in, 67–68

Institutional innovation, 10

Institutional limits, expanding, 79; improving performance within existing, 78–79

Interest rates, subsidies of to state-owned enterprises, 33

Intermediate input deflator, total factor productivity and, 132

International enterprises, rising competition from, 36

International quality ladder, hierarchy of, 70

Intrafirm decision rights, creation of, 47–51

Investment behavior, desired capital stock model of, 225–31; investment demand model of, 231–33; investment demand II model of, 233–37

Investment resources, captured by state-owned enterprises, 16

Investment spending, allocation of funds for, 222; background on, 218–21; banking system modification and, 223; decentralization of, 217; institutional setting for, 222–24; as key to economic activity, 217; models, 224–37; sources of funds for, 221–22

Jiangsu Province, exports and, 241; rural enterprise development in, 71

Joint stock companies, state-owned enterprises reorganizing to, 38

Joint ventures, described, 39–40

Labor, estimating output elastics for, 157–58; incentives and, 58–60; market regulation and reform, 172–75 overemployment of, 15

Labor productivity, 175, 176t; bonuses relationship to, 177–78; review of, 128–31. *See also* Productivity; Total factor productivity

Living standards, Pareto efficient allocation and, 89

Loans, forgiveness given to state-owned enterprises, 33; policy, 81; seeking rent in form of soft, 79

Losses, industrial, 35; as percent of GDP and FDP, 143–44; by state-owned enterprises, 144t

Luoyang Tractor Works, 76

Macao, export performance of Guangdong and, 244

Management, objectives of, 56–57, 58t; reforming property rights by reforming, 107; state-owned enterprises appointment of, 46; types of, 52t

Management responsibility contracts, 181–82. *See also* Contracts

Managerial incentives, importance of, 13

Market based economy, created by reform process, 84–85; announcement of creation of a goal of a, 84; technical change, 9

Market conditions, equation to measure impact of, 82

Market environment, 60–63; capacity to adjust and, 62–63; competition and, 61–62; oversupply and response and, 61; price autonomy and, 60–61

Market pressure, enterprise strategy toward, 77–80

Market segmentation, eroded by partial reforms, 73–75

Mining, price controls effect on, 32

Mismatch hypothesis, on incentives and autonomy, 93; innovation activity model and, 98–101; versus catch-up hypothesis, 91–98

Monopsony power, end of, 15

for decline of, 144–45; shortcomings of data on, 32–33

Profit-capital ratios, 75t

Profits, among large and medium sized enterprises, 147–49; bonuses and retention of, 13, 52; distribution of, 52–54; emphasis on, 56–57, 94; eroded by competition, 76–77; fiscal dependence on industrial, 69; forms of sharing of, 53t; paradoxes of, 145–47; expenditures on new product development and, 102; rates of, 143–44; rates of for total production and new product production, 102t; state-owned enterprise emphasis on, 56–57; upper-level technicians contribution to, 102–03; 103t

Property rights, allocation of, 12t; capture hypothesis and, 115–17; clarifying, 10; Coase theorem and property rights, 120–23; congruence of, 111–14, 114t; consistency needed in, 17–18; endogenous reform hypothesis and, 117–20; importance of better specified, 12, 19; institutional innovation and, 10; means of indexes of, 113t; reform by ownership, 113t; reform incentive structure and, 55; reforming, 107–25; relationship of enterprise performance and, 114–23; reforms impact on enterprise performance, 110; in township and village enterprises, 108–10

Public enterprises, devolution of, 29–30; dominant role of in reforms, 29, 66

Public ownership, decentralization of, 29–30; limiting externalities arising from, 12

Pudong, development of, 245

Pure ownership, estimating effects of, 153–69

Quality ladder, hierarchy of, 70

Rates of return, to capital, 77t; effect of competition on, 76–77

Reform, endogenous. *See* Endogenous reform

Reforms, causality in process of, 10–11; centrally directed, 65–66; characteristics of, 66–68; Coase theorem and, 11–12; costs of, 272–73; dynamics of partial, 72–85; effective transition through incremental, 7; enterprise contributions to, 37–40; feedback mechanisms and, 83; groping strategy of, 8–9; highlights of, 4–5; impact of on export performance, 242–44; impact on performance, 110–11; improved productivity linked to, 13; of the labor market, 172–75; market-based economy created from, 84–85; market environment and, 60–63; model for analyzing, 68–72; model of economic, 265–77; Open Door policy, 4–5; paradoxes of, 6–7; property rights and, 107–25; rural reform program, 4–5; society's preferences for, 274–76; sustainability of, 18–20. *See also* Economic reforms

Regulation, of the labor market, 172–75

Research and development, township and village enterprises and, 9

Resource cost ratios, in different policy environments, 247–55

Resources, contract responsibility system and, 120; innovation and, 97–98; partial reforms lower barriers to, 73–75

Retained earnings, bonuses and, 185–86

Retirement costs, state-owned enterprises, 72

Revenues, decline of government, 80; eroded by competition, 76–77; government source of, 38

Rural enterprises, growth of, 5; importance of, 39; in Jiangsu Province, 71; ownership in, 155–56; people's communes and, 156. *See also* Township enterprises; Village enterprises

Rural reform program, impact of, 4–5

Salaries. *See* Wages

Savings rates, 19

Schumpeterian competition, entrance into, 90

Shangdong Province, exports and, 241

Shanghai, export performance of, 241; 244–46

Shareholding enterprises, profitability of, 13

Socialist countries, lack of innovation in, 89

Soft loans, seeking rent in form of, 79

Special Economic Zones, imports and, 36

State sector, growth outside of, 27–29

State-owned enterprises, 23; behavior of consistent with neoclassical firms, 14–15; benefits of productivity increases in, 18; conversion of, 11; cooperation with township and village enterprises by, 71; cost disadvantages of, 71–72; declining profitability of, 14; described, 37–39; economic breaks given to, 33; equation to test enterprise efficiency, 78; as government's chief source of revenue, 38; growth of, 5;

improved efficiency in, 12–13; improved performance of, 66–67; investment resources captured by, 16; lack of autonomy of, 44, 46, 174–75; losses by, 144t; lack of exit and business failure of, 90–91; managerial objectives of, 56–57, 58t; outstripped by collective enterprises, 16; overemployment of labor in, 15; paradoxes of, 6, 145–47; pension costs of, 33t; percentage of industrial output by, 26; price controls effect on, 32; price regulation and, 60–61; productivity of converted and loss-making, 130t; profits rates of, 143–44; welfare costs of, 33

Statistics, falsification of, 134–35

Stock exchanges, companies listings on, 38

Structure-conduct-performance (S-C-P) paradigm, 127

Subsidies, seeking rent in form of, 79

Surveys, used in this study, 2, 91. *See also* State Statistical Bureau; World Bank Enterprise Survey

Taxes, breaks given to state-owned enterprises, 33; fiscal dependence on industrial, 69; sources of, 38

Technical change, industrial innovation ladder and, 9; market based, 9; rural communities research and development and, 9; total factor productivity gains and, 142–43

Technicians, in the workforce, 93t

Technology, diffused from state-owned enterprises, 37; econometric specification of, 203; partial reforms lower barriers to, 73–75; sustainability of advances in, 19

Textile industry, deregulation of, 82

Thousand-Firm Reinvigoration Program, 123

Total factor productivity, 131–43; capital stock deflators and, 133; collective enterprises and, 153; equation, 131, 246; estimates of, 159–60; estimation results, 163–68; export orientation and, 246–47; external constraints on, 62–63; gains in allocative efficiency and; 140–42 growth rates of, 31t; improvement of, 12–13, 30–31; literature review on, 136–37, 138t; new output bias and, 134; nonproduction inputs and, 135–36; output bias of, 133–35; output deflators and, 131–33; performance conclusions about, 137; shortages cited by, 62; sources of growth of, 137–43; studies of, 138–39t; in township and village enterprises compared to state-owned enterprises, 16–17. *See also* Labor productivity; Productivity

Total wage bill, 182–83

Township enterprises, autonomy of, 44, 156 174–75; budget constraints on, 156; cooperation with state-owned enterprises by, 71; cooperative culture of, 156–57; employment and wages in, 197–215; Hengdian township development case study, 279–87; industrial output by, 26–27; loss-making enterprises closed, 80; property rights in, 108–10; as pure wage maximizers, 210; rapid growth of, 28; research and development in, 9; total factor productivity in, 16–17; wage systems of, 60

Trade reforms, impact of on export performance, 242–44

Urban Survey Team, total factor productivity and, 134

Village enterprises, autonomy of, 44, 156, 174–75; budget constraints on, 156; cooperation with state-owned enterprises by, 71; cooperative culture of, 156–57; employment and wages in, 197–215; external constraints on, 62–63; growth of, 5; industrial output by, 26–27; loss-making enterprises closed, 80; property rights in, 108–10; as pure wage maximizers, 210; rapid growth of, 28; research and development in, 9; shortages cited by, 62; total factor productivity in, 16–17; wage systems of, 60

Wage bill equation, 187–88; estimates of, 187t

Wage setting behavior, linked to labor productivity, 14; model, 180–87; reward and effort and, 15

Wage-employment system, importance of reforms on, 13

Wages, 175–79; average, 177t; basic rate of, 181, 183–84; bonuses as share of total, 178t–79t; equation of basic, 184; 188–89; "floating" system of, 173; Hengdian Company, 283–87; hierarchy of, 71; quota equation for, 186; relationship between productivity and, 176; setting, 58–59; tied to performance, 58–59, 178t; total bill of, 182–83; in township and village enterprises, 197–215. *See also* Bonuses

Welfare costs, to state-owned enterprises, 33

Woolen textile industry, deregulation of, 82

World Bank Enterprise Survey, assignment of decision rights explored in, 44–47; on enterprise autonomy, 174; industrial investment, finance and enterprise performance and, 217–18, 222; on labor productivity, 175; new product defined in, 91; performance of rural enterprises compared to state enterprises, 154; on structure, authority and incentives, 43–63; on transfer of property rights, 111–14; wage and employment behavior in, 173

Zhejiang Province, exports and, 241